HIDDEN ®
Montana

D0367093

HIDDEN®

Montana

Including Missoula, Helena, Bozeman, and
Glacier and Yellowstone National Parks

John Gottberg

FIFTH EDITION

Ulysses Press®
BERKELEY, CALIFORNIA

Published by: ULYSSES PRESS
P.O. Box 3440
Berkeley, CA 94703
www.ulyssespress.com

ISSN 1524-1297
ISBN 1-56975-491-8

Printed in Canada by Transcontinental Printing

10 9 8 7

MANAGING EDITOR: Claire Chun
PROJECT DIRECTOR: Laura Brancella
COPY EDITOR: Steven Schwartz
EDITORIAL ASSOCIATES: Lily Chou, Leona Benten, Kate Allen,
    Amy Hough, Alice Riegert, Rachel Rubin
TYPESETTER: Lisa Kester, Matt Orendorff, Tamara Kowalski
CARTOGRAPHY: XNR Productions; Yellowstone map
    by Pease Press
HIDDEN BOOKS DESIGN: Sarah Levin
COVER DESIGN: Sarah Levin, Leslie Henriques
INDEXER: Sayre Van Young
COVER PHOTOGRAPHY: Jupiterimages.com
ILLUSTRATOR: Doug McCarthy

Distributed in the United States by Publishers Group West

Write to us!

If in your travels you discover a spot that captures the spirit of Montana, or if you live in the region and have a favorite place to share, or if you just feel like expressing your views, write to us and we'll pass your note along to the author.

We can't guarantee that the author will add your personal find to the next edition, but if the writer does use the suggestion, we'll acknowledge you in the credits and send you a free copy of the new edition.

ULYSSES PRESS
P.O. Box 3440
Berkeley, CA 94703
E-mail: readermail@ulyssespress.com

What's Hidden?

At different points throughout this book, you'll find special listings marked with this symbol:

◄ HIDDEN

This means that you have come upon a place off the beaten tourist track, a spot that will carry you a step closer to the local people and natural environment of Montana.

The goal of this guide is to lead you beyond the realm of everyday tourist facilities. While we include traditional sightseeing listings and popular attractions, we also offer alternative sights and adventure activities. Instead of filling this guide with reviews of standard hotels and chain restaurants, we concentrate on one-of-a-kind places and locally owned establishments.

Our authors seek out locales that are popular with residents but usually overlooked by visitors. Some are more hidden than others (and are marked accordingly), but all the listings in this book are intended to help you discover the true nature of Montana and put you on the path of adventure.

Contents

Maps

OUTDOOR ADVENTURE SYMBOLS

The following symbols accompany national, state and regional park listings, as well as beach descriptions throughout the text.

▲	Camping		Snorkeling or Scuba Diving
	Hiking		Waterskiing
	Biking		Windsurfing
	Horseback Riding		Canoeing or Kayaking
	Downhill Skiing		Boating
	Cross-country Skiing		Boat Ramps
	Swimming		Fishing

ONE

Exploring Montana

Montana is known as "Big Sky" country, and that label is no accident. From the vast prairies that swathe the eastern half of this fourth-largest of the United States, one's view of the heavens seems endless. The handful of rural individualists and urban refugees who make their home here, where the Rocky Mountains flow into Canada, would argue that heaven is everywhere in Montana.

Two of America's greatest national parks frame Montana. On the state's northern edge are the spectacularly chiseled peaks of Glacier National Park, the roof of the Rockies: Glacier's watershed flows in not two but three directions, to the Pacific Ocean, the Gulf of Mexico and Hudson Bay. On Montana's southern border with Wyoming lies the thermal wonderland of Yellowstone National Park, whose geysers and hot springs, canyons and waterfalls, and rich and varied wildlife led most Americans to consider it a myth until little more than a century ago.

In the state's far west, stands of huge and ancient firs and cedars dominate the landscape. The Continental Divide follows the Rocky Mountain backbone in a southeasterly direction from Glacier to Yellowstone, dividing Montana into two unequal halves. Two great rivers, the Missouri and the Yellowstone, drain the eastern prairies where huge dinosaurs once roamed and where Crow, Cheyenne and Blackfeet Indians pursued the world's largest herds of American bison across the plains.

History is everywhere in Montana. The American Indian culture lives on in seven different Indian reservations and numerous state parks and historic sites. Among them is the Little Bighorn Battlefield National Monument; General George Armstrong Custer is popularly cited as having made his "last stand" here, when in fact the demise of Custer's cavalry was the last hurrah for Sioux and Cheyenne warriors in their struggle against white domination. The Meriwether Lewis and William Clark expedition is well chronicled; the explorers twice transited Montana, in 1805 and 1806, opening the way for subsequent settlement. Myriad 19th-century ghost towns still speckle the landscape, remnants of a boom-and-bust mining era when fortunes were made and lost in the same day and vigilante justice ruled many towns.

Montana's urban centers are few and far between. A scant 877,000 people live in this state of just over 147,000 square miles. Billings, Montana's largest city, has fewer than 100,000 residents. People come to Montana to get away from city life, not to find it. As a result, outdoor opportunities abound. Fishing and hunting are religions in the northern Rockies and upper Great Plains, and the less aggressively inclined will find wide-ranging opportunities for boating and whitewater rafting, hiking and horseback riding, skiing and bicycling. Montana is, indeed, a state for all seasons.

Hidden Montana is designed to help you take full advantage of your vacation. It covers popular, "must-see" places, offering advice on how best to enjoy them. It also tells you about many off-the-beaten-path spots, the kind you might find by talking with folks at the local café or with someone who has lived in the area all of his or her life. It describes the state's history, its natural areas and its residents, both human and animal. It suggests places to eat, to stay, to play, to camp. Taking into account varying interests, budgets and tastes, it provides the information you need whether your vacation style involves backpacking, golf, museum browsing, shopping or all of the above.

After providing introductory information, this book starts its statewide tour in northwest Montana (Chapter Two) and adjacent Glacier National Park (Chapter Three). Straddling the Continental Divide on the Canadian border, Glacier is a vast region of chiseled peaks and broad valleys, of deep blue lakes and racing rivers. South and west of Glacier Park, waves of mountain ranges shelter the likes of enormous Flathead Lake; the National Bison Range, within the Flathead Indian Reservation; the city of Missoula, and the lovely Bitterroot Valley.

Chapter Four (north central Montana) reaches east from the high Rockies into Charles M. Russell country. The life of this cowboy artist (1864–1926), who made his home in Great Falls, paralleled the emergence of the American West. Visitors search out the museum complex and enormous Missouri River wildlife refuge named in his honor, and visit the historic steamboat port of Fort Benton less than an hour's drive from either.

Chapters Five and Six visit southern Montana. Five delves into the rich gold-rush history of southwest Montana. Some ghost towns, such as Bannack and Virginia City, survive as historical monuments. Other towns, like Butte, with its open-pit copper mines, and Helena, the state capital whose heart and soul is Last Chance Gulch, are unique combinations of past and present. Six reaches into south central Montana's "Yellowstone Country," so named for its central river. Burgeoning Bozeman, with its Museum of the Rockies, is the heart of a region that includes historic Livingston and Red Lodge, outstanding ski resorts, the headwaters of the Missouri River and other attractions.

Chapter Seven zooms in on Yellowstone National Park. Although the world's first national park is almost entirely in Wyoming, three of its five gateways are in Montana, and it should be an integral part of any visitor experience here. The expansive park preserves thermal and geological wonders and a remarkable range of wildlife, and is renowned worldwide.

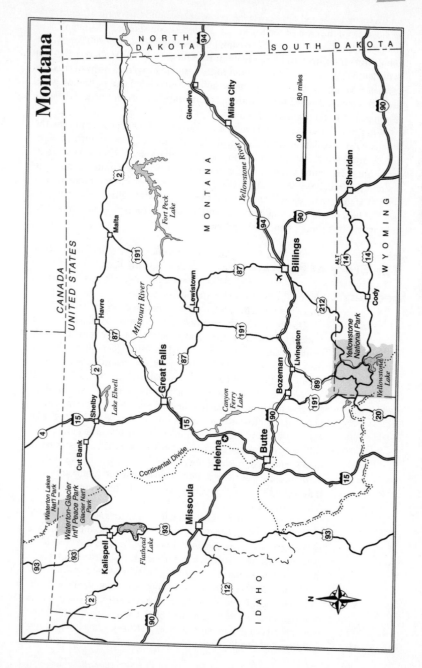

Montana

NORTH DAKOTA

SOUTH DAKOTA

94

Glendive

Miles City

80 miles

40

0

Sheridan

90

2

Fort Peck Lake

M O N T A N A

Yellowstone River

94

90

Billings

W Y O M I N G

Malta

191

Lewistown

87

ALT 14

14

212

Cody

Havre

Missouri River

87

191

Yellowstone National Park

87

2

Great Falls

Livingston

Bozeman

89

Yellowstone Lake

Lake Elwell

Shelby

15

Canyon Ferry Lake

15

90

191

20

Cut Bank

Continental Divide

Helena

Butte

Waterton Lakes Nat'l Park

4

Waterton-Glacier Int'l Peace Park

Glacier Nat'l Park

Missoula

15

93

CANADA

UNITED STATES

93

93

Kalispell

Flathead Lake

93

2

12

I D A H O

90

N

Chapters Eight and Nine cover eastern Montana, and the vast prairies that extend east from the crest of the Rockies. Eight focuses on southeast Montana, a region dominated by the lower Yellowstone River. It includes Bighorn Canyon National Recreation Area and Little Bighorn Battlefield National Monument, as well as the large range towns of Billings and Miles City. Nine explores often-overlooked northeast Montana. Bisected by 134-mile-long Fort Peck Lake on the Missouri River, this region is noted for its history, its recreation, and its amber fields of grain rustling right to the Canadian border.

What you choose to see and do is up to you. One of the joys of exploring this state is its very isolation, and along with that, its decided lack of traffic congestion. Many Montana highways are so wide open that there is no formal daytime speed limit. For some visitors, that means you can scoot from attraction to attraction that much faster, so long as you drive in a "reasonable and prudent manner," as state law requires. For others, it means that while others may race past you like bats out of hell, you can relax and watch the scenery go past: mile after mile after mile of mountain, river and prairie.

▼▼▼▼▼▼▼▼▼▼▼▼▼▼▼

The Story of Montana

GEOLOGY

Montana was once a vast and shallow inland sea, its bedrock dating back two and a half billion years and longer. It was only about 100 million years ago, with the formation of the Rocky Mountains, that it began to take on the appearance we recognize today.

The modern Rockies consist mainly of granite, an igneous rock made up of quartz, feldspar and granite, along with traces and veins of metals such as gold, silver, lead and zinc. As molten elements, these minerals blended deep within the earth and welled upward, to the great sea plain and marshy wetlands on the surface.

Very slowly, the two tectonic plates that make up most of the North American continent—the Canadian Shield and the Pacific Plate—drifted toward each other, floating on the molten rock that still bubbled and brewed far under the earth's surface. In a slow collision, the plates crushed against each other and started to buckle and fold, pushing the granite layer upward. This process continues even now, though so slowly that the mountains have only gained a few inches in height during the time humankind has walked the earth.

Dinosaurs, which were abundant in the area when the formation of the Rockies began, would have experienced the buckling phenomenon as occasional earthquakes. Perhaps not coincidentally, the granite mass cracked through the sandstone surface at about the time of the great beasts' extinction, 60 million years ago.

As the north–south block of mountains tilted upward, the softer sedimentary rocks at the surface slid eastward, their waters draining ahead of them. On these often treeless plains, water and wind have been the principal geological forces, sometimes carving fantastic "badland" formations.

The Rocky Mountains as we see them today, however, were shaped by glaciers. A series of ice ages, the last of which ended 10,000 years ago—less than an eyeblink in geological time—covered the high country in accumulations of snow and ice. These glaciers flowed slowly down the mountainsides in solid frozen rivers that gouged deep valleys creating steep mountain faces and marking the courses for the turbulent rivers that would slice canyons hundreds of feet deep. Nowhere is this natural drama so evident as in Glacier National Park, which takes its name from the forces that carved its unforgettable face.

The lofty mountains attract storm clouds like a magnet, making for rainfall and snowfall many times greater than in the semi-arid prairies to their east. Runoff, from the melting snowpack in spring and the thunderstorms of summer, gives birth to Montana's rivers: notably the great Missouri and Yellowstone, with their myriad forks and tributaries, in the east, but also the Flathead, Bitterroot, Clark Fork and other streams in the west.

> Hot springs, geysers, fumaroles and boiling mud appear in the Yellowstone area in greater concentration than anywhere else on earth. Hot springs throughout the Montana Rockies prove that volcanism remains an active force.

The rivers give significance to the Continental Divide, the dotted line on maps that meanders through the wilderness connecting the highest mountain passes. All precipitation that falls east of the Continental Divide flows eventually to the Atlantic Ocean, via either the Gulf of Mexico or, nearer Glacier Park, via Canada's Hudson Bay. West of the Divide, it flows to the Pacific. In some places, the backbone of the continent is marked by nothing more spectacular than a point-of-interest sign at a roadside rest area. In others, as in Glacier Park, crossing the Continental Divide means climbing a switchback road up a wall of granite to the summit of a pass more than a mile above sea level.

Volcanism has had a profound effect in parts of Montana. The earth remains especially restless around the Yellowstone National Park area, which encompasses a giant ancient caldera. More earthquakes occur here than anywhere in the lower 48 states outside of California.

AMERICAN INDIANS   American Indians touched the Montana Rockies lightly and with reverence. The Flatheads and Kootenais lived as nomads, huddling around fires in bison-leather tents through thousands of long, brutal winters along the foothills, waiting to follow the spring snowmelt into hidden canyons and ancient forests of the high country. Their population was never large, and these mountain tribes rarely came into conflict—in fact, they rarely encountered one another except on purpose. Intertribal pow-

HISTORY

Text continued on page 8.

A Story
of Glaciers

Perhaps the most striking features of Montana's varied landscape are the sheer-sided mountains, the deep lakes and the broad valleys typical of Glacier National Park and adjacent regions of the northern Rocky Mountains.

These are a direct result of glaciation during two million years of ice ages, the most recent of which retreated from Montana's high country barely 10,000 years ago. At its peak, this thick layer of snow and ice was several thousand feet deep.

Glaciers are formed under climactic conditions in which winter snowfall exceeds summer snowmelt over an extended period of time. Eventually, the intensive pressure of snow buildup on an alpine icefield causes underlying layers to compress into an almost plastic glacial ice: extremely hard, but able to flow like viscous water. This ice squeezes out between mountain peaks like toothpaste from a tube; gravity keeps the glacier grinding its way downhill at speeds that can reach several miles a day.

So powerful is this unremitting natural force that it acts as a giant conveyor belt. Montana's ancient glaciers flowed in "gelid" rivers, gouging deep valleys, scouring mountain faces, and establishing courses for turbulent rivers that today slice canyons hundreds of feet deep.

Geologists can measure a glacier's advance by the composition of its moraine: the rock, mud and other debris torn from mountain walls and deposited at the glacier's terminus. This marks the point at which the rate of melting equaled the rate of accumulation, and is a reliable indicator of climactic conditions at any particular time in history.

As conditions change, a glacier will advance or retreat; this is true of the 50-some small glaciers remaining in Glacier National Park today. In the century-plus since their discovery by white explorers, they have shrunken periodically, and their future is indeterminate.

The best known of these are Grinnell Glacier, a prominent landmark of the Many Glacier region and accessible by trail from the Many Glacier Lodge, and Jackson Glacier, which flows east off the Continental Divide at Gunsight Pass and is easily visible from the Logan Pass overlook.

Possibly the most remarkable of the few glaciers still to be found in Montana is the Grasshopper Glacier, high on the Beartooth Plateau above Cooke City near the northeastern entrance to Yellowstone National Park. One of the largest icefields in the continental United States, the glacier takes its name from the millions of grass-hoppers—of a now-extinct species—frozen in its sheer 80-foot ice cliff. A 14-mile wilderness trek is required to reach its base, and if winter snow hasn't sufficiently melted, you won't see the insects even then. August is your best bet.

Three or four other glaciers envelop the flanks of 12,799-foot Granite Peak (Montana's highest) and the surrounding Absaroka-Beartooth Wilderness Area, but serious Montana glacier seekers head north to Glacier Park.

Incidentally, when you look at a glacier, the deep blue you see comes from the great compression of glacial ice. It is especially visible in fractures and is intensified on cloudy days. The glacial ice crystals are so dense that they act as prisms, absorbing all colors of sunlight except the blue wavelength, which is reflected back.

wows were held at traditional times and places for purposes of trade, social contests, spiritual ceremonies and political diplomacy.

Where warfare did occur, it was mainly among the Plains Indians tribes east of the mountains. The Blackfeet and Crow, Cheyenne and Dakota (Sioux) would send hunting parties into the rich high-country valleys of the mountain people. Before the arrival of the whites, intertribal battles bore little resemblance to the bloodbaths that would come. War parties were generally small and had no firearms, steel or horses. The limited supply of arrows a warrior could carry did not last long in battle, and it was better to save them for hunting if possible, since each handmade arrow represented hours of work.

At least two non-Indian influences—horses and guns—began to change the tribes' way of life long before the first white man set foot in what is now Montana at the beginning of the 19th century. Horses had first come into Indian hands in northern New Mexico in 1680, via the Spanish. By the 1750s, virtually every tribe in the Rockies and Great Plains had bought, captured or stolen enough horses to breed its own herd. Many others were driven off or escaped; these wild steeds spawned the herds of mustangs that even today inhabit remote areas of Montana. Horses let the Indians travel much farther and faster, bringing more frequent contact—friendly or hostile—between tribes.

Guns spread more slowly among American Indians. In the British and French settlements along America's east coast, armies of both colonial powers gave rifles to tribes that helped fight the Seven Years' War (1756–63). Guns meant power to conquer other tribes. Fur traders on what was then the American frontier found that the self-defense needs of the tribes made guns extremely valuable as items of exchange, as well as empowering the tribes to hunt more efficiently (and therefore to trade larger quantities of valuable furs for more guns). As a tribe got guns by trading with whites from the east, it often turned them against rival tribes to the west in order to expand its hunting territory. In this way, firearms often made their way westward ahead of the first white explorers.

The popular notion that all American Indians were infallible defenders of their environments is challenged by what next happened in the northern Great Plains. Utilizing different hunting methods that relied on guns and horses, the Plain tribes slaughtered tens of millions of bison in the four decades ending with the 1880s. This event, among others, resulted in extreme hardship for American Indian tribes who relied on buffalo meat and hides to support their culture.

EXPLORERS AND MOUNTAIN MEN   At the time of the first incursion into Montana by white men, the Indian culture was still strong. The region was a part of the vast Louisiana Purchase, acquired from Spain by France in 1800 and sold to the United States for $15 million in 1803. Some 150 wilderness-bound French trappers and traders penetrated the Rockies shortly thereafter, ignorant of the fact that the territory was now American. But that didn't matter much, since virtually all of these frontiersmen took Indian wives and never returned to civilization.

The first official U.S. foray into what is now Montana was the famous Lewis and Clark expedition. In the spring of 1805, 45 men led by Army Captain Meriwether Lewis and soldier William Clark made their way up the Missouri River and across Montana. They found willing guides in Shoshone interpreter Sacajawea and her French fur-trader husband, who led them all the way to the mouth of the Columbia River on the Pacific coast. In 1806, Lewis and Clark took separate routes back east across Montana, Lewis via the Missouri, Clark via the Yellowstone River, rejoining at the confluence of the two streams near what is now Montana's eastern border. The two leaders' published reports of their remarkable expedition opened the gates to generations of subsequent 19th-century exploration and settlement.

> John Colter, a member of Lewis & Clark's expedition, was the first white man to lay eyes on what would become Yellowstone National Park.

Not all of Lewis' and Clark's men returned home with them. In 1806, for instance, expedition member John Colter left the party to seek his fortune as a trapper and trader on the new frontier. He returned to St. Louis four years later with stories of boiling springs and smoke spewing from the earth: He was the first white man to see the strange landscape that would become Yellowstone National Park. Although most people dismissed Colter's tales as the product of an imagination gone mad in the wilderness, no one ignored the fact that he had also brought back a fortune in beaver pelts.

In 1811, less than a year after Colter's return from the wilderness, John Jacob Astor's American Fur Company sent its first expedition into the Rockies. As large international fur-trading companies established trading posts along the eastern edge of the Rockies, hundreds of freelance adventurers set off to probe deeper into the mountains in search of pelts. These "mountain men"— men like Jim Bridger, Jedediah Smith, David Jackson, Jeremiah "Liver Eatin'" Johnston and Thomas "Broken Hand" Fitzpatrick —explored virtually every valley in the Rockies during the next 30 years, bringing back more than half a million beaver pelts each year. In order to kill animals in such phenomenal numbers, the mountain men not only set their own traps but also traded gunpowder and bullets to the Indians for more furs. By the 1840s, beavers had become nearly extinct in the Rockies. The last of the old-time fur trappers became guides for army expeditions and pioneer wagon trains, or established their own trading posts, where they continued to sell ammunition to the tribes—a practice that soon would become controversial, then illegal.

PIONEERS AND PROSPECTORS   The first wagon train crossed the Continental Divide in 1842. It was made up of 100 frontier families, traveling in Conestoga wagons with a herd of cattle, bound for Oregon. The route they took, which came to be known as the Oregon Trail, would be used by just about all pioneers en route to the western territories for the next 27 years. But the trail through future Wyoming and Idaho bypassed Montana.

Montana grew around mining booms, cattle ranching and a transcontinental railroad. Only one of the trappers' early trading posts had become a permanent town. Fort Benton, established in 1846, was an important Missouri River port: It was the head of navigation for steamboats from St. Louis for many decades, and was the prime shipping port in Montana until the advent of the railroad.

The first permanent white settlement in Montana was a Jesuit mission established by Belgian Father Pierre-Jean de Smet in the Bitterroot Valley in 1841. Other missions soon followed. But the riches of the earth did far more to attract settlers than did riches from heaven.

Rich placer gold strikes at Bannack in 1862, Virginia City in 1863 and Last Chance Gulch in 1864 led to the creation of the Montana Territory, with its capital (after 1875) at Helena, a small city that grew up around the third gold strike. The first two communities were briefly territorial capitals, but lawlessness made them bad choices. When Henry Plummer, the sheriff of Bannack, was found to be the secret leader of a band of highway robbers and murderers preying on unprotected miners, a vigilante committee took matters into its own hands. Plummer and his gang were hunted down, and the sheriff was hanged on the gallows he built himself. (Today Bannack's population of 3000 has dwindled to about three—it is now a state park—while Virginia City has found new gold in tourism dollars.)

The Northern Pacific Railroad provided Montana with its first direct rail link with east (Minneapolis) and west (Portland, Oregon) upon its completion in 1883. Cities like Billings, Livingston and Missoula owe their existence to the railroad: Each began as a construction camp before developing into a regional center.

The grasslands of central and eastern Montana were ideal for cattle ranching. With the depletion of the native bison herds to feed railroad crews, boundless grazing land was left empty. The first cattle herds were being driven overland from Texas as early as 1866, but it was the new transportation network that really made Montana's cattle industry economically feasible. Beginning in the mid-1870s, vast ranches that measured in the millions of acres were established in eastern and central Montana under absentee, often British, ownership. These ranches thrived, employing thousands of cowboys and earning their owners bigger profits, in many cases, than the gold and silver mines had ever yielded. (The Grant-Kohrs Ranch National Historic Site, near Deer Lodge, is testimony to this era.) On some of these ranches, cattle numbered in the millions—on paper, at least.

> The unfenced rangeland was so big that to actually count all the cattle, let alone round them up and brand them, was impossible.

The demand for more land for railroads, ranches and mines led to conflict between the settlers and the Indians, who fought to protect their traditional hunting grounds. They won a few battles, but inevitably, they lost the war. The last major Sioux and Cheyenne victory was at the Battle of the Little Bighorn in June 1876, when 260 U.S. cavalrymen under the command of General George Armstrong Custer were annihilated. (The site is today a national monument.) The following year, Nez Perce rebel Chief Joseph and his followers, fleeing toward Canada from Oregon and Idaho, were captured a few miles south of the international border. Nez Perce National Historical Park commemorates their flight.

THE DECLINE OF THE OLD WEST When statehood was granted to Montana in 1889, the frontier already was changing more rapidly than anyone could have predicted. The beginning of the end came with the brutal winter of 1887, when a single blizzard heaped snow higher than the cattle's heads and was followed by weeks of record cold temperatures. When the spring thaw came, few cattle could be found alive: Most had frozen or starved. Some ranch owners lost 90 percent of their herds and went bankrupt, turning their backs on the former ranches.

Newcomers rushed in to seize pieces of the abandoned land. Many started more modest cattle ranches. Others raised sheep—which ruined the rangeland for cattle. These dry-land agricultural farms were hated by both sheep and cattle ranchers because they fenced open rangeland and built roads. Legal title to land that had been part of bankrupt ranches was vague at best, so violent clashes—known as "range wars"—erupted among cowboys, sheepmen and grangers. The chaos was made worse when some cowboys from the early ranches turned to crime after losing their jobs, forming outlaw bands that lived by armed robbery. Rampant lawlessness continued into the early years of the 20th century. Eventually, when landholders had occupied their ranches and farms long enough to file for legal title under the law of adverse possession, the violence ebbed.

Most mining districts of the Rockies continued to flourish until 1893, when the U.S. Congress ended silver subsidies, bringing about a collapse in the market. The gold-mining industry prospered until 1933, when a similar change in federal law ruined the market. World demand for copper, however, increased. Immense ore deposits at Butte, which came to be known as "the richest hill on earth," created a city of 100,000 people at the turn of the 20th century. Here, too, lawlessness and corruption prevailed as three fabulously wealthy "copper kings"—William A. Clark, Marcus Daly and Frederick A. Heinze—fought for control of the mines and state government.

MODERN TIMES Yellowstone became the world's first national park in 1872; the rail junction of Livingston, Montana, founded in 1882, became its first real gateway. Tourists changed here from the main east–west line to a spur line up the Yellowstone River to Gardiner, near Mammoth Hot Springs. This remained the best way into Yellowstone until the 1920s, when many Americans owned automobiles and the first main highways were paved. Ever since, tourism has been central to the Montana economy and has increased steadily.

Today Butte's population is only about 33,000, but its open-pit mines remain productive and the town is a living museum of mining prosperity.

The homesteading era of 1910–1925 brought thousands of new settlers to Montana, as a new wave of immigrants claimed 320-acre Great Plains farms. Unfortunately, they were not well trained in methods of productively farming semi-arid terrain. At first, the grain-growing land of the north and east produced bumper crops of wheat, but a cycle of drought years that began about 1920 led to bank closures, mortgage foreclosures and general economic disaster. When the Great Depression struck in 1929, Montana had a long head start. Soon the mines and lumber mills were closing as well.

President Franklin Roosevelt's New Deal and other Depression-era programs tied to irrigation and soil conservation helped boost Montana out of the hole. Most important was the construction of the Fort Peck Dam on the Missouri River. Completed in 1940, the dam created a 134-mile-long reservoir that not only helps farms, but also has a major hydroelectric and recreational function. With Fort Peck's boost, Montana agricultural and mining sectors returned to their previous era of productivity.

In the late 20th century, Montana has become a key national producer of petroleum and natural gas. The Kevin-Sunburst Field on the Canadian border near Shelby, the Williston Basin Field on the North Dakota border near Sidney, and the Belle Creek Field near Broadus, in the southeast, are all rich in fossil fuels. However, with the fall of oil prices in recent years, petroleum production is not what it once was.

While agriculture continues to play a vital role in Montana, the greatest number of jobs is now in the service industry.

Altitude and rainfall are the primary factors when it comes to plant life in Montana. In the arid prairies that blanket the eastern part of the state (except in the major river valleys that draw their water from the mountains to the west) irrigation is essential—it takes 25 to 40 acres here to graze a single cow. The closer the land is to the base of the Rocky Mountains, the drier it is, with natural vegetation that consists mainly of thin layers of grass. This is because the Rockies cast a rain shadow. As weather patterns move from west to east, clouds dump most of their rain or snow on the high, cool mountains, leaving little moisture to fall on the prairies.

The foothills along the eastern edge of the Rockies are even drier than the prairies, since they are not only in the rain shadow but also are steep enough that whatever rain does fall quickly spills away. The foothills are just high enough, however, that cooler temperatures let snow melt more slowly, seeping into the top layer of earth to sustain scrub trees like juniper and numerous flowering shrubs.

Mountain forests change with elevation, forming three distinct bands. On the lower slopes of the mountains, ponderosa pine stand 50 feet tall and more. Spirelike Douglas fir and spruce dominate the higher reaches of the mountains. Between the two bands of evergreen forest, shimmering stands of aspen trees fill the eastern mountainsides and paint them bright yellow in September. On the wetter western slopes, lodgepole pine forests are more frequently found in this transitional zone. Both the aspen and lodgepole pine are what forestry experts call opportunistic species. Stands grow wherever clearings appear in the evergreen woods, because of forest fires, clearcutting or pine beetle infestations. Gradually, over a span of centuries, the taller evergreens will crowd out old aspen and lodgepole stands as new stands appear elsewhere. The distinctive aspen, in particular, is a delicate tree that cannot tolerate high- or low-altitude extremes.

The upper boundary of the deep-green conifer forests is known as timberline, the elevation above which nighttime temperatures drop below freezing year-round and trees cannot grow. Timberline is around 8500 feet in Yellowstone National Park on the southern Montana border, 6000 feet in Glacier National Park on the state's northern border. Above timberline lies the alpine tundra, a delicate world of short grasses and other green plants rooted in permafrost where tiny flowers appear for brief periods each summer.

At the highest elevations, above 10,000 feet, summer freezing prevents even the small plants of the tundra from growing. Clinging to the granite cliffs and boulders grows lichen, a symbiotic combination of two plants that survive in partnership: A type of moss forms a leathery shell that protects an alga, which in turn provides nutrients by photosynthesis to feed the moss. This ingenious arrangement is perhaps the ultimate tribute to life's amazing capacity for adapting to even the harshest environments.

FAUNA

An abundance of wildlife is one of Montana's greatest attractions. You are most likely to get a good look at large animals in Yellowstone and Glacier parks, where long-standing prohibitions against hunting have helped them lose their fear of humans. The wildlife populations are about the same in national forests and wilderness areas, but sightings are much less common because animals generally keep their distance from roads, trails, and human scent.

The eastern foothills and high plains are a favorite habitat of jackrabbits and prairie dogs, coyotes and pronghorn antelope, as well as prairie birds such as hawks, grouse and pheasants.

As the number of coyotes in an area declines, the number of coyote pups born in a litter increases; so although states have paid hundreds of thousands of dollars every year for nearly a century to eliminate these wild canines because ranchers believe they may pose a threat to livestock, coyote populations are on the increase just about everywhere in the west. They are commonly seen not only in open grasslands, but also on the outskirts of urban areas. Intelligent and curious, coyotes can often be spotted observing humans from a distance. They are not generally dangerous to humans, though they may lure and attack small pets.

Pronghorn antelope, once hunted nearly to extinction and until recently listed as a threatened species under the federal Endangered Species Act, are again a common sight on the high plains. They are most common in Montana's southeast. Although these tan-black-and-white deerlike creatures with short legs and large heads are commonly called antelope, they are not related to the true antelope of Africa and Asia—in fact, they are not related to any other living species.

American bison, more often called buffalo (although they are unrelated to Asian buffalo), once roamed throughout the Great Plains and Rocky Mountains. Today they are only found on buf-

WHO'S AFRAID OF THE BIG GRAY WOLF?

Wolves were virtually extinct in the region until 1995, when in a highly controversial move the first gray (timber) wolves were reintroduced to the backcountry of Yellowstone National Park. Current reports are that more than 300 canine relatives in 31 packs are flourishing—much to the chagrin of area ranchers, whose forebears paid bounty hunters for their slaughter.

falo ranches, a growing industry here, and in a few protected areas including Yellowstone National Park and the National Bison Range north of Missoula. When this range was established by President Theodore Roosevelt in 1908, only about 20 wild bison survived from an estimated 50 million a century earlier. Today the 19,000-acre grassland preserve has as many as 500 of the great beasts.

Rattlesnakes are also in the lower mountains and high plains. The good news is that they rarely venture into the higher mountains. Snakes and other reptiles are coldblooded and cannot function in low temperatures, so they are hardly ever found at elevations above about 7000 feet. When hiking at lower elevations, walk loudly and never put your hand or foot where you cannot see it.

Deer, mountain lions and bobcats inhabit the lower mountain ranges, foothills and plateaus. While white-tailed deer and mule deer may be spotted anywhere in the mountains, they prefer to graze in areas where they can browse on undergrowth. Mountain lions hunt deer and prefer areas with high rocks, where they can spot both danger and prey from a distance. Since mountain lions (also known as cougars) are nocturnal and reclusive, it's a stroke of luck to glimpse one darting across the road in your headlights at night. Wild horses graze some remote areas on the west side of the Rockies, including the Bighorn Canyon on Montana's southern border with Wyoming.

Small mammals commonly found in Rocky Mountain forests and meadows include squirrels, chipmunks, raccoons, porcupines and skunks. Large animals include elk and black bears. Because elk prefer high mountain meadows in the warm months, they are rarely seen outside of national parks except by serious hikers who venture deep into the wilderness. Sightings are more common in winter, when the elk descend to lower elevations where grass is easier to reach under the snow. In some areas, usually marked by signs and sometimes offering observation areas, herds of elk may be spotted from the road in winter. The world's largest concentration of elk is in Yellowstone National Park, especially in the Mammoth Hot Springs area. Moose also are found in the Montana Rockies, most frequently in marshy areas at dawn or dusk. These herbivores, the largest members of the deer family (they may weigh over 1000 pounds at full maturity), are hard to spot because of their ability to blend into forest surroundings.

Black bears are elusive, but more common than most hikers realize. In times of drought, when food is scarce, it's not unusual for a bear to raid trash cans along the fringes of civilization. Black bears rarely attack people, but they are unpredictable and can be dangerous because of their size—they typically run 250 to 350 pounds. Most injuries involving bears happen because campers store their food inside tents with them at night. When camping in the forest, it's a better idea to leave all food inside a closed vehicle or suspended from a tree limb.

Grizzly bears, the larger and more aggressive cousins of black bears, live in the backcountry of Glacier and Yellowstone national parks and adjacent wilderness areas, but are extinct in most other parts of Montana. They are listed as a threatened species by the federal government. Attacks on campers and hikers by the 600- to 1000-pound bears are rare but not unheard of.

Beavers once inhabited nearly every stream in Montana and adjacent states. Trapped by the millions for their pelts in the early 19th century, these largest of North American rodents stood at the brink of extinction. More recently, they have too often been considered pests: Beavers build dams in streams, to create ponds around their dome-shaped stick-and-mud lodges. Their dams flood the most desirable areas of mountain valleys. Landowners persisted for many years in poisoning the beavers, or dynamiting their dams and putting up low electric fences to keep them away. Now a protected species, beavers seem to be making a slow comeback. It's not unusual to discover beaver ponds on backcountry streams, and if you watch a pond near sunset, you may get a look at the animals themselves.

Near timberline, Rocky Mountain bighorn sheep are common and easy to spot in alpine meadows. Herds of ewes are protected by a single ram, while other males lead a solitary existence elsewhere until mating season. Then the high crags echo with the crash of horns as young rams challenge their elders for dominance over the female herd. Mountain goats—shaggy, snow-white and solitary—may also be seen in some high mountain areas, especially in Glacier National Park. The small animals most often seen above timberline are golden marmots—large, chubby rodents nicknamed whistlepigs because they communicate with shrill whistles. Smaller rodents called pikas colonize high-altitude rockpiles, where swarms of hundreds of them are sometimes seen.

▼▼▼▼▼▼▼▼▼▼

Where to Go

Montana is too big a place to cover in one two-week trip. Any attempt to visit all the areas described in this book in a single vacation is doomed from the outset. If you try to "see it all," you may find yourself so focused on covering large distances that you sacrifice quiet moments to appreciate the natural beauty you came to see.

Deciding what to see and where to go is a tough choice. The good news is that no matter how many times you visit, Montana will still have plenty of places to discover the next time you come.

Many tourists head straight away to **Northwest Montana**, the state's least arid region on the western slope of the Continental Divide and (aside from its national parks) the most frequently visited. Its mountains enclose the university city of Missoula; the Bitterroot Valley, flanked on both sides by steep ridges; and the National Bison Range, within the Flathead Indian Reservation. Extending north from Flathead Lake, the largest natural freshwater lake west of the Mississippi River, is the recreational paradise of the Flathead Valley and its central town, Kalispell.

On the northeast rim of this corner of Montana, bordering the Canadian province of Alberta, is **Glacier National Park**, the "roof of the Rockies." Straddling the Continental Divide, its watershed flows in not two but three directions: to the Pacific Ocean, the Gulf of Mexico and Hudson Bay. The park boasts hundreds of miles of trails and thousands of large animals. Its surrounding area includes the Blackfeet Indian Reservation and Canada's Waterton Lakes National Park, together with which Glacier forms the world's only "international peace park."

The Rocky Mountain Front drops dramatically from Glacier National Park to the east, where the prairies slope gently downward to the Missouri River. The regional focus of **North Central Montana** is Great Falls, Montana's second-largest city. The area includes everything from dinosaur digs and ancient "buffalo jumps" to the historic steamboat port of Fort Benton. This is Russell Country, named for turn-of-the-20th-century cowboy artist Charles M. Russell, whose Great Falls studio is now a popular museum of Western art. From Fort Benton, intrepid river runners can launch a fascinating voyage down the wild and scenic Missouri River Breaks.

The world's first national park (it was established in 1872), Yellowstone National Park is undoubtedly the most famous.

Southwest Montana is mining country, past and present. Gold rush history lives on here in ghost towns like Bannack, established as the first territorial capital after ore was discovered here in 1862, and Virginia City, which tourism has kept alive and well and far more law-abiding than it was in the 19th century. Butte, whose copper mines once earned it the label "the richest hill on earth," has a stately and historic hillside downtown more reminiscent of old San Francisco than of any other city in the Rockies. Last Chance Gulch remains Helena's main street. The charming state capital is just a short drive from a spectacular Missouri River gorge known as the Gates of the Mountains.

South Central Montana is also known as "Yellowstone Country." Headwaters of the Missouri and Yellowstone rivers, with their sources in Yellowstone National Park (itself only a short drive from the region's major towns), flow northward through Bozeman, Livingston and other towns. Montana State University and its grand Museum of the Rockies are in sophisticated Bozeman, which has become a magnet for out-of-state immigrants. The former coal-mining town of Red Lodge is located right at the foot of the

Absaroka-Beartooth Wilderness and Montana's highest mountains. Other attractions include major ski resorts and the subterranean network of Lewis and Clark Caverns.

Although 2.2-million-acre **Yellowstone National Park** is almost entirely in Wyoming, three of its five gateways are in Montana. A remarkable thermal wonderland of more than 10,000 geysers, hot springs and boiling mud caldrons, plus impressive canyons, waterfalls and high-elevation lakes, Yellowstone sits on the crest of an ancient volcanic crater. It also has perhaps the Rocky Mountains' most varied and accessible wildlife, from elk and moose to bison and grizzly bears.

The prairies of **Southeast Montana** and the lower Yellowstone River Valley were once were the domain of Plains Indians, who hunted bison, deer and pronghorn antelope by the thousands. Eons before them, this area was a veritable Jurassic Park; modern fossil hunters find paradise here. Montana's largest city, the ranching center of Billings, is a gateway to the Crow and North Cheyenne Indian Reservations, the Bighorn Canyon National Recreation Area, and the Little Bighorn Battlefield National Monument, where General Custer met his match in 1876. Nearby is Miles City, which bills itself as "Montana's cowboy capital."

Bisected by 134-mile-long Fort Peck Lake and its surrounding Charles M. Russell National Wildlife Refuge on the Missouri River, **Northeast Montana** offers fine recreational opportunities. And history stays alive through a strong American Indian presence and the Fort Union Trading Post National Historic Site at the confluence of the Missouri and the Yellowstone rivers.

When to Go

SEASONS

Though it may sound romantic, springtime in Montana is less than appealing. Cold winds, occasional avalanches, brown vegetation and plenty of mud are a few of the reasons why many people in the tourist business shut down their shops and motels in April and take their own vacations to more southerly climes. Just about any other time of year, however, the climate is ideal for one kind of outdoor recreation or another, giving rise to a distinctive summer-and-winter double tourist season.

The traditional summer tourist season, which runs from Memorial Day to Labor Day, is characterized by cool nights, mild days, colorful wildflowers and sudden, brief afternoon rainstorms. In most parts of the Montana Rockies, it's a good idea to start outdoor activities early and carry ponchos or waterproof tarps on all-day hikes, since rain is almost inevitable in the afternoon.

In a common yet peculiar phenomenon, wind currents called "waves" can carry precipitation for long distances from clouds hidden behind the mountains, causing "sun showers." Old-timers say that if it rains while the sun is shining, it will rain again tomorrow. This adage almost always holds true—but then, if it doesn't rain in the sunshine, it's still likely to rain tomorrow. The good news is, summer rains rarely last more than an hour, and skies generally clear well before sunset.

Above timberline, temperatures may fall below freezing at night all summer and typically reach only 40° to 50° Fahrenheit at midday. It is not unusual for Glacier's Going-to-the-Sun Road and other alpine byways to be closed by blizzards even in August, sometimes stranding motorists for an hour or two before snow-plows clear the road.

Early fall—around mid-September—is one of the most delightful times to visit the Montana Rockies, as the turning of the aspens paints the mountainsides in yellow with splashes of orange and red, brilliant against a deep green background of evergreen forests. Mountain highways tend to be crowded with carloads of leaf-gawkers on weekends but not on weekdays, while hiking and biking traffic on forest trails is much lighter than during the summer. The weather is generally dry and cool in early fall, making it a great time to take a long wilderness hike or mountain bike trip. The first light snowfall can be expected in the high country toward the end of September; the first heavy snow typically comes around Halloween. November is hunting season, a good time to stay out of the mountains unless you're armed and dangerous.

The official ski season runs from Thanksgiving Day through March—the period in which all ski areas expect a reliable snow base and within which all ski events and package tours are scheduled. If you're planning ahead for a major ski vacation, you'll want to schedule it between those dates, too. In reality, snowfall amounts, as well as winter temperatures in the mountains, can vary a lot from year to year, so the actual dates of operation at various resorts can be somewhat unpredictable. These days, the huge artificial snowmaking capacity of most ski areas almost always assures a Thanksgiving opening day. While snowmaking usually ceases after March when advance-reservation business slows down, skiing continues until spring temperatures rise enough

"SNOW EATERS"

East of the Continental Divide, clouds typically build in the early afternoon and then burst into thunder, lightning and sometimes hail. But North Central Montana is more noted for a unique winter weather phenomenon called "snow eaters" by the Blackfeet Indians. Warm "chinook" winds that sometimes sweep down the Rocky Mountain Front in midwinter have been known to raise temperatures by 40 or more degrees (Fahrenheit) in ten minutes or less. Great Falls gets the brunt of these, but their effect is felt as far east as Billings.

to erode the snow base. In some years, at some ski areas, late-season skiing may continue well into April. Uncrowded ski trails, discount lift tickets and lots of sunshine make the late season a favorite time for many local ski enthusiasts.

CALENDAR OF EVENTS

JANUARY   **North Central Montana**   The Montana Pro Rodeo Circuit Finals are held in Great Falls in the middle of the month.

FEBRUARY   **Northwest Montana**   The Whitefish **Winter Carnival** includes parades, fireworks and a formal dance, plus torchlight skiing and races on the Big Mountain.
Southwest Montana   The four-day, 350-mile **Race to the Sky Dog Sled Race** traverses spectacular trails bordering the Bob Marshall and Scapegoat wildernesses. The **Winternational Sports Festival** in Butte features a variety of outdoor and indoor events. Anaconda's **Chocolate Festival** gives town residents a midwinter caffeine and sugar buzz.
South Central Montana   The Red Lodge **Winter Carnival** climaxes the ski season in this old mining town.

MARCH   **Northwest Montana**   Arts, crafts, music and dancing round out the activities for Libby's **Irish Fair and Music Festival**.
Glacier National Park   As the winter snow melts near Essex, the **Snow Rodeo and Spring Ski Race** gives cross-country skiers one final, late-season fling.
North Central Montana   The four-day **C. M. Russell Auction of Original Art** in Great Falls is widely regarded as the nation's largest and finest auction of original Western art of the 19th and 20th centuries.
Southwest Montana   As many as 50,000 people are Irish for two days around **St. Patrick's Day** in Butte.

APRIL   **Northwest Montana**   Near Whitefish, the exciting Big Mountain celebrates the end of ski season with its annual **Furniture Race**: Participants test chairs and sofas, fitted with skis, on the slopes. In Missoula, the **International Wildlife Film Festival** screens videos from around the world for a full week and offers workshops, lectures and seminars.
Glacier National Park   **Essexpress** is a weekend devoted to railroad history at the Izaak Walton Inn.
Southwest Montana   The **Helena Railroad Fair** is the largest convention of model train enthusiasts in the northern Rockies.
South Central Montana   Montana State University-Bozeman hosts the **Indian Club Powwow**, featuring dancing, drumming, singing and food from a number of local tribes.

Northeast Montana Glendive hosts the **Spring Fling** with home and garden booths and exhibitions.

Northwest Montana Bigfork's **Whitewater Festival** is highlighted by kayak races on Class V rapids and a triathlon.

Southeast Montana In Billings, an MSU **Wine & Food Festival** has six days of tastings and auctions to benefit Montana State University. Miles City's **Bucking Horse Sale** features three days of bucking-bronc riding, thoroughbred and wild-horse racing, street dances and a parade.

Northwest Montana Lovers of Rocky Mountain oysters throng to the **Mission Mountain Testicle Festival** in Charlo to see bull privates cleaned, breaded and deep-fried before serving.

North Central Montana The **Lewis & Clark Festival** in Great Falls includes a re-enactment of the explorers' 1805 passage and encampment on the Missouri River. Fort Benton's **Summer Celebration** includes a parade, concert, art show and fireworks.

Southwest Montana Helena hosts the **Governor's Cup**, the state's biggest annual road-running event with more than 7000 entries. **Western Heritage Days** at the Fort Owen Inn Arena in Stevensville celebrate 19th-century ranch life with packing demonstrations, chuckwagon cookery and performances of cowboy music.

Yellowstone National Park The **Upper Yellowstone Roundup** offers a rodeo, parade and community dance in Gardiner, at the park's north entrance.

Southeast Montana The highlights of **Little Big Horn Days** in Hardin are a full-scale re-enactment of Custer's Last Stand and a "military ball" in 1880s period wardrobe. **Buzzard Day** at Makoshika State Park, near Glendive, includes a variety of outdoor events to celebrate the buzzards' annual return.

Northeast Montana The **Fort Union Rendezvous** near Sidney is an authentic re-creation of historic trapping and trading days. The **Red Bottom Powwow** in Frazer, on the Fort Peck Indian Reservation, is a traditional Assiniboine fete. **Frontier Days** bring rodeos, parades, a barn dance and the Dirty Shame dance show to Culbertson.

Northwest Montana The **Standing Arrow Powwow**, at Elmo on Flathead Lake, is highlighted by Kootenai dancing. Missoula hosts an **International Choral Festival** for five days at mid-month. Hamilton has two big events: the **Bitterroot Valley Bluegrass Festival**, with banjo and fiddle workshops and music for the whole family, and the **Bitterroot Valley Good Nations Powwow** featuring American Indian music and arts. **Libby Logger Days** are highlighted by a parade and widespread entertainment.

Glacier National Park   At Browning on the Blackfeet Indian Reservation, **North American Indian Days** focus on the dancing, singing, drumming and games of this Plains Indian tribe; there's a parade and a rodeo.

North Central Montana   From late July into early August, the **Montana State Fair** dominates life in Great Falls with top-name entertainment, rodeos and horse races, art and trade shows, and a carnival. Late in the month, Lewistown is at center stage again with its **Central Montana Horse Show, Fair and Rodeo.** The **Great Northern Fair** in Havre includes a rodeo, a demolition derby and a large midway. The Fort Belknap Indians convene their annual powwow as part of **Milk River Indian Days** in Harlem, also including a parade and crafts exhibits.

Southwest Montana   Butte takes six days to celebrate July 4 with parades, concerts, dances and fireworks in its annual **Freedom Festival.** Helena's big event is the **Last Chance Stampede and Fair,** a classic four-day Western rodeo with great entertainment. The quiet streets of Bannack State Park, west of Dillon, come to life for **Bannack Days,** featuring pioneer craft demonstrations and activities that include horse-and-buggy rides, black-powder shooting and panning for gold. **Twin Bridges' Floating Flotillas and Fish Fantasies,** a weekend of arts, dances and entertainment, concludes with a floating parade on the Beaverhead River.

South Central Montana   Red Lodge's **Home of Champions Rodeo and Parade** and the **Livingston Roundup Rodeo and Parade** are weekend-long tributes to Independence Day. Bozeman's **Gallatin County Fair** runs for five days at mid-month. The **Red Lodge Mountain Man Rendezvous** re-creates the fur-trader era of the 1820s and 1830s.

Southeast Montana   On the Northern Cheyenne Indian Reservation at Lame Deer, the **Northern Cheyenne Powwow** on the July 4 weekend features parades, dancing, drumming, singing and feasting. There are also big **4th of July celebrations** in Laurel and Roundup and a major rodeo in Harlowton. **Summerfair** in Billings is an arts festival that draws more than 100 artisans from 15 states to benefit the Yellowstone Art Center. **Homesteader Days** in Huntley include such old-style entertainment as a parade, concerts and a big barbecue.

Northeast Montana   The granddaddy of all Montana rodeos is the **Wild Horse Stampede** at Wolf Point on the Fort Peck Indian Reservation; evolved from traditional powwows and bucking contests, it features wild-horse races and other events. The **Old Fashion Fourth** in Lambert includes 19th-century diversions. Glasgow hosts the **Montana Governor's Cup Walleye Tournament,** which brings 200 teams of fishermen to Fort Peck Lake to compete for a $15,000 prize, and the **Northeast Montana Fair & Rodeo.**

Northwest Montana The **Western Montana Fair & Horse-racing** in Missoula and **Northwest Montana Fair** in Kalispell, scheduled one after the other, highlight the August calendar. Each is several days long and feature rodeos, horse racing, demolition derbies, country-and-western concerts, parades and fireworks. Musicians stroll Bigfork's main street and artists display their creations during the Flathead Lake community's annual **Festival of the Arts**. Ever since Trout Creek, near Thompson Falls on Noxon Reservoir, was proclaimed "Huckleberry Capital of Montana" in 1981, it's held an annual **Huckleberry Festival**, including an arts fair and parade. **Buffalo Days** in Gardiner includes a parade, street dance and buffalo-meat barbecue.

North Central Montana Lewistown's **Montana Cowboy Poetry Gathering** is three days of authentic rhymes and recitations, music and dance. **Rocky Boy's Annual Powwow** at the reservation south of Havre honors native heritage with dances and crafts.

Southwest Montana The **Commemoration of the Battle of the Big Hole**, at Big Hole National Battlefield Park, recalls one of the major conflicts of the 1877 Nez Percé War. Helena celebrates Montana artists with the juried **Western Rendezvous of Art**.

South Central Montana The **Sweet Pea Festival of the Arts** in Bozeman attracts big-name musicians for rock and jazz concerts; there are also sporting events, a parade, arts and crafts and a climactic ball. In Red Lodge, the **Festival of Nations** pays homage to immigrants from many countries who built the old mining town; highlights include traditional dances, craft demonstrations, an international cooking pavilion and a parade.

Southeast Montana The **MontanaFair** brings rodeos, livestock exhibitions, concerts and a carnival to Billings. Miles City's **Eastern Montana Fair & Rodeo** is scheduled the last full weekend of the month. Crow Agency, located on the Crow Indian Reservation, becomes the "tepee capital of the world" for five days during the **Crow Fair and Rodeo**, when hundreds of tepees rise from the banks of the Little Bighorn River: events include parades, dancing, singing, feasting and horse races. At Huntley's annual **Threshing Bee**, visitors can see antique farming equipment used by early-20th-century homesteaders in operation, and enjoy arts and music.

Northeast Montana **Wadopana Powwow** is celebrated at Wolf Point on the Fort Peck Indian Reservation.

Northwest Montana Libby's **Nordicfest** is a three-day celebration of the logging town's Scandinavian heritage, featuring traditional crafts, food, dancing and sporting events.

North Central Montana Lewistown hosts the **Montana State Chokecherry Festival**, in which a parade, arts exhibit and duck races share time with the tasting and judging of preserves and wine. There are old-fashioned **Threshing Bees** in Choteau.

Southwest Montana   The **North American Indian Alliance Powwow** takes place in Butte. The **Last Chance Community Powwow** gets Helena dancing and singing late in the month.

South Central Montana   The **Running of the Sheep** at Reedpoint, about halfway from Bozeman to Billings, is vaguely reminiscent of the famous running of bulls in Pamplona, Spain, as a herd of woolies is driven down the six-block-long Main Street. There's also a parade and a log throwing contest.

Southeast Montana   In Laurel, the **Canyon Creek Battlefield Pipe Ceremony** honors all veterans of the battle between the Nez Perce and the U.S. Army with a peace pipe ritual, rifle salute and riderless horse procession.

Northeast Montana   The **Milk River Wagon Train** is reason for a community parade and festival in Malta. A parade of 80 antique tractors, a barbecue and fiddle music highlight the **Threshing Bee and Antique Show** in Culbertson.

OCTOBER   **Northwest Montana**   Bigfork's **Tamarack Time** is a harvest festival in which individual community members prepare their favorite recipes. The four-day **Glacier Jazz Stampede** in Kalispell presents all kinds of jazz music, from ragtime and big-band to modern improv.

Glacier National Park   Railroad buffs again gather at the Izaak Walton Inn in Essex for the **Alta/Mont Railfan Weekend**.

South Central Montana   As hunting season kicks off, the restaurants of Ennis host **Hunters Feed and Wildgame Cookoff**, competing for prizes with their wild-game recipes.

Southeast Montana   The NILE **Stock Show and Rodeo** in Billings has five rodeo performances in eight days, livestock shows and a trade exhibit with more than 150 presenters.

NOVEMBER   **Northwest Montana**   Missoula gears up for the holiday season with the **Festival of Gifts Art & Craft Show**. Bigfork also gets ready for Christmas when **Bigfork Elves Decorate for Christmas** with a tree lighting ceremony.

Southwest Montana   The **Downtown Helena Fall Art Walk** features horse-drawn carriage rides, music and demonstrations by local artists.

Southeast Montana   Billings slips into the holiday spirit with its **Holiday Parade**.

Northeast Montana   The **Christmas Stroll & Parade of Lights** on Thanksgiving Friday launches the holiday season in Sidney.

DECEMBER   **Northwest Montana**   Bigfork's **Christmas Parade** features colorful lighting displays and a variety of special holiday events.

North Central Montana During Great Falls' **Christmas Stroll**, fiddlers, cowboy poets and wagonrides usher in the holiday season.

Southwest Montana Butte holds its **Festival of Trees** and a **Christmas Stroll** the first weekend of the month.

South Central Montana Downtown streets close to vehicle traffic and merchants stay open late during **Christmas Strolls** in Bozeman and Red Lodge.

Southeast Montana Other cities have embraced the **Christmas Stroll** idea, including Billings and Broadus.

▼▼▼▼▼▼▼▼▼▼▼
Before You Go

VISITORS CENTERS

For free visitor information packages, including the annual *Montana Vacation Guide*, state highway map and current details on special events, accommodations and camping, contact **Travel Montana**. ~ P.O. Box 200533, Helena, MT 59620-0133; 406-841-2870, 800-847-4868; www.visitmt. com. In addition, most towns have chambers of commerce or visitor information centers. Tourist information centers are usually not open on weekends. For information on Yellowstone National Park, contact the **Wyoming Division of Tourism**. ~ 122 West 25th Street, Herschler Building, Cheyenne, WY 82002; 307-777-6323; www.wyomingtourism.org. For information on Canada's Waterton Lakes National Park, contact **Waterton Park Information Services**. ~ Box 100, Waterton Lakes National Park, Alberta T0K 2M0, Canada; 403-859-2252, fax 403-859-2342; www.watertoninfo.ab.ca, e-mail travel@watertoninfo.ab.ca.

PACKING

The adage that you should take along twice as much money and half as much stuff as you think you'll need is sound advice as far as it goes. In the more remote reaches of Montana, though, stores selling something more substantial than beef jerky and country-and-western cassettes are few and far between.

Westerners in general, and Montanans in particular, are casual in their dress and expect the same of visitors. Leave your suit and tie at home. Even in summer, you should pack a couple of long-sleeve flannel shirts, jeans and your cowboy boots for evening or ranch wear, but most of the time, you'll be happy in shorts and a T-shirt. In spring and fall, layers of clothing are your best bet, since the weather can change dramatically from day to day and region to region. Winters are downright cold, so pack your very warmest clothing for this time of year!

Other essentials to pack or buy along the way include a good sunscreen and high-quality sunglasses. Cool temperatures often lull newcomers into forgetting that thin high-altitude air filters out far less of the sun's ultraviolet rays; above timberline, exposed skin will sunburn faster than it would on a Florida beach.

For outdoor activities, tough-soled hiking boots are more comfortable than running shoes on rocky terrain. Even RV travelers and those who prefer to spend most nights in motels may want to take along a backpacking tent and sleeping bag in case the urge to stay out under star-spangled Western skis becomes irresistible. If you're planning to camp in the mountains during the summer months, don't forget to pack lots of mosquito repellent. A canteen, first-aid kid, flashlight and other routine camping gear are also likely to come in handy. Both cross-country and downhill ski rentals are available everywhere you look in the mountains during the winter, though serious skiers may find that the quality and condition of rental skis leave something to be desired. In the summer, mountain bikes may be rented as well. Other outdoor-recreation equipment—kayaks, fishing tackle, golf clubs and gold pans—generally cannot be rented, so you'll want to bring the right gear for your special sporting passion.

Umbrellas are oddities around these parts: A Montanan keeps chilly afternoon rain from running down the back of his or her neck by wearing a cowboy hat.

A camera, of course, is essential for capturing your travel experience; of equal importance is a good pair of binoculars, which let you explore distant landscapes from scenic overlooks and bring wildlife up close. And don't, for heaven's sake, forget your copy of *Hidden Montana*.

LODGING   Accommodations in Montana run the gamut from tiny one-room cabins to luxury hotels that blend traditional alpine-lodge ambience with contemporary elegance. Bed and breakfasts can be found in most of the larger or more tourist-oriented towns you'll visit, and even in such obscure places as Absarokee and Bigfork. They come in all types, sizes and price ranges. Typical of the genre are lovingly restored Victorian-era mansions comfortably furnished with period decor, usually having fewer than a dozen rooms.

The abundance of motels in towns along all major highway routes presents a range of choices, from name-brand motor inns to traditional ma-and-pa establishments that have endured since motels were invented. While rather ordinary motels in the vicinity of major tourist destinations can be pricey, lodging in small towns away from major resorts and interstate routes can offer friendliness, quiet and comfort at ridiculously low rates.

At the other end of the price spectrum, peak-season rates at a handful of leading ski resorts can be very costly. To save money, consider staying in more affordable lodging as much as an hour away and commuting to the ski slopes during the day, or plan your vacation during "shoulder seasons," before and after the peak seasons. Even though the summer is a lively time in many ski towns, accommodations are in surplus and room rates often drop to less than half the winter rates.

In some Montana towns, you'll find lavishly restored historic hotels that date back to the mining-boom days of the late 19th century. Many combine affordable rates with plenty of antique decor and authentic personality. Both Glacier and Yellowstone national parks have lodges that offer distinctive accommodations at mid-range rates: the Glacier Park Lodge and Yellowstone's Old Faithful Inn rank high among the Rockies' most memorable historic inns.

Guest ranches are located throughout the state. Horseback riding is the common theme of all. Some offer luxury lodging, spa facilities, and a full range of activities that may include fishing, boating and swimming. Others operate as working ranches, providing lodging in comfortably rustic cabins and offering the opportunity to participate in roundups, cattle drives and other ranching activities. Rates at most guest ranches are comparatively expensive, but include all meals and use of recreational facilities. Most guest ranches have minimum-stay requirements ranging from three days to a week.

Whatever your preference and budget, you can probably find something to suit your taste with the help of this book. Remember, rooms can be scarce and prices may rise during peak season: summer in most of the state, winter in ski resorts. Travelers planning to visit a place in peak season should either make advance bookings or arrive early in the day, before the "No Vacancy" signs start lighting up. National park lodges are highly sought after, so travelers must make reservations several months in advance.

Lodging prices listed in this book are high-season rates. If you are looking for off-season bargains, it's good to inquire. *Budget* lodgings generally run less than $50 per night for two people; while satisfactory and clean, they are modest. *Moderate* motels and hotels range from $50 to $90; what they have to offer in the way of luxury will depend on where they are located, but they generally offer larger rooms and more attractive surroundings than budget lodgings. At *deluxe*-priced accommodations, you can expect to spend between $90 and $130 for a homey bed and breakfast or for a double in a hotel or resort. In hotels of this price you'll generally find spacious rooms, a fashionable lobby, a restaurant and often a bar or nightclub. *Ultra-deluxe* facilities, priced above $130, are the finest in the state, offering all the amenities of a deluxe hotel plus plenty of extras.

Room rates vary as much with locale as with quality. Some of the trendier destinations have no rooms at all in the budget price range. In other communities—those where rates are set with truck drivers in mind and those in out-of-the-way small towns—every motel falls into the budget category, even though accommodations may range from $19.95 at rundown, spartan places to $45 or so at the classiest motor inn in town. The price categories listed in this book are relative, designed to show you where to get the most out of your travel budget, however large or small it may be.

DINING

Fine dining in Montana tends to focus on the region's traditional cuisine: beef and trout. Buffalo steaks and wild-game dishes also are popular throughout the state. Most cities have Italian, Mexican and Chinese restaurants, but only in the more sophisticated university towns of Bozeman and Missoula and in scattered resort communities will you find a wide selection of gourmet foods.

Restaurants listed in this book offer lunch and dinner unless otherwise noted. Dinner entrées at *budget* restaurants usually cost $7 or less. The ambience is informal, service usually speedy and the crowd often a local one. *Moderate*-priced restaurant entrées range between $7 and $12 at dinner; surroundings are casual but pleasant; the menu offers more variety and the pace is usually slower than at budget restaurants. *Deluxe* establishments tab their entrées from $12 to $20; cuisines may be simple or sophisticated, depending on the location, but the decor is plusher and the service more personalized than at moderate-priced restaurants. *Ultra-deluxe* dining rooms, where entrées begin at $20 and cooking is a fine art, are virtually nonexistent in Montana.

If your idea of an ideal vacation includes savoring epicurean delights, then by all means seize opportunities whenever they arise. When traveling in Montana, you can go for days between gourmet meals.

Some restaurants change hands often and are occasionally closed in low seasons. Efforts have been made in this book to include places with established reputations for good eating. Compared to evening dinners, breakfast and lunch menus vary less in price from restaurant to restaurant.

DRIVING

Some first-time visitors to the Rocky Mountains wonder why so few mountain roads have guard rails to separate motorists from thousand-foot dropoffs. The truth of the matter is, highway safety studies have found that far fewer accidents occur where there are no guard rails. Statistically, edgy, winding mountain roads are much safer than straight, fast interstate highways. Unpaved roads are another story. While many unpaved roads are wide and well graded, weather conditions or the wear and tear of heavy seasonal use can create unexpected road hazards. Some U.S. Forest Service and Bureau of Land Management roadways are designated for four-wheel-drive or high-clearance vehicles only. If you see a sign indicating four-wheel-drive only, believe it. These roads can be very dangerous in a standard passenger car without the high ground clearance and extra traction afforded by four-wheel drive—and there may be no safe place to turn around if you get stuck.

Montana has its share of those straight, fast highways, however, especially in the eastern prairies. For cars, 75 miles per hour is the maximum speed limit on interstates and 70 miles per hour on other roads during the day. Violators are subject to speeding tickets. At night, speed limits for cars are 75 miles per hour on interstate highways, 65 on other roads, and 35 (day or night) in construction zones. Trucks, RVs, and cars with trailers are limited to 65 miles per hour on interstates at all times, 60 miles per hour on other roads during the day, and 55 miles per hour on other roads at night.

Some Montana side roads will take you quite far from civilization, so be sure to have a full radiator and a full tank of gas. Carry spare fuel, water and food. Should you become stuck, local people are usually helpful about offering assistance to stranded vehicles.

Montana gets a lot of snow in the winter months. Mountain passes, not to mention the eastern prairies, frequently become snowpacked. Under these conditions, tire chains are always advised and often required, even on main highways. State patrol officers may make you turn back if your car is not equipped with chains, so make sure you carry them along. At the very least, studded tires—legal in the state from October through May—are recommended. In winter it's wise to travel with a shovel, gravel or cat litter for traction, and blankets or sleeping bags.

If your car does not seem to run well at high elevations, you should probably have the carburetor adjusted at the next service station. The air at Rocky Mountain altitudes is "thin"—that is, it contains considerably less oxygen in a given volume than air at lower altitudes. The carburetor or fuel-injection unit should be set leaner to achieve an efficient fuel-to-air mixture.

You can get full information on statewide road conditions for Montana at any time of year by calling 800-226-7623; for conditions in Yellowstone National Park, call 307-772-0824.

TRAVELING WITH CHILDREN

Any place that has wild animals, cowboys and Indians, rocks to climb and limitless room to run is bound to be a hit with youngsters. Plenty of family adventures are available in Montana, from manmade attractions to experiences in the wilderness. A few simple guidelines will help make traveling with children a pleasure.

Book reservations in advance, making sure that the places you stay accept children. Many bed and breakfasts do not. If you need a crib or extra cot, arrange for it ahead of time. A travel agent can be of help here, as well as with most other travel plans.

If you are traveling by air, try to reserve bulkhead seats: they have more room. Carry on extras you may need such as diapers, changes of clothing, snacks, toys and small games. When traveling by car, be sure to take along those extras, too. Make sure you have plenty of water and juices to drink; dehydration can be a subtle but serious problem. Larger towns, and some smaller ones, have all-night convenience stores that carry diapers, baby food, snacks and other essentials; national parks also have such stores, though they usually close early.

A first-aid kit is essential for any trip. Along with adhesive bandages, antiseptic cream and something to stop itching, include medicines your pediatrician might recommend to treat allergies, colds, diarrhea or chronic problems your child might have. Mountain sunshine is intense, so take extra care to limit youngsters' exposure for the first few days. Children's skin is usually more tender than adult skin, and severe sunburn can happen before you realize it. A hat is a good idea, along with a reliable sunblock. It's advisable to ask your physician if high altitude is a problem for you.

Many national parks, monuments and historic sites offer special activities just for children, and some state parks do so as well. Visitors center film presentations and rangers' campfire slide shows can help inform children about natural history, and head off some questions. Still, kids tend to find a lot more things to wonder about than adults have answers for. To be as prepared as possible, seize every opportunity to learn more, particularly about wildlife, source of consistent curiosity for young minds.

TRAVELING WITH PETS

Montana is big dog country. Throughout the Rockies, you may notice more vacationers traveling with their pets than in other parts of the country. Pets are permitted on leashes in virtually all campgrounds. But few bed and breakfasts or guest ranches will accept them, and more run-of-the-mill motels seem to be adopting "No Pets" policies with each passing year.

Otherwise, the main limitation of traveling with a canine companion is that national parks and monuments prohibit pets on trails or in the backcountry. You are supposed to walk your dog on the roadside, pick up after it, then leave it in the car while you go hiking. Make sure the dog gets adequate shade, ventilation and water. Fortunately, dogs are free to run in national forests; leashes are required only in designated camping and picnic areas.

Visit www.travelpets.com for a list of a few pet-friendly lodgings in Montana and other states.

Wildlife can pose special hazards in the backcountry. At lower elevations in the plains and foothills, campers should not leave a cat or small dog outside at night because coyotes may attack it. In remote forest areas, it's especially important to keep on eye on your dog at all times. Bears are upset by dogs barking at them and may attack even very large dogs. Porcupines, common in pine forests, are tempting to chase and slow enough to catch; if your dog *does* catch one, a mouthful of quills means painfully pulling them out one by one with pliers, or making an emergency visit to a veterinary clinic in the nearest town.

Traveling solo grants an independence and freedom different from that of traveling with a partner, but single travelers are more vulnerable to crime and must take additional precautions.

WOMEN TRAVELING ALONE

It's unwise to hitchhike and probably best to avoid inexpensive accommodations on the outskirts of town; the money saved does not outweigh the risk. Bed and breakfasts, youth hostels and YWCAs are generally your safest bet for lodging, and they also foster an environment ideal for bonding with fellow travelers.

Keep all valuables well-hidden and clutch cameras and purses tightly. Avoid late-night treks or strolls through undesirable parts of town, but if you find yourself in this situation, continue walking with a confident air until you reach a safe haven. A fierce scowl never hurts.

These hints should by no means deter you from seeking out adventure. Wherever you go, stay alert, use your common sense and trust your instincts. If you are hassled or threatened in some way, never be afraid to call for assistance. It's also a good idea to carry change for a phone call and to know a number to call in case of emergency.

For more helpful hints, get a copy of *Safety and Security for Women Who Travel* (Travelers' Tales, 2004).

Montana is a conservative state and not among the more sympathetic to sexual minorities. Nonetheless, you'll find social and support groups in a handful of towns, especially those with larger and more liberal university populations—specifically, at the University of Montana in Missoula as well as Montana State University in Bozeman.

GAY & LESBIAN TRAVELERS

Montana is a friendly and hospitable state for senior citizens to visit, especially in the mountains in summer, when cool and sunny weather offers respite from the hot, humid climate of many other parts of the country. Many hotels, restaurants and attractions offer senior discounts that can cut a substantial chunk off vacation costs.

SENIOR TRAVELERS

The national park system's Golden Age Passport allows free admission for anyone 62 and older to the numerous national parks, monuments and historic sites in the region; apply in person at any national-park unit that charges an entrance fee. The passports are also good for a 50 percent discount on fees at most national-forest campgrounds. Many private sightseeing companies also offer significant discounts for seniors. ~ 888-467-2757; www.nationalparks.org.

The **American Association of Retired Persons** (AARP) offers membership to anyone age 50 or over. AARP's many benefits include travel discounts with several firms and escorted tours on Gray Line buses. ~ 601 E Street NW, Washington, DC 20049; 888-687-2277; www.aarp.org.

Elderhostel offers all-inclusive packages with educational courses at colleges and universities, some in Montana. ~ 11 Avenue de Lafayette, Boston, MA 02111; 617-426-7788, 877-426-8056, fax 617-426-0701; www.elderhostel.org.

A CB radio or cell phone isn't a bad idea for extended backcountry driving.

Be extra careful with your health. High altitude is the biggest risk factor: some driving routes through Montana cross mountain passes that exceed 10,000 feet in elevation. Check with your physician about problems it may pose for you. People with heart problems are commonly advised to avoid all physical exertion above 10,000 feet, and those with respiratory conditions such as emphysema may not be able to visit high altitudes at all. In the changeable climate of the Rockies, seniors are more at risk of suffering hypothermia. Tourist destinations may be a long way from any hospital or other health care facility.

In addition to the medications you normally use, it's wise to bring along your prescriptions in case you need replacements. Consider carrying a medical record with you, including your history and current medical status as well as your doctor's name, phone number and address. Make sure that your insurance covers you while you are away from home.

DISABLED TRAVELERS

Montana is striving to make more destinations, especially public areas, fully accessible to persons with disabilities. Parking spaces and restroom facilities for the physically challenged are provided according to both state law and national park regulations. National parks and monuments also post signs that tell which trails are wheelchair accessible.

Golden Access Passports, good for free admission to all national parks and monuments as well as discounts at most federal public campgrounds, are available at no charge to persons who are blind or have a permanent disability. You must apply in person at any national park unit that charges an entrance fee. ~ 888-467-2757; www.nationalparks.org.

For more information contact the **Society for Accessible Travel & Hospitality**. ~ 347 5th Avenue, Suite 610, New York, NY 10016; 212-447-7284, fax 212-725-8253; www.sath.org. For additional valuable tips, contact **MossRehab ResourceNet**. ~ MossRehab Hospital, 1200 West Tabor Road, Philadelphia, PA 19141; 215-456-9600; www.mossresourcenet.org.

Flying Wheels Travel is a travel agency specifically for disabled people. ~ 143 West Bridge Street, Owatonna, MN 55060; 800-535-6790, fax 507-451-1685; www.flyingwheelstravel.com. You can also contact **Travelin' Talk**, a networking organization. ~ P.O. Box 1796, Wheat Ridge, CO 80034; 303-232-2979; www.travel

intalk.net. **Access-Able Travel Service** has worldwide information online. ~ 303-232-2979; www.access-able.com.

The **North American Riding for the Handicapped Association** promotes the benefits of horseback riding for those with disabilities. They run therapeutic riding centers throughout the state. ~ P.O. Box 33150, Denver, CO 80233; 800-369-7433; www.narha.org.

Passports and Visas Most foreign visitors, other than Canadian citizens, must have a valid passport and tourist visa to enter the United States. Contact your nearest U.S. embassy or consulate well in advance to obtain a visa and to check on any other entry requirements.

FOREIGN TRAVELERS

Customs Requirements Foreign travelers are allowed to import the following: 200 cigarettes (1 carton), 50 cigars or 2 kilograms (4.4 pounds) of smoking tobacco; one liter of alcohol for personal use only (you must be at least 21 years old to bring in alcohol); and US$100 worth of duty-free gifts that can include an additional 100 cigars. You may bring in any amount of currency, although amounts in excess of US$10,000 require a declaration form. Carry any prescription drugs in clearly marked containers; you may have to provide a written prescription or doctor's statement to clear customs. Meat or meat products, seeds, plants, fruit and narcotics are not allowed to be brought into the United States, and there is a long list of other contraband items, from live birds and snakes to switchblade knives, which vacationers hardly ever have with them. For further information, contact the **United States Customs Service.** ~ 1300 Pennsylvania Avenue NW, Washington, DC 20229; 202-354-1000; www.cbp.gov.

Driving If you plan to rent a car, an international driver's license should be obtained prior to arrival. United States driver's licenses are valid in Canada and vice versa. Some rental car companies require both a foreign license and an international driver's license along with a major credit card and require that the lessee be at least 25 years of age. Seat belts are mandatory for the driver and all passengers. Children under the age of 6 or under 60 pounds should be in the back seat in approved child safety restraints.

Currency U.S. money is based on the dollar. Bills come in denominations of $1, $2, $5, $10, $20, $50 and $100. Every dollar is divided into 100 cents. Coins are the penny (1 cent), nickel (5 cents), dime (10 cents) and quarter (25 cents). Half-dollar and dollar coins exist but are rarely used. You may not use foreign currency to purchase goods and services in the United States. Consider buying travelers' checks in dollar amounts. You may also use credit cards affiliated with an American company, such as American Express, VISA, Barclay Card and Interbank.

Electricity and Electronics   Electric outlets use currents of 110 volts, 60 cycles. To use appliances made for other electrical systems, you need a transformer or other adapter. Travelers who use laptop computers for telecommunication should be aware that modem configurations for U.S. telephone systems may differ from their European counterparts. Similarly, the U.S. format for videotapes is different from that in Europe; National Park Service visitor centers and other stores that sell souvenir videos often have them available in European format on request.

Weights and Measurements   The United States uses the English system of weights and measures. American units and their metric equivalents are as follows: 1 inch = 2.5 centimeters; 1 foot (12 inches) = 0.3 meter; 1 yard (3 feet) = 0.9 meter; 1 mile (5280 feet) = 1.6 kilometers; 1 ounce = 28 grams; 1 pound (16 ounces) = 454 grams or 0.45 kilogram; 1 quart (liquid) = 0.9 liter.

▼▼▼▼▼▼▼▼▼▼▼▼▼

Outdoor Adventures

CAMPING

RV or tent camping is a great way to tour Montana's national and state parks and forests during the summer months. Besides saving substantial sums of money, campers enjoy the freedom to watch sunsets from beautiful places, spend nights under spectacular starry skies, and wake up to find themselves in lovely surroundings that few hotels can match.

Most towns have commercial RV parks of some sort, and long-term mobile home parks often rent spaces to RVers by the night. But unless you absolutely need cable television, none of these places can compete with the wide array of public campgrounds available in government-administered sites. Federal campgrounds are typically less developed. You won't find electric, water or sewer hookups in campgrounds at national forests, national monuments or national recreation areas (with the exception of one campground in Bighorn Canyon National Recreation Area). As for national parks, there are more than 300 hookups in Yellowstone and more than 200 in Glacier. The largest campgrounds offer tent-camping loops separate from RV loops, as well as hike-in backcountry camping by permit. A few state park campgrounds in Montana have hookups, notably the various units of Flathead Lake State Park near Kalispell. You won't find much in the way of sophisticated reservation systems in Montana. In July and August, the largest campgrounds in Yellowstone National Park require reservations by calling 307-344-7311 (credit card only); reservations are not accepted at Glacier National Park, nor are they taken for most Yellowstone campgrounds. The general rule in public campgrounds is still first come, first served, even though they fill up practically every night during peak season. For campers, this means traveling in the morning and reaching your intended campground by early afternoon—or, during peak season at Yellowstone, by late morning. In the national parks, campers may find it more convenient to keep a single location for as much as a week and explore surrounding areas on day trips.

For a listing of state parks with camping facilities and reservation information, contact the **Montana Department of Fish, Wildlife & Parks.** ~ 1420 East 6th Avenue, Helena, MT 59620; 406-444-2535; www.fwp.state.mt.us. For information on camping in Montana's national forests, call 877-444-6777 or contact the **U.S. Forest Service-Northern Region.** ~ P.O. Box 7669, Missoula, MT 59807; 406-329-3511; www.fs.fed.us/r1. For information on camping in national parks and monuments, contact the **National Park Service Inter-Mountain Regional National Park Visitor Information.** ~ P.O. Box 25287, Denver, CO 80225; 303-969-2000.

WILDERNESS AREAS AND PERMITS   The passage of the Wilderness Act of 1993 represented a major expansion of federal wilderness protection. Today more than 4.3 million acres of national forest and Bureau of Land Management (BLM) land in Montana has been designated as wilderness. To be considered for federal wilderness protection, an area must consist of at least five contiguous square miles without a road of any kind. At the time it is declared a wilderness area, the land is limited to uses that existed as of that date. Since most wilderness areas in Montana were created quite recently, since 1978, it is generally the highest peaks, where roads are few and far between, that qualify for wilderness status. Besides protecting ancient forests from timber cutting by newly developed methods like skylining or helicopter airlifting, federal wilderness designation prohibits all mechanized transportation: no jeeps, motorcycles or all-terrain vehicles, and (after years of heated controversy) no mountain bikes. Wilderness areas usually have well-developed trail networks for hiking, cross-country skiing and pack trips using horses or llamas.

Some national forest recreation areas have Braille nature trails with marked points of interest appealing to the senses of touch and smell.

You do not need a permit to hike or camp in most wilderness areas, but plan to stop at a ranger station anyway for trail maps and advice on current conditions and fire regulations. Tent camping is allowed without restriction in wilderness areas and almost all other backcountry areas of national forests, except where posted signs prohibit it. Throughout the national forests in dry season and in certain wilderness areas at all times, regulations may prohibit campfires and sometimes ban cigarette smoking, with stiff enforcement penalties.

For backcountry hiking in Glacier and Yellowstone national parks and most other National Park Service–administered sites, you must first obtain a permit from the ranger at the front desk in the visitors center. The permit procedure is simple and free. It helps park administrators measure the impact of hiking in sensitive ecosystems and distribute use evenly among the major trails.

If you frequent national parks, consider purchasing a National Parks Pass. It's good for a year from first use in a park and allows you and your family (or passengers) free entrance into all national parks that charge an entrance fee. ~ 888-467-2757; www.nationalparks.org.

BOATING & RAFTING

Many of Montana's large natural lakes and manmade reservoirs have large sections administered by federal or state agencies. Flathead Lake, for example, has several state park units on its shores; Bighorn Lake is contained within the Bighorn Canyon National Recreation Area; Fort Peck Lake is entirely encompassed by the Charles M. Russell National Wildlife Refuge. Federal boating safety regulations may vary slightly from state regulations, while Indian reservations have separate rules for boating on tribal lakes. (The southern half of huge Flathead Lake is contained within the reservation of the same name.) More significant than any differences between federal, state and tribal regulations are the local rules in force for specific lakes, which are posted near boat ramps. Ask for applicable boating regulations at a local marina or fishing supply store, or use the addresses and phone numbers listed in "Parks" or other sections of each chapter in this book to contact the headquarters for lakes where you plan to use a boat. The same is true if you're planning a trip on the Missouri or Yellowstone rivers, Montana's two major navigable streams.

Boats—from small motorized skiffs, big, fast bass boats, sometimes even houseboats—can be rented by the half-day, day, week or longer at marinas on many of the larger lakes. At most marinas, you can get a boat on short notice on a weekday, since much of their business comes from weekend recreationists.

Whitewater rafting is a very popular sport in many areas of the Montana Rockies, notably the Flathead River near West Glacier Park, the Smith River south of Great Falls, the Clark Fork and Blackfoot rivers east of Missoula, and a series of rivers flowing north out of Yellowstone Park: the Madison, Gallatin, Boulder, Stillwater and upper Yellowstone. Independent rafters are welcome, but because of the bulky equipment and specialized knowledge of river hazards involved, most adventurous souls stick with group tours offered by the many rafting companies located throughout the state (see "Outdoor Adventures" in the appropriate chapters). State and federal regulations require rafters, as well as people using canoes, kayaks, sailboards or inner tubes, to wear life jackets.

Since the splash made by the 1992 Robert Redford movie *A River Runs Through It,* based on the Norman Maclean book of the same title, Montana fishing has received the kind of attention it has always deserved. The state has thousands of miles of streams and hundreds of lakes. The more accessible a shoreline, the more anglers you'll find there, especially in summer. You can beat crowds by hiking a few miles into the backcountry or, to some extent, by fishing on weekdays.

FISHING

Fish hatcheries stock mountain streams with trout, especially rainbows, the Rockies' most popular game fish. Many coldwater lakes also offer fishing for cutthroat and golden trout, kokanee salmon and mountain whitefish. Catch-and-release fly-fishing is the rule in some popular areas, allowing more anglers a chance at bigger fish. Be sure to inquire locally about eating the fish you catch, since some seemingly remote streams and rivers have been contaminated by old mines and mills.

Sought for their delicious meat and caviar-like roe, paddlefish, which weigh well over 100 pounds at maturity, must be snagged with huge treble hooks and stout casting gear.

In the warmer lakes and reservoirs of eastern Montana's Great Plains, the most popular game fish is walleye, a large and hard-fighting member of the perch family common in Missouri River reservoirs and other waters. There are also largemouth and smallmouth bass, northern pike, catfish, crappie, and various other species. Most exotic is the paddlefish, an enormous bottomfeeder with a two-foot snout; it hasn't evolved much over 70 million years. You can chase these fish from May to July in the Missouri and Yellowstone rivers, near their confluence.

For copies of the state's fishing regulations, inquire at a local fishing supply or marina, or contact the **Montana Department of Fish, Wildlife & Parks**. ~ 1420 East 6th Avenue, Helena, MT 59620; 406-444-2535; www.fwp.state.mt.us. Montana state fishing licenses are required for fishing in national forests and national recreation areas, but not on Indian reservations, where short-term permits are sold by the tribal governments. Yellowstone National Park has a seven-day fishing license, which is sold at any of the park's visitors centers for $15.

An annual nonresident fishing license is costly compared to the resident fee. Short-term licenses (ten days or less) are the best bet for nonresident visitors. Nonresident children normally fish free with a licensed adult. High-lake and stream fishing seasons begin in late spring and run through the fall; most lower-elevation lakes and reservoirs are open year-round for fishing.

Downhill and cross-country skiing and snowmobiling are all extremely popular in Montana, along with less common cold-weather sports such as dog-sledding. If you're a snowsport lover, you can

WINTER SPORTS

call **Travel Montana** for current information, updated daily, on weather and snow conditions at downhill ski resorts throughout the state. ~ 406-841-2870, 800-847-4868; www.visitmt.com. You can also call for winter road conditions. ~ 800-226-7623.

Montana has 16 downhill ski areas, the largest of which are The Big Mountain (Whitefish), Big Sky, Bridger Bowl (Bozeman), and Red Lodge. There are more than two dozen groomed cross-country trails in six national forests, extensive backcountry trail systems in Yellowstone and Glacier national parks, and several lodges that cater specifically to Nordic adventurers. Additionally, more than 20 designated snowmobiling areas in the state connect more than 3500 miles of groomed trails, 600 of them at the self-proclaimed "snowmobile capital of the world": West Yellowstone.

Vehicle "snow parks" in national forests and other recreation areas are closely monitored. Before you can use these to unload your skis or snow machine and head into the backcountry, you must buy a season parking permit, available at most sporting-goods shops. The permit fee is much less than the fine you will be paying if you're caught without one.

GUIDES & The best way to assure the reliability of the folks guiding you into **OUTFITTERS** the wilderness by horse, raft or cross-country skis is to choose someone who has met the standards of a statewide organization of their peers. For a membership list, contact the **Montana Outfitters and Guides Association.** ~ 2033 11th Avenue, #8, Helena, MT 596001; 406-449-3578; www.moga-montana.org. For guides and outfitters in Yellowstone Park, contact the **National Park Service.** ~ P.O. Box 168, Yellowstone National Park, WY 82190; 307-344-2271; www.nps.gov/yell.

TWO

Northwest Montana

Northwest Montana is a child of the last Ice Age.

Glacial ice caps and inland seas receded from the Rockies only about 12,000 years ago. Their legacy—a wonderland of steep-sided mountains and broad valleys, of deep blue lakes and racing rivers extending south and west from Glacier National Park—can be enjoyed by all who visit the region today.

Waves of mountain ranges enclose myriad river valleys and lakes, including Flathead Lake, the largest natural freshwater lake west of the Mississippi River.

American Indians, of course, were the first permanent residents of northwest Montana. Nomadic tribes hunted Montana's plains and foraged its valleys for thousands of years before the Flathead settled west of the Continental Divide around A.D. 1500.

French and British trappers may have preceded American explorers Meriwether Lewis and William Clark (1805 and 1806) as the first whites to penetrate the region. In 1841, the first permanent white settlement—a Jesuit mission—was established in the Bitterroot Valley. Gold and silver rushes in the 1850s and 1860s soon led to Montana becoming a territory (in 1864) and a state (in 1889).

Traditionally, the economy of northwest Montana depended heavily upon agriculture and logging. Those trends continue, but today tourism plays an increasingly important role in the economy. The environmental ethic is strong in this mountainous region and that sentiment is particularly evident among the liberal thinkers in the university town of Missoula.

The tourist economy is tied closely to outdoor sports and wildlife viewing. Fishing and hunting, hiking and horseback riding, and skiing and river rafting are some of the more popular pastimes. Five national forests and eight designated wilderness areas provide ample opportunities.

Off-track adventurers are guaranteed to see many nonhuman denizens of the forests, mountains and riverbanks—like elk, deer, antelope, bighorn sheep and mountain goats. They may also encounter grizzly or black bears. Backcountry visitors should consult forest or park rangers to learn appropriate precautions before proceeding into the backcountry.

As elsewhere in Montana, habitation is sparse. There are really only two significant population centers: Missoula, home of the University of Montana and a focus for the state's wood-products industry amid the mountains and valleys of the southwest; and the Flathead Valley, between Flathead Lake and Glacier Park, encompassing Kalispell, Whitefish, Columbia Falls and several other small northwestern towns heavily dependent on tourism.

You can start an exploration of the region from Missoula, at the foot of the Bitterroot Valley, where Montana's first white settlement took place. Route 93 continues north, passing through the Flathead Indian Reservation and skirting the National Bison Range, the Mission Range and Flathead Lake, to Kalispell. West from here, Route 2 extends into the tall timber country around Libby and its nearby Cabinet Mountains Wilderness.

Author Norman Maclean wrote his classic *A River Runs Through It* about life on the Blackfoot River, which runs through the Garnet Range and Lolo National Forest just east of Missoula. The spirit of a people in love with their natural environment, as portrayed in the book and 1992 movie, is typical of the entire region.

Missoula

Sitting on the Clark Fork River at the intersection of five river valleys, surrounded by mountains on all sides, the university town of Missoula is unquestionably one of Montana's most attractive communities. It's an intellectually and artistically oriented city, perhaps Montana's most cultured; yet its proximity to outdoor recreation—the Rattlesnake Wilderness Area, which bans motorized travel, begins just a mile from the city limits—makes it a mecca for backpackers, river rafters and anglers alike.

Missoula (pop. 60,700) got its name from British explorer David Thompson, who mapped the area in 1812 and dubbed it *Ne-missoola-takoo,* meaning "at the cold chilling waters" in the native Salish language. The first settlement here was in 1860, but the town grew quickly as a regional center for mining, logging and the railroad industry.

SIGHTS

Twenty-seven city buildings are today on the National Register of Historic Places, including the old **Northern Pacific Depot,** at the north end of Higgins Avenue, in downtown Missoula's main street. ~ 100 West Railroad Avenue. The biweekly Farmers Market spreads around its portals, and city trolley tours begin at the circle in front. Inquire at the **Missoula Convention & Visitors Bureau** for details on this and other organized tours. ~ 1121 East Broadway #103; 406-543-6623, 800-526-3465; www.missoula chamber.com, e-mail info@missoulachamber.com.

Just three blocks southeast of the depot is the west end of the **East Pine Street Historic District.** Beginning at Pattee Street and extending five blocks east to Monroe, the thoroughfare boasts fine Queen Anne houses facing a central park strip. Turrets and

One-day Getaway

Missoula to Bigfork

- Leaving Missoula early, follow Route 93 to Ravalli (37 miles). Take Route 12 (six miles) and Route 212 (four miles) to the **National Bison Range** (page 57) in Moiese. Stop at the visitors center for a crash course on bison history then drive the beautiful 19-mile road across Red Sleep Mountain. Watch for bison, pronghorn sheep and birds.

- Five miles north of Ravalli on Route 93, take a self-guided tour of **St. Ignatius Mission** (page 58) with its many hand-painted murals. Allow 30 minutes.

- Back on Route 93, stop 20 miles down the road at **Sqelix'u-Aqsmakni'k Cultural Center (The People's Center)** (page 58), a small Indian museum near Pablo that's worth visiting. Allow about one hour.

- Drive seven miles to **Polson** (page 59). Eat lunch and meander through the gift shops and galleries. Tour either the **Miracle of America Museum** (page 59) or the **Polson-Flathead Historical Museum** (page 59). Then check out the impressive views near the 204-foot-high **Kerr Dam** (page 59).

- Backtrack briefly to Route 35 at the foot of Flathead Lake. Then follow Route 35, the scenic east shore route around the lake to Bigfork (34 miles). Seasonal roadside stands sell a variety of fresh fruits, with cherries topping the list. If you spot an open stand, pull over.

- Spend the rest of the afternoon and night at **Bigfork** (page 60). Shoppers will need a couple of hours to saunter through the lakeside village's wonderful art galleries, gift shops and clothing stores. For dinner, reserve a table at the acclaimed Showthyme or the equally popular La Provence or **Bigfork Inn** (page 62). Cap off the evening with a musical at the **Bigfork Summer Playhouse** (page 64).

asymmetrical features intersperse with more neo-classical styles to make this a must-see for architecture buffs.

The **Art Museum of Missoula,** a half block south of Pine, specializes in art of the western states. A permanent collection of contemporary Montanan artists includes works by Monte Dolack. The museum also offers traveling exhibits, a museum shop and a full slate of community events. Closed Sunday. ~ 335 North Pattee Street; 406-728-0447, fax 406-543-8691; www.missoula artmuseum.org, e-mail museum@missoulaartmuseum.org.

Three blocks west is the **Missoula County Courthouse,** a 1910 building with a distinctive copper-domed clock tower that contains a two-ton bell. Painter Edgar Samuel Paxson, best known for his 1899 painting of "Custer's Last Stand," created a series of eight murals depicting different eras of Montana history for the courthouse. Completed in 1914, they surround the upper landing of the main inside staircase. Closed Saturday and Sunday. ~ 200 West Broadway; 406-721-5700, fax 406-721-4043.

Nearby **St. Francis Xavier Catholic Church** also boasts outstanding artistry in its steeple, its stained-glass windows and its paintings. The church was constructed in 1891; the 66 early Renaissance–style murals in its sanctuary were the work of Jesuit Brother Joseph Carignano, who created them in just 18 months of 1901 and 1902. Call for hours. ~ 420 West Pine Street; 406-542-0321.

A Carousel for Missoula is just what it claims: a fully hand-carved wooden carousel, the first in the U.S. built by community volunteers. Local schoolchildren even raised and donated one million pennies toward its construction. Opened in 1995 in Caras Park, a few steps from downtown near the Clark Fork, the charming and colorful merry-go-round is housed in a pavilion that also features a band organ, gift shop, concession stand and open restoration shop. Adjacent to the carousel is Dragon Hollow, a community-built play area with swings, slides and a three-headed guardian dragon. Admission. ~ 101 Carousel Drive; 406-549-8382; www.carrousel.com.

A short distance southeast of downtown Missoula, the **University of Montana** (UM) spreads across 150 acres and some 64 buildings at the foot of Mount Sentinel, characterized by a giant M on its slopes. Chartered in 1893, UM has an enrollment of 13,558 students and is an integral part of life in Missoula. A student group offers tours of the tree-lined campus; you can also guide yourself around the University Center student union building, modern Washington-Grizzly Stadium, the Maureen and Mike Mansfield Library and the Paxson and Maloy Fine Art galleries. ~ Campus Drive; 406-243-0211, fax 406-243-4087; www.umt. edu. For tours call 406-243-6266.

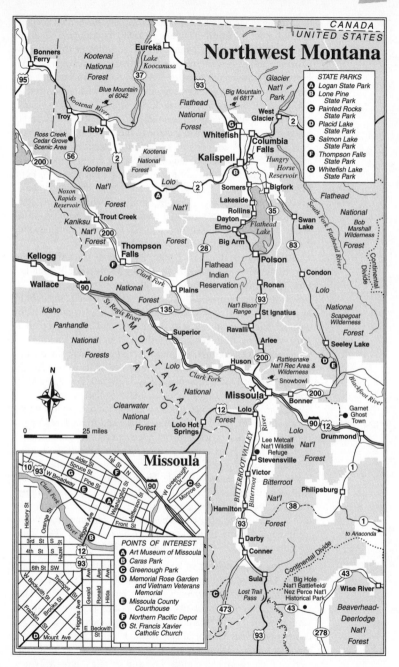

Northwest Montana

CANADA
UNITED STATES

Bonners Ferry

Kootenai National Forest

Eureka
Lake Koocanusa

95

37

93

Blue Mountain el 6042

Big Mountain el 6817

Glacier Nat'l Park

Troy

Kootenai River

Libby

Flathead National Forest

West Glacier

2

Ross Creek Cedar Grove Scenic Area

56

2

G Whitefish

Columbia Falls

STATE PARKS

A Logan State Park
B Lone Pine State Park
C Painted Rocks State Park
D Placid Lake State Park
E Salmon Lake State Park
F Thompson Falls State Park
G Whitefish Lake State Park

200

Kootenai National Forest

Kalispell

Noxon Rapids Reservoir

Kootenai Nat'l

Lolo

Hungry Horse Reservoir

Kaniksu

Trout Creek

Forest

Nat'l

200

Nat'l Forest

Somers

Lakeside

Rollins

Dayton

2

A

Flathead Lake

Bigfork

Flathead National Forest

South Fork Flathead River

35

Bob Marshall Wilderness

Continental Divide

Kellogg

Thompson Falls

Forest

Elmo

Big Arm

Swan Lake

83

F

Clark Fork

28

Wallace

90

Lolo National Forest

St. Regis River

Plains

135

Polson

Ronan

93

Condon

Lolo

Idaho

Panhandle

National

Forests

I D A H O

M O N T A N A

Superior

Nat'l Bison Range

St Ignatius

Ravalli

Arlee

National Scapegoat Wilderness Forest

Seeley Lake

D **E**

Flathead Indian Reservation

Lolo

Clark Fork

National

Clearwater National Forest

N

0   25 miles

Huson

200

Rattlesnake Nat'l Rec Area & Wilderness

Snowbowl

Missoula

Bonner

200

Blackfoot River

Garnet Ghost Town

Lolo

12

Lolo River

Lolo Hot Springs

BITTERROOT VALLEY

Lee Metcalf Nat'l Wildlife Refuge

Lolo

90

12

Drummond

1

Missoula

10

93

W Broadway

Clark Fork River

Alder St

Spruce St

Pine St

1st St N

F

G

90

W Greenough Dr

Monroe St

C

Washington St

Jefferson St

Higgins Ave

Front St

A

Hickory St

Orange St

B

Stevensville

Victor

Bitterroot

Nat'l

Nat'l

Forest

Philipsburg

38

1

3rd St   S S

4th St   S

12

93

Hazel

Hamilton

93

6th St SW

POINTS OF INTEREST

A Art Museum of Missoula
B Caras Park
C Greenough Park
D Memorial Rose Garden and Vietnam Veterans Memorial
E Missoula County Courthouse
F Northern Pacific Depot
G St. Francis Xavier Catholic Church

W Beckwith St

Tremont

Brooks St

Gerald Ave

Ronald Ave

Hilda

Higgins Ave

Franklin

E Beckwith

D   Mount Ave

Darby

Conner

Sula

Lost Trail Pass

473

93

Big Hole Nat'l Battlefield/ Nez Perce Nat'l Historical Park

Continental Divide

to Anaconda

1

43

Wise River

Beaverhead- Deerlodge Nat'l Forest

43

278

Missoula Memorial Rose Garden was established in 1946 to remember World War II casualties. In 1989, the Montana Vietnam Veterans Memorial—a 12-foot-tall bronze sculpture by Deborah Copenhaver—was dedicated in the northeast corner of the park. Forty-four flower beds nurture 326 rose bushes, including a variety of hybrid teas, grandifloras, floribundas and miniatures. ~ 700 block of Brooks Street at Bickford Street.

If you leave the city center area and head west of Reserve Street on South Avenue, you'll come to the **Historical Museum at Fort Missoula**. A complex of 13 historical structures, including an early U.S. Forest Service lookout and a one-room schoolhouse, spreads across 32 acres right in the heart of what was once Fort Missoula (1877–1947). Indoor galleries display thousands of artifacts in permanent and changing exhibits. There's even an area for picnicking. Closed Monday in winter. ~ Off of South Avenue West; 406-728-3476, fax 406-543-6277; www.montana.com/ftmslamuseum, e-mail ftmslamuseum@montana.com.

As Broadway (Business Route 90) extends northwest from downtown Missoula, it passes the **Rocky Mountain Elk Foundation**, which appeals to those who like their animals stuffed. A couple dozen creatures, including hunters' trophy elk, are exhibited in the taxidermy section. There's also an art gallery with original paintings and bronze sculptures, and a gift shop that sells everything from books to T-shirts. The nonprofit foundation claims to have conserved and restored more than three-and-a-half million acres of natural wildlife habitat across North America. ~ 2291 West Broadway; 406-523-4500, 800-225-5355; www.elkfoundation.org, e-mail info@elkfoundation.org.

HIDDEN ► About seven miles from downtown, next to Johnson Bell International Airport, is the **Smokejumper Base and Aerial Fire Depot**. Here, U.S. Forest Service smokejumpers are trained to parachute into remote areas to fight wild fires. Throughout the summer, five daily guided tours of one of the largest smokejumper bases in the United States are available. Historical photos and dioramas explain how fires are detected and squelched, sometimes (as in July 1994) at the cost of firefighters' lives. The adjacent Intermountain Sciences Laboratory continues research into new firefighting technologies. Tours available in winter by request. ~ 5765 West Broadway; 406-329-4934, fax 406-329-4955.

DETOURS FROM ROUTE 90 From 1930 to 1953, **Ninemile Remount Depot** was a Forest Service dispatch center that supplied pack animals for firefighting and other backcountry work. The Civilian Conservation Corps built the Cape Cod–style ranger station in the 1930s; today, it is a working ranch with a visitors center open from Memorial Day through Labor Day. Scheduled guided tours are available; you can also take a self-guided tour of the saddle shop, blacksmith shop and corrals. To reach Nine-mile from Route 90, take Exit 82, 22 miles northwest of Missoula, and follow the signs four miles north. ~ 20325 Remount Road, Huson; 406-626-5201, fax 406-626-5403.

Route 90 West enters the Idaho Panhandle at Lookout Pass, 105 miles from Missoula. The interstate follows the Clark Fork and St. Regis rivers along the flank of the Bitterroot Range through Lolo National Forest.

For wallet watchers, the **Best Inn & Conference Center South** is a leading example of a regional chain. The motel has 84 rather sterile-looking guest rooms, all off indoor corridors, with queen beds and air conditioning. There's a large hot tub in a solarium, and an adjacent restaurant; the lobby contains all manner of books, magazines and tourism literature. ~ 3803 Brooks Street; 406-251-2665, 800-272-9500, fax 406-251-5733; www.bestinn.com, e-mail bst2137@montana.com. If this one's full, check out **Best Inn North**. ~ 4953 North Reserve Street; 406-542-7550, 800-272-9500, fax 406-721-5931; www.bestinn.com, e-mail bst2137@montana.com. Both motels are MODERATE.

LODGING

The historic **Goldsmith's Inn** is a charming piece of Missoula history. A 1911 manse that was home to an early University of Montana president, it was moved to its present site on the Clark Fork River and restored in 1989. There's reproduction Victorian antique decor throughout, from the beds to the wallpaper to the tiled baths (every room has its own). The wraparound porch is perfect for taking a snooze or watching the river. Gourmet breakfasts are served. ~ 809 East Front Street; 406-728-1585, 866-666-9945; www.goldsmithsinn.com, e-mail dickgsmith@aol.com. DELUXE TO ULTRA-DELUXE.

Ruby's Inn and Convention Center, just off Route 90 at the north end of Missoula, is a new entrant in the upscale sweepstakes.

AUTHOR FAVORITE

Missoula's foremost property just might be the **Holiday Inn Missoula-Parkside,** beside the Higgins Avenue bridge overlooking the Clark Fork River. Every one of the hotel's 200 rooms has either a mountain view or a balcony overhanging its spacious atrium lobby, which resembles a Midwest town square with its brickwork, trees, benches and gaslight lamps. Rooms have queen- or king-size beds, air conditioning and desks. Within the inn is a restaurant, a lounge (featuring casino machines), an indoor swimming pool, a hot tub, a sauna, a workout room and a game room. ~ 200 South Pattee Street; 406-721-8550, 800-399-0408, fax 406-728-3472; www.park-side.com, e-mail info@park-side.com. DELUXE.

Its 126 units are smaller than the Holiday Inn's or Doubletree Edgewater's (see below), but have similar facilities and are neat and clean. In addition to an outdoor swimming pool, hot tub and sauna available to all guests, the motel has a guest room with a jacuzzi tub, as well as larger family units. Complimentary breakfast and light evening snacks are served. ~ 4825 North Reserve Street; 406-721-0990, 800-221-2057, fax 406-721-0990; www. montana.com/rubys, e-mail rubys@montana.com. MODERATE.

Just two blocks from the University of Montana is the **Creekside Inn**, whose 54 rooms all have queen-size beds and cable television. There's also an outdoor pool and an adjacent 24-hour restaurant. Don't expect to get a room here, however, when the UM football team is playing a home game. ~ 630 East Broadway; phone/fax 406-549-2387. BUDGET TO MODERATE.

A highly regarded place overlooking the Clark Fork is the **Doubletree Edgewater** just east of downtown Missoula. Its 171 rooms are spacious but otherwise pretty standard motel fare—queen beds, desk, air conditioning and so forth—but the extras are big city: a gift shop with espresso bar, a fine-dining restaurant, cocktail lounge, pool, workout facility and hot tub. ~ 100 Madison Street; 406-728-3100, 800-222-8733, fax 406-728-2530. DELUXE.

The **Gelandesprung Hotel** provides Swiss-chalet lodging at the Montana Snowbowl ski resort. Rooms and suites are available, some with private baths. A hot tub and kitchen facilities are available. Ask about lodging/lift ticket package deals. ~ 1700 Snowbowl Road; 406-549-9777, 800-728-2695; www.montanasnowbowl. com, e-mail info@montanasnowbowl.com. BUDGET TO MODERATE.

DINING

HIDDEN ►

Three dozen area restaurants team with local musicians every summer Wednesday from 11 a.m. to 1:30 p.m. for **Out to Lunch at Caras Park**. More than 3000 local residents typically attend this Clark Fork riverside gathering each week. Music changes

AUTHOR FAVORITE

Locals never seem to have trouble finding the **Dinosaur Café**, but visitors sometimes do: it's tucked in the back of Charlie B's Bar. Don't let the sometimes-rowdy bar front stop you from wandering inside. This place is where I head to satisfy my craving for bayou classics; they serve some of the best Cajun fare north of Louisiana—and lots of it. They dish up some 50 gallons of gumbo weekly plus scores of po'boy sandwiches including homemade andouille sausage, fried oyster, and catfish. And just to show they're not prejudiced, the Dinosaur also caters to more timid taste buds with their chargrilled burgers and six-ounce sirloins. Closed Sunday. ~ 428 North Higgins Avenue; 406-721-3808. BUDGET.

weekly, from big band to acoustic rock to country; admission is free, and the food booths are inexpensive. You can also play on the antique carousel here. A free shuttle bus serves downtown from outlying areas. Closed weekends. ~ Beneath Higgins Avenue Bridge; 406-543-4238, fax 406-543-9831; www.missoula downtown.com, e-mail mda@missouladowntown.com. BUDGET.

Housed in a former railroad stop/motel, **The Depot** is the place to go for local color and tantalizing prime rib (blackened or grilled). This lively two-story restaurant also offers fresh seafood (including crab and lobster); a lighter menu is served on the deck. Need you be told to save room for Montana mud pie and banana/macadamia-nut pie? Dinner only. ~ 201 West Railroad Street; 406-728-7007, fax 406-721-8410. DELUXE.

Locals flock to **Red Bird**, tucked back in an alley between ◄ HIDDEN
Ryman and Higgins streets near West Front Street, within the historic Florence Hotel (still undergoing renovation). For an alley hideaway, though, this restaurant sets a very high standard. The seasonal menu emphasizes fresh local ingredients and features soups, pastas, fish and meat entrées, including roast lamb. Dinner only. Closed Sunday and Monday. ~ 120 West Front Street; 406-549-2906. MODERATE TO DELUXE.

Get your pub grub at the **Iron Horse Brew Pub**, which serves burgers, salads and sandwiches alongside a selection of locally brewed beer. ~ 501 North Higgins Avenue; 406-728-8866. BUDGET.

A favorite student hangout is **Food for Thought**, located just across the street from the University of Montana campus. Its in-house bakery draws the biggest "aahs" for its fresh-from-the-oven bread and triple-berry muffins, but a full menu is served here from morning 'til way past dark. Check out their omelettes, burgers and burritos any day of the week. The bargain bookstore is a plus. ~ 540 Daly Avenue; phone/fax 406-721-6033. BUDGET TO MODERATE.

At **The Mustard Seed**, non-traditional Asian dishes, from subtle Cantonese to tangy Thai, are given a contemporary treatment in original recipes with fresh ingredients. The restaurant is low-lit, modern and efficient. ~ Southgate Mall, 406-542-7333, fax 406-721-3621; www.mustardseedasiancafe.com. MODERATE.

The Bridge takes pride in its casual neighborhood bistro atmosphere. Gourmet pizzas, pasta and seafood are served in a homey candlelit dining room. Dinner only. ~ 515 South Higgins Avenue; 406-542-0638, fax 406-543-7525; www.bridgebistro. com. MODERATE TO DELUXE.

SHOPPING

For a quarter-century and running, the crops and creations of gardeners and produce growers, bakers and coffee vendors, tinkers and tailors have been offered for sale at the **Missoula Farmers Market** in the area fronting the Northern Pacific Depot, now usually overflowing onto Railroad Avenue and Alder Street. Closed in winter. ~ Circle Square, north end of Higgins Avenue; 406-721-5652

The **Gallery Blue** has rotating monthly exhibits of current work by many of the region's leading contemporary painters, sculptors, potters and jewelers. Closed Sunday and Monday. ~ 121 West Broadway; 406-721-5460, www.gallery-blue.com The **Monte Dolack Gallery** offers the work of a nationally known poster artist who lives and works in Missoula. Closed Sunday in winter. ~ 139 West Front Street; 406-549-3248, www.dolack.com. Antiques and collectibles are displayed en masse at the **Montana Antique Mall** in the historic Montana Hotel building. ~ 331 West Railroad Street; 406-721-5366.

The leading local bookstore is **Fact & Fiction**, which often highlights Montana authors with readings and signings. ~ 220 North Higgins Avenue; 406-721-2881. **Garden City News** has more than 800 magazines on its racks, as well as a variety of national newspapers and detailed maps. ~ 329 North Higgins Avenue; 406-543-3470.

Montana visitors are always delighted to learn that the state has no sales tax, so visits to **Southgate Mall**, the largest shopping center within a 200-mile radius, often seem like Christmas. More than 100 stores are open daily. ~ 2901 Brooks Street; 406-721-5140.

NIGHTLIFE   As Montana's undeclared "culture capital," Missoula has more choices of sophisticated nightlife than anywhere else in the state.

For stage aficionados, the **Montana Repertory Theatre**, a top-notch professional company, tours nationally. ~ University of Montana Performing Arts Center; 406-243-6809. The MCT **Community Theatre** gives classes and performs year-round; the associated **Missoula Children's Theatre** visits nearly 1000 communities a year, making it one of the largest touring children's theaters in America. ~ 200 North Adams Street; 406-728-1911; www.mctinc.org.

Music lovers have the **Missoula Symphony Orchestra & Chorale**, whose five-concert subscription series features outstanding guest artists between September and May. ~ 225 West Front Street; 406-721-3194. The **String Orchestra of the Rockies** performs throughout Montana. ~ P.O. Box 8265, Missoula, MT 59807; www.sor-montana.org. Missoula also has a dance troupe, the **Garden City Ballet Company**. ~ www.gardencityballet.org. In addition, the **International Wildlife Film Festival** is presented in Missoula every May. ~ 406-728-9380; www.wildlifefilms.org.

The **University of Montana Department of Drama/Dance** serves up student theater and dance from September through April in the Masquer and Montana theaters. ~ UM Performing Arts Center; 406-243-4481, box office: 406-243-4581.

You can find live music of all kinds around the city. For rhythm-and-blues, visit the **Union Club**. ~ 208 East Main Street; 406-728-7980. For bluegrass or rockabilly on Thursday and Friday, there's the **Old Post Pub**. ~ 103 West Spruce Street; 406-721-7399. Since 1952 blues and folk-music lovers have gone to **The Top Hat**. Reggae, Brazilian and classic rock also make appearances. There's a large dancefloor. Occasional cover. ~ 134 West Front Street; 406-728-9865.

Pick up the daily *Missoulian* or the weekly *Missoula Independent* for schedules, prices, and venues for the International Wildlife Film Festival and other happenings around town.

The **Iron Horse Brew Pub** serves up old-style German pilsners, ambers, lagers, ales and stout produced at the Missoula Brewery and the Bayern Brewing Co. The pub has a full bar, a beer garden and more than 15 beers on tap. They also serve a variety of pub food. ~ 501 North Higgins Avenue; 406-728-8866. **The Press Box**, across a footbridge from the university's Washington-Grizzly Stadium, is a sports bar featuring three satellite dishes, 33 TVs, 20 casino gaming machines and a full menu, as well as karaoke on Thursday. ~ 835 East Broadway; 406-721-1212.

There's no shortage of casino action. One local favorite is the **Lucky Strike Casino**. Just off Brooks Street one block from South Avenue, it's open 24 hours and offers poker and keno machines, live poker tables and off-track betting on horse and greyhound races. There's live entertainment on weekends. ~ 1515 Dearborn Street; 406-549-4152, fax 406-728-3365.

GREENOUGH PARK 🚶 🚴 🏛 Enjoy this city park by following a one-mile paved path along Rattlesnake Creek, or taking a short drive that parallels it through lush vegetation. Interpretive signs remind visitors of the excellent birdwatching in the park, once part of a Missoula estate. The facilities include picnic areas and restrooms. ~ From East Broadway, take Madison Street north to Duncan Drive. Turn right on Vine Street and left on Monroe Street to the park; 406-721-7275, fax 406-523-2765.

PARKS

RATTLESNAKE NATIONAL RECREATION AREA AND WILDERNESS 🚶 🚴 🐴 🏛 These 61,000 acres of rugged mountain country begin just a few miles north of Missoula. Numerous creeks tumble from the high country, where craggy peaks and tiny lakes speckle the alpine landscape. Motorized vehicles and bicycles are permitted in the recreation area—which includes the Montana Snowbowl ski area—but not in the wilderness. Despite its name, rattlesnakes are not a problem. Restrooms are located at some trailheads. ~ Principal access is off Sawmill Gulch Road, which turns off Rattlesnake Drive about four miles north of downtown Missoula; 406-329-3814, fax 406-329-1049.

▲ No-trace camping is permitted beyond a three-mile radius from the main trailhead at Sawmill Gulch Road.

LOLO NATIONAL FOREST 🚶 🚴 🐎 ⛷ 🏕 🏊 ⛴ 🚣 Based in Missoula, this forest encompasses much of four counties from the Idaho border (east of Sandpoint) to the Continental Divide, excluding Flathead Indian Reservation. It surrounds or borders five wilderness areas and many lakes and rivers. Anglers cast for trout, whitefish, kokanee, bass, pike and perch. There are picnic areas and restrooms. ~ From Missoula, travel southwest on Route 12, west on Route 90, northwest on Route 200, or northeast via Route 200 to Route 83; 406-329-3750, fax 406-329-3795.

▲ There are 416 RV/tent sites and 80 for tents only at 30 campgrounds, none with hookups; $5 to $10 per night; 14-day maximum stay.

WELCOME CREEK WILDERNESS AREA 🚶 🐎 🏕 This small wilderness, in the northwest corner of Granite County, extends from the crest of the Sapphire Mountains to Rock Creek, about 20 miles southeast of Missoula. Several trails, including those for Welcome Creek and Sawmill Creek, begin from Forest Road 102. ~ To Forest Road 102, take Exit 126 from Route 90 east of Missoula and follow Rock Creek south; 406-329-3814, fax 406-329-1049.

▲ No-trace camping only.

▼▼▼▼▼▼▼▼▼▼▼▼
Bitterroot Valley
    •

The Bitterroot River flows almost due north for 100 miles from the Continental Divide to enter the Clark Fork River just west of Missoula. The valley it has carved, between the Bitterroot and Sapphire Mountains, was the site of the first pioneer settlement in Montana. In 1841, Jesuit Father Pierre De Smet established a Roman Catholic mission at what is now Stevensville. A nearby fort soon followed, and the onrush of settlers wasn't far behind. Today the valley is a thriving grain-growing region with access for visitors to numerous historical locations and outdoor adventures.

Route 93 follows the Bitterroot Valley south from Missoula to Lost Trail Pass, where it enters Idaho.

HISTORICAL HOT SPRINGS

American Indians knew Lolo Hot Springs as a meeting place and bathing spot, and as a mineral lick for animals. Lewis and Clark camped here in September 1805 and once again in June 1806. William Clark wrote in his journal that he "found this water nearly boiling hot at the places it spouted from the rocks. . . ." Today you can immerse yourself in the pools and contemplate days of yore at The Fort at Lolo Hot Springs.

Many Missoula workers commute daily from **Lolo**, 11 miles south at the junction of Route 12, which continues to Lewiston, Idaho. **Lolo Hot Springs**, 26 miles west of Lolo, has been a popular getaway for area residents for more than a century. An outdoor hot-springs swimming pool and an indoor soaking pool are both open to the public for a fee. You'll also find four fully-equipped cabins available. ~ Route 12, Lolo Hot Springs; 406-273-2290, 800-273-2290; www.lolohotsprings.com, e-mail stoen@lolohotsprings.com.

The **Lolo Pass Visitors Information Center**, seven miles farther west on the Montana–Idaho border, is located at 5235 feet at the intersection of ancient Indian trade routes from north, south, east and west. The center, staffed by Clearwater National Forest, contains displays describing the natural and human history of the pass, including Lewis and Clark's passage along the Lolo Trail. Displays on Nez Perce Indian culture and history are also featured. Reduced hours from early September to late May. ~ Route 12, Lolo Pass; 208-942-3113, fax 208-942-3311.

Twenty-eight miles south of Missoula, and just over a mile east of Route 93, is historic **Stevensville**. Here is Father De Smet's **St. Mary's Mission**, the first Catholic mission and permanent white settlement in the American Northwest. The grounds of the restored Italianate mission include the chapel and priest's residence, a log house, a pharmacy, an American Indian museum, a cemetery, a visitors center, the mission's original apple orchard and a picnic area. Tours are offered daily mid-April to mid-October. Admission. ~ De Smet Park, West 4th Street, Stevensville; phone/fax 406-777-5734.

Major John Owen built nearby **Fort Owen** of adobe and logs in 1850, and it soon became a regional trade center. Brochures and interpretive displays lend themselves to self-guided tours of the fort, which is a free state park located a half mile east of Stevensville junction. ~ Route 269, Stevensville; 406-542-5500, fax 406-542-5529.

The life of northern Bitterroot Valley residents through the last half of the 19th century is related at the **Stevensville Historical Museum**. Closed Thursday through Sunday and Labor Day through Memorial Day. ~ 517 Main Street, Stevensville; 406-777-2269.

The **Lee Metcalf National Wildlife Refuge** encompasses 2800 acres of wetland along the east bank of the Bitterroot River, two miles north of Stevensville. Named for the late Senator Metcalf, a Stevensville native, the refuge is home to many deer and birds, including osprey, bald eagles and a wide variety of migratory waterfowl. A self-guided auto tour, interpretive trails, a wheelchair-accessible path and a picnic area are open year-round. ~ Route

203, Stevensville; 406-777-5552; leemetcalf.fws.gov, e-mail bob_
danleye@fws.gov.

Other Bitterroot Valley towns, including Victor, Hamilton
and Darby, feature more historical sites. The **Victor Heritage
Museum**, housed in an old train depot 35 miles from Missoula,
features early railroad artifacts in its collection. Closed Sunday
and Monday, closed in winter. ~ Main and Blake streets, Victor;
406-642-3997.

Twelve miles farther, near **Hamilton**, population center of the
Bitterroot Valley (pop. 2700), is the valley's preeminent manmade
attraction: the **Marcus Daly Mansion**. "Copper King" Daly, an
Irish immigrant, and his family used the Georgian revival–style
estate as a summer escape from New York between 1890, when
it was remodeled, and 1941, when Mrs. Daly died. The three-
story mansion—which contains 56 rooms, 25 bedrooms, 15
baths and 5 Italian marble fireplaces in its 24,000-plus square
feet—is now owned by the state. Located two miles north of
Hamilton on a secondary highway, it is surrounded by 50
planted acres, a tiny fraction of the 22,000-acre Bitter Root
Stock Farm that Daly owned. Tours are conducted daily from
Memorial Day to Labor Day, by appointment the rest of the year.
Admission. ~ Eastside Highway, Hamilton; 406-363-6004, fax
406-375-0048; www.dalymansion.org, e-mail developmentdi-
rector@dalymansion.org.

The ornate brick **Tammany Castle**, a mile south of the mansion, was a stable for race horses; it is not open to the public but
can be viewed from the highway. ~ Eastside Highway, Hamilton.

Ravalli County Museum preserves pioneer and Indian artifacts
in the old 1900 Ravalli County Courthouse. Of note is a display
honoring scientists at Hamilton's Rocky Mountain Laboratories
who discovered the causes and cures for Rocky Mountain tick
fever. Closed Tuesday and Wednesday. Admission. ~ 205 Bedford
Street, Hamilton; 406-363-3338.

Little Darby, 17 miles south of Hamilton, boasts the **Darby
Pioneer Memorial Museum**, an 1886 log cabin moved from
nearby Tin Cup Creek. It now features pioneer home goods, family histories and the original Darby phone switchboard. Closed
Labor Day through Memorial Day. ~ Council Park, Main Street,
Darby; 406-821-3753. Also here is the **Darby Historic Ranger
Station**, which displays early-20th-century U.S. Forest Service
memorabilia and offers current information on Bitterroot National Forest recreation. Closed late November through April. ~
712 North Main Street, Darby; 406-821-3913, fax 406-821-4264.

About four miles south of Darby, consider turning off Route
93 onto Route 473. The road is mostly paved for 28 miles to
Painted Rocks State Park. ~ West Fork Road, Darby.

Five miles south of the state park, look for the **Alta Ranger**   ◄ HIDDEN
Station, the first Forest Service ranger station in the United
States. It was built in 1899 by two men using cross-cut saws and
axes.

Route 93 climbs 31 miles beyond Darby to 7014-foot Lost
Trail Pass and the **Lost Trail Powder Mountain** ski area on the
Montana–Idaho border. Route 93 continues south into Idaho.
Route 43 turns east, climbing Chief Joseph Pass to the Big Hole
Battlefield unit of Nez Perce National Historical Park (see
Chapter Four).

The Fort at Lolo Hot Springs creates a wilderness feeling while   **LODGING**
providing a thimbleful of luxury. Standard rooms have twin or
double beds, a desk and a chair; deluxe rooms have one or two
queen beds, dinettes and sleeper sofas. All have private baths.
The resort has a restaurant, a saloon-casino and gift shops, and
is adjacent to the hot springs pools. ~ Route 12, Lolo Hot
Springs; 406-273-2201, 800-273-2290, fax 406-273-2201;
www.lolotrailercenter.com. MODERATE TO DELUXE.

With its 200 avian species, river frontage and fly-fishing
streams, **Teller Wildlife Refuge** makes a peaceful getaway for
birders, anglers and just about anyone who ap-
preciates the great outdoors. This nonprofit refuge   Though only traces of
sprawls across some 1300 acres in the Bitterroot   the settlement remain,
Valley and is home to foxes and pheasants as well as   Alta was once a tent
moose and sandhill cranes. Two furnished houses and   city inhabited by
two fishing cabins all have room for at least six people,   more than 500
and you can either cook your own food or get catered   gold miners.
food delivered. If you stay with a group, the rates are quite
reasonable. While Teller is geared to overnight guests, day visitors are welcome. ~ 1292 Chaffin Road, Corvallis; 406-961-3507;
www.tellerwildlife.org, e-mail tamia@tellerwildlife.org. DELUXE.

In the heart of the Bitterroot Valley, **Deffy's Motel** offers a lot
for the price. Air-conditioned rooms have queen-size beds, TV and
phones (of course), and the motel has a hot tub for soaking tired
driving muscles. ~ 321 South 1st Street, Hamilton; 406-363-1244,
800-363-1305. BUDGET.

Best Western Hamilton Inn has 36 spacious rooms. All have
desks, queen- or king-size beds and other standard furnishings.
The two-story motel has a large outdoor hot tub, and it offers
free continental breakfast. ~ 409 South 1st Street, Hamilton; 406-
363-2142, 800-426-4586, fax 406-363-2142. MODERATE.

The Lost Horse Creek Lodge offers accommodations for up
to 62 people. Hiking, biking and horse trails crisscross the property. Sledding and fishing are also great ways to relax. The lodge
features a popular restaurant. ~ 1000 Lost Horse Road (on Forest

Service Road 429), Charlos Heights; 406-363-1460, fax 406-363-6107; www.losthorsecreeklodge.com, e-mail info@losthorse creeklodge.com. DELUXE.

HIDDEN ▶

A full range of guest ranches are located at the head of the valley. A rustic fly-fishing haven, the **Nez Perce Ranch** offers three out-of-the-way log cabins (including lofts; each sleeps four) on the Nez Perce Fork of the Bitterroot River. The ranch offers *no* planned activities: You fish, hike and canoe on your own, and if you want to ride, the owners will line you up with an area outfitter. Prepare meals in your own cabin or drive 10 to 40 miles for a restaurant. Clearly, this is designed for the independent, outdoor-oriented vagabond. Cabins rent weekly; shorter stays are available by prior arrangement. Closed September through May. ~ 7206 Nez Perce Road, Darby; 406-349-2100, fax 406-349-2171; www.nezperceranch.com, e-mail nezperceranch@ blackfoot.net. DELUXE TO ULTRA-DELUXE.

Perched atop a mountain, the **Tin Cup Lodge Bed & Breakfast** enjoys lovely views of the valley below. The four Western-themed rooms in the main building are furnished with handmade log furniture, and have easy access to the B&B's rec room (complete with pool table and large-screen TV), laundry facilities (free for guests) and dining area. For more privacy (and a few more dollars), you can opt for cabins with private hot tubs and fireplaces. ~ 582 Tin Cup Road, Darby; 406-821-1620; www.tincup lodge.com, e-mail tincuplodge@aol.com. DELUXE TO ULTRA-DELUXE.

Nestled against the Selway-Bitterroot Wilderness Area near the foot of lofty Trapper Peak, the **Triple Creek Ranch** combines outdoor programs with luxury accommodations. The adults-only ranch has plush cabins and poolside suites for up to 21 couples and 28 single visitors, each with stocked refrigerators and complimentary liquor; some have private hot tubs. Gourmet meals are served in the lodge. ~ 5551 West Fork Road, Darby; 406-821-4600, fax 406-821-4666; www.triplecreekranch.com, e-mail tcr@bitterroot.net. ULTRA-DELUXE.

DINING

HIDDEN ▶

Seeming out of place in the central Bitterroot Valley, **The Hamilton** in tiny Victor is a throwback to the traditional pubs of the British Isles. Between games of darts you can enjoy fish and chips or fresh fruit cobbler and sip imported and microbrewed ales and stouts. Closed Sunday. ~ 104 Main Street, Victor; 406-642-6644. BUDGET.

The Bitterroot's leading restaurant may well be **The Banque Club**, located in an old downtown bank building on two floors. Downstairs, creative moderate-to-deluxe-priced Continental cuisine is served nightly for dinner in elegant ambience; upstairs, **The Exchange Bar & Grill** offers more casual chowing and drinking at budget prices. The Exchange serves lunch and dinner; closed Sunday. ~ 225 West Main Street, Hamilton; 406-363-1955. BUDGET TO DELUXE.

In fact, you can bank on finding a good place to eat in Hamilton because **The Spice of Life Cafe** also occupies a turn-of-the-20th-century financial institution. Today, money changes hands for its bistro fare (pastas, chicken, fish, steaks and the like) and its great chardonnay cake. Lunch is served Monday through Friday, dinner Wednesday through Saturday. ~ 163 South 2nd Street, Hamilton; 406-363-4433; www.thespiceinhamilton.com. MODERATE TO DELUXE.

Even more out of the way is the **Lost Horse Creek Lodge**, in a century-old log cabin next to Lolo National Forest. Inside, you eat steak, chicken and burgers; outside, you play horseshoes or volleyball in summer, or sled in winter. Friday night offers all-you-can-eat shrimp dinners. From Route 93 eight miles south of Hamilton, turn west three miles on Lost Horse Road, then west another one and one quarter miles on dirt Forest Road 429. ~ 1000 Lost Horse Road, Charlos Heights; 406-363-1460, fax 406-363-6107; www.losthorsecreeklodge.com, e-mail info@lost horsecreeklodge.com. MODERATE TO DELUXE.

◀ HIDDEN

For fine dining amid rustic beauty, visit the **Triple Creek Ranch Restaurant**, where a fireplace blazes in the corner of this bright, high-ceilinged space. The ever-changing gourmet menu is prepared with fresh, seasonal ingredients. At breakfast try the macadamia-nut bread french toast, or order broccolini salad with miso-marinated chicken at lunch. Evening diners enjoy diver scallops served three ways, natural beef short ribs with chipotle–dried cherry barbecue sauce or balsamic-grilled quail with roasted beets, sautéed fennel and orange-glazed carrots. Reservations required. The restaurant is closed to nonguests on Sunday and Monday. ~ 5551 West Fork Road, Darby; 406-821-4600, fax 406-821-4666; www.triplecreekranch.com, e-mail tcr@ bitterroot.net. ULTRA-DELUXE.

A SCENIC MOUNTAIN REPAST

There may be no better view in the Bitterroot Valley than from **The Grub-stake**, located on the slope of Downing Mountain 2000 feet above the valley floor. The unique 16-sided building has a huge central fireplace, a great salad bar and a menu that features steaks, prime rib, chicken and Montana mountain trout. Dinner is served at 4:30 nightly. Call for reservations and directions, then plan a half-hour to switchback the eight miles to the restaurant. Closed October through April. ~ Hamilton; 406-363-3068; www.grubstake.com, e-mail eat@grubstake.com. MODERATE TO DELUXE.

Satisfy your craving for hickory-smoked ribs at **Rocky Knob Lodge,** a log structure redolent of rustic atmosphere. In addition, steak, trout, chicken and lobster appear on the menu. ~ Route 93, 13 miles south of Darby; 406-821-3520. MODERATE TO ULTRA-DELUXE.

SHOPPING   Art lovers traveling south through the Bitterroot Valley won't want to miss the **Bronze Horse Foundry and Gallery,** the oldest foundry in the Northwest. The gallery offers collectible sculptures and limited-edition bronze castings. ~ 599 Popham Lane, Corvallis; 406-961-2999; e-mail bronzehorse@onewest.net.

PARKS   **BITTERROOT NATIONAL FOREST** 🚶🚴🐎🛶 The forest blankets most of the Sapphire Mountains and the lower slopes of the Bitterroots (below the Selway-Bitterroot Wilderness Area) on either side of the Bitterroot Valley. It also shrouds the upper forks of the Bitterroot River. Headquarters are in Hamilton. Facilities include picnic areas and restrooms. ~ Most recreational sites are a short distance off Route 93 between Stevensville and Lost Trail Pass; 406-363-7100, fax 406-363-7159.

▲ There are 137 RV/tent sites and 10 for tents only at 15 campgrounds (no hookups); no charge to $14 per night; 5-, 7- or 14-day maximum stay. There are also seven cabins; $25 to $50 per night.

SELWAY-BITTERROOT WILDERNESS AREA 🚶🐎 Some 1.3 million acres in Montana and Idaho are contained in this massive wilderness. Crowned by the crest of the dramatic Bitterroot Range, it extends about 60 miles from 9075-foot Lolo Peak to 10,157-foot Trapper Peak. In Montana, the main attraction to hikers and horseback riders is a series of gorgeous, wildlife-rich creek canyons. Cutthroat trout thrive in alpine lakes and streams, but be aware that they're a catch-and-release species. ~ Easiest access to trailheads is from the Twin Lakes campground, reached via Forest Road 429 and Lost Horse Road, which turns west off Route 93 eight miles south of Hamilton; 406-821-3269, fax 406-363-7159; e-mail bshay@fs.fed.us.

▲ Primitive only.

LAKE COMO RECREATION AREA 🚶🚴🐎🏊⛵ Rock Creek rushes from the Bitterroots to feed this three-mile-long reservoir. Facilities include picnic areas and restrooms. Day-use fee, $5. ~ Route 93 south from Hamilton 12 miles, then Lake Como Road four miles west; 406-821-3913, fax 406-821-4264.

▲ There are 10 tent sites, $8 per night; 11 RV sites with water and electric hookups, $14 per night (Closed mid-September through April); and 10 horse campsites, $4 per night.

PAINTED ROCKS STATE PARK 🏃 🚴 🏕 🎣 ⛴ 🚤 🛶

Built along the shore of pretty Painted Rocks Reservoir, deep in the southern Bitterroot Range, this park is open year-round. Picnic areas and restrooms round out the amenities. ~ From Route 93 five miles south of Darby, turn south on paved West Fork Road (Route 473) for 23 miles; 406-542-5500, fax 406-542-5529.

▲ There are 25 primitive sites (no hookups); no charge; 14-day maximum stay.

▼▼▼▼▼▼▼▼▼▼▼▼▼

Flathead Indian Reservation & Lake

Spanning 1942 square miles of land surrounding the meandering Flathead River and broad Flathead Lake between Missoula and Kalispell, the Flathead Indian Reservation is the home of the Confederated Salish and Kootenai tribes.

Within this vast and scenic swath of landscape are located the impressive National Bison Range, the charming St. Ignatius Mission, several units of Flathead Lake State Park and other attractions, not the least of which is the foreboding Mission Range that marks the reservation's eastern boundary.

SIGHTS

Most travelers cross the reservation via Route 93 between Missoula and Kalispell. Probably the most intriguing detour along the way—for nature lovers, at least—is the **National Bison Range**. When it was established by President Theodore Roosevelt in 1908, less than 100 wild bison survived from an estimated 50 million a century earlier; most had been wantonly slaughtered during the four decades between 1840 and 1880.

A 19-mile scenic drive begins and ends at the visitors center; it climbs a well-maintained dirt road over Red Sleep Mountain, enabling observation of bison herds (including, in the spring and early summer, many calves). Allow at least 90 minutes. The reserve also harbors herds of elk, mule deer, whitetail deer, bighorn sheep and pronghorn antelope, along with numerous other smaller mammals, ground birds and migratory waterfowl.

◆◆◆◆◆◆◆◆◆◆◆◆◆◆◆◆◆

Today up to 500 bison, each of which can weigh a ton or more, roam the National Bison Range's 19,000 acres of natural grassland and scattered woods.

To reach the main entrance, turn west off Route 93 on Route 200 at Ravalli, 37 miles north of Missoula; after six miles, turn north again on Route 212 and proceed about four miles to the bison range. The visitors center is closed weekends in winter. Admission in summer. ~ Route 212, Moiese; 406-644-2211, fax 406-644-2661; www.bisonrange.fws.gov, e-mail bisonrange@fws.gov.

Beyond Ravalli on Route 93, you'll surmount a saddle and find yourself staring into the spectacular **Mission Range** of the Rockies. Sheer, glacier-carved cliffs drop dramatically from the stark, snow-specked, 8000- to 9000-foot climes of Mount Hard-ing, Mountaineer Peak and Daughter of the Sun Mountain, presenting a stunning backdrop for the farms and communities of the Mission Valley below its western flank.

Perhaps no view of the Mission Range is more spiritually uplifting than one taking in the **St. Ignatius Mission**. A designated national historic site, the mission was established by the wide-ranging Jesuit Father Pierre De Smet in 1854, 13 years after he founded St. Mary's Mission at modern Stevensville. Flathead and other tribes erected the current church in 1891 from lumber and a million kiln-baked bricks. Brother Joseph Carignano, whose work also adorns St. Francis Xavier Church in Missoula, painted the mission's 58 wall and ceiling murals. Nineteenth-century artifacts and American Indian crafts are exhibited in the original log chapel and priest's residence, located next to the current church. ~ Off Route 93, St. Ignatius; 406-745-2768, fax 406-745-0010.

Beyond St. Ignatius, you're deep in the heart of the **Flathead Indian Reservation** on which more than half of the 6700 enrolled tribal members live. Powwows are held in July at opposite ends of the reserve in the villages of Arlee and Elmo. The southeast and northwest corners of the reservation are open to tribal members only. Most of the eastern flank of the reservation, from Flathead Lake to the Jocko River, comprises the **Mission Mountains Tribal Wilderness Area**, with public trailheads providing access to high-country lakes and peaks. Permit required. ~ P.O. Box 278, Pablo, MT 59855; 406-675-2700, fax 406-883-2896.

Four large rooms of exhibits at the **Ninepipes Museum of Early Montana**, halfway between Ravalli and Flathead Lake, trace not only Flathead Indian history but also that of early miners, loggers, ranchers and other pioneers. A gallery of historical photographs is even more impressive if Bud Cheff, Sr., born on the Flathead reservation in 1915 and a lifelong resident, is around to spin a yarn or two. Admission. ~ 40962 Route 93, Charlo; 406-644-3435; www.ninepipes.org.

A mile north of Pablo, where tribal headquarters are located, the **Sqelix'u-Aqsmakni'k Cultural Center**, "The People's Center," includes an exhibit gallery of Salish, Pend d'Oreille and Kootenai

SIGHTSEEING BY SAIL

Boat tours are a great way to see Flathead Lake. Go for a ride on either the *Nor'easter* or the 51-foot racing sloop *Questa*, which won the 1930 Americas Cup for financier J. P. Morgan. Closed October through May. ~ Averill's Flathead Lake Lodge, Bigfork; 406-837-4391, fax 406-837-6977; www.averills.com, e-mail flatheadlakelodge@centurytel.net.

tribal life. Guided interpretive tours and educational programs are also offered, and there is an excellent gift shop. Closed weekends fall through spring. ~ Route 93, Pablo; 406-675-0160, 800-883-5344, fax 406-675-0260; www.peoplescenter.org, e-mail tours@peoplescenter.org.

On either side of Pablo are the **Ninepipe National Wildlife Refuge** and the **Pablo National Wildlife Refuge,** both part of the National Bison Range complex, which contains more than 4500 acres of pond-and-wetland habitat for waterfowl and for the day use of curious visitors. Closed during spring nesting season and fall hunting season. ~ Ninepipe is off of Route 93, about five miles south of Ronan; Pablo is on Reservoir Road, about three miles south of Polson; 406-644-2211, fax 406-644-2661; e-mail bisonrange@fws.gov.

FLATHEAD LAKE   At the town of Polson, seven miles north of Pablo and just over halfway from Missoula to Kalispell, Route 93 meets **Flathead Lake,** the largest natural freshwater lake west of the Mississippi River. Twenty-eight miles long and 15 miles at its widest, the lake boasts 185 miles of shoreline. A driving loop of the lake is 86 miles by paved highway.

Polson, the largest town on the lakeshore with 4000 people, has a thriving resort business heavily oriented toward boating and fishing. Anglers come from all over North America to test the deep waters of Flathead Lake, gouged by the last glaciers. It is likewise popular with other boating enthusiasts, from motorboaters to sailboaters. A good way to explore is aboard the 41-foot tour boat **Port Polson Princess.** Closed in winter. ~ Polson; 406-883-2448, 800-882-6363, fax 406-883-5392.

Polson has two interesting museums. The **Polson-Flathead Historical Museum** focuses on Polson's pioneer heritage as the Flathead's earliest settlement and includes a saddle that once belonged to notorious "Calamity Jane" Canary. Admission. Closed September through May. ~ 802 Main Street, Polson; 406-883-3049.

The **Miracle of America Museum,** a mile south, features changing exhibits of Americana, including American Indian artifacts, homestead items, vintage vehicles and a variety of antique tools. You'll also find a re-created pioneer village, complete with a schoolhouse, a general store and a jail. Admission. ~ 58176 Route 93, Polson; 406-883-6804; www.cyberport.net/museum, e-mail museum@cyberport.net.

Bunyan is said to have gouged the sheer walls of the Flathead River Gorge, which drains the lake. Water, regulated by the **Kerr Dam,** flows through the channel at a rate of a half-million gallons a second. At 204 feet, the dam is more than 54 feet higher than Niagara Falls. Tours are temporarily suspended; call ahead for details. ~ Kerr Dam Road, Polson; 406-883-4450, fax 406-533-3151.

Around the lakeshore northeast and northwest of Polson are six separate units of **Flathead Lake State Park** (see "Parks" section below).

The hamlet of Dayton, 23 miles northwest of Polson with a view toward Wild Horse Island, is the site of Montana's only winery: **Mission Mountain Winery**. Because the winter climate is harsh for viticulture, some grapes are imported from Washington's Columbia Valley and then blended here. But the rest come from Mission's four vineyards near Flathead Lake and one near Thompson Falls. The cabernet sauvignon and Johannesburg riesling are surprisingly good; other vintages include chardonnay, pinot noir, merlot and pinot grigio. The tasting room is open daily from May through October. ~ Route 93, Dayton; 406-849-5524; www.missionmountainwinery.com, e-mail info@mission mountainwinery.com.

North from Dayton along Route 93, around the western lakeshore, you'll spot numerous residences overlooking Flathead Lake, often spectacularly situated in beautiful communities like Rollins and Lakeside. On the way, the highway passes the West Shore Unit of Flathead Lake State Park. West Shore's rock formations attract hikers and photographers.

At Somers, Route 93 breaks away from Flathead Lake and continues to Kalispell, only eight miles farther north. Lower Valley Road (Route 82) continues east, along the north end of the lake and across the Flathead River, to Route 35. The town of **Bigfork** is two miles south of this junction.

Located where the Swan River enters Flathead Lake, Bigfork blossoms with the spring flowers that line its main street and hang outside its sidewalk cafés and restaurants. The village is rapidly gaining a statewide reputation as a center for the fine and performing arts. The **Bigfork Art & Cultural Center**, for instance, exhibits the paintings, sculptures and crafts of Montana artisans. Closed January through March; closed Sunday and Monday the rest of the year. ~ 525 Electric Avenue, Bigfork; 406-837-6927. Across the street, the million-dollar **Bigfork Summer Playhouse** presents popular live theater. ~ 526 Electric Avenue, Bigfork; for ticket information write P.O. Box 456, Bigfork, MT 59911; 406-837-4886; www.bigforksummerplayhouse.com.

From Bigfork, Route 35 returns to Polson down the east shore of the lake, a distance of 32 miles. The orchards along this shore were famous for their plump, sweet cherries until a 1989 cold snap temporarily destroyed the industry. Determined growers have successfully replanted with hardier cold-resistant cherries and other fruits.

The **Swan Lake Road** (Route 83), which tucks itself behind the Mission Range and takes the 124-mile backdoor route to Missoula, begins near Bigfork. It follows the Swan River south

nearly to its source, crosses a saddle and proceeds down the
Clearwater River to its confluence with the Blackfoot. The principal resort communities along this route are **Swan Lake**, at the
southern end of the 12-mile-long lake of the same name, and
Seeley Lake. Near Seeley Lake are state parks at **Salmon Lake**,
five miles south, and **Placid Lake**, six miles southwest.

LODGING

Low-cost accommodations are hard to come by in this region,
especially in peak summer months. One reasonable option is the
Ninepipes Lodge, which offers modern conveniences in a rustic
setting. The lodge's cozy atmosphere is enhanced by stone fireplaces and exposed beams. Twenty-five rooms feature all of the
standard amenities. ~ 41000 Route 93, Charlo; 406-644-2588,
fax 406-644-2928; www.ninepipes.com, e-mail ninepipes@nine
pipes.com. MODERATE.

On Flathead Lake, you can't do better than the **KwaTaqNuk
Resort at Flathead Bay**, where you can get lakefront accommodation and a hefty helping of American Indian culture with it.
The 112 high-ceilinged rooms have Salish-Kootenai motifs and all
the standard amenities, including private baths. The Best Western–
associated resort offers a restaurant, a lounge and 24-hour casino,
a gift shop and an art gallery, two swimming pools (one indoor)
and a whirlpool; it also offers boating and water-sports rentals
from its marina. ~ 303 Route 93 East, Polson; 406-883-3636,
800-882-6363, fax 406-883-5392; www.kwataqnuk.com. DELUXE.

Port Polson Inn is a standard motel in an outstanding location. Perched on the southern end of Flathead Lake, it has water
and mountain views. You'll find 44 rooms,
some with kitchens, and a fitness center and a hot
tub. The staff can inform you about boat tours and
white-water rafting trips. Continental breakfast is
included in the rate. ~ 502 Route 93, Polson; 406-883-
5385, 800-654-0682. MODERATE TO ULTRA-DELUXE.

At Averill's Flathead Lake
Lodge, team roping is
taught to guests by
rodeo-loving owner
Doug Averill.

Only a mile from Bigfork, **Averill's Flathead Lake
Lodge** is a 2000-acre ranch with a dual emphasis: riding
and water sports. For horse lovers, there's morning instruction and trail rides. The lodge's lakeside setting provides excellent opportunities for fishing and a variety of water sports. In
the afternoon, attention shifts to the lake, where guests learn to
sail and team aboard J. P. Morgan's Americas Cup prototype, the
51-foot *Questa*, in match racing with other yachts. Lodging is in
two lodges and 20 two- and three-bedroom log cottages. Full
family-style meals are served in the central lodge. Open May
through September, with a one-week minimum stay during peak
season. ~ P.O. Box 248, Bigfork, MT 59911; 406-837-4391, fax
406-837-6977; www.averills.com, e-mail flatheadlakelodge@
century.net. ULTRA-DELUXE.

Located at the south end of town, the two-story **Timbers Motel** has 40 nicely furnished units, all with full baths and in-room coffee; facilities include an outdoor swimming pool, a whirlpool and a sauna. ~ 8540 Route 35, Bigfork; 406-837-6200, 800-821-4546, fax 406-837-6203; www.timbersmotel.com, e-mail timbers@digisys.net. DELUXE.

A lovely bed and breakfast is **Burggraf's Countrylane B&B**, on Swan Lake nine miles southeast of Bigfork. With seven lakefront acres and a selection of fishing boats and canoes for guests, it's a rural getaway. There are five rooms, each with private bath; a honeymoon suite has a jacuzzi tub and walk-in shower. A full breakfast is served. No smoking, pets or children under 12. Closed October through April. ~ 1 Rainbow Drive on Swan Lake, Bigfork; 406-837-4608, 800-525-3344, fax 406-837-2468; e-mail nburggraf@yahoo.com. DELUXE.

DINING

It would be hard to find a setting more peaceful than at the **Ninepipes Lodge and Restaurant**, which sits at the edge of the Ninepipe National Wildlife Refuge at the foot of the striking Mission Range. Dinner entrées here focus on steaks, seafood and pasta; soups and sandwiches are popular at lunch. Big picture windows offer a fine view of the refuge's ducks and other waterfowl. ~ 41000 Route 93, Charlo; 406-644-2588, fax 406-644-2928; www.ninepipes.com, e-mail ninepipes@ninepipes.com. MODERATE TO DELUXE.

The **China Gate** is one of Montana's better Asian restaurants—at least if you like Americanized dishes like chop suey and egg foo yung. They're accompanied by a pleasant view across Flathead Lake. Closed Monday. ~ Routes 93 and 35, Polson; 406-883-4048. BUDGET.

There's more dining by the lake at **Showthyme**. Chef Blu Funk serves imaginative American and Continental dishes blending global flavors with a casually elegant style. Located in an early 1900s bank building that still has its original brick walls, hardwood floors and pressed-tin ceiling, Showthyme rates high with locals as well as travelers. Dinner only. ~ 548 Electric Avenue, Bigfork; 406-837-0707; www.showthyme.com. DELUXE.

The **Bigfork Inn** offers a country-style Swiss-chalet atmosphere with outdoor dining just down the block from the Bigfork Summer Playhouse, so it's a hit with theatergoers. Fresh seafood, pasta, chicken and steaks are the fare. A children's menu and lighter entrées ensure something for the whole family. Dinner only. ~ 604 Electric Avenue, Bigfork; 406-837-6680, fax 406-837-5658. MODERATE TO DELUXE.

At the **Swan River Cafe**, you can get European and American dishes geared to the diner who prefers his or her cuisine on the lighter side. Breakfast, lunch and dinner are served every day, with Sunday featuring a brunch and a prime-rib buffet dinner.

The remodeled building has a garden terrace and six antique-filled hotel rooms that overlook Bigfork Bay on Flathead Lake. Closed two weeks in late winter. ~ 360 Grand Avenue, Bigfork; 406-837-2220. DELUXE.

SHOPPING

Col. **Doug Allard's Flathead Indian Museum and Trading Post** is worth a stop if only to sample some of the huckleberry products made here, including jams, syrups, ice cream and milkshakes. Adjoining the expansive souvenir shop is a museum display of beaded Flathead tribal clothing from the early 1900s. Beadwork is sold, as are a wide range of souvenirs. ~ 1 Museum Lane, off of Route 93, St. Ignatius; 406-745-2951.

◄ HIDDEN

The **Four Winds Indian Trading Post** is a private venture featuring several 19th-century buildings from around the Mission Valley that were reassembled at this site. The active trading post, which re-creates a store of a similar era, is almost a museum in its own right. You'll find everything from Nez Perce cornhusk bags, porcupine-hair headdresses and cedar-bark baskets to beaded moccasins, books, T-shirts and cassette tapes of traditional music. ~ Route 93, three miles north of St. Ignatius; 406-745-4336.

The Four Winds Indian Trading Post is home to the biggest bead selection in the state.

On the south side of Flathead Lake, **Three Dog Down** has been rated "best in the world" by *Glamour* magazine for its down bedding, pillows and comforters. ~ 61547 Route 93, Polson; 406-883-3696.

One of the region's biggest antique markets, with 6000 square feet of display space, is **The Osprey Nest Antiques** at the north end of Flathead Lake. Closed Sunday and Monday in summer; call for winter hours. ~ Milepost 101, Route 93, Somers; 406-857-3714.

You'll also find paintings, sculptures and carvings by many contemporary Montana artisans at the **Kootenai Galleries**, open May through September and by appointment. ~ 573 Electric Avenue, Bigfork; 406-837-4848.

There are numerous galleries in the artists' community of Bigfork, especially along **Electric Avenue**.

◄ HIDDEN

Quilters, take note: It may be out of the way, but **Deer Country Quilt** is just the shop you've been looking for. Buy locally made quilts or the supplies to make them with; if you've got an idea in your mind but lack the skills to produce it yourself, order a hand-crafted quilt to your own design and specifications. ~ Route 83, Seeley Lake; 406-677-2730.

NIGHTLIFE

The **Port Polson Players** present three plays, which run through July and August at the John Dowdall Theatre in Boettcher Park. ~ P.O. Box 1152, Polson, MT 59860; 406-883-9212; www.port polsonplayers.com.

The **Bigfork Summer Playhouse** is the area's most acclaimed theater company, offering productions of a variety of popular shows, every summer night except Sunday. ~ 526 Electric Avenue, Bigfork; for ticket information write to P.O. Box 456, Bigfork, MT 59911; 406-837-4886; www.bigforksummerplayhouse.com.

Bigfork locals tipple at the **Tall Pine Lounge & Casino**. ~ Old Town Shopping Center, Bigfork; 406-837-6714. Or they head to the **Garden Bar**, an informal bar and restaurant that serves burgers and soups along with Western microbrews. ~ 451 Electric Avenue, Bigfork; 406-837-9914.

PARKS

MISSION MOUNTAINS WILDERNESS AREA 🚶🐎🏕️🎣 The majestic peaks and high alpine lakes of the Mission Range are preserved within this wilderness, which extends north–south for about 30 miles (beginning opposite the southern end of Flathead Lake) and tilts eastward toward the Swan River Valley. Panoramic views and wildlife are memorable. Some alpine lakes are home to the rare golden trout, worth a trip in itself for many anglers. The wilderness is abutted on the west by the Mission Mountains Tribal Wilderness. ~ Easiest access is from the east, off Route 83 north of Seeley Lake. There are trailheads at the ends of Forest Roads 79 (Lindbergh Lake Road) and 561, both a short distance south of Condon; 406-758-5204, fax 406-758-5363.

▲ Primitive camping; there are also three cabins; $25 to $50 per night.

FLATHEAD LAKE STATE PARK 🚶🚴🏊⛵🎣🚣🛶 Comprising six separate units around the circumference of Flathead Lake—two on the west shore, three on the east, plus Wild Horse Island—this park offers water-sports access to the huge lake. Anglers consider its lake trout legendary. Traveling clockwise around the lake from Polson, the park units are: *Big Arm* (406-849-5255); *Wild Horse Island* (406-849-5255), a 2892-acre wilderness in the lake's west arm that is indeed home to a handful of wild horses, as well as bighorn sheep and bald eagles, restricted to day use only; *West Shore* (406-884-3044), known for its intriguing rock formations; *Wayfarers* (406-837-4196), featuring a full-access disability campsite; *Yellow Bay* (south of Bigfork; 406-982-3034), in the heart of the cherry-orchard country; and *Finley Point* (near Polson; 406-887-2715), with a marina set on a forested peninsula at the south end of the lake, closed in winter. Facilities include picnic areas and restrooms. Day-use fee, $6. ~ On Route 93 on the lake's west side, Big Arm is two miles east of Elmo and West Shore is four miles south of Lakeside; take a boat from Big Arm to Wild Horse Island. On Route 35 along the east shore, Wayfarers is at Bigfork; Yellow Bay is 13 miles south of

Gouged by glaciers more than 10,000 years ago, Flathead Lake has a surface area of 188 square miles and a maximum depth of 386 feet.

Bigfork; Finley Point is 6 miles northeast of Polson, then 3 miles north via Finley Point Road; 406-751-4577, fax 406-257-0349.

▲ There are 113 RV/tent sites at five campgrounds, including 16 hookups at Finley Point and marine-kayak campsites around the lake; $15 per night; seven-day maximum stay.

LAKE MARY RONAN STATE PARK 🏇 🏕 🏊 🎣 🚤 ⛵ 🛶
Shrouded in a forest of Douglas fir and Western larch west of Flathead Lake, this pleasant lakefront park is a favorite of bird-watchers, huckleberry pickers and mushroom hunters. The heart-shaped, two-mile-wide lake is also frequented by trout, bass and kokanee fishermen. There are picnic areas and restrooms. Day-use fee, $5. ~ Seven miles northwest from Route 93 at Dayton via Lake Mary Ronan Highway; 406-752-5501.

▲ There are 27 primitive sites (no hookups); $14 per night; 14-day maximum stay.

JEWEL BASIN HIKING AREA 🚶 🛶 This unique, specially de-   ◀ HIDDEN
signed recreation area is northeast of Bigfork in the northern Swan Range. Neither horses nor mountain bikes are permitted on the 50 miles of trails that wind through its 15,349 acres of mountains and lakes, streams and wildflower-rich meadows west of Hungry Horse Reservoir. ~ From Route 83 northeast of Bigfork, take Echo Park Road north three miles to Jewel Basin Road, then proceed about seven miles farther to trailheads off Forest Road 5392; 406-387-3800.

▲ Primitive only.

PLACID LAKE AND SALMON LAKE STATE PARKS 🚶 🚴 🏊
🏊 🚤 ⛵ 🛶 Located four miles apart, very near Seeley Lake in the Clearwater Valley, these parks are popular with water-sports enthusiasts. Canoeing in particular is excellent in this area. Snowfall keeps both closed from November through April. Facilities include picnic areas and restrooms. Day-use fee, $5 ~ Salmon Lake is five miles south of Seeley Lake on Route 83. Placid Lake is three miles south of Seeley Lake via Route 83 and three miles west on Placid Lake Road; 406-542-5500, fax 406-542-5529.

▲ There are 40 RV/tent sites at Placid Lake, 25 RV/tent sites at Salmon Lake, none with hookups; $15 per night; 14-day maximum stay.

Stretching about 40 miles north from the top end of Flathead Lake, flanked on the east by the lofty peaks of Glacier National Park and on the west

▼▼▼▼▼▼▼▼▼▼▼▼▼▼
The Flathead Valley

by the evergreen-shrouded Salish Mountains, the Flathead Valley nestles around the meandering Flathead River. A bustling tourist region with lumber and fruit-growing industries (especially cherries), it has not one but three regional centers, all situated within 15 miles of one another: Kalispell, Whitefish and Columbia Falls.

SIGHTS   As the largest town for more than 100 miles in any direction, **Kalispell** is a good place to begin an exploration of the region. The town of 13,000 people is 32 miles from West Glacier and only 8 miles north of Flathead Lake.

Worth a look is Kalispell's art museum, the **Hockaday Center for the Arts**. The work of regional and national artists is exhibited in six galleries; there's also a permanent collection of Western art and a sales gallery. Closed Sunday and Monday in winter. ~ 302 2nd Avenue East and 3rd Street, Kalispell; 406-755-5268, fax 406-755-2023; hockadaymuseum.org, e-mail hockaday@centurytel.org.

Whitefish, 15 miles north of Kalispell via Route 93, is a friendly resort community with a proud railroading heritage. The town's growth spurt began in 1904 when the Great Northern Railway moved its division point here from Kalispell. For an introduction to local railroad and logging history, visit the **Stumptown Historical Society Museum** in the half-timbered train depot. Daily hours vary; call ahead. Closed Sunday. ~ 500 Depot Street, Whitefish; 406-862-0067; www.whitefishmt.com/stumphis.

Located on the main east–west Amtrak line, Whitefish hugs the south shore of seven-mile-long **Whitefish Lake**. Today, this year-round playground lures dedicated golfers and shoppers as well as younger adults who like to play hard day and night. Summertime, the lake beckons boaters and swimmers while **Big Mountain** ski resort—just eight miles away—opens a gondola (admission) to a summit viewing station and Forest Service Visitor Center. In winter, the resort is a popular ski and snowboard destination. ~ Big Mountain Road, Whitefish; 406-862-1900, 800-858-4152, fax 406-862-2922; www.bigmtn.com, e-mail big mtn@bigmtn.com.

Aluminum and timber are the economic mainstays in **Columbia Falls**, but the town's position as western gateway to Glacier

AUTHOR FAVORITE

sights   Whenever I have company, I take them to see Kalispell's crown jewel, the **Conrad Mansion**. Founding father Charles Conrad made a fortune as a Missouri River trader after his family lost its Virginia plantation during the Civil War. In 1895 he built a new estate here in Kalispell. The three-story, 26-room Norman-style home, set amid three acres of gardens, still contains most of its original Victorian decor: oak woodwork in the Great Hall, sleigh-style beds, imported marble in the bathrooms. Period-attired guides offer one-and-a-half-hour tours daily from mid-May to mid-October. Admission. ~ On Woodland Avenue between 3rd and 4th streets East, Kalispell; 406-755-2166; www.conradmansion.com.

Park, only 15 miles east, is almost equally as important. Attractions here range from the sublime to the ridiculous. On the one hand, there's quaint **St. Richard's Catholic Church**, which dates from 1892. ~ 1210 9th Street West, Columbia Falls; 406-892-5142. On the other hand, you might opt to pass an afternoon at the **Big Sky Waterpark & Miniature Greens**, a water park with ten slides. Closed in winter. Admission. ~ Route 2 East, Columbia Falls; 406-892-5025.

You can stay downtown at the **Kalispell Grand Hotel**. The refurbished 1909 hotel houses two restaurants, a casino with a classy lounge and an art gallery. Guest rooms, on the second and third floors, are comfortably spacious with modern baths and queen- and king-sized beds. A complimentary continental breakfast featuring homemade biscotti and coffee cake is served. Pets are welcome. ~ 100 Main Street, Kalispell; 406-755-8100, 800-858-7422, fax 406-752-8012; www.kalispellgrand.com, e-mail grand@kalispellgrand.com. MODERATE.

LODGING

Kalispell's leading lodging is the **WestCoast Outlaw Hotel**, which comes with all the bells and whistles: indoor swimming pools, jacuzzis, a sauna, tennis and racquetball courts, a restaurant, a lounge and a casino. The 218 guest rooms are sufficiently spacious but are otherwise just standard motel rooms. ~ 1701 Route 93 South, Kalispell; 406-755-6100, 800-325-4000, fax 406-756-8994; www.westcoasthotels.com/outlaw. DELUXE.

The **Cottonwood Hill Farm Inn**, housed in a renovated farmhouse on 14 acres, is a cozy getaway situated between Kalispell and Whitefish. With just three elegantly decoated rooms (all with private baths and four-poster beds), guests get plenty of attention—or privacy. Breakfast, an afternoon snack and a late-night dessert are all included in the price. Closed in winter. ~ 2928 Whitefish Stage Road, Kalispell; 406-756-6404, 800-458-0893, fax 406-756-6404; www.cottonwoodhillfarm.com, e-mail info@cottonwoodhillfarm.com. ULTRA-DELUXE.

If you like being pampered, you'll adore the classy yet unpretentious **Garden Wall Inn**. Within walking distance of downtown, this charming 1920s-era hostelry has five bedrooms furnished with period antiques and fresh flowers. You'll love the complimentary hors d'oeuvres and three-course breakfasts prepared by the inn's trained chefs. ~ 504 Spokane Avenue, Whitefish; 406-862-3440, 888-530-1700; www.gardenwallinn.com, e-mail garden@digisys.net. DELUXE TO ULTRA-DELUXE.

Whitefish is home to several excellent bed and breakfasts. With its Western motif and hearty buffet breakfast, the cedar-timbered **Good Medicine Lodge** is a class act. There are nine rooms, some with fireplaces and balconies. All have private baths and comfy lodgepole beds. ~ 537 Wisconsin Avenue, Whitefish;

Architectural Kalispell

For the past century, genteel Kalispell has served as Flathead Valley's business center. Starting life as a railroad division point, Kalispell grew into a charming town full of Victorian- and Craftsman-style dwellings as well as grand public and commercial buildings. Park outside meter-maid territory by the 26-room Conrad Mansion to begin your tour.

CONRAD MANSION   Take a one-and-a-half-hour tour of this Norman-style mansion built by Kalispell founder Charles Conrad. Costumed interpreters relate Conrad-family and Kalispell histories. Afterward, stroll the grounds. Admission. ~ On Woodland Avenue between 3rd and 4th streets, East.

6TH AVENUE EAST   Head south on 6th Avenue, where you'll pass several historic homes. Built in 1892 for a railway superintendent, the house at **312 6th Avenue East** received a Tudor-style makeover during the 1940s. The 1907 **Conrad/Tobie House** was the home of Charles Conrad's son. ~ 428 6th Avenue East. The 1910 **Elliot House** once served as Glacier National Park's winter headquarters. ~ 505 6th Avenue East. At **540 6th Avenue East** stands a half-timbered Craftsman-style home, built in 1924. Walk west one block.

5TH AVENUE EAST   More eye-catching houses line this street. The 1913 Prairie-style **Sickler/Edmiston House** has a distinctive low-pitched hipped roof and widely overhanging eaves. Notice the leaded-glass window transoms and front-door sidelights. ~ 535 5th Avenue East. The 1911 Colonial Revival–style **Keith House** was once an upscale bed and breakfast, among other incarnations. ~ 538 5th Avenue East. The 1910 **Agather House** is another Colonial Revival–style dwelling. Watch for the ornate ironwork, native rock porch and dual chimneys. ~ 604 5th Avenue East. Walk west on 6th Street a block. Turn north.

406-862-5488, 800-860-5488, fax 406-862-5489; www.good medicinelodge.com, e-mail info@goodmedicinelodge.com. DELUXE TO ULTRA-DELUXE.

Up on The Big Mountain you'll find the **Hibernation House**, an old-style economy ski lodge in the village at the foot of the chairlifts. Each of the 24 basic rooms has a queen-size bed, a set of bunks, a phone, a private bath with shower, and cable TV. Shared facilities include a laundry and a hot tub. A full breakfast

4TH AVENUE EAST   Note the fishscale shingles and front gable sunray pattern at the 1894 Queen Anne–style **McIntosh House**. ~ 511 4th Avenue East. You can't miss the front-entry rotunda and corner quoins of the lovely Georgian Revival–style **Conlon House**. ~ 305 4th Avenue East. **302 4th Avenue East** is another classic Queen Anne–style residence, built in 1900. Walk two blocks west on 3rd Street.

HOCKADAY CENTER FOR THE ARTS   Originally a Carnegie library that supplied logging camps with books and magazines, the 1903 Hockaday Center for the Arts (see page 66) is now a regional center for contemporary art. A domed octagonal entry graces the front of this masonry Classical Revival–style building. ~ 302 2nd Avenue East and 3rd Street.

MAIN STREET   Head two blocks west, into the business district, where the 1904 **Masonic Temple** stands. ~ 241 Main Street. Next door, the 1908 **Knight & Twining Block** is where Glacier Park photographer T. J. Hileman once had his studio. ~ 237 Main Street. An unexpected Art Nouveau–style façade graces the early 1940s building at **222 Main Street**. The 1900 structure at **140 Main Street** was an early-day bar. Stop to read the plaque on the corner of 2nd Street; it recounts Kalispell's beginnings. The **Hamm Brewing Company of St. Paul** built the spiffy 1901 building with the pressed metal façade. ~ 127 Main Street.

KALISPELL GRAND HOTEL   With its brass light fixtures, oak staircase, and pressed-tin ceilings, the Kalispell Grand Hotel (page 67) was the height of luxury in its early days. Travelers paid $2 nightly to sleep here when other rooms cost half that sum. ~ 100 Main Street.

CENTRAL SCHOOL MUSEUM   Walk east two blocks and head south on 2nd Avenue East until you hit the Central School Museum. This 1894 Richardsonian Romanesque building functioned as a school for almost a century. Today, the renovated building houses permanent and changing exhibits portraying Flathead Valley and Northwest Montana history. If you're hungry, eat lunch at the museum's Central School Café. ~ 124 2nd Avenue East; 406-756-8381. To return to the Conrad Mansion, follow 2nd Street three blocks east. Go south one block and east two blocks.

is included. Closed April and May and from mid-September through Thanksgiving Day. ~ 3812 Big Mountain Road, Whitefish; 406-862-1982, 800-858-5439, fax 406-862-1956; www.big mtn.com, e-mail cenres@bigmtn.com. MODERATE TO DELUXE.

The Flathead Valley is bed-and-breakfast country: there are at least 40, and the number is growing. The **Bad Rock Country B&B** stands out in the Columbia Falls area. Old West antiques and majestic mountain views typify the seven guest rooms (all with private baths) in this elegant country house, set on ten acres near the west entrance to Glacier Park. Four rooms in log cabins have fireplaces and patios. Guests enjoy gourmet breakfasts and hot-tub relaxation. ~ 480 Bad Rock Drive, Columbia Falls; 406-892-2829, 888-892-2829, fax 406-892-2930; www.bad rock.com, e-mail stay@badrock.com. ULTRA-DELUXE.

For a full listing of accommodations or assistance in finding a room, contact the **Flathead Convention & Visitors Association**. Closed weekends. ~ 15 Depot Park, Kalispell; 406-756-9091, 800-543-3105.

DINING

For refined dining you can't beat chef-owned **Café Max**. It's earned well-deserved kudos for innovative Pacific Northwest cuisine. Specialties include whiskey-marinated cowboy steak seasoned with cracked pepper and sage, and chargrilled Columbia River surgeon with lemon. Dinner only. Closed Sunday and Monday. Reservations recommended. ~ 121 Main Street, Kalispell; 406-755-7687; www.cafemaxmontana.com. DELUXE TO ULTRA-DELUXE.

HIDDEN ▶

You may not find cheaper meals anywhere than at **Sykes' Grocery, Market & Restaurant**. In business since 1905, Sykes' serves three meals a day, seven days a week. Coffee is still just a dime a cup, quarter-pound burgers cost $1.95, pork chop dinners run $4.95. Besides a deli and ice-cream counter, Sykes' sells fresh produce and camping gear, and operates a pharmacy—all in the same shop. ~ 202 2nd Avenue West, Kalispell; 406-257-4304, fax 406-755-3058. BUDGET.

Both Kalispell and Whitefish provided the backdrop for the 1994 Meryl Streep film *The River Wild*.

The **Bulldog Pub & Steakhouse** is at the head of the pack for Old World ambience and hearty steaks. Shrimp, chicken and prime rib are good, too. Enter off a parking lot around the corner from Kalispell City Hall; expect an intriguing weapons collection mounted on the walls, smoky air and loud blues. Closed Sunday. ~ 1701 Route 93 South, Kalispell; 406-752-7522, fax 406-756-8160. BUDGET TO DELUXE.

Located midway between Kalispell and Whitefish, **Fenders Restaurant & Lounge** is built around a classic automobile theme. Antique vehicles, like a '57 Ford and a '56 Chevy, have been remodeled into restaurant booths, and other period memorabilia decorate the walls. The menu is heavy on steak and seafood, as well as pasta and chicken. A children's menu is available. ~ 4090 Route 93 North, Kalispell; phone/fax 406-752-3000. MODERATE TO DELUXE.

Hankering for Cajun food? Then make tracks for the casual, New Orleans-style **Tupelo Grille**. Look for bayou classics such as the blackened tilapia with crawfish étouffée or the pan-fried chicken and dumplings. Tamer tastebuds should try the low-country shrimp and grits or jerked pork tenderloin. Dinner only. Closed the first two weeks in November. ~ 17 Central Avenue, Whitefish; phone/fax 406-862-6136; www.tupelogrille.com. MODERATE TO DELUXE.

With a name like **Truby's Wood Fired Pizza**, it's not hard to guess what the star attraction is at this welcoming Whitefish eatery. Their thin-crusted gourmet pizzas baked to order in a brick oven make tempting dinner fare, especially when partnered with a crispy Caesar salad. If you don't see toppings that dazzle you, create your own pizza. (Hint: gorgonzola with pine nuts is quite a tasty combination.) Truby's has also earned kudos for its barbecued baby back ribs smoked on the premises as well as its pastas and steaks. Dinner only. ~ 115 Central Avenue, Whitefish; 406-862-4979. MODERATE TO DELUXE.

The **Dire Wolf Pub** offers an imaginative twist on the usual pub fare: try the blackened Cajun chicken sandwich or the pasta with fresh basil, spinach and tomatoes. A variety of salads, pizzas and burgers round out the menu. Kick back on the breezy deck with one of the local brews in hand. ~ 845 Wisconsin Avenue, Whitefish; 406-862-4500. BUDGET TO MODERATE.

Drawing raves on the east side of Flathead Valley is the **Back Room**. Located behind the Nite Owl restaurant in Columbia Falls, the Back Room has built its reputation on smoked baby back ribs and broasted chicken, partnered with homemade fry bread and baked beans. It's unpretentious, friendly and probably the best meal-deal around. Thursday you can watch a magician bamboozle diners of all ages. Dinner only. ~ Route 2 East, Columbia Falls; 406-892-3131. MODERATE.

SHOPPING

If you're looking for Montana crafts and products, visit **The Melon Basket** in the 50-store Kalispell Center Mall. ~ 20 North Main Street, Kalispell; 406-752-8778. There's also **Montana Expressions**, which carries an assortment of locally made furniture, accessories and textile art. Closed Sunday. ~ 123 Main Street, Kalispell; 406-756-8555.

The place to go for collectibles is the **Kalispell Antiques Market**, which represents 35 different dealers. ~ 48 Main Street, Kalispell; 406-257-2800.

One of the area's best bookstores is **Bookworks**, a locally owned shop that emphasizes subjects of regional interest, especially nature and the outdoors. Closed Sunday from January through May. ~ 244 Spokane Avenue, Whitefish; 406-862-4980.

NIGHTLIFE

The performing arts are lively in the Flathead. The **Whitefish Theatre Company**, a community troupe, offers everything from musicals to dramas in a September-to-May season, including a world music series. ~ 1 Central Avenue, Whitefish; 406-862-5371; www.

whitefishtheatreco.com. The **Glacier Orchestra & Chorale** presents concerts year-round, often with guest conductors and performers. ~ 140 Main Street, Kalispell; write to P.O. Box 2491, Kalispell, MT 59903; 406-257-3241; www.glaciersymphony chorale.org.

Popular among the valley's poker-and-keno crowd is the **Montana Nugget Casino**. ~ 740 West Idaho Street, Kalispell; 406-756-8100. Locals frequent **Moose's Saloon** every day for video poker and lively conversation on a sawdust floor. ~ 173 North Main Street, Kalispell; 406-755-2337. The lively **Blue Moon**, at the Whitefish-Kalispell junction, rages on weekends with live country-and-western music and dancing. ~ 6105 Route 2, Columbia Falls; 406-892-9925.

For loud rock music and general rowdiness, you can't top a two-block stretch of Central Avenue in downtown Whitefish. Try the **Great Northern Bar** for a rocking good time, with live music Thursday through Saturday. ~ 27 Central Avenue; 406-862-2816. Hang at **Casey's Casino, Pub & Liquor Store** for video games. ~ 101 Central Avenue; 406-862-8150. **Palace Bar** has casino machines, sports on the TVs and the cheapest beers in Whitefish. ~ 125 Central Avenue; 406-862-2428. Play live or video poker at **Bulldog Saloon**. ~ 144 Central Avenue; 406-862-5601. Another great spot is the **Great Northern Brewery**, with a tasting room for local microbrews. ~ 2 Central Avenue; 406-863-1000.

PARKS

WOODLAND WATER PARK 🚲 🏊 A lagoon runs through the heart of this Kalispell municipal park, providing a serene setting for a variety of activities, from strenuous sports to strolls through a rose garden. Swans, geese and ducks inhabit the lagoon. The park has a municipal swimming and diving pool and water slides; other facilities include a skating park, horseshoe pits and a walking trail. In winter, there's ice-skating. Picnic areas and restrooms round out the amenities. ~ Follow 2nd Street East from downtown Kalispell to Woodland Park Drive; 406-758-7718.

LONE PINE STATE PARK 🚶 🚲 🐎 Located just outside Kalispell, 280-acre Lone Pine occupies a glacial knoll overlooking the Flathead Valley. With its interpretive programs, pine-and-fir forest, wildflowers and bird life, it's an educational resource for valley schools. Facilities include a visitors center, an archery range, volleyball courts, picnic areas, restrooms and a handicapped-accessible overlook. Closed October through April. Day-use fee, $5. ~ Four miles southwest of Kalispell on Foys Lake Road, then one mile north on Lone Pine Road; 406-752-5501, fax 406-257-0349.

WHITEFISH LAKE STATE PARK 🚶 🏕 🏊 🎣 🚤 🚣 Providing water-sports access to beautiful, seven-mile-long Whitefish Lake, this state park is one of Montana's most popular. Visiting

anglers can pursue northern pike, lake whitefish and trout. Facilities include picnic areas and restrooms with showers. Closed
October through April. Day-use fee, $5. ~ One-
half mile west of downtown Whitefish on Route
93, turn north a mile on West Lakeshore Drive;
406-862-3991, 406-752-5501 (winter), fax 406-
257-0349.

Huckleberries abound in
Flathead National Forest
from mid-July to Octo-
ber. Try looking in
areas cleared by tim-
ber cutting or forest
fires, and along
roads.

▲ There are 25 RV/tent sites (no hookups); $12
per night; seven-day maximum stay.

FLATHEAD NATIONAL FOREST 🏃 🚴 🐎 🦌 🏕 🏊
🛶 🎣 🚤 ⛴ 🎿 Covering more than two million
mountainous acres south and west of Glacier National
Park, this forest encompasses Hungry Horse Reservoir, the Jewel
Basin Hiking Area, The Big Mountain ski resort and many other
important recreational sites. There are picnic areas and restrooms. ~ Most highways and secondary roads that lead out from
the Flathead Valley penetrate the forest. The greatest concentration of sites are off the East Side and West Side roads that flank
Hungry Horse Reservoir, joining near the Spotted Bear Ranger
Station; 406-758-5204, fax 406-758-5363.

▲ There are 322 RV/tent sites in 22 campgrounds (no hookups); up to $12 per night; 14-day maximum stay.

The region west of Kalispell is a land of
dense, Pacific Northwest–like forests of
towering pines and firs, jagged peaks rich

The Northwest Corner

in timber and silver ore, and mountain streams harnessed for hydroelectric power. Route 2 is the artery of this district; the main centers are Libby, on the Kootenai River, and Eureka, near the Canadian border.

If you discover an unusual percentage of tall, blue-eyed blonds
among Libby's 2600 residents, blame it on a Norwegian lumber
mill operator named J. Neils. In the late 1800s, he wrote friends
and relatives in Minnesota, seeking people to work for him. Several hundred Scandinavian loggers migrated west with their families. Today their contributions are recalled every September in
the Nordicfest celebration.

Libby is located 89 miles from Kalispell and 92 miles from Sandpoint, Idaho. It is the home of **Libby Dam**, 17 miles north on the
Kootenai River. Completed in 1975 for hydroelectricity and
flood control, the dam is 420 feet high, 310 feet wide at its base
and more than a half-mile long at its crest. Guided tours of the
dam's powerhouse are offered four times a day between 10 a.m.
and 4 p.m., daily from Memorial Day to Labor Day, and by appointment the rest of the year. ~ Route 37 North, Libby; 406-
293-5577, fax 206-764-3681.

SIGHTS

The Libby Dam has created serpentine, 90-mile-long, 370-foot-deep **Lake Koocanusa,** which extends north into Canada's British Columbia province. It's name comes from combining "Kootenai" and "Canada" with "USA." Along its shores are several recreation areas and campgrounds; you may also see bald eagles and osprey fishing, and bighorn sheep on steep slopes.

Every September, Libby celebrates Nordicfest to pay homage to its fore-fathers' Scandinavian heritage.

Back in Libby, the **Heritage Museum** features area history, wildlife and economy, though perhaps most interesting is the 12-sided log building in which it's housed. The grounds also include a miner's cabin and a loggers' cookhouse. Open summer only. ~ 1367 Route 2 South, Libby; 406-293-7521; www.lincolncountylibraries.com/museum; e-mail museum@libby.com.

The **Ross Creek Cedar Grove Scenic Area** is 25 miles south of Troy near Bull Lake; it boasts a wheelchair-accessible interpretive trail, less than a mile long, that leads among giant old-growth western red cedar trees, some 175 feet tall and estimated at more than 500 years old. Closed in winter. ~ Route 56; 406-295-4693, fax 406-295-7410.

Equidistant (67 miles) from both Libby and Kalispell, eight miles south of the Canadian border on Route 93, the Christmas tree-farming center of **Eureka** is at the heart of Kootenai National Forest. In the little town, the **Tobacco Valley Historical Village** relates area history museum-style. Closed September through May. ~ Main Street, Eureka; 406-297-7654; e-mail historicalvillage@interbel.net. To the northeast, the **Ten Lakes Scenic Area** invites visitors to follow a mountain road to lakes renowned for their hiking and fishing. Get the hiking guide from the ranger station for detailed information on specific trails. ~ Grave Creek Road, Eureka; 406-882-4451.

LODGING

In the heart of Libby, the **Caboose Motel** has 28 comfortable, air-conditioned rooms with queen- and king-size beds. ~ 714 West 9th Street at Route 2, Libby; 406-293-6201, 800-627-0206, fax 406-293-3621; www.mtwilderness.com, e-mail info@mt wilderness.com. MODERATE.

Play cowpoke at **McGinnis Meadows Cattle & Guest Ranch,** a working ranch situated on a breathtaking 500 acres adjacent to the Lost Trail Wildlife Refuge. Week-long stays here mean horses, horses and more horses. You'll work on your riding skills and have plenty of opportunities to herd, rope and pen cattle. After a hard-day's ride, soak those saddle-sore bones in the communal hot tub. Accommodations are in the cozy, Western-style lodge or in well-appointed cabins. All meals are included in the rate. Closed November through March. ~ 6600 McGinnis Meadows

Road, Libby; 406-293-5000, 866-764-5569; www.mmgranch.net, e-mail info@mmgranch.net. ULTRA-DELUXE.

In the tiny town of Eureka is **The Corner Cottage**, a restored 1919 Victorian that has just one upstairs suite with two guest rooms, perfect for two couples traveling together (or you can also just rent one of the rooms). The larger room has a queen-size bed and overstuffed chair; the other holds a full-size bed and antique rocker. Hiking, mountain biking and fishing opportunities are close by; Glacier National Park is about an hour away. Despite (or perhaps because of) the remote location, high-speed internet is available. ~ 509 2nd Avenue East, Eureka; 406-297-2098; www.acornercottage.com, e-mail info@acornercottage.com. DELUXE.

DINING

Beck's Montana Cafe, located at the western edge of Libby, serves three square meals a day. Roasted chicken and the salad bar are popular every night, as are homemade soups and daily specials, such as chicken enchiladas and prime rib. ~ 2425 Route 2 West, Libby; 406-293-6687. MODERATE.

Here's honesty in advertising. This corner of Montana is clearly off the beaten track, as **The Boondocks** so eloquently admits. Three blocks north of the main highway through Troy, it serves three meals daily, including homemade Mexican food, sourdough pizza and sandwiches. This is also the place to catch all the local gossip, and there's a deck for soaking up nice weather. ~ 407 North 2nd Street, Troy; 406-295-5780. BUDGET TO MODERATE.

For all-American fare served in a charmingly rustic setting, make tracks for the **Antler Inn**. This cozy log-cabin restaurant comes complete with family antiques, old-time oil lamps and tantalizing wafts of fresh-baked pie—all of which make you feel right at home the moment you walk in the door. Dinner entrées of note include roast duck glazed with a wild plum sauce, and prime rib. Remember to leave room for a piece of five-fruit pie after you've cleaned your plate. Dinner only. Closed Monday and Tuesday in summer, Monday through Thursday in winter. ~ 2225 Grave Creek Road (Mile Marker 170 on Route 93), Eureka; 406-882-4408. DELUXE.

SHOPPING

Kootenai Fine Art displays the works of noted Montana painter Marjorie D. Caldwell and other artists of the Western genre. Closed weekends, except by appointment. ~ 580 Greers Ferry, Libby; 406-293-9320; www.kootenaifineart.com.

PARKS

KOOTENAI NATIONAL FOREST 🚶 🚴 🐎 🏹 🏠 🛶 ⛷ 🚣 🛶 🛷 It's almost a given that this 2.2-million-acre national forest contains more board feet of lumber than any other in Montana. Within its boundaries are 90-mile-long Lake Koocanusa and the Cabinet Mountains Wilderness. Picnic areas and restrooms are among the facilities. ~ Route 37, which follows the Lake Koocanusa shoreline, connects Route 2 at Libby with Route 93 at Eureka; 406-293-6211.

▲ There are 509 RV/tent sites (no hookups), and 60 sites for tents only at 39 campgrounds; $5 to $10 per night; 14-day maximum stay.

CABINET MOUNTAINS WILDERNESS AREA 🚶 🐎 🏕️ 🚣 Comprising 94,000 acres west of Libby along the spiny crest of the Cabinet Mountains, this wilderness extends 33 miles, climaxed by 8712-foot Snowshoe Peak. Trails lead to alpine lakes and streams. Vegetation is denser here than in most other mountain districts of Montana. Denizens include deer, elk, bighorn sheep, mountain goats and an occasional grizzly bear. ~ Many trails begin from logging roads branching off Route 2. Or take Flower Creek Road, just south of Libby, to several other trailheads; 406-827-3533, fax 406-827-0718.

> With an average summer high of 88°F and an average winter low of 22°F, Thompson Falls has the mildest weather in the state, earning it the nickname "banana belt."

▲ Primitive only.

LOGAN STATE PARK 🚶 🚴 🏊 🚣 🛶 🚤 ⛴️ 🚣 Once called Thompson Chain of Lakes State Park, this park near the source of the Thompson River is the focal point of a necklace of small lakes and ponds. The park is on the north shore of Middle Thompson Lake, largest of the group. Fishing and birdwatching are the main attractions. Facilities include picnic areas and restrooms. Day-use fee, $5. ~ Off Route 2, 39 miles southeast of Libby; 406-752-5501, fax 406-293-7190; www.fwp.state.mt.us.

▲ There are 41 RV/tent sites (no hookups); $15 per night; 14-day maximum stay.

Thompson Falls Area   The meandering, and sometimes thundering, Clark Fork River is the focal point of this region, best explored on Route 200 west of Missoula. It includes Thompson Falls, an outdoor recreational gateway about 100 miles northwest of Missoula, and long, skinny Noxon Rapids Reservoir.

SIGHTS   Thompson Falls' **Old Jail Museum** was built in 1907 as a prison and sheriff's residence; it offers an interesting depiction of early settlement and law enforcement. Closed September through April. ~ Madison Street and Maiden Lane, Thompson Falls; 406-827-3496.

The pine-forested mountains of Lolo National Forest are home to bighorn sheep; there's a **viewing station** on the highway eight miles east of Thompson Falls.

The head of 27-mile-long **Noxon Rapids Reservoir** is about six miles northwest of Thompson Falls along Route 200. The reservoir was created by the earth-filled Noxon Rapids Dam on the Clark Fork River. Another dam forms Cabinet Gorge Reservoir on the state's western border, just east of Idaho's majestic Lake Pend Oreille.

The **Bighorn Lodge Bed & Breakfast**, located on the Bull River adjacent Cabinet Mountain Wilderness, is a country inn with seven guest rooms (all with private baths), an outdoor spa and a big deck with fine mountain views. There's hiking, riding, canoeing and fishing in the surrounding national forest. A full breakfast is served; dinner may be arranged by request. ~ 2 Bighorn Lane, Noxon; 406-847-4676, 800-347-8477, fax 406-847-0069; www. bighornlodgemontana.com, e-mail bhl@blackfoot.net. DELUXE.

LODGING

Located in the foothills of the Bitterroots overlooking Noxon Rapids Reservoir, the **Blue Spruce Lodge** consists of two log chalets, each with three bedrooms, two baths and a kitchen and living area. The chalets comfortably sleep six or more, and one is wheelchair accessible. The lodge provides dinner and a continental breakfast. Two-night minimum. ~ 451 Marten Creek Road, Trout Creek; 406-827-4762, 800-831-4797; www.montana lodge.com, e-mail bluesprucelodge@blackfoot.net. DELUXE.

◄ HIDDEN

The usual fare in this corner of the state is traditional home cooking, and no one does it better than **Minnie's Café**, which serves three meals daily; try the salad bar, hand-pressed burgers and homemade pies. ~ 921 Main Street, Thompson Falls; 406-827-3747. MODERATE.

DINING

THOMPSON FALLS STATE PARK 🏊 🚣 🚤 🛥️ ⛵ Nature walks and birdwatching along the Clark Fork River, and boating and fishing access to Noxon Rapids Reservoir, are the highlights of this park. There are picnic areas and restrooms. Closed October through April. Day-use fee, $5. ~ Two miles northwest of the town of Thompson Falls off Route 200; 406-752-5501.

PARKS

▲ There are 20 primitive sites; $12 per night; 14-day maximum stay.

Robert Redford's 1992 movie *A River Runs Through It* may have brought Montana fly-fishing to the awareness of the nation, but the richness of the fishing life has never been a secret to anyone who lives in the state. That's especially true in northwest Montana. The streams and lakes flowing from the Rockies' western slopes offer trout, walleye and many other species worthy of *any* fish story.

▼▼▼▼▼▼▼▼▼▼▼▼▼▼
Outdoor Adventures

FISHING

Huge populations of trout—rainbow, brook, cutthroat and brown, in particular—inhabit the creeks and rivers that flow from the Continental Divide. In the Missoula and Flathead Valley areas, this is the predominant fish. Mountain whitefish and bull trout are also widely found in rivers and lakes, and many lakes have yellow perch.

Other species may not be as widely distributed. Huge Flathead Lake and nearby Whitefish Lake are known for their lake trout and lake whitefish. Whitefish Lake also has northern pike, as do several lakes in the Seeley-Swan region. You will find kokanee salmon, a favorite of gourmets, in lakes Koocanusa and Mary Ronan, among others. Noxon Rapids Reservoir, on the Clark Fork near the Idaho border, boasts ten different species of fish, more than anywhere else on the west side of the Continental Divide.

Many fishing equipment companies also operate guided tours to area rivers and lakes as an adjunct service. Contact **Grizzly Hackle International Fishing Company** for trips to the Bitterroot, Blackfoot, Clark Fork, Rock Creek and Missouri rivers. ~ 215 West Front Street, Missoula; 406-721-8996, 800-297-8996; www.grizzlyhackle.com. **Lakestream Fly Fishing Co.** is another option for trips on the Flathead River and Cedar Lake, its own private lake. ~ 334 Central Avenue, Whitefish; 406-862-1298; www.lakestream.com. One leading company is **Wilderness Outfitters**, specializing in horseback trips in summer through the Bob Marshall Wilderness. ~ 11500 Frenchtown Frontage Road, Missoula; 406-728-0550; www.montanawildernesstrips.com. In Columbia Falls, call **Glacier Fishing Charters** for fishing on Flathead Lake January through September. ~ 375 Jensen Road, Columbia Falls; 406-892-2377.

BOATING

On Flathead Lake, numerous marinas will rent boats of all sizes for fishing or pleasure boating. One such establishment is **Absolute Water Sports**, which rents everything from ski boats to canoes. Closed October through Memorial Day. ~ 303 Route 93, Polson; 406-883-3900, 800-358-8046. Owned and operated by the confederated Salish and Kootenai tribes, **S & K Marina** rents jet skis, boats and boat slips, and provides a variety of repair services. Closed October through March. ~ 1501 Route 93, Polson; 406-883-1902; www.s-kmarina.com.

Also in the Flathead Valley, instruction and rentals for boating activities on Whitefish Lake are available from **Whitefish Lake Lodge Resort**. ~ 1399 Wisconsin Avenue, Whitefish; 406-862-2929, 800-735-8869; www.wfll.com.

RIVER RUNNING

The River Wild, Meryl Streep's 1994 adventure movie about whitewater rafting, was filmed in Montana. And while few would challenge a Class VI rapid of the type Streep and co-star Kevin Bacon

Fly-fishing Haven

The prospect of laying a hand-tied lure on a placid stretch of river and reeling in a giant trout has a romance shared by few outdoor recreations. And few places are better suited to the sport of fly-fishing than western Montana.

Here, after all, runs the Blackfoot River, scene of Norman Maclean's classic novel, *A River Runs Through It*, whose film success popularized fly-fishing for a whole new generation of anglers. The Clark Fork and the Bitterroot and Swan rivers rank among the best trout streams in North America, along with the Big Hole, the Madison and others in the southern part of the state.

The roots of fly-fishing date back at least two thousand years. Macedonians were known to have used artificial flies in upland lakes and streams. The first known sport fishing manual, published in England in 1496, described a dozen hand-tied flies (six of them still in use today). But fly-fishing as it's known in the 1990s did not become possible until now when the horsehair line was reinvented. The modern flycasting line—typically nylon with a plastic covering, tapered to a monofilament leader—provides the weight for casting the virtually weightless fly; it can float atop the water or sink below the surface.

A flexible fiberglass or graphite rod, usually about eight feet long, is whipped in a motion that sends the line and lure to a precise location in the water. This is the true test of the skilled angler: the ability to "read" the water, to know where fish are most likely to strike, and to place the fly to drift over that exact spot.

Artificial flies may be made from silk, fur, feathers or other materials, but they usually resemble a natural food source for the fish: insects (such as mayflies, caddis flies and midges), freshwater shrimp or snails, for instance.

The angler's challenge is to simulate the insect's natural behavior and outwit the fish—either by "wet-fly" fishing with the lure underwater, or "dry-fly" fishing on the surface of the water. Dry-fly anglers try to cast a slack line, allowing their lure to remain naturally on the surface as long as possible before it is caught in the current.

Lodges throughout western and southern Montana provide fly-fishing guides and instruction. See individual chapters for details.

tackled, there are floating opportunities of all kinds available throughout northwest Montana. That goes for kayakers and canoeists as well as rafters.

In the Missoula area, popular trips are through Hell Gate Canyon and Alberton Gorge on the Clark Fork River, and down the Blackfoot.

Northwest Montana's most popular area for rafting is on the various forks of the Flathead River, on the west side of Glacier National Park. If you're not an experienced rafter, the best and safest way to go is with an outfitter.

For seasonal rentals of river equipment, check out **The Trailhead**. ~ 221 East Front Street, Missoula; 406-543-6966.

KAYAKING & CANOEING   Kayakers enjoy the same rivers as rafters. But if you prefer lake water to whitewater, **Glacier Sea Kayaking** allows you to explore Flathead Lake's coastline and islands. Reservations required. ~ 390 Talley Lake Road, Whitefish; 406-862-9010; www.digisys.net/seakayak.

The region's best canoeing is in the Seeley-Swan area and at the Thompson Chain of Lakes. On Route 83, the **Clearwater Canoe Trail** has a put-in four miles north of Seeley; canoeists can glide down the Clearwater River for an hour or two to the north end of Seeley Lake, then take a footpath back along the stream.

An hour's drive west of Kalispell at **Logan State Park**, the ten-mile Thompson Chain of Lakes beside Route 2 demands only a few very short portages.

DOWNHILL SKIING   Montana's largest destination ski resort, and one of its oldest, is **The Big Mountain**, overlooking Whitefish Lake about 12 miles (as the eagle flies) west of Glacier National Park. Established in the 1960s, The Big Mountain is just that: It has more than 3000 acres of skiing and snowboarding terrain and 90 runs, served by 11 chairlifts and two surface lifts. The vertical drop is 2500 feet from a summit elevation of 7000 feet. Here there are gentle groomed slopes for beginning skiers, steep and deep powder for experts. Base facilities include lodge and condominium accommodations, restaurants and bars, and ski shops with full rentals.

AUTHOR FAVORITE

To really appreciate magnificent Flathead Lake, you need to get out of your car, jump into a canoe, and paddle till you can't stand looking at one more gorgeous mountain view. I know it's a tall order, but if you stop at one of the marinas along the lake they will gladly help you overdose on the scenery.

~ Big Mountain Road, Whitefish; 406-862-2900, fax 406-862-2955; www.bigmtn.com, e-mail bigmtn@bigmtn.com.

Montana Snowbowl Ski Resort, 12 miles northwest of Missoula, has a vertical drop of 2600 feet from a summit elevation of 7600 feet. Advanced skiers appreciate the steep-sided bowls, but there are also beginners' slopes. There's a terrain park for snowboarders. Two chairlifts and two surface tows serve more than 30 runs. Facilities include a rental shop, a café, a bar and chalet-style lodging. Closed April to late November. ~ 1700 Snowbowl Road, Missoula; 406-549-9777, 800-728-2695; www.montana snowbowl.com, e-mail info@montanasnowbowl.com.

Day-use ski areas (with no on-site lodging) in northwest Montana include:

Lost Trail Powder Mountain Ski Area, straddling the Montana–Idaho border above the Bitterroot Valley, 91 miles south of Missoula. The snow arrives here early in the season and stays late. Five chairlifts and three rope tows serve 43 runs in the Bitterroot National Forest. There's an 1800-foot vertical drop from a top elevation of 8200 feet. Closed Monday through Wednesday. ~ Route 93, Conner; 406-821-3211, fax 406-821-3742; www. losttrail.com, e-mail ski@losttrail.com.

Check out **Turner Mountain Ski Area** in the Purcell Mountains west of Lake Koocanusa in northwesternmost Montana. A double chairlift climbs to the top of the 5952-foot peak; 90 percent of the 14 runs that descend 2110 feet of vertical to the base area are deemed expert. It's only open Friday through Sunday in season (usually December through May), and daily during holidays. ~ Located 22 miles north of Libby on Pipe Creek Road; 406-293-4317; www.skiturner.com, e-mail skier@libby.org.

The Big Mountain boasts an excellent 15-kilometer track for cross-country skiers; in fact, it's occasionally used as a training center for U.S. Olympic bi-athletes and Nordic racers. ~ Big Mountain Road, Whitefish; 406-862-1900. **Holland Lake Lodge** has a 25-kilometer trail system and full lodging and rental packages in the Swan River Valley. ~ Route 83, Condon; 406-754-2282. At **Chief Joseph Pass,** near Lost Trail Pass, a 24-kilometer network of rated trails, groomed weekly, has been developed by the Bitterroot Cross Country Ski Club. ~ Route 43, Conner.

CROSS-COUNTRY SKIING

When the snow disappears, the golf courses flourish. Among the leading public courses in northwest Montana is the **Buffalo Hill Municipal Golf Club,** a 27-hole championship course with views from The Big Mountain to Flathead Lake. ~ 1176 North Main Street, Kalispell; 406-756-4530, 800-342-6319. The 18-hole **Larchmont Municipal Golf Course** hosts the Montana Open golf tournament. ~ 3200 Fort Missoula Road, Missoula; 406-721-4416.

GOLF

In the Glacier Park area, the **Flathead Valley Golf Association** will make advance tee-time reservations for visiting golfers at any of the area's nine 18-hole courses. ~ 500 Depot Street #5, Whitefish; 406-862-7970, 800-392-9795; www.golfmontana.net. It seems as though every community of any size throughout the region has its own municipal nine-hole course. In Missoula, it's the **Highlands Golf Club**. ~ 102 Ben Hogan Drive; 406-728-7360.

TENNIS

Local parks and recreation offices are happy to share the locations and open hours of municipal courts. Call for information in Missoula at 406-721-7275. In Kalispell, contact 406-758-7717. Missoula's **Playfair Park** is a good place to swing a racket. ~ 3001 Bancroft. **Fort Missoula** also has 8 unlit courts. Or you can try Kalispell's **Northridge Park**. ~ Northridge Drive.

RIDING STABLES

If you want to embark on a modern-day Lewis and Clark excursion, **Lolo Hot Springs** offers one- to two-hour and half-day rides from Memorial Day to Labor Day. ~ 38500 Route 12 West, Lolo; 406-273-2290; www.lolohotsprings.com.

Guests of **L-Diamond-E Ranch Outfitters** get to go by horse to mine sapphires. ~ Rock Creek Road, Clinton; 406-825-6295, 888-725-8747; www.ldiamonde.com.

PACK TRIPS & LLAMA TREKS

While many horse-packing outfitters serve hunters in particular, others prefer riders who simply enjoy the outdoors. They'll take you anywhere, even through the most remote reaches of wilderness. Try **Lion Creek Outfitters** for a range of daily trips—kid-friendly or with elevation and incredible views. ~ 610 Patrick Creek Road; Kalispell; 406-755-3723; www.lioncreekoutfitters.com.

Guided llama pack trips—you walk, the llama carries your load—are an unusual way to explore Montana's wilderness. In July and August in the Glacier Park area check out the **Great Northern Llama Co.** ~ 600 Blackmer Lane, Columbia Falls; 406-755-9044; www.greatnorthernranch.com.

BIKING

Missoula has been called "one of the top ten bicycling cities in the United States" by *Bicycling* magazine. The sentiment clearly carries north into the Flathead Valley area.

So important is bicycling to northwest Montana that the **Adventure Cycling Association** (ACA), formerly known as BikeCentennial and regarded as America's leading bike-touring organization, has established its national headquarters here. The ACA publishes touring maps and supports a national network of touring routes. ~ 150 East Pine Street, Missoula; 406-721-1776; www.adventurecycling.org.

Local bicycle shops also have information on planned activities and mountain-biking routes. Favorite locations for the latter include the **Rattlesnake National Recreation Area** near Missoula and **The Big Mountain Ski and Summer Resort** outside of White-fish, where you can also rent digglers. Another popular area is **Kreis Pond**, with 35 miles of designated mountain-bike trails near the Ninemile Ranger Station and Remount Depot, 27 miles northwest of Missoula. The Park publishes a pamphlet showing bike trails in Lolo National Forest. ~ Lolo National Forest; write to 20325 Remount Road, Huson, MT 59846; 406-626-5201.

Note: National forest roads and trails are generally open to mountain biking, but wheeled vehicles—motorized or not—are not allowed in designated wilderness areas.

Bike Rentals **Open Road Bicycles** is a full-service shop that rents mountain and road bikes equipped with helmets, pumps and bags. ~ 517 South Orange Street, Missoula; 406-549-2453. You'll find mountain, road and kids' bikes (helmets and water bottles included) at **Glacier Cyclery**. Reservations recommended during peak season. Closed Sunday from mid-September to mid-May. ~ 326 East 2nd Street, Whitefish; 406-862-6446; www.glaciercyclery.com.

Northern Montana is one of the greatest places on earth for hiking, backpacking and mountaineering. Quite aside from Glacier National Park, there are thousands of miles more throughout the national forests and wilderness areas of the region. All distances listed are one way unless otherwise noted.

HIKING

MISSOULA **Crazy Canyon Trail** (3.4 miles), in the Pattee Canyon Recreation Area near Missoula's southeastern city limits, presents a moderate climb to the top of 5158-foot Mount Sentinel, overlooking Missoula from the south side of the Clark Fork River. You can descend from here via the **Hellgate Canyon Trail** (2.1 miles) to the banks of the Clark Fork, or via the **"M" Trail** (1.8 miles) to the University of Montana campus.

Stuart Peak Trail (12 miles) is a strenuous ascent through the Rattlesnake National Recreation Area and Wilderness. Beginning at the Sawmill Gulch Road trailhead, it traverses Spring

WALKS THROUGH THE WOODS

The **Montana Wilderness Association** organizes free day and weekend hikes throughout the state, including excursions into the Cabinet Mountains, Bitterroot National Forest and Kootenai National Forest. Each trip is limited to a few hikers, though, so advance reservations are necessary. Contact the MWA for a free booklet of the more than 140 statewide hikes offered from May through October. ~ P.O. Box 635, Helena, MT 59624; 406-443-7350 ext. 107, fax 406-443-0750; www.wildmontana.org.

Gulch and then rises above the timberline for great views from the upper slopes of 7960-foot Stuart Peak. The loop trail returns past Twin Lakes and Lake Creek. The elevation gain is more than 3800 feet from the trailhead.

BITTERROOT VALLEY Lake Como Trail (7 miles) circles a reservoir popular among water-sports enthusiasts, 14 miles south of Hamilton at the foot of the Bitterroot Mountains. With virtually no elevation gain, it's an easy walk. A trailhead is at Lake Como Recreation Area; from the trail's end, a one-mile walk along the road beside the dam will return you to your start.

The best way to hike the **South Lost Horse Creek Trail** (13 miles) is from the top down. The trailhead is on the Idaho border at the west end of 18-mile-long Lost Horse Road (Forest Road 429), nine miles south of Hamilton off Route 93. From Bear Creek, cross a 6100-foot Bitterroot Mountain pass to Fish Lake, then descend 1700 feet down the steep-sided canyon of South Lost Horse Creek. Moderate.

FLATHEAD INDIAN RESERVATION & LAKE Numerous trails penetrate the Mission Mountains Wilderness Area. One of the shortest and most spectacular is the **Turquoise Lake Trail** (4.6 miles), which climbs to a sparkling glacial lake nestling beneath a sheer cliff at the 5800-foot-level of Daughter of the Sun Mountain. The moderately strenuous trail begins at the end of 12-mile-long Forest Road 561 southwest of Condon, halfway between Swan Lake and Seeley Lake.

The **Jewel Basin Hiking Area** has been set aside by the U.S. Forest Service and Flathead National Forest for foot travel only. Located 15 miles from Kalispell and about five miles from Bigfork, it has 35 miles of trails. Access is from West Side Road (Hungry Horse Reservoir) or from Jewel Basin Road, off Foothill Road (northeast of Bigfork). There's fishing and camping at 25 alpine lakes, wildlife and seasonal floral displays.

FLATHEAD VALLEY The **Danny On Memorial Trail** (5.6 miles) climbs The Big Mountain, seven miles north of Whitefish, from the lodge at the foot of the slopes. Named for a noted botanist and photographer of the region, the trail passes through beautiful meadows with views across the Flathead Valley. For a shorter (3.8-mile) hike, take the gondola up the mountain and hike back down.

Equipment If you didn't come properly equipped for back-packing, you can buy boots, packs, tents, sleeping bags and warm clothing at many places throughout the region. Bargain hunters who don't mind buying used should try **Runner Up** in Whitefish for camping and hiking equipment as well as boots and clothes. ~ 550 1st Street East, Whitefish; 406-862-8880. **Glacier Wilderness Guides** near West Glacier has sleeping bags, ground pads, backpacks and tents. Closed weekends in winter. ~ 11970 Route 2 East, West Glacier; 800-521-7238.

Route 90, the main east–west interstate highway through
Montana, connects Missoula with Seattle and Coeur
d'Alene, Idaho, to the west; with Butte, Bozeman and
Billings to the east. The primary north–south artery is **Route 93**;
from the Idaho border at Lost Trail Pass, it runs north through
the Bitterroot Valley to Missoula, where it crosses Route 90. It
then continues north to the Canadian border via Flathead Lake,
Kalispell and Eureka. **Route 2**, which runs east from Sandpoint,
Idaho, through Libby and Kalispell to Glacier National Park and
beyond, is the other important route in northwest Montana.
  For road reports, call 800-226-7623 or 511 statewide.

▼▼▼▼▼▼▼▼▼▼▼
Transportation

CAR

The **Missoula International Airport** is served by Delta, United,
Big Sky and Northwest, as well as regional carrier Horizon. ~
5225 Route 10 West, Missoula; 406-728-4381; www.msoair-
port.org. Kalispell's **Glacier Park International Airport** is served
by America West, Big Sky, Delta, Horizon and Northwest. ~ 4170
Route 2 East, Kalispell; 406-257-5994; www.glacierairport.com.

AIR

Greyhound Bus Lines runs east–west through Montana from
Seattle to Missoula, Billings and points east. ~ 800-231-2222;
www.greyhound.com. **Rimrock Trailways** provides regional bus
service. ~ 1301 South Main Street; 406-755-4011.
  Major stations for Greyhound are in Missoula. ~ 1660 West
Broadway; 406-549-2339. There's also a station in Kalispell. ~
1301 South Main Street; 406-755-4011.

BUS

Amtrak's Seattle–Chicago "Empire Builder" cuts across northern
Montana, stopping at Whitefish en route from Idaho to North
Dakota. ~ 500 Depot Street, Whitefish; 406-862-2268, 800-872-
7245; www.amtrak.com.

TRAIN

Missoula has 10 agencies and the Flathead Valley has 12 in Kalispell and Whitefish. At Missoula International Airport, you'll
find **Avis Rent A Car** (800-230-4898), **Budget Rent A Car** (800-
527-0700), **Hertz Rent A Car** (800-654-3131) and **National Car
Rental** (800-227-7368).
  At Glacier Park International Airport east of Kalispell are
Avis Rent A Car (800-230-4849), **Budget Rent A Car** (800-527-
0700), **Hertz Rent A Car** (800-654-3131) and **National Car Rental**
(800-227-7368).

**CAR
RENTALS**

Missoula's **Mountain Line** is an extensive citywide bus system
with reasonable fares. ~ 406-721-3333; www.mountainline.com.

**PUBLIC
TRANSIT**

Transportation in the Missoula area is provided by **Yellow Cab**.
~ 406-543-6644. In the Flathead Valley, **Kalispell Taxi & Airport
Shuttle** offers 24-hour service. ~ 406-752-4022.

TAXIS

THREE

Glacier National Park

Spectacular Glacier National Park is the crown jewel of the Montana Rockies. Embracing some 1600 square miles of mountain scenery where the Continental Divide meets the Canadian border, the park is known for its chiseled peaks (six of which exceed 10,000 feet), some 200 deep turquoise lakes, and over 700 miles of hiking trails: the most of any national park in America. Many of these trails may also be traveled on horseback. Glacier's watershed flows in not two but three directions: to the Pacific Ocean, the Gulf of Mexico and Hudson Bay.

Glacier National Park takes its name not from the snowfields that cap its highest peaks, but from the dramatic geological activity that created its stunning landscapes. Ending about 10,000 years ago, the series of ice ages that cloaked much of North America saved their finest artistry for this mountainous region. As rivers of ice forced their way down mountainsides, they sculpted sheer cliff walls, gouged valleys and lakes, and laid the future foundation for alpine meadows and streaming waterfalls and cascades. The panorama is best seen from Going-to-the-Sun Road, the lone highway to cross the park. This engineering marvel has been termed "the most beautiful 50 miles in the world."

Beasts are far more at home here than man. Elk, deer, mountain goats and bighorn sheep range widely throughout Glacier, and several hundred grizzly and black bears make their homes in the park. Bird life includes the white-tailed ptarmigan and numerous raptors, while more than 1400 species of plants have been identified in the park, including many colorful wildflowers best seen in the early summer months.

Archeological findings indicate that American Indians knew this terrain as long ago as 11,000 years. In the modern era, Blackfeet and other Plains tribes—who migrated to the east side of the mountains in pursuit of bison about A.D. 1600—have used the park area for hunting and spiritual purposes. Even today, the Blackfeet, whose reservation borders the park to the east, revere Glacier as a sacred place.

Hudson's Bay Company fur trappers were the first white men to penetrate the region; miners and ranchers followed. But Glacier's very ruggedness saved it from exploitation. It was brought to the attention of the American public by the Great Northern Railway, which joined in competition with other transcontinental railways (Northern Pacific in Yellowstone, Canadian Pacific in Banff) in routing its track around the park and promoting Glacier as the "Switzerland of America."

Glacier National Park was formally created in 1910, and the Great Northern undertook the building of hotels and chalets to match the Swiss image. Many of them remain today, magnificent tributes to a bygone era. Going-to-the-Sun Road was completed in 1932 to coincide with the creation of the world's first "international peace park": Glacier and Alberta's adjacent Waterton Lakes National Park were given this designation by acts of both the U.S. Congress and Canadian Parliament, with a push from regional chapters of Rotary International. Today, more than two million visitors a year swarm through the two parks.

Alberta's Waterton Lakes National Park, smaller by far than Glacier (covering just over 200 square miles), nevertheless features similarly striking mountain terrain and offers many of the same activities and services. Several trails cross the frontier between the two parks; the primary road access is the Chief Mountain International Highway, at the extreme northeast edge of Glacier Park. The year-round access point is via Cardston and the Port of Piegan.

If you're approaching Glacier from Kalispell and the west, you'll take Route 2 to West Glacier, then detour onto Going-to-the-Sun Road. If you're proceeding north from Great Falls to Glacier, you can take Going-to-the-Sun Road west off Route 89 in the Blackfeet Indian Reservation on the east side of the park.

Western Gateways

East of Columbia Falls, itself at the edge of the Flathead Valley only 15 miles from West Glacier, Route 2 knifes through a string of small communities: Hungry Horse, Martin City, Coram. These Flathead Riverside villages, each at an elevation slightly higher than the last, lead the traveler to Glacier National Park's west entrance. Unfortunately, these settlements come with baggage: the sort of unabashedly commercial "attractions" that are the bane of too many national park gateways.

SIGHTS

There is, for instance, the **Montana Vortex**, said to be situated on—you guessed it—a vortex. Closed mid-October through March. Admission. ~ 7800 Route 2 East, Columbia Falls; 406-892-1210. At the **North American Wildlife Museum** you needn't remain in your car—the creatures are stuffed. Closed November through April. Admission. ~ 10780 Route 2, Coram; 406-387-4018.

Better you should inhale the view from **Hungry Horse Dam**. The reservoir formed by this 564-foot dam, four miles off Route 2, extends snakelike for 33 miles between the rugged Swan and Flathead ranges of the Rockies. A visitors center describes the dam's construction on the South Fork of the Flathead River. Free guided tours of the top of the dam are offered daily from Memorial Day through Labor Day. ~ West Side Road, Hungry Horse; 406-387-5241, fax 406-387-4012.

The South, Middle and North forks of the Flathead are part of the **Flathead National Wild and Scenic River** system. Together they stretch 219 miles across spectacular wilderness and near-wilderness. The North and Middle forks define the western boundary of Glacier National Park. Whitewater rafters, kayakers and fly-fishermen are regular visitors. ~ West Glacier; 406-387-3800, fax 406-387-3889.

At **West Glacier**, where many of the Flathead River rafting companies are headquartered, is the west entrance to the national park. Nontourists who want to avoid the twisty-turviness of Going-to-the-Sun Road can stay on Route 2, crossing the Continental Divide at mile-high Marias Pass and reaching East Glacier Park, 55 miles away, in about an hour.

This southern highway follows the original (and still highly operational) Great Northern route up the Middle Fork of the Flathead. One essential stop is at the old rail camp of Essex, whose **Izaak Walton Inn** is a veritable museum of railroad memorabilia. ~ 290 Izaak Walton Inn Road, off of Route 2, Essex; 406-888-5700; www.izaakwaltoninn.com, e-mail info@izaakwalton inn.com.

The isolated community of **Polebridge**, about 32 miles north of West Glacier and 41 miles from Columbia Falls, offers access to Glacier Park's northwest frontier across the Flathead River's North Fork. Rough gravel roads lead to this outpost, boxed in on either side by high mountains. There are cabins, a hostel, a mercantile and a popular saloon/café here, and until very recently everything ran on kerosene or propane.

LODGING   Just outside Glacier National Park are several comfortable motels to choose from. Eleven miles from West Glacier, the **Mini Golden Inns Motel** has 38 rooms, including rooms with kitchenettes. From November through April bargain off-season rates kick in. ~ 8955 Route 2 East, Hungry Horse; 406-387-4313. MODERATE TO DELUXE.

Opposite the Amtrak station in West Glacier is the **Glacier Highland Motel**, especially appealing to winter visitors with its very large jacuzzi tub. The Highland has 33 rooms, a restaurant and a gift store. ~ Route 2 East, West Glacier; 406-888-5427, 800-766-0811, fax 406-888-5764. MODERATE.

Two of the West Glacier whitewater raft companies also offer cozy log cabin rentals. **Great Northern Whitewater Raft and Resort** has five log homes that each accommodate four to six guests.

Text continued on page 92.

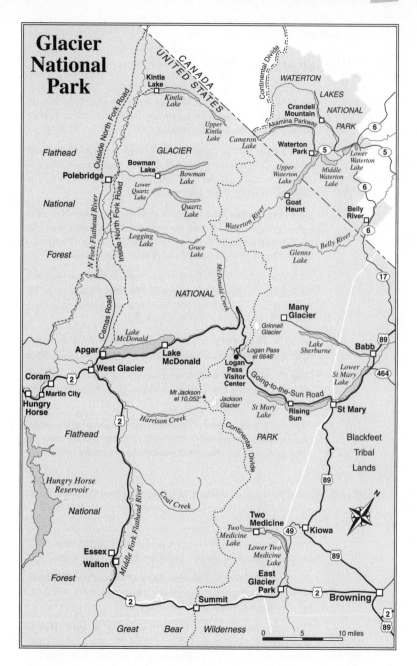

Glacier National Park

Three-day Weekend

Glacier National Park

Day 1
- This itinerary starts in **West Glacier** (page 88). After breakfast, buy a picnic lunch then, begin the spectacular 50-mile journey to St. Mary via **Going-to-the-Sun Road** (page 94).

- Make **Apgar Village** (page 94), with its gorgeous lake view, your first stop. Continue along Going-to-the-Sun Road, remembering to pull over occasionally and burn up some film. At Avalanche Creek, stroll the **Trail of the Cedars** (page 106).

- You'll reach **Logan Pass** (page 94) atop the Continental Divide in a slow-going 16 miles. Peruse the visitors center exhibits then hike the **Hidden Lake Trail** (page 106) to Hidden Lake Overlook, a favorite haunt of mountain goats. Eat lunch near the overlook.

- Follow Going-to-the-Sun Road to Sun Point, an ideal starting point for walking .7 miles along wind-rippled **St. Mary Lake** (page 95) to Baring Falls. Feeling energetic? Trek another 1.6 miles to St. Mary Falls or .7 miles beyond that to Virginia Falls.

- At the **St. Mary Visitors Center** (page 95) attend the slide presentation and check out the special exhibits; have dinner in St. Mary.

- Drive 21 miles to **Many Glacier** (page 95) and stay at the National Historic Landmark **Many Glacier Hotel** (page 96) or **Swiftcurrent Motor Inn** (page 96).

- Watch for grizzlies, mountain goats and bighorn sheep on the mountain slopes (binoculars help). Afterward, catch the evening naturalist program. Don't miss **Native America Speaks** if it's scheduled.

Day 2
- Drive one hour to **Waterton Lakes National Park** (page 100) via Route 89 and scenic Chief Mountain International Highway.

- At the **Information Centre** (page 100), pick up maps and brochures about evening interpretive programs. For great views of the town and lakes, hike the nearby **Bears Hump Trail** (page 108).

- To savor the distinctly Canadian flavor of **Waterton Townsite**, browse the village's many shops (including its grocery store) and the **Heritage Centre museum** (page 100).

- Time permitting, eat lunch before hopping on an **Inter-Nation Shoreline Cruise** (page 100) of Upper Waterton Lake. Otherwise, order a sandwich to bring along for the two-hour cruise.

- Stop at the **Prince of Wales Hotel** (page 101) to check out the gift shop and incredible scenery. Need a break? Indulge in afternoon high tea at the hotel. Or forego refreshments and drive the nine-mile **Red Rock Parkway** to **Red Rock Canyon** (page 101). At the parkway's end, you'll find several short trails to roam.

- Dine at the Kilmorey Lodge's casually elegant **Lamp Post Dining Room** (page 102).

- After dinner, stroll the two miles from Waterton Townsite to Cameron Falls, stopping at the outdoor Peace Park Pavilion. You can also attend a 60-minute evening slide presentation at the Falls Interpretive Theater.

- Overnight at **Kilmorey Lodge** (page 101) or **Prince of Wales Hotel** (page 101).

Day 3
- Drive 48 miles to St. Mary. Hankering for outdoor adventure? Grab a portable lunch in town then head south to peaceful **Two Medicine** (page 95) via Route 89. At Kiowa Junction (20 miles), turn onto curvy Route 49, a scenic (and some say, nerve-wracking) foothills road. Go nine miles to Two Medicine Junction, turn, and travel nine more miles into Glacier Park.

- Walk to Running Eagle Falls, an easy half-mile loop trail. At nearby **Two Medicine Lake** (page 95), combine a boat ride on the Sinopah with a .9-mile hike to Twin Falls or 2.2-mile jaunt to Upper Two Medicine Lake. Afterward, mosey on to East Glacier.

- If you prefer civilization to wilderness, forget Two Medicine and aim for **Browning** (page 98). At Kiowa Junction, stay on Route 89 another 12 miles to reach the Blackfeet Reservation's business hub and **Museum of the Plains Indian** (page 98).

- Drive Route 2 for 13 miles to **East Glacier** (page 97) for lunch. Then browse the local shops, art galleries and **Glacier Park Lodge** (page 97).

- Dine at **Serrano's** (page 100) or drive 30 minutes to Essex and sample the fare at the **Izaak Walton Inn** (page 92), a mecca for railfans.

- For fashionably late dining, hold out for another half-hour ride to West Glacier's **Belton Chalet** (page 92). Stay overnight at this National Historic Landmark.

Every chalet has a fireplace and kitchen, and the resort includes an indoor hot tub, a sun room, and a restaurant. All the rooms are nonsmoking. Guests are invited to join rafting, fishing and horseback trips in summer, cross-country skiing and snowmobile excursions in winter. Three-night minimum in July and August. ~ 12127 Route 2 East, West Glacier; 406-387-5340, 800-735-7897, fax 406-387-9007; www.gnwhitewater.com. ULTRA-DELUXE.

Glacier Raft & Outdoor Center has nine handsome log cabins for rent, all with gas fireplaces, full kitchens, bathrooms and living rooms. They also include linens and dishes and you can rent equipment for skiing, rafting and biking. ~ 11957 Route 2 East, West Glacier; 406-888-5454; www.glacierraftco.com. ULTRA-DELUXE.

When you step inside the authentically restored **Belton Chalet** it's easy to imagine what yesteryear's travelers to Glacier Park experienced when they came West. Built in 1910 to accommodate well-heeled visitors who traveled to Glacier Park by train, this lovely hostelry is now a National Historic Landmark. The 25-room lodge is closed mid-October through May; the two three-bedroom cabins are open year-round. ~ 12575 Route 2 East, West Glacier; 406-888-5000, 888-235-8665, fax 406-888-5005; www.beltonchalet.com, e-mail belton@digisys.net. DELUXE TO ULTRA-DELUXE.

The **North Fork Hostel** might be booked months ahead in summer. But if you can reserve a bunk at this rustic house, you'll have ready access to recreation around Bowman, Kintla and several other long glacial lakes. Mountain bikes and some backpacking equipment can be rented. Tepees, two small cabins and several large log homes are also available. Hostelers share a kitchen, washrooms and other facilities. Closed mid-January

AUTHOR FAVORITE

At the **Izaak Walton Inn**, just across the Middle Fork of the Flathead from the national park, diesel helper engines idle near the inn's front door and hilltop cabooses shelter overnight hikers and Nordic skiers. These are testimony to its railroad heritage: the Izaak Walton was built in 1939 to lodge Great Northern Railway service crews. Today it is a National Historic Register property surrounded by trestles and tunnels. The rustic lobby, simple wood-paneled rooms and country-style restaurant hold a museum's worth of memorabilia. In addition, the inn maintains some 22 miles of groomed cross-country trails, a telemark hill and two back-country bowls; ski rentals are available. ~ 290 Izaak Walton Inn Road, off of Route 2, Essex; 406-888-5700, fax 406-888-5200; www.izaakwaltoninn.com, e-mail info@izaakwaltoninn.com. DELUXE.

through May. ~ 80 Beaver Drive, Polebridge; 406-888-5241; www.nfhostel.com, e-mail nfhostel@nfhostel.com. BUDGET.

In Coram, you can get a good breakfast at the **Spruce Park Café**. Look for such delights as homemade cinnamon rolls and fresh-baked pie. ~ 10045 Route 2 East, Coram; 406-387-5614. BUDGET.

DINING

◀ *HIDDEN*

Nearer the west entrance, the **Glacier Highland Motel and Restaurant** serves up staunchly Montana cuisine: big omelettes for breakfast, oversized sandwiches for lunch, and pizza, chicken and steak for dinner. Open daily in Summer; otherwise, call for hours. ~ 12555 Route 2, West Glacier; 406-888-5427. MODER-ATE TO DELUXE.

The historic **Belton Chalet** serves gourmet fare in a memorable setting, either outdoors on the expansive deck or inside the restored early-20th-century dining room. Dinner entrées include cowboy cut ribeye steak, salad nicoise with ahi tuna and vegetarian options such as vegetarian leek pastry. Save room for the huckleberry peach pie. Appetizers and lighter fare are served in the cozy tap room. Closed from mid-October through May. ~ 12575 Route 2 East, West Glacier; 406-888-5000, 888-235-8665, fax 406-888-5005; www.beltonchalet.com, e-mail belton@digisys.net. DELUXE TO ULTRA-DELUXE.

Just outside Glacier National Park, **Heaven's Peak Dining & Spirits** offers fine views along with upscale cuisine. Look for seafood, steak and local game dishes, as well as fancy variations on local desserts. Huckleberry crème brûlée, anyone? Dinner only. ~ 12130 Route 2, West Glacier; 406-387-4754; e-mail thepeak@cyberport.net. DELUXE.

GREAT BEAR WILDERNESS AREA 🚶 🐎 🚲 ⛵ Wedged between Glacier National Park and the Bob Marshall Wilderness Area ("The Bob"), the Great Bear Wilderness is indeed one of the principal remaining strongholds of the grizzly bear. It encompasses the sources and upper reaches of the Middle Fork of the Flathead River, with alpine lakes and peaks ranging above 8000 feet. ~ Most trails that penetrate this wilderness begin either off Route 2 on the south side of Glacier Park, principally in the Essex area, or from the Spotted Bear Ranger Station near the head of Hungry Horse Reservoir; 406-758-5200, 406-387-3800. ▲ Primitive only.

PARKS

From its magnificent sculpted peaks to its abundant pristine lakes, Glacier National Park is a natural wonderland, one that no traveler can afford to miss. It's also a hiker's paradise with scores of trails to choose from; anglers will find its lakes stocked with trout.

Glacier National Park

SIGHTS   Entering the park at West Glacier, stop at **Glacier National Park Headquarters** for maps and information. ~ West Glacier; 406-888-7800; www.nps.gov/glac. Nearby is the splendid **Alberta Visitors Center**. A replica *Tyrannosaurus rex* skeleton greets you at the door, and elsewhere there are impressive displays and detailed information for motorists who plan to continue north of the international border, perhaps to Waterton Lakes National Park, after their visit to Glacier. ~ West Glacier; 406-888-5743.

Apgar Village, located two miles from West Glacier where McDonald Creek flows out of **Lake McDonald**, has a visitors center as well as a lodge and motel, a campground, a restaurant, a general store, three gift shops and boat rentals. Apgar Village is at the junction of Camas and Going-to-the-Sun roads. Two miles farther up Camas, look for the Fish Creek Campground, where you'll hit the 40-mile gravel **Inside North Fork Road**, which leads to Bowman and Kintla lakes and other sites in the park's rarely visited western boundary region, and Going-to-the-Sun Road. ~ 406-888-7800, fax 406-888-7868; www.nps.gov/glac.

For its first ten miles, this 50-mile highway traces the southeastern shore of Lake McDonald, the park's longest and deepest (464 feet) body of water, through forests of larch and lodgepole pines. Near the head of the lake is the full-service **Lake McDonald Lodge**, complete with general store; narrated one-hour lake cruises (admission) begin here four times daily. ~ 406-257-2426.

Surrounded by snow drifts as late as July, Logan Pass sits on the Continental Divide. Its visitors center offers a variety of interpretive programs, guided hikes and other activities, many of them focusing on the natural history of the high country.

Going-to-the-Sun Road is kept open year-round as far as Lake McDonald Lodge, which is at 3153-foot elevation. (Larger trailers and recreational vehicles—those longer than 21 feet and wider than 8 feet—are prohibited in the highest stretches of the road over Logan Pass.) The lodge, like the road over Logan Pass, usually opens in early June and is typically closed by November. But cross-country skiers frequently begin winter explorations of Glacier National Park from this point.

As the road begins to climb beyond Lake McDonald, the mountains' western slopes come into view. The increased precipitation on this side of the mountains has yielded extensive groves of old-growth cedar and hemlock.

About eight miles from Lake McDonald, Going-to-the-Sun Road makes a 90-degree turn to the northwest and begins a rapid climb (with but a single hairpin switchback) to subalpine meadows and 6646-foot **Logan Pass**. It traverses the precipitous **Garden Wall**, passes the **Weeping Wall** (where springs pour from the side of the cliff) and affords unparalleled panoramas of mountains, glaciers, waterfalls and the McDonald River valley.

Descending the east side of the Divide, the road offers several views south toward 10,052-foot Mount Jackson and **Jackson Glacier**, a source of the St. Mary River.

The descent ends at **St. Mary Lake**, another long, narrow body of water. The **St. Mary River** flows north from here, making its way to Hudson Bay in northern Ontario. At **Rising Sun**, about midway along the lake's northwestern shore, there's a campground, motor inn and restaurant; 90-minute, naturalist-led boat tours (admission) of St. Mary Lake begin here. ~ 406-257-2426.

Another visitors center with activities and interpretive programs is located at **St. Mary**, where Going-to-the-Sun Road terminates at its junction with Route 89 outside the park entrance. Here also you'll find a campground and other lodging, restaurants, a garage and a general store. A historic ranger station, built in 1913 at the Red Eagle Lake trailhead, has been refurbished to its original appearance; it is not often open, unfortunately, but visitors can peer into its windows.

Two of Glacier Park's most scenic locations—Many Glacier and Two Medicine—aren't accessible from Going-to-the-Sun Road; instead, there are separate approaches to each from the east side of the park.

To get to **Many Glacier**, head north on Route 89 from St. Mary, as if you were proceeding to Canada's Waterton Lakes. After nine miles, turn left at Babb junction; then follow Many Glacier Road about 12 miles west, along the Swiftcurrent River and Lake Sherburne, to the **Many Glacier Hotel**. Surrounded by some of the park's most starkly magnificent summits—one of whose cliffs drops an amazing 4200 feet, farther than any in California's world-renowned Yosemite National Park—the hotel sits on turquoise **Swiftcurrent Lake**, one of a series of small lakes fed by Grinnell Glacier. Classic wooden boat tours across Swiftcurrent and Josephine lakes, boat rentals and guided horse trips are available at Many Glacier. There are also guided naturalist walks; wildlife watching, especially for bears, is excellent here.

Two Medicine is the name given to three lakes, a river and a park community in the southeastern section of Glacier. It's reached by traveling 20 miles south from St. Mary on Route 89, another nine miles west and south toward East Glacier on Route 49, and then nine miles west past Lower Two Medicine Lake on Two Medicine Road. A historic chalet near the shore of Two Medicine Lake has a general store and snack bar (but no lodging), and there are lake cruises (the *Sinopah* schedules four trips a day on the lake; fee) and boat rentals as well as a campground.

The **Lake McDonald Lodge**, built in 1913, is one of several impressive national historic landmarks in or adjacent to the national park. Set on the west side of the park, near the north end

LODGING

of Lake McDonald in a grove of giant cedars, the lodge has 100 guest units—individual cabins and double rooms in the main lodge and motel annex—all with private bathrooms. Its huge lobby contains a big stone fireplace and collection of big-game trophies. Facilities include a restaurant, a coffee shop, a lounge and a camp store. Closed October to late May. ~ Going-to-the-Sun Road, Glacier National Park; 406-892-2525, fax 406-892-1375; www.glacierparkinc.com, e-mail info@glacierparkinc.com. MODERATE TO DELUXE.

The **Many Glacier Hotel** offers unquestionably the most awesome view of any lodge in the park: across Swiftcurrent Lake toward spectacular Grinnell Glacier, which tumbles down the east face of the Continental Divide from 9500 feet. The hotel has 211 guest rooms—small, basic, but with private baths—and a spacious lobby and dining area. Request a lakeside room. Closed mid-September through May. ~ Many Glacier Road, Glacier National Park; 406-892-2525, fax 406-892-1375; www.glacier parkinc.com, e-mail info@glacierparkinc.com. DELUXE TO ULTRA-DELUXE.

Glacier Park, Inc. (known to locals as GPI) is the operator of six National Park inns, with a common reservation line travelers can call for rates and information. In addition to the Lake McDonald Lodge, the Many Glacier Hotel, and Glacier Park Lodge, the company also operates a number of motels. ~ 406-892-2525, fax 406-892-1375; www.glacierparkinc.com, e-mail info@glacierparkinc.com.

Village Inn has 36 guest rooms located at the south end of Lake McDonald. Closed October to early May. ~ South Going-to-the-Sun Road, Apgar Village, Glacier National Park; 406-892-2525, fax 406-892-1375; www.glacierparkinc.com, e-mail info@glacierparkinc.com. DELUXE TO ULTRA-DELUXE.

Rising Sun Motor Inn on the northern shore of St. Mary Lake has 72 cabins and rooms. Closed early September to early June. ~ Going-to-the-Sun Road, Glacier National Park; 406-892-2525, fax 406-892-1375; www.glacierparkinc.com, e-mail info@glacier parkinc.com. MODERATE.

Swiftcurrent Motor Inn has 88 motel rooms and rustic cabins. Closed early September to early June. ~ Many Glacier Road, Glacier National Park; 406-892-2525, fax 406-892-1375; www. glacierparkinc.com, e-mail info@glacierparkinc.com. BUDGET TO MODERATE.

DINING   **Eddie's Restaurant** is a good choice on the west side of Glacier Park. Families enjoy a wide-ranging menu—everything from hamburgers, pan-fried trout and fresh salads to steak and chicken entrées—in a casual atmosphere near Lake McDonald. Closed mid-September to late May. ~ Camas Road, Apgar Village; 406-888-5361, fax 406-888-5242. MODERATE.

Other meals are available in park lodges and motels, or in gateway communities like East Glacier Park and St. Mary.

Every lodge and store in the park has a souvenir outlet. The best of the bunch—and the one with the longest season, open from the second week of May through October—may be the **Montana House**, a regional craft shop at Apgar Village, on the west side of the park. ~ Main Street, Apgar Village; 406-888-5393.

SHOPPING

GLACIER NATIONAL PARK

PARKS

Though there are many small glaciers on its higher peaks, Glacier Park was named for the geologic glaciation that carved its features, rather than for its rivers of ice. The 50-mile Going-to-the-Sun Road connects its green western boundary with the striking Rocky Mountain Front that marks its eastern flank. Picnic areas, restrooms, amphitheaters and visitors centers round out the amenities. Lodges and restaurants are located at several sites, and groceries are in Apgar and West Glacier, St. Mary and East Glacier. ~ Enter from the west at West Glacier, 32 miles northeast of Kalispell on Route 2; from the east at St. Mary, 155 miles northwest of Great Falls on Route 89; 406-888-7800; www.nps.gov/glac, e-mail glac_information@nps.gov.

Rugged mountains and deep glacial lakes, as well as 700-plus miles of hiking trails, are the highlights of Glacier National Park, a wildlife-rich, 1600-square-mile preserve that crowns the Continental Divide.

There are 1001 RV/tent sites in 13 campgrounds; $12 to $17 per night. Seven-day maximum stay. Primitive camping is permitted at Apgar Village and St. Mary through the winter. Reservations are accepted for Fish Creek and St. Mary campgrounds. Reserved campsites are $17 per night; 800-365-2267; http://reservations.nps.gov.

Eastern Gateways

The entire eastern edge of Glacier National Park is bounded by the Blackfeet Indian Reservation, which is one-and-a-half times the size of the park itself. This land of sharp geological contrast, one and a half million acres in extent, contains all of the park's eastern gateways.

St. Mary, located where Going-to-the-Sun Road meets Route 89, is one of about ten communities on the reservation. **East Glacier Park**, at the southeastern corner of the national park, 31 miles from St. Mary, is another. It is most notable for its historic **Glacier Park Lodge**. ~ Route 49, East Glacier Park; 406-892-2525, fax 406-892-1375; www.glacierparkinc.com, e-mail info@glacierpark

SIGHTS

inc.com. The adjacent community of East Glacier that has grown up nearby has an Old West facade and a keen orientation toward outdoor recreation, mainly in the Two Medicine Lake region to its west.

The shield-shaped **Blackfeet Indian Reservation** stretches from the dramatic Rocky Mountain Front across some 50 miles of prairies to the town of Cut Bank, and a similar distance south from the Canadian border. It is the home of the Blackfeet tribe, Montana's largest. Of its nearly 15,000 members, approximately half live on the reservation. ~ P.O. Box 850, Browning, MT 59417; 406-338-7521, fax 406-338-7530; www.blackfeetnation.com.

Browning is the seat of tribal government and the site of the North American Indian Days celebration in mid-July. Located 13 miles northeast of East Glacier Park, it is the focus of most visitor interest in the reservation.

The **Museum of the Plains Indian** is one of Montana's finest small museums. Its galleries include an interpretive collection of traditional clothing and artifacts of the Blackfoot and other northern Great Plains tribes, contemporary paintings and sculptures by tribal artists, an audio-visual presentation and changing exhibits. The museum shop is a good place to find authentic arts and crafts. Closed weekends in Winter. Admission in Summer. ~ Route 89 opposite Route 2 West junction, Browning; 406-338-2230; e-mail mti@3rivers.net.

For tours of Glacier and the Blackfeet Reservation emphasizing American Indian heritage, try **Sun Tours** (406-226-9220, 800-786-9220), which offers summer and fall bus tours from East Glacier Park and the St. Mary Lodge, or **Curly Bear Wagner's** tours (317-443-1450 or 406-338-2058; www.curlybear.org), which focus on Blackfeet history.

LODGING   Nearby, for the budget backpacker, there's **Brownie's** AYH **Hostel**. This two-story log hostel has 25 beds in male and female dormitories, ten private rooms with full-sized beds and a family room with two queen-sized beds. A community kitchen, showers, laundry and equipment storage are available. Downstairs there are a convenience store and a deli. Reservations recommended. Closed October to mid-May. ~ 1020 Route 49, East Glacier Park; 406-226-4426. BUDGET.

The **Glacier Park Lodge** is a tourist attraction in its own right. The huge structure, built of fir and cedar logs at the end of World War I, has a four-story atrium supported by tree trunks, and a brilliant wildflower garden in front of its entrance. All 161 guest rooms are clean and well maintained. Facilities include a restaurant, coffee shop and lounge, as well as a swimming pool, a nine-hole golf course and horse stables. Closed early September to mid-May. ~ Route 49, East Glacier Park; 406-892-2525, fax

406-892-1375; www.glacierparkinc.com, e-mail info@glacier
parkinc.com. DELUXE TO ULTRA-DELUXE.

You'll find another seasonal hostel back behind Serrano's
restaurant. The **Backpacker's Inn** consists of an eight-bed coed
cabin and two private cabins (with queen-size beds and linens).
Each of these rustic cabins has a full bathroom. Bring your own
sleeping bag (if you're staying in the dorms), or rent one for $1.
Closed October through April. ~ 29 Dawson Avenue, East Glacier
Park; 406-226-9392, e-mail serranosmex@centurytel.net. BUDGET.

Two of the more affordable East Glacier motels are open from
May through September and are handicapped-accessible. The **Mountain Pine Motel** has 25 rooms and two cottages with kitchens, on
lovely pine-shaded grounds. ~ 909 Route 49, East Glacier Park;
406-226-4403. BUDGET TO MODERATE.

Jacobson's Scenic View Cottages include 12 units and a playground for kids. The cottages have TVs but no phones; one has
a kitchen. Closed mid-October to late April. ~ 1204 Route 49,
East Glacier Park; 406-226-4422; e-mail jacobcot@gec-isp.net.
MODERATE.

The family-run **St. Mary Lodge and Resort** offers a variety of
lodging choices, ranging from spacious rooms with balconies,
jacuzzi tubs and fireplaces to cozy mountain cottages. You'll find
a fine-dining restaurant, two kid-friendly eateries, a lounge and
several shops; laundry facilities and a gas station round out the
amenities. Closed mid-October to mid-May. ~ Route 89 at
Going-to-the-Sun Road, St. Mary; 406-732-4431, 208-726-6279
(winter), 800-368-3689, fax 406-732-9265; www.glcpark.com,
e-mail stmary@glcpark.com. DELUXE TO ULTRA-DELUXE.

If you want to stay near the Museum of the Plains Indian on
the Blackfeet Indian Reservation, try the **War Bonnet Lodge**. The
modern motel has 35 units, a restaurant and lounge. ~ Routes 2
and 89, Browning; 406-338-7610. MODERATE.

AUTHOR FAVORITE

"No vegetarians: We eat beef!" proclaims the **Bear Creek Guest Ranch.**
Established in 1933 a quarter-mile outside the national park boundary, the
ranch provides accommodation in rustic private cabins and lodge rooms, as
well as full board (bed and breakfast only in fall and winter). A visit to
Bear Creek is highlighted by its riding program, with a variety of pack
trips and cattle drives offered. Customized trips are also available.
Three-day minimum stay in summer. ~ P.O. Box 151, East Glacier
Park, MT 59434; 406-226-4489; www.bearcreekranch.com, e-mail
speidell@3rivers.net. ULTRA-DELUXE.

DINING   For a surprisingly authentic taste of Mexico, stop by **Serrano's**, where the rustic atmosphere is every bit as appealing as the tempting chili-flavored fare, which includes generous portions of enchiladas and tacos. The restaurant, open evenings only, occupies a historic log home. Closed October 1 to May 1. ~ 29 Dawson Avenue, East Glacier Park; 406-226-9392; e-mail serranosmex@ centurytel.net. MODERATE TO DELUXE.

SHOPPING   Don't miss the excellent gift shop at the **Museum of the Plains Indian**, offering authentic Plains Indian arts and crafts. ~ Route 89 opposite Route 2 junction, Browning; 406-338-2230.

In East Glacier, be sure to check out the **John L. Clarke Western Art Gallery and Memorial Museum**. Prints, wood carvings, turquoise jewelry and other original works of art, most by Montana artists, can be found here. Closed October through mid-May. ~ 900 Route 49, East Glacier Park; 406-226-9238.

Also drop by **The Spiral Spoon**, which features hand-carved wooden spoons and other items made of cherrywood, Montana birch, and exotic woods. Closed October through April. ~ 1012 Route 49, East Glacier Park; 406-226-4558; www.thespiral spoon.com.

▼▼▼▼▼▼▼▼▼▼▼▼
Waterton Lakes National Park

The three interlocked Waterton Lakes and scenic Cameron Lake are the main attractions of Alberta's Waterton Lakes National Park. Make your headquarters in the Waterton Park townsite, 21 miles northwest of the nearest U.S.–Canada border crossing (at Chief Mountain). Situated on a small promontory that extends into Upper Waterton Lake, it is framed to the north and west by lofty peaks and steep cliffs. In summer, the town bustles with tourist vehicles and wandering wildlife; in winter, when the Chief Mountain International Highway is closed, it's just the animals, cross-country skiers and a handful of hardy year-round residents.

SIGHTS   The **Information Centre** offers lots of information on the park, and park staff provide guided walks and evening interpretive programs on a regular basis in summer. ~ Park Entrance Road near the Prince of Wales Hotel. For information year-round, contact the **Park Headquarters**. ~ 403-859-2224, fax 403-859-2650; parkscanada.gc.ca/waterton, e-mail waterton.info@pc.gc.ca.

The townsite has a small **Heritage Centre** museum and art gallery open mid-May to the end of September. ~ 403-859-2624.

One of the most popular activities in the park is taking the narrated two-hour voyage through windy Upper Waterton Lake with **Waterton Inter-Nation Shoreline Cruise Company**. From June through September, hikers can take the Waterton Inter-Nation Shoreline cruise aboard a 200-passenger boat one way to

Goat Haunt, then enjoy a ten-mile return trek along the shoreline. Admission. ~ Waterton Marina; 403-859-2362.

Numerous short scenic drives lead to other attractions. The **Akamina Parkway** winds through the narrow Cameron Valley, where Alberta's first producing oil well was drilled almost a century ago, for ten miles west to Cameron Lake. The nine-mile **Red Rock Parkway** to Red Rock Canyon follows the much wider Blakiston Valley, passing exhibits on Waterton geology, prehistory and history en route.

LODGING

Waterton Park's accommodations are all solidly booked well in advance for the peak summer months. Unless you're camping, reserve months ahead or plan to drive at least 27 miles (from Cardston, the next closest town with lodging) to reach the park. For assistance, contact the **Waterton Chamber of Commerce**. ~ P.O. Box 55, Waterton Lakes National Park, AB T0K 2M0, Canada; 403-859-2224; e-mail waterton.info@pc.gc.ca. Or try the **Alberta Tourism Office**. ~ 800-252-3782; www.travelalberta.com, e-mail travelinfo@travelalberta.com.

The national park's landmark is the stately and majestic **Prince of Wales Hotel**, built in 1927 on a grassy knoll just north of the townsite. Its Bavarian-style architecture is only one lure of this 87-room hotel; another is its unforgettable view of the length of Upper Waterton Lake all the way into Montana. The hotel has a fully licensed restaurant and lounge, and a British-style high tea is served every afternoon in Valerie's Tea Room. Elevators rise only to the fourth floor, which means guests staying in the fifth- and sixth-story rafters will have to do some stair climbing. Closed mid-September to mid-May. ~ Prince of Wales Road, Waterton Park; 406-892-2525, fax 406-892-1375; www.glacierparkinc.com, e-mail info@glacierparkinc.com. ULTRA-DELUXE.

Just north of Waterton Lakes National Park's northeastern entrance on Alberta Route 6, a small herd of bison can be observed from an overlook at the Buffalo Paddocks.

My favorite among the in-town motels is the **Kilmorey Lodge**. With 23 guest rooms and suites on the shore of Emerald Bay, this country inn has drawn national accolades for its personalized service and its housekeeping. Furnishings are antique, and there are eider-down comforters on all the beds. Most units are nonsmoking; children 16 and under stay free with parents. The Lamp Post Dining Room is Waterton's best restaurant, and the lodge has a separate lounge. The Kilmorey is a rarity in Waterton in that it's open year-round. ~ 117 Evergreen Avenue, Waterton Park; 403-859-2334, 888-859-8669, fax 403-859-2342; www.kilmoreylodge.com, e-mail kilmorey@telusplanet.net. DELUXE TO ULTRA-DELUXE.

Another upscale accommodation is the 51-room **Aspen Village Inn**. The inn has a hot tub and cottages available. Closed mid-October through April. ~ P.O. Box 100, Waterton Park T0K

2M0, Canada; 403-859-2255, 888-859-8669, fax 403-859-2033; www.aspenvillageinn.com, e-mail info@watertonpark.com. ULTRA-DELUXE. There's also the 70-room lakeside **Bayshore Inn**. Closed mid-October to mid-April. ~ 111 Waterton Avenue, Waterton Park; 403-859-2211, 888-527-9555; www.bayshoreinn.com, e-mail info@bayshoreinn.com. DELUXE TO ULTRA-DELUXE. For mountain lodging, stay at the **Crandell Mountain Lodge**. ~ P.O. Box 114, Waterton Park AB T0K 2M0, Canada; phone/fax 403-859-2288, 866-859-2288; www.crandellmountainlodge.com. ULTRA-DELUXE.

The clean and comfortable **Bear Mountain Motel** has 35 rooms with TVs and free coffee; kitchenettes and family-size units cost extra. Closed mid-October through April. ~ 208 Mountainview Road, Waterton Park; 403-859-2366. BUDGET TO MODERATE.

Within earshot of Cameron Falls is the **Northland Lodge**, with nine rooms, two of them budget-priced and sharing a bath. Guests here can watch TV in a central lounge with a fireplace or hang out on a balcony with a beautiful view. The lodge's secluded location ensures a large dose of peace and quiet. Closed mid-October to mid-May. ~ 408 Evergreen Avenue, Waterton Park; 403-859-2353. MODERATE TO DELUXE.

DINING

The best restaurant in Waterton National Park is **The Lamp Post Dining Room**. Three gourmet meals a day are served in a casual atmosphere at this lakeside country lodge, open year-round. The restaurant is fully licensed and service is superb. ~ Kilmorey Lodge, 117 Evergreen Avenue; 403-859-2334, fax 403-859-2342; www. kilmoreylodge.com, e-mail kilmorey@telusplanet.net. DELUXE.

At **Valerie's Tea Room** you can get a formal English-style high tea every afternoon, complete with scones, jam and cream. ~ Prince of Wales Hotel, Prince of Wales Road; 403-859-2231. MODERATE.

PARKS

WATERTON LAKES NATIONAL PARK 🚶 🚴 🐎 🎣 🏕 ⛵ 🛶 ⚓ 🎿 🚤 Much of the same rugged mountain scenery of Glacier National Park extends across the Canadian border to this park, whose centerpiece is the three interlocked Waterton Lakes. Wildlife, including bears and bighorn sheep, is equally impressive here. There are 190 miles of hiking and horse trails in the park, which covers more than 200 square miles. Facilities include picnic areas, restrooms, amphitheaters and visitors centers. ~ By road from the east side of Glacier National Park, take Route 89 north 13 miles from St. Mary, then Route 17 (the Chief Mountain International Highway) 14 miles to the U.S.–Canada border. Waterton Park townsite is another 20 miles northwest; 403-859-5133, fax 403-859-2650; www.parkscanada.gc.ca/waterton, e-mail waterton.info@pc.gc.ca.

▲ There are 367 RV/tent sites, and 24 for tents only, at three campgrounds, including 95 with hookups in the Waterton Townsite Campground; $19 to $30 (Canadian) per night; 13-day maximum stay. No reservations. Campgrounds are open early May to late September. Primitive camping is permitted at the Pass Creek Picnic Area during fall, winter and spring.

You don't need a license to fish in Glacier National Park; this makes fishing an especially popular activity among visitors. Be sure to pick up a pamphlet describing park regulations, however, from any ranger station or visitors center.

Outdoor Adventures

FISHING

Rainbow, brook, cutthroat and lake trout, as well as mountain whitefish, may be difficult to catch, but anglers consider them worth the effort. (Fishing for bull trout is prohibited.) You'll have best luck from a boat over the large lakes' deepest holes, or casting from the shore of smaller alpine lakes.

If you prefer to fish with an outfitter, try **Glacier Fishing Charters**. They take groups of four trolling for lake trout; off-season trips can be arranged. ~ 375 Jensen Road, Columbia Falls; 406-892-2377.

> Glacier naturalists ceased stocking the park's lakes and rivers a number of years ago when they found that the introduced fish were curtailing the reproduction of native species.

Licenses are required in Waterton Lakes National Park. They may be purchased from the national park visitor reception center in Waterton townsite.

BOATING

In Glacier National Park, the **Glacier Park Boat Company** rents a variety of vessels—including rowboats, canoes and motorboats—on several lakes. Scenic launch tours are also offered. Closed October through May. ~ 406-257-2426; www.glacierparkboats.com, e-mail gpboats@montanaweb.com.

In Waterton Lakes National Park, you'll find boat tours at the Emerald Bay Marina on Upper Waterton Lake (in Waterton Park townsite), and boat ramps on both the Upper and Middle lakes. The only boat rentals are at Cameron Lake. Sailing and wind surfing, as well as scuba diving, are popular on windy Upper Waterton Lake, but less stable craft are discouraged.

RIVER RUNNING

The Middle and North forks of the Flathead River, which define the western boundary of Glacier National Park and converge near the community of West Glacier, are very popular whitewater rivers. The **Montana Raft Company** runs eight-day combination backpacking/rafting expeditions in summer. They are the oldest of several outfitters that run these rivers. ~ Route 2, West Glacier; 406-387-5555, 800-521-7238; www.glacierguides.com. For multiday trips on several forks of the Flathead, try **Glacier Raft Company**. ~ P.O. Box 210, West Glacier, MT 59936; 406-888-5454, 800-235-6781; www.glacierraftco.com. For an unforgettable adventure on Class IV rapids on the Middle Fork, contact **Great Northern Whitewater**. ~ P.O. Box 270, West Glacier, MT 59936; 800-735-7897; www.gnwhitewater.com. Horseback/rafting combination trips are the specialty of **Wild River Adventures**. ~ P.O. Box 272, West Glacier, MT 59936; 406-387-9453, 800-700-7056; www.riverwild.com.

Kayaking and canoeing can be hazardous in larger lakes of both parks, especially Lake McDonald, St. Mary and Upper Waterton Lakes, and East Side lakes, which often funnel heavy western winds toward the drier eastern prairies. Stay close to shore if you're paddling here. Wilderness lakes such as Bowman and Kintla, in the far northwest of Glacier Park, are especially popular among canoeists. Both craft can be rented at McDonald, Two Medicine and Swiftcurrent lakes in Glacier National Park (see "Boating"), and at Cameron Lake in Waterton Lakes National Park.

CROSS-COUNTRY SKIING

Near Glacier Park, the **Izaak Walton Inn** has extensive backcountry packages. The Inn maintains some 33 kilometers (21 miles) of groomed trails, as well as a telemark hill and two backcountry bowls. Ski rentals are available here. A trail-use fee is charged to skiers who do not stay at the inn (see "Western Gateways Lodging"). ~ Route 2, Essex; 406-888-5700; www.izakwalton inn.com, e-mail info@izaakwaltoninn.com.

For those with their own equipment, there are numerous popular Nordic ski trails in and around Glacier National Park, in the Lake McDonald, Polebridge, St. Mary and East Glacier areas.

Waterton Park has no organized Nordic facility, but many of its 160 miles of hiking trails are employed by cross-country skiers in winter. A five-kilometer (three-mile) trail along the shore of Cameron Lake is groomed weekly.

The nearest downhill ski resort is the Big Mountain at Whitefish in the Flathead Valley (see Chapter Two).

GOLF

Golfers passing through West Glacier won't want to miss the **Glacier View Golf Course** with its scenic 18-hole course. Closed mid-October through April. ~ West Glacier; 406-888-5471.

AUTHOR FAVORITE

Nothing is more invigorating than a brisk jaunt across the snowy wonderland that is Glacier National Park in winter. Beautiful views of the mountains around St. Mary's Lake can be had from the **Red Eagle Lake Trail** (8 miles roundtrip). Contact the park for more trail information. ~ 406-888-7800; www.nps.gov/glac.

The 18-hole **Waterton Lakes Golf Course**, built in 1929, is renowned for its scenic beauty. For non-duffers, it also has a panoramic restaurant. Closed mid-November through April, other times, open when weather permits. ~ 403-859-2114.

RIDING STABLES

In Glacier National Park, **Mule Shoe Outfitters** operate small corrals at Many Glacier and Lake McDonald for guided rides through the park. Beginning June and continuing to mid-September, they range from an hour to all day. First-timers are welcome. ~ Many Glacier, 406-732-4203, 520-684-2328 (winter); Lake McDonald, 406-888-5121; mule-shoe.com.

In Waterton Lakes National Park, **Alpine Stables**, just east of the Waterton Park townsite, offers hour-long, half-day and overnight trips in the park from May 1 to the end of September. ~ 403-859-2462, 403-653-2449 (winter); www.alpinestables.com.

PACK TRIPS & LLAMA TREKS

The 900-odd miles of backcountry trails in the combined national parks, not to mention the expansive adjacent wilderness areas and national forests, are open to horses as well as hikers. Outfitters can take you practically anywhere with advance notice. **Spotted Bear Outfitters** is a fly-fishing guest ranch that leads treks through the Bob Marshall Wilderness, combining horseback riding, rafting and fly-fishing. ~ 115 Lake Blaine Drive, Kalispell; 406-755-7337, 800-223-4333; www.spottedbear.com. For six-day pack trips in the Bob Marshall Wilderness, try **Bear Creek Outfitters**. ~ Box 151, East Glacier Park, MT 59434; 406-226-4489, 800-445-7379; www.bearcreekranch.com. In Waterton Park, contact **Alpine Stables**. ~ 403-859-2462, 403-653-2449 (winter).

For late summer llama treks into the Swan Divide Area of the Flathead National Forest, consult the **Great Northern Llama Co.** ~ 600 Blackmer Lane, Columbia Falls; 406-755-9044; www.gnranch.com.

BIKING

Bike touring is encouraged through **Glacier National Park**, and several tour operators lead groups across the Continental Divide on Going-to-the-Sun Road. But because of the increased danger of accidents during the peak travel season—mid-June to Labor Day—bicyclists are restricted from hazardous sections of the narrow, winding highway between 11 a.m. and 4 p.m. Bicycles are not permitted on park trails or off-road.

National forest roads and trails are generally open to mountain biking, but wheeled vehicles—motorized or not—are not allowed in designated wilderness areas. Bike rentals are hard to come by around Glacier National Park and Waterton Lakes National Park, so if you're intent on hitting a few trails, be sure to bring along your own bike.

Bike Rentals   There are no bike-rental companies in the actual parks. Nearby, though, is Whitefish's **Glacier Cyclery**, where you'll find hybrid, full suspension mountain bikes, touring, tandem and kids' bikes (helmets and water bottles included), as well as car racks that they will install and all kinds of touring gear; reservations recommended during peak season. Closed Sunday from early September to late May. ~ 326 East 2nd Street, Whitefish; 406-862-6446; www.glaciercyclery.com. Or try **Glacier Raft Company** in West Glacier. ~ 406-888-5454, 800-235-6781; www.glacieroutdoorcenter.com.

HIKING   Glacier National Park itself has some 730 miles of trails. Waterton Park has another 190 miles. And there are hundreds of miles more throughout the adjoining national forests and wilderness areas. (All distances listed for hiking trails are one way unless otherwise noted.) Backcountry permits are required for overnight camping, so be sure to obtain one from a national park visitors center.

The best available guide to hiking this region is *Hiking Glacier and Waterton Lakes National Parks* by Erik Molvar (Falcon Guide, 1999).

Guided day and weekend hikes through the Montana backcountry are organized by the **Montana Wilderness Association**. Each trip is limited to 14 or fewer hikers, though, so advance reservations are necessary. ~ 307 1st Avenue East, Suite 20, Kalispell; 406-755-6304; www.wildmontana.org.

GLACIER NATIONAL PARK   The **Avalanche Lake Trail** (2 miles) begins at the Avalanche Creek campground, four miles from Lake McDonald. Its first section—the broad and paved 300-yard **Trail of the Cedars**—is a wheelchair-accessible route that loops through an old-growth forest of western red cedars. Then it rambles up the churning gorge of Avalanche Creek to the lake itself, fed by a series of waterfalls that tumble down 2000-foot cliffs on its far side.

The **Highline Trail** (11.8 miles) traverses the Garden Wall, a thin, 20-mile wall of rock perhaps more appropriate for mountain goats than for people. It starts from the Logan Pass Visitors Center, then makes a moderate descent to "The Loop," a 150-degree switchback on Going-to-the-Sun Road.

The **Hidden Lake Trail** (3 miles) is among the park's most popular. Starting from the Logan Pass Visitors Center, it begins with a one-and-a-half-mile-long boardwalk across a fragile alpine meadow, a natural amphitheater of wildflowers called the Hanging Gardens of Logan Pass. You can return to the visitors center from a scenic overlook, where the boardwalk ends, or continue another mile and a half on a rough trail that drops rapidly to Hidden Lake.

Beware the Bear

Of all the great mammals of the Rocky Mountains, none is as feared or as respected as the grizzly bear. Once numbering at about 50,000 in the lower 48 states, ranging from the Mississippi River west to the Pacific Ocean, this great bear was reduced by white settlement to fewer than 1000 on 2 percent of its former range. Today, most grizzlies—protected as a threatened species under the federal Endangered Species Act—inhabit the national parks and wilderness areas running down the spine of the Rockies from the Canadian border through Yellowstone National Park. In western Montana, Glacier National Park and the adjacent Great Bear Wilderness are two of its strongholds. Biologists estimate there are several hundred resident grizzlies.

Ursus arctos horribilis is the second largest omnivore (that is, meat and plant eater) in North America, superseded only by the polar bear. Males can weigh more than 1000 pounds, females 600. Though nocturnal, an adult can be aggressive if intruders disturb it . . . or its cubs.

The grizzly is easily distinguished from the more docile American black bear (*Ursus americanus*) by its broad head; a well-defined shoulder muscle, which helps it dig for rodents, insects and roots; and its frequently silver-tipped, or "grizzled," fur coat. Grizzlies don't climb trees as well as black bears, but they can outrun horses and people in a sprint.

Only occasionally do backcountry visitors see grizzlies today. Even in Yellowstone Park, once renowned for its begging roadside bears, they have been removed to the wilderness. Wildlife watchers who want to observe grizzlies should look during the dawn and dusk hours around the fringes of woodlands and meadows . . . from a distance.

To avoid grizzly encounters, travel in numbers, make plenty of noise (by talking frequently or singing loudly) and avoid hiking at night. Clean cooking gear immediately after use, and store food in airtight containers away from your campsite. Don't bury your garbage; pack it out.

If confronted by a grizzly while hiking, do *not* turn your back and run. Move slowly away, avoiding eye contact. If the grizzly charges, stand your ground: Bears often feign a charge or run past you. As a last resort, curl into a ball and play dead, covering your neck and head with your hands and arms. If a grizzly invades your camp, find a tree or boulder to climb as high as you can. If you are attacked, fight back with any weapon, including your fists. Playing dead will *not* work here.

Grizzlies kill humans only infrequently; more often they die at the hands of man. But like the wise Scout, it's best to be prepared.

The **Grinnell Glacier Trail** (5.5 miles) leaves from the Many Glacier Hotel, climbing slowly past Lake Josephine, then rapidly (about 1500 feet) to Upper Grinnell Lake and the glacier. The scenery is spectacular—if you've never been close to a glacier before, grab this opportunity to get a close-up look at crevasses, bergschrunds and nunataks.

The **Two Medicine Lake Circuit** (7.2 miles) loops around the most southerly of Glacier's large lakes. Most of this relatively easy hike, which includes crossing a swaying suspension bridge, is through woodlands. It offers some of Glacier's finest hiking, among colorful foliage and twisting valleys. An additional 1.7-mile, gently rising side trip will bring you to pretty Upper Two Medicine Lake.

The **Boulder Pass Trail** (31 miles) is one of the park's most challenging. It can be done either eastbound from Kintla Lake (near Polebridge) or westbound from Goat Haunt at the south end of Upper Waterton Lake. In either case, you'll have a climb of well over 3000 feet to the summit of 7470-foot Boulder Pass on the Continental Divide.

Alpine meadows, rocky summits and a wealth of wildlife are the highlights of a hike through the Boulder Pass Trail.

The official park guided hiking and backpacking concessionaire, **Glacier Wilderness Guides** has been hiking the backcountry since 1983. Trips range from one to ten days. Experienced guides carry all the group equipment and most of the food; participants handle only their personal gear and some food. Among the trails explored: **Belly River** (12 miles), **Cut Bank Creek** (14 miles), **Stoney Indian Pass** (56 miles), **Two Medicine** (7 miles) and **Waterton Lake–Bowman Lake** (26 miles). ~ Route 2, West Glacier; 406-387-5555; www.glacierguides.com.

WATERTON LAKES NATIONAL PARK   Short but strenuous is the **Bears Hump Trail** (1.5 miles roundtrip), which climbs 650 feet from the national park visitor reception center, opposite the Prince of Wales Hotel, to one of the best viewpoints in the park.

The **Bertha Lake Trail** (4.3 miles) begins at the Waterton Lake townsite and climbs 1500 feet up a series of steep switchbacks to the lovely lake, wedged in a deep subalpine valley. En route, just 1.8 miles from the trailhead, Bertha Falls cascade over a cliff face.

The **Twin Lakes Loop Trail** (15.5 miles) is usually regarded as a weekend backpack. Hikers slowly ascend the forested Bauerman Valley from the end of Red Rock Parkway before stopping overnight at Upper Twin Lake, one of two small alpine tarns. Bighorn sheep and mountain goats are often seen here. The return trail climbs through Blue Grouse Basin, then descends the valleys of Lone and Blakiston creeks back to Red Rock Canyon.

Able hiking companions staff the **Canadian Wilderness Tours**. Trained naturalists take individuals or groups of any size and of any age or ability on walks emphasizing Waterton's fauna, flora, history and geology. ~ 800-408-0005; www.whitemountainad ventures.com.

Transperation

Route 2, which runs eastbound through Kalispell and West Glacier, then skirts the south side of Glacier National Park en route to East Glacier Park, Browning and points east, is the most important access route to the national park. In Browning, this highway crosses northbound Route 89 from Great Falls. This route transits St. Mary and extends to the Canadian border.

CAR

The 50-mile **Going-to-the-Sun Road** links West Glacier and St. Mary through the heart of Glacier National Park. Because the road is steep and narrow, no vehicles or car trailers longer than 20 feet, or wider than seven and a half feet including mirrors, are permitted over Logan Pass.

Principal access to Waterton Lakes National Park is the **Chief Mountain International Highway,** which branches west off Route 89, 13 miles north of St. Mary.

Kalispell's **Glacier Park International Airport** is served by America West Airlines, Big Sky, Delta, Horizon and Northwest. ~ 4170 Route 2 East, Kalispell; 406-257-5994; www.glacierairport.com.

AIR

Regional bus service is available through **Rimrock Trailways,** which connects to Greyhound routes in Missoula and other cities. ~ 403 2nd Street East, Whitefish; 406-862-6700, 800-255-7655; www.rimrocktrailways.com.

BUS

Amtrak's "Empire Builder" stops daily in each direction, at Browning, East Glacier Park, Essex, West Glacier and Whitefish, en route between Chicago to Seattle. Some stops are seasonal only; check schedule information. ~ 800-872-7245; www.amtrak.com.

TRAIN

A limited choice of rentals is available in West Glacier. For a better selection, contact one of the agencies at Glacier Park International Airport between Kalispell and Columbia Falls (see Chapter Two).

CAR RENTALS

Glacier National Park provides scheduled transportation between its various lodges and railway stations in touring vans. There's also a daily service from the Glacier Park Lodge (at East Glacier Park) to the Prince of Wales Hotel (at Waterton Park). ~ 406-756-2444; www.glacierparkinc.com.

PUBLIC TRANSIT

FOUR

North Central Montana

Montana's north-central region encompasses many of the extremes of the Montana experience. Extending from the Bob Marshall Wilderness Area east across the Missouri River to the wide-open rangeland "where the buffalo roam, where the deer and the antelope play," this is an area that is both as old and as new as you'll find in the state.

Stand atop the Continental Divide west of Great Falls, where the Rocky Mountain Front drops dramatically to the northern Great Plains, and you may get some idea of the region's geographical magnitude. This broad, slow-flowing stream provides water for the arid farmland, habitat for waterfowl and other wildlife, recreation for the sportsman and sportswoman.

Two centuries ago, tens of millions of American bison, in herds of thousands, cavorted through these mountains and prairies. Hunted to near-extinction in the 19th century, they nearly met the same fate as their reptilian Jurassic predecessors, whose bones and other fossil remains have been found en masse along the Rockies' eastern slope. More skeletons of *Tyrannosaurus rex,* believed to have been the largest dinosaur ever to walk the earth, have been found in Montana than in all other discovery areas put together.

Blackfoot Indians, horsemen and hunters who relied heavily on bison to provide food and hides for clothing and shelter, once dominated this region. Around the turn of the 19th century, the first whites penetrated the upper Missouri: first French Canadian trappers, and soon thereafter the trailblazing Lewis and Clark expedition. The American explorers followed the Missouri upstream in 1805, taking two weeks to portage around the Great Falls. In the mid-19th century, Fort Benton became the single most important port on the Missouri, with steamboats traveling upstream all the way from New Orleans to deliver and receive goods.

Today, north-central Montana's economy focuses on Great Falls. With 50,000 people, this trade and industrial center on the Missouri River is a haven for outdoor sports lovers and the site of a major Air Force base. Havre, with a population of 9000, is one of the only other towns in the region with more than 3000 people.

Great Falls is Montana's heartland. Not a "mountain town," not a "cowboy town," the state's second-largest city is near enough to the Rocky Mountain crest to be a recreational gateway, near enough to eastern Montana's semiarid ranch country to be an agricultural center. It's a place in between, straddling history as it does the Missouri River, mindful of its roots as a 19th-century trade hub but also a thoroughly modern center of national air defense and a hydroelectric power industry.

Great Falls

Great Falls is best known, in fact, as "The Electric City." The series of dams on the Missouri just below the community provide power to a huge area, and the river's water supports a thriving wheat and barley industry in the rolling hills north of here.

When Lewis and Clark first ventured into this stretch of the Missouri in 1805, they discovered a different river from the one visitors see today. Over a ten-mile stretch there were five cataracts, which they called the "Great Falls of the Missouri": "A sublimely grand spectacle," Lewis wrote in his journal. He quickly noted that "the river was one continued sene of rappids and cascades which I readily perceive could not be encountered with our canoes." The party was forced to portage their equipment around the falls; the 18-mile ordeal took 15 days to complete.

SIGHTS

Today, as a result of five hydro projects, the falls are not the spectacles that Lewis observed. The feature usually called the Great Falls—the farthest downstream (located ten miles from downtown) and, at 80 feet, the largest of the five falls—is now contained by Ryan Dam, built in 1915. **Broadwater Overlook Park** features a heroic bronze sculpture by Montana artist Bob Scriver that commemorates the portage and has a visitors center with interpretive displays. ~ 15 Overlook Park; 406-771-0885, fax 406-761-6129; www.greatfallschamber.org, e-mail mmartinson@great fallschamber.org.

Undoubtedly the best place to experience the river locally is **Giant Springs/Heritage State Park**, three miles east of the city off River Drive. "The largest fountain I ever saw" is how Clark described the springs, which bubble from the earth at a rate of nearly eight million gallons per hour and flow 201 feet to the Missouri. (The spring is one of the world's largest; the *Guinness Book of World Records* lists the outflow, named the **Roe River**, as the world's shortest river.) The day-use park also features a visitors center and rainbow trout hatchery that offers self-guided and interpretive tours. On the premises is the Lewis & Clark National Historic Trail Interpretive Center, featuring a video presentation, gift shop, displays and botanical gardens. Downriver a mile by car or trail are blufftop lookouts over scenic Rainbow Falls. ~ 4600 Giant Springs Road; 406-454-5840, 406-454-5858, fax 406-761-8477.

Great Falls was also the home of C. M. Russell (1864–1926), the nation's most acclaimed frontier artist. (See "Charles M. Russell: The Cowboy Artist" in this chapter.) The **Charles M. Russell Museum Complex** includes his home, his original log-cabin studio and an outstanding art museum. The world's most extensive collection of Russell's original works is here: oils, watercolors, pen-and-ink sketches, sculptures, even some accompanying poetry. All of it focuses on the cowboys, American Indians and wildlife of the West. Also displayed are works by Russell's contemporaries and current artists of the American West, as well as the Browning Firearms Collection. There is an excellent gift shop. Closed Monday in winter. Admission. ~ 400 13th Street North; 406-727-8787, fax 406-727-2402; www.cmrussell.org, e-mail keri@cmrussell.org.

Another center for the arts is **Paris Gibson Square Museum of Art,** an imposing stone building constructed in 1895. Its galleries include permanent and changing exhibits, a fine-art shop and a café. Closed Sunday in winter and Sunday and Monday in summer. ~ 1400 1st Avenue North; 406-727-8255, fax 406-727-8256; www.the-square.org, e-mail info@the-square.org.

And the **Montana Cowboys Association Museum** has a log-cabin display of Old West memorabilia at the fairgrounds. ~ 311 3rd Street Northwest; 406-761-9299.

West of the Russell Museum and Paris Gibson Square is Great Falls' most architecturally interesting neighborhood, the **Northside Residential Historic District,** dating from 1885. Thirty-nine homes on 3rd and 4th Avenues North, between Park Drive and 10th Street, are described in a walking tour pamphlet. The self-guided tour begins at the **Cascade County Historical Society.** ~ 422 2nd Street South; 406-452-3462; e-mail hphc@highplains heritage.org.

It's not something most visitors are immediately aware of, but the Great Falls area is Ground Zero. That is to say, some 200 long-range nuclear missiles are buried in silos just beneath the surface of the innocent-looking plains that surround the city. The 341st Space Wing, based at **Malmstrom Air Force Base,** has command of the site. ~ 2nd Avenue North, east of 57th Street. Visitors with an interest in this sort of thing can learn more at the **Base Museum and Air Park,** just inside the main gate, where a Minuteman missile, numerous historic aircraft and other military vehicles are displayed. Closed weekends; call ahead for special arrangements. ~ 406-731-2705, fax 406-731-2769; www.malmstrom.af.mil, e-mail curtis.shannon@malmstrom.af.mil.

LODGING

The **Best Western Heritage Inn** is at the head of the class in Great Falls. Its central atrium/courtyard, designed in a loose French Quarter–style, has an indoor swimming pool, hot tubs, saunas

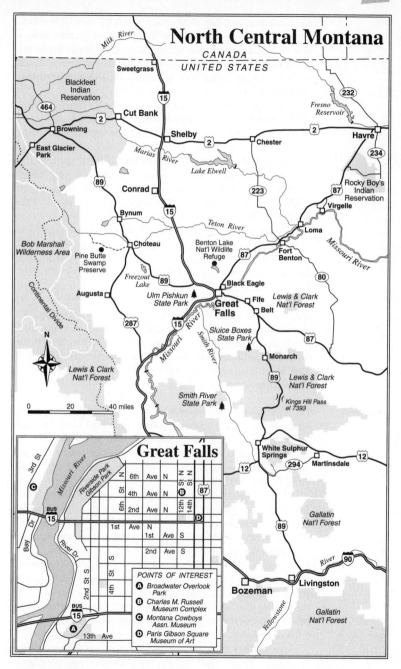

North Central Montana

Milk River

CANADA
UNITED STATES

Sweetgrass

Blackfeet
Indian
Reservation

464

15

2

Cut Bank

Browning

Shelby

Chester

Havre

East Glacier
Park

Marias River

2

Fresno
Reservoir

232

234

89

Conrad

Lake Elwell

223

Rocky Boy's
Indian
Reservation

87

Bynum

15

Teton River

Virgelle

Bob Marshall
Wilderness Area

Choteau

Benton Lake
Nat'l Wildlife
Refuge

Loma

87

Missouri River

Pine Butte
Swamp
Preserve

Fort
Benton

Continental Divide

Freezout
Lake

89

Black Eagle

80

Augusta

Ulm Pishkun
State Park

Great
Falls

Fife

Belt

Lewis & Clark
Nat'l Forest

287

15

Missouri River

Smith River

Sluice Boxes
State Park

87

N

Monarch

Lewis & Clark
Nat'l Forest

Lewis & Clark
Nat'l Forest

89

0   20   40 miles

Smith River
State Park

Kings Hill Pass
el 7393

Great Falls

White Sulphur
Springs

12

12

294

Martinsdale

3rd St

Missouri River

Riverside Park
Gibson Park

N   6th Ave N

N
12th St
14th St

N

87

Gallatin
Nat'l Forest

BUS
15

St

4th Ave N

6th St

2nd Ave N

89

Bay Dr

River Dr

1st   Ave N

1st   Ave S

2nd Ave S

River

90

S

2nd St S

St

4th St

S

Bozeman

Livingston

BUS
15

POINTS OF INTEREST

13th Ave

Yellowstone

Gallatin
Nat'l Forest

Ⓐ Broadwater Overlook
   Park
Ⓑ Charles M. Russell
   Museum Complex
Ⓒ Montana Cowboys
   Assn. Museum
Ⓓ Paris Gibson Square
   Museum of Art

and a fitness center. Just off the courtyard is a family-style restaurant and a bustling casino/sports bar. The two-story motor inn—near the south freeway entrance to Great Falls—has 236 spacious and modern rooms with queen and king beds and writing desks. ~ 1700 Fox Farm Road; 406-761-1900, 800-548-8256, fax 406-761-0136. MODERATE.

The **Triple Crown Motor Inn** is located in the heart of downtown Great Falls. All 49 rooms are air-conditioned, with cable television. Children 12 and under stay free with adults. ~ 621 Central Avenue; 406-452-1470. BUDGET.

The **Old Oak Inn Bed & Breakfast** has four country-cozy rooms and two suites set in a restored 1908 Victorian. Watch Great Falls wake up from the front porch before heading back inside for a full breakfast. ~ 709 4th Avenue North; 406-727-5782. MODERATE TO DELUXE.

The **Wagon Wheel Motel** aims to please the romantic. Some of its rooms have heart-shaped beds and hot tubs. Even unromantic travelers will enjoy the in-room jacuzzi. ~ 2620 10th Avenue South; 406-761-1300, 800-800-6483, fax 406-761-7320. BUDGET.

The four-story **Great Falls Inn** delivers quality for price. Its 60 spacious rooms have queen-size beds and wood furnishings; 48 are equipped with refrigerators and microwaves. A continental breakfast comes with the room price. There's a laundry on the third floor, a fireplace in the lobby and a fitness room. ~ 1400 28th Street South; 406-453-6000, fax 406-453-6078; www.great fallsinn.com. MODERATE.

DINING

For Mexican food, **El Comedor** is a pleasant, off-the-main-drag establishment. There's nothing too gourmet here—you'll get the standard enchiladas and burritos along with fajitas and smoked pork. The decor is a medley of sombreros, serapes and a wooden Aztec calendar. ~ 1120 25th Street South; 406-761-5500, fax 407-761-5502. BUDGET.

The best place to get your morning coffee is at **Morning Light**. The beans are roasted on the premises, and a selection of homemade pastries greet early risers. ~ 900 2nd Avenue North; 406-453-8443, fax 406-761-8221; www.morninglight.com. BUDGET.

Eddie's Supper Club is a long-established local favorite. Eddie's pioneered the "campfire" steak; some argue that it's the best steak in Montana. Breakfast, lunch and dinner are served in the coffee shop, furnished with formica-topped tables, and after 3 p.m. in the low-lit, vinyl-upholstered dining room. The lounge boasts a twin piano bar. ~ 3725 2nd Avenue North; 406-453-1616. BUDGET TO ULTRA-DELUXE.

Jaker's offers steak and seafood specialties in an atmosphere of casual elegance. Pasta and chicken entrées are also popular. ~

Charles M. Russell:
The Cowboy Artist

Perhaps no artist more exemplified the American West than Charles Marion Russell, a hard-drinking, tough-talking, whimsical whisper of a man who learned to punch cows and ride with the Indians, but who attracted a circle of friends that included presidents and movie stars.

Born in St. Louis, Missouri, in 1864, Russell was never cut out for his parents' high-society lifestyle. When Charles was 16, his father shipped him off to Montana to what was hoped would be a "school of hard knocks" for the rebellious youth ... but the lad thrived on it.

A failure as a sheepherder, Russell was befriended by a mountain man, Jake Hoover, who taught him how to survive in the Wild West. The pair shared a tiny sod-roofed cabin in the Little Belt Mountains until Russell got a job as a night wrangler at a cattle ranch. That left his days open to paint, draw and sculpt.

One reason Russell's works stand out from those of other Western artists is that he lived what he put on canvas. Although his vivid depictions of the West began to earn him a profit, he continued to wrangle cattle for another decade. He also spent a full winter with the Blackfeet, learning their spoken language as well as a sign language that any Plains Indian tribe could understand.

Eventually, Russell found it expedient for his artistic career to move from the prairie. He relocated to Great Falls in 1897, married, and three years later built a home in a fashionable neighborhood near downtown. In 1903, he constructed a separate log studio—"a cabin just like I used to live in," he said. Until his death in 1926, this was Russell's sanctuary, a place where he surrounded himself with his personal collections of cowboy and American Indian lifestyles, and where he produced every last work he painted or sculpted. Both the house and the studio are now a part of the C. M. Russell Museum Complex, donated by Russell's widow, Nancy, to the city of Great Falls.

Russell's works—more than 4500 oils and watercolors, pen-and-ink drawings, clay and wax sculptures and illustrated letters (he was a renowned storyteller) —symbolize the adventure and the freedom of the West as he knew and loved it. For many easterners, the work of "America's Cowboy Artist" was their principal link to the romance of the Old West.

Russell was a lifelong defender of the pre-20th-century West, and he decried the rapid changes he saw during his lifetime.

"I liked it better when it belonged to God," he said.

1500 10th Avenue South; 406-727-1033, fax 406-727-9997; www.jakers.com, e-mail jim@jakers.com. MODERATE TO DELUXE.

HIDDEN ► Families enjoy **Borrie's** on the north side of the Missouri River opposite downtown Great Falls. Established in 1938, the hard-to-find restaurant serves up traditional Italian (ravioli, spaghetti) and American (steaks, seafood, chicken) fare with an ebullient ambience. Dinner only. ~ 1800 Smelter Avenue, Black Eagle; 406-761-0300, fax 406-761-2021. MODERATE TO ULTRA-DELUXE.

The kids want spaghetti, the wife wants prime rib, but you feel like a plate of chow mein? No problem. **3D International**, owned and operated by the Grassechi family for five decades, has it all. Located like Borrie's across the 10th Street Bridge, this art deco–style restaurant also has one of Montana's few Mongolian grills. ~ 1825 Smelter Avenue, Black Eagle; 406-453-6561, fax 406-453-9947. MODERATE TO DELUXE.

SHOPPING Perhaps the best place to claim memories of Great Falls is the shop at the **Charles M. Russell Museum Complex**. The museum shop specializes in reproductions of Western art but has a good selection of books and various quality souvenirs, not to mention the largest selection of C. M. Russell prints around. Closed Monday in winter. ~ 400 13th Street North; 406-727-8787; www.cmrussell.org, e-mail keri@cmrussell.org.

Great Falls' Farmers Market takes place throughout the summer, 5 to 6:30 p.m. on Wednesday and 7 a.m. to noon on Saturday. Fruit, vegetables, baked goods and craft items are sold at **Whittier Park** on the south side of the Civic Center. May through October only. ~ Central Avenue and 1st Street; 406-761-4434, fax 406-761-6129; e-mail admin1@greatfallschamber.org.

AUTHOR FAVORITE

If you're interested in Plains Indian history, it's worth braving the long dusty road leading to **Ulm Pishkun State Park**, an ancient buffalo jump. You'll find the interpretive exhibits in the visitors center as intriguing as the wide-open views at the actual jump site. For thousands of years, American Indians drove herds of bison up this mile-long *pishkun*, or buffalo jump, from which the beasts plunged to their deaths. Arrowheads, knives, hide scrapers, hammers and other tools have been discovered at this site, believed to be the largest of its kind in the United States. To reach it, take Route 15 south ten miles from Great Falls to Ulm (Exit 270); then follow signs four miles north. Closed Monday and Tuesday in winter. Admission. ~ Ulm-Vaughn Road at Goetz Road; 406-866-2217, fax 406-866-2218.

One of Great Falls' main shopping centers is the **Holiday Village Mall**. ~ 1200 10th Avenue South; 406-727-2088. There's also **Westgate Mall**, with restaurants and gift shops. ~ 1807 3rd Street Northwest; 406-761-2464.

As befits a city of 50,000, Great Falls has an active music scene. It's headed by the **Great Falls Symphony**, which plays an October-to-May classical season and a free pops concert in June. Besides a 65-member orchestra, the symphony includes a string quartet, a wind quintet, a youth orchestra and a 90-voice choir. ~ Civic Center; 2 Park Drive South; 406-453-4102; www.gfsymphony.com.

NIGHTLIFE

Between October and April, the **Great Falls Community Concert Series** stages four to six cultural events with guest artists. Performances may range from Broadway show tunes to ethnic choirs; diverse musicians may include renowned classical artists and popular ensembles. ~ Civic Center, 2 Park Drive South; 406-453-9854.

From mid-June to mid-August, the **Great Falls Municipal Band**—which has been playing every year since 1895—performs free Wednesday-night concerts at the Gibson Park bandshell.

For drinks, **Philly's** in the Holiday Inn Great Falls has as many regulars as any lounge in town. ~ 400 10th Avenue South; 406-727-7200. **Club Cigar** wins kudos for its historic downtown atmosphere. There's often live music on Friday and Saturday. Closed Sunday. Occasional cover. ~ 208 Central Avenue; 406-727-8011. **The Max** in the Best Western Heritage Inn is clearly Great Falls' number-one casino. ~ 1700 Fox Farm Road; 406-761-1900.

GIANT SPRINGS/HERITAGE STATE PARK 🏃 🚲 🛶 One of the world's largest freshwater springs (7.9 million gallons per hour) bubbles into the world's shortest river (the Roe River, 201 feet) by the banks of the Missouri River. The springs were discovered by Lewis and Clark in 1805. The Lewis & Clark National Historic Trail Interpretive Center here features a video presentation, gift shop and botanical garden. An adjacent fish hatchery is open for public viewing. There are picnic areas and restrooms. Day-use fee, $2 per person. ~ Three miles east from downtown Great Falls via River Drive; turn left onto Giant Springs Road; 406-454-5840, 406-454-5858, fax 406-761-8477.

PARKS

ULM PISHKUN STATE PARK 🏃 The largest buffalo jump yet identified in the United States, this was a site where ancient American Indians drove herds of bison off a cliff. A variety of primitive tools have been uncovered—if you find one, leave it where it is and tell a park ranger (removal of artifacts is a punishable offense). Picnic tables, restrooms and interpretive displays round

Text continued on page 120.

DRIVING TOUR
Lewis & Clark's Route

This all-day walking/driving tour will be just the ticket for Lewis and Clarkers as well as families unfamiliar with the Corps of Discovery's exploits. It covers a ten-mile stretch of the Missouri River where five waterfalls forced the expedition to make a torturous 18-mile overland portage.

RIVER'S EDGE TRAIL   Pack a picnic lunch and drive to the Lewis & Clark National Historic Trail Interpretive Center in Giant Springs/Heritage State Park, where you'll park. Feeling energetic? Take the stairs (by the center) that lead to River's Edge Trail (page 133). Retrace some of the explorers' footsteps (minus the annoying prickly pear cactus) by walking a mile west (left) along the scenic Missouri to Black Eagle Falls. Then backtrack. Early morning (start by 8) is the best (i.e., coolest) time for strolling and spotting herons and pelicans.

LEWIS & CLARK NATIONAL HISTORIC TRAIL INTERPRETIVE CENTER   By the time you return (after 9 a.m.), the Lewis & Clark National Historic Trail Interpretive Center will be open. For the first 15 minutes, cruise the gift shop and entrance exhibits. Then catch the superb half-hour film on the Corps of Discovery. Spend the next 90 minutes on a self-guided tour of the well-designed, kid-friendly exhibits. They detail the captains' 1804–1806 odyssey and their encounters with the Plains Indians who helped in the trek westward. Outside, partake in a variety of live programs for more living history. Closed Monday during the winter. Admission. ~ 4201 Giant Springs Road; 406-727-8733.

GIANT SPRINGS/HERITAGE STATE PARK   Giant Springs/Heritage State Park (page 111) holds the largest freshwater spring in America in addition to the shortest river in the world, the 201-foot Roe. Read the interpretation, stroll through the park and photograph Canada geese. You can also visit a fish hatchery here. This takes an hour if you also go to the hatchery. ~ 4600 Giant Springs Road; 406-454-5840.

BLACK EAGLE FALLS OVERLOOK   Drive a mile southwest on Giant Springs Road to River Drive. Turn west and go .3 mile to Black Eagle Falls Overlook. Park and read the interpretive sign. According to the Hidatsa Indians, Lewis & Clark would know they'd followed the correct river if they found an eagle's nest on an island by a waterfall. The good news for the explorers was sighting the nest perched in a cottonwood. The bad news was this was the last in a series of five waterfalls requiring portage. ~ River Drive and 25th Street North.

RAINBOW DAM AND OVERLOOK   Backtrack to River Drive and drive just over one mile east past Giant Springs/Heritage State Park to Rainbow Dam. The best views here are from the second (upper) parking area. Read the interpretive exhibits that cover Lewis & Clark as well as Rainbow Dam history. And don't forget to look for rainbows! ~ River Drive.

RYAN DAM PARK, DAM AND OVERLOOK   Now head west on River Drive. When you reach 15th Street, you'll cross the Missouri River by turning right. At this point, 15th Street becomes Route 87. Travel north on Route 87 to the Ryan Dam turnoff. Make a right (east) at the sign, then follow the signs along this winding, bumpy road. You can picnic at Ryan Dam Park (open seasonally) and jounce across a swaying cable suspension bridge to Ryan Island. You'll find extensive interpretation here as well as restrooms. Lewis' journal describes this waterfall as "a roaring too tremendous to be mistaken for any cause short of the great falls of the Missouri." Give yourself about an hour and a half for this stop. ~ Off Route 87 North.

WEST BANK PARK   Back on Route 87, drive south and take the Northwest Bypass turn. Go downhill then turn right (west) onto Smelter Avenue (the turn sign reads "Northwest Bypass"). You'll veer left and the street will become 3rd Street Northwest. Turn left (east) just past Westgate Shopping Mall and follow the signs to West Bank Park. Near the south end of this park you'll find interpretive panels. This is where a grizzly bear charged Meriwether Lewis. It's also a good wildlife viewing area along the Missouri. ~ 17th Avenue Northeast and 3rd Street Northwest.

BROADWATER OVERLOOK PARK   Go back to 3rd Street Northwest and drive south. Turn left (east) at the intersection onto Central Avenue West, then turn right (south) on River Drive and go 1.1 miles. Veer left at 10th Avenue South to head uphill to Broadwater Overlook Park (page 111). A heroic bronze sculpture depicting a few members of the Corps of Discovery and a huge American flag mark this site. The visitors center holds more displays on the explorers and regional history. From the overlook, you get neat views of the city and the confluence of the Sun and Missouri rivers. Give yourself about 30 minutes here if you go inside the visitors center. ~ 10th Avenue South and 2nd Street; 406-771-0885.

out the amenities. Day-use fee, $2 per person. Call ahead for seasonal hours. ~ Ten miles south from Great Falls on Route 15 to Ulm (Exit 270), then three and a half miles north; 406-866-2217, fax 406-866-2218.

BENTON LAKE NATIONAL WILDLIFE REFUGE 🚶 🚲 Nine-mile-long, gravel-surfaced Prairie Marsh Drive loops through the marshy lakes and wetlands of this 12,300-acre reserve, where more than 260 species of birds and land animals have been observed. Pick up a brochure at the visitors center; its numbers correspond to ten interpretive stops along the road. Restrooms and a visitors center are among the facilities. The tour route may be closed in inclement weather. ~ Take Bootlegger Trail north 9.2 miles from Great Falls to the refuge's visitors center. ~ 406-727-7400, fax 406-727-7432; http://bentonlake.fws.gov, e-mail benton lake@fws.gov.

▼▼▼▼▼▼▼▼▼▼▼▼
The Rocky Mountain Front

Route 89 north, connecting Great Falls with Glacier National Park's eastern portals, draws ever closer to the dramatic Rocky Mountain Front, where the range's craggy peaks drop suddenly to the prairies, unbuffered by the waves of lower mountains found to the west.

SIGHTS

The largest town in these environs is **Choteau**, a center for outdoor recreation and dinosaur digging, with a population of about 1800. Choteau (pronounced "SHO-toe") is the gateway to the nation's best-known wilderness area, several wildlife refuges and a paleontological reserve.

Displays of fossils and artifacts in the town's **Old Trail Museum** interpret some of these regional attractions. Attached to the museum, located at the north edge of town, is a block of frontier-style displays, including a craft shop, a grizzly bear exhibit, a schoolhouse, an ice-cream parlor, the log-cabin studio of artist Jesse Gleason and a visitors center with ample parking. Closed Monday and Tuesday in winter. Admission. ~ Route 89, Choteau; 406-466-5332; www.oldtrailmuseum.org, e-mail otm@ 3rivers.net.

Two roads head west from Choteau into **Lewis and Clark National Forest** and toward the fringe of the **Bob Marshall Wilderness**. Neither motorized vehicles nor bicycles are permitted in this land of grizzly bears and mountain lions. ~ 406-466-5341, fax 406-466-2237.

At the foot of the Rocky Mountain Front, the Teton River flows through a wetland that is a spring feeding ground for grizzlies and home to a herd of bighorn sheep. The Nature Conservancy purchased and set aside 18,000 acres as the **Pine Butte Swamp Preserve**, 17 miles west of Choteau, to protect the flora and fauna of this unique region. ~ Bellview Road; 406-466-5526, fax 406-466-5674.

The conservancy also owns the adjoining **Egg Mountain** ◄HIDDEN
Paleontological Site. This site on the Willow Creek Anticline, 12 miles west of Choteau, is where the first dinosaur eggs (42 of them, in 14 nests) were discovered in North America. Admission. ~ 823 North Main Street, Choteau; 406-466-5332, fax 406-466-5874; e-mail otm@3rivers.net.

There are state wildlife management areas near Choteau at Pishkun Reservoir, Willow Creek Reservoir, Ear Mountain, Sun River, Blackleaf Creek and elsewhere. The most accessible—because the highway to Great Falls runs right through its heart—is the **Freezout Lake Wildlife Management Area.** A birdwatcher's checklist of 187 species spotted here is available from area headquarters. Winter visitors may want to drive through the rural village of Augusta, 26 miles southwest of Choteau, then 15 miles west to the **Sun River Game Range,** where herds of elk and deer find a welcome cold-weather sanctuary. ~ Route 89, four miles northwest of Fairfield; 406-467-2646.

The **Bunkhouse Inn** is housed in a grey, two-story building that **LODGING** was hauled from Gilman, three miles up the road, to its present location in the 1920s. Coincidentally, the building had been the Gilman Hotel. You'll find nine rooms with shared baths; quilts are a cozy touch. The porch is a great spot to take in local activity. ~ 122 Main Street, Augusta, south of Choteau on Route 287; 406-562-3387. BUDGET.

There are numerous guest ranches along the Rocky Mountain Front. An especially good one, not far from the Bob Marshall Wilderness, is the **Seven Lazy P Ranch.** Located 30 miles west of Choteau on the North Fork of the Teton River, it focuses on horse pack trips into The Bob and seasonal fishing and hunting. Guests stay in nine rustic cabins and duplexes, eight with private

AUTHOR FAVORITE

Thirty-five miles west of Augusta on Gibson Lake, at the edge of "The Bob," is **Klicks' K Bar L Ranch.** This rustic ranch, in the Klick family since 1927, cannot be reached by road: You arrive either by horseback or via jetboat across the lake. Thirteen cabins share toilet/shower facilities, as well as a natural hot-springs pool. Activities include riding and catch-and-release fly-fishing. Six-day minimum. ~ Box 287, Augusta, MT 59410; 406-562-3551 (summer and fall), 406-562-3589 (winter and spring). ULTRA-DELUXE.

baths; most socializing is around the large stone fireplace in the main lodge. Meals are hearty and ranch-style. Four-day minimum stay, American plan. Closed December through April. ~ Canyon Road, Choteau; 406-466-2044; e-mail sevenlazyp@mon tana.com. ULTRA-DELUXE.

DINING

Three meals a day, six days a week, the **Log Cabin Café** dishes up ample portions of good American food: pancakes, burgers, steaks, pasta and seafood; in summer you'll find elk and buffalo. There's a children's menu, too. Closed Monday. ~ 102 South Main Street, Choteau; 406-466-2888. MODERATE TO DELUXE.

The **Outpost Deli** provides a more casual alternative for less-hearty appetites. Deli sandwiches and soups are the popular choices here, as well as ice cream on hot summer days. ~ 819 North Main, Choteau; 406-466-5330. BUDGET.

Start your day with a huge breakfast at **Mel's Ice Cream Shop & Diner**, where you can choose from different egg, french toast and pancake combinations. A variety of burgers, sandwiches, fish and chicken are offered for lunch and early dinner. Breakfast, lunch and dinner. ~ Kittycorner to Bunkhouse Inn on Main Street, Augusta; 406-562-3408. BUDGET.

HIDDEN ►

Well off the beaten track some 22 miles north of Choteau is **The Rose Room**, a supper club that is well known to area residents but which sees few visitors. In the heart of downtown Pendroy (population 25), the club does business in an old Farmers State Bank building—blink and you'll miss it. Call for reservations, then try the locally produced beef or the deep-fried shrimp. Dinner only. Closed Monday. ~ Route 219, Pendroy; 406-469-2205. DELUXE TO ULTRA-DELUXE.

NIGHTLIFE

HIDDEN ►

Katy's Wildlife Sanctuary is a very rustic local bar in a village some 14 miles north of Choteau. The only wildlife you'll find within its doors, however, is of the two-legged variety. It's a fun place to catch some true Montana flavor. Closed Monday. ~ 11 Front Street North, Bynum; 406-469-2214.

PARKS

LEWIS AND CLARK NATIONAL FOREST 🏃 🚴 🏇 🏊 🛶 The eastern edge of the Rocky Mountain Front, below the Bob Marshall Wilderness, and a handful of small mountain ranges southeast of Great Falls—the Little Belt, Big Snowy, Little Snowy, Highwood, Crazy and Castle mountains—are encompassed by this national forest. Facilities here include picnic tables and restrooms. ~ Reach the Rocky Mountain Front section of the forest via various secondary roads that lead west off Routes 89 and 287 from Choteau and Augusta. Route 89 (Kings Hill Scenic Byway) cuts through the Little Belt Mountains section of the forest between Great Falls and White Sulphur Springs; 406-791-7700, fax 406-731-5302.

▲ There are 241 RV/tent sites and 29 for tents only at 15 campgrounds, none with hookups; no charge to $10 per night; 14-day maximum stay. Closed mid-November to mid-May.

BOB MARSHALL WILDERNESS AREA 🕴 🐎 🏕️ 🎣 The second-largest wilderness in the lower 48 states, "The Bob" and its adjoining preserves (the Great Bear and Scapegoat wilderness areas) occupy more than one and a half million very wild, rugged and mountainous acres on the Continental Divide. Some 1800 miles of trails crisscross the region. ~ From the east, main access to "The Bob" is via Teton Canyon Road (off Route 89 near Choteau), which follows the Teton River nearly to its headwaters; Sun River Road (off Route 287 in Augusta), which ends at Gibson Reservoir; and Augusta Ranger Station Road (also from Augusta), which extends up Wood Creek. There are major trailheads at the terminus of each. You can also approach the wilderness from the west (off Route 83) or from the north (at Spotted Bear Ranger Station southeast of Hungry Horse). There are five major ranger stations: Rocky Mountain Ranger District, 406-466-5341, fax 406-466-2237; Spotted Bear Ranger Station, 406-758-5376, 406-387-3800; Lincoln Ranger District, 406-362-4265; Swan Lake Ranger District, 406-837-7500; and Seeley Lake Ranger District, 406-677-2233.

"The Bob," as it is known to wilderness lovers, preserves more than a million acres of rugged mountains, rivers and lakes.

▲ Primitive only.

The Western Hi-Line

Route 2, running east about 400 miles along the Canadian border from the Blackfeet Indian Reservation to Williston, North Dakota, and paralleled by the Great Northern Railway line, is known to Montanans as "the Hi-Line." The western section of this route runs from Cut Bank to Havre. Cattle ranching and grain production, notably wheat, sustain the economy of this northernmost tier of the state, which extends more than one-eighth of the way across the United States.

SIGHTS

At the eastern edge of the Blackfeet Indian Reservation, still within the shadow of the high peaks of Glacier National Park, is **Cut Bank,** a major grain-storage center that marks the western corner of Montana's Golden Triangle. This region, which stretches from Great Falls (100 miles southeast of Cut Bank) to Canada, from the Rocky Mountain Front to the Missouri River, is literally one of the breadbaskets of the nation. Farms between Havre and Cut

Bank produce more than half of the wheat and barley grown in Montana, one of the top five states in those commodities. You may see huge combine harvesters in the fields in late August and September.

Routes 2 and 15 intersect at the grain and railroad town of **Shelby**, 23 miles east of Cut Bank. Shelby's **Marias Museum of History and Art** recalls such snippets of past glory as the 1923 world heavyweight championship fight here between Jack Dempsey and Tommy Gibbons. In all, the ten-room museum displays 10,000 items, including several re-created early-20th-century rooms. The free museum is open daily except Sunday in summer; from September to May it's open Tuesday afternoons only. ~ 206 12th Avenue, Shelby; 406-424-2551.

> Between Shelby and the border, the Kevin-Sunburst Oil Field is Montana's largest: it has pumped some 80 million barrels of oil since its discovery in 1922.

Shelby is just 35 miles south (via Route 15) of the Canadian border at **Sweetgrass**, the busiest international port of entry between Blaine, Washington (connecting Seattle and Vancouver), and Pembina, North Dakota (connecting Minneapolis and Winnipeg).

Several Hutterite colonies are located in the region north of Great Falls and east of Glacier Park. People of German descent, the **Hutterites** follow a simple lifestyle similar in many ways to the Amish of the eastern United States. The men are always clad in black suits and hats, the women in colorful homemade skirts and kerchiefs on their heads. Communities include Rimrock (near Sunburst), Hillside (near Sweetgrass), Eagle Creek (near Galata), Rockport (near DuPuyer) and Miller (near Bynum). To visit one of their communities, inquire at the **Shelby Chamber of Commerce**. ~ 100 2nd Avenue South, Shelby; 406-434-7184; www.shelbymontana.org.

Along the eastern edge of the Kevin-Sunburst Oil field runs the **Whoop-Up Trail,** which connected the steamship port of Fort Benton with Fort Whoop-Up, on Canada's Old Man River, beginning in 1868. An important transportation link, it was partially restored by Boy Scouts in the 1960s; where the deeply rutted "bulltrain" trail crosses the Marias River southeast of Shelby, a historical marker notes the site of old Fort Conrad. Tepee rings left by nomadic Indian tribes are still visible along the Whoop-Up Trail.

In the little town of **Chester**, almost midway from Shelby to Havre, you'll find the **Liberty County Museum**. Housed in a former Methodist church, the museum is a repository of fascinating items and photographs from northern Montana's late-19th-century homesteading era. Closed in winter except by appointment. ~ 210 2nd Street East, Chester; 406-759-5256; in winter call Betty at 406-759-5274.

The area's leading recreational center is **Lake Elwell**, on the Marias River southwest of Chester. A marina near the Tiber Dam, open mid-May to mid-September, is a center for boating, fishing and camping, as well as autumn bird hunting.

Havre, the largest town on the Hi-Line (and the home of Montana State University–Northern), benefits economically from both the 100 miles of grain fields to its west and the 300 miles of ranch country to its east. The city hopes to attract history buffs with **Havre Beneath the Streets**, a four-year project (completed in 1994) ◄ HIDDEN that restored long-disused tunnels and underground corridors beneath the community. Developed around 1900 in the early days of the Great Northern Railway and last put to serious use by Prohibition-era bootleggers, they now welcome visitors. Public tours include a saloon, drugstore, meat market, bakery, barber shop, laundry, tack shop, hardware store and even a brothel and Chinese opium den. Closed Sunday in winter. Admission. ~ 120 3rd Avenue, Havre; 406-265-8888.

Havre got its start in 1879 when **Fort Assiniboine** was constructed; it was then the largest military fort west of the Mississippi River. ~ Route 87, six miles southwest of the current town site. Guided tours of the fort are offered through the **H. Earl Clack Memorial Museum**, which features archaeological and area history displays. Closed Monday and Tuesday. ~ 306 3rd Avenue, Havre; 406-265-4000.

The museum also organizes one-hour guided tours of the **Wahkpa Chug'n** archaeology site, a prehistoric campsite and bison kill ground on the banks of the Milk River, believed to have been used as long as 2000 years ago. ~ Behind Holiday Village Shopping Center, Route 2 West; 406-265-6417.

Twenty miles south of Havre is the **Rocky Boy's Indian Reservation**. Located in the foothills of the Bears Paw Mountains, the reservation is home to about 2500 Chippewas and Crees. ~ Box Elder; 406-395-4282.

How could you go wrong with a motel that matter-of-factly lists **LODGING** its location as "next to a 27-foot-tall Talking Penguin"? That Chilly Willy–looking fellow standing outside **Glacier Gateway Inn** trumpets the town's distinction as the "coldest spot in the nation," which it has been on occasion. The motel is not so ostentatious; its 18 rooms have queen-size beds and air conditioning (the latter presumedly for summers). There's also an exercise room, pool access and hot tub. Breakfasts are complimentary. ~ 1121 East Railroad Street, Cut Bank; 406-873-5544, 800-851-5541, fax 406-873-5546; www.glaciergatewayinn.com, e-mail glacierg@northerntel.net. MODERATE.

In Shelby, the **O'Haire Manor Motel** has 37 rooms in a two-story establishment with a modern fitness room and hot tub. All rooms have cable TV and phones, and there's a coin laundry as well. ~ 204 2nd Street South, Shelby; 406-434-5555, 800-541-5809, fax 406-434-2702. BUDGET.

TownHouse Inns of Havre boasts the most full-service accommodation on Montana's northern plains. There's an atrium swimming pool, spa, fitness room and sauna. The casino claims to be "Havre's most liberal." Wood furnishings are a nice touch, as are the whirlpool baths. ~ 601 West 1st Street, Havre; 406-265-6711, fax 406-265-6213. MODERATE.

El Toro Inn is a good alternative for wallet watchers. With 41 rooms off two floors of inside corridors, this is a cozy motel with cable TV and a guest laundry. Microwave ovens and refrigerators come with every room, and children 11 and younger stay free with adults. ~ 521 1st Street, Havre; 406-265-5414, 800-422-5414. MODERATE.

DINING   **Uncle Joe's** has two distinct dining atmospheres. The dimly lit, downstairs dining room is the setting for a romantic dinner of moderate-to-deluxe-priced steak and seafood. Upstairs, lively patrons enjoy budget-to-moderate-priced ribs, chicken and burgers. No lunch downstairs. Closed Monday. ~ 1400 1st Street, Havre; 406-265-1013. BUDGET TO DELUXE.

Boxcars appeals to the northern palate with its menu of Mexican cuisine, fried chicken, panini sandwiches and the like. The restaurant, done up in the decor of an old railroad station, has an adjoining lounge and casino. Closed Sunday. ~ 619 1st Street, Havre; 406-265-2233. BUDGET.

A few doors down, **4B's Restaurant** is open 24 hours for family-style fare such as burgers and prime rib. ~ 604 West 1st Street, Havre; 406-265-9721. BUDGET.

NIGHTLIFE   The back bar at the **Palace Bar** was built in St. Louis in 1883 and carried up the Missouri River on a steamboat. Towering and ornate, it is worth a visit just to see it. ~ 228 1st Street, Havre; 406-265-7584.

PARKS   **BEAVER CREEK COUNTY PARK** Extending for 16 miles along Beaver Creek Road south of Havre, this is one of the nation's largest county park, covering approximately 10,000 acres. There's fishing in two lakes and many fine scenic views. Facilities include picnic tables and restrooms. ~ Take Route 234 (Beaver Creek Road) south from Havre toward Rocky Boy's Indian Reservation; 406-395-4565.

▲ There are 100 RV/tent campsites, no hookups; $8 per night.

Historic Fort Benton, 42 miles northeast of Great
Falls via Route 87, has been called "the birthplace
of Montana." Established as a Missouri River

Fort Benton Area

trading post for buffalo robes by the American Fur Company in
1846, it was named for Missouri senator Thomas Hart Benton.
Its importance mushroomed in 1860, when steamboats began
docking here after journeying from St. Louis or New Orleans; no
port in the world was farther (3485 miles) from an ocean.

For the next 27 years, until the Great Northern Railroad arrived
in 1887, effectively ending river trade, Fort Benton was the most
important city in Montana. The **Riverfront Steamboat Levee**, now
a National Historic Landmark, became the rowdiest four blocks
in the West after gold was discovered in the nearby hills in 1862.
Saloons and brothels were open 24 hours a day,
and gunfights were more common than royal
flushes. ~ Front Street between 14th and 18th
streets; www.fortbenton.com. The restored **I.G.
Baker House** once was the headquarters for the most
powerful trading company in the territory. ~ Front
Street between 16th and 17th streets. **St. Paul's
Episcopal Church** was built in Norman-Gothic style by
stonemasons in 1880. ~ Choteau and 14th streets.

SIGHTS

Many of the buildings facing
the Riverfront Steamboat
Levee date from the
steamboat era, including
the Grand Union Hotel,
the mercantile T. C.
Power & Co. and the
city's first firehouse.

The only building still standing on the site of **Old Fort
Benton** is an adobe blockhouse, believed to be the oldest
standing building in Montana. Reconstructions of the trade
store, warehouse, blacksmith shop and carpenter shop are un-
derway. Interpretive signs describe the layout of the rest of the
fort, some ruins of which remain. ~ Old Fort Park, Front Street.
Artifacts from the fort and the town's heyday are on display next
to the fort in the **Museum of the Upper Missouri**. Open summers
only, or in winter by appointment. Admission. ~ Front and 19th
streets; 406-622-5905; www.ftbenton.com.

Opposite the museum, on the riverbank, stands the **Lewis
and Clark State Memorial**, a bronze sculpture of the two explorers with their native guide, Sacajawea, by Bob Scriver. About
four blocks north, the **Museum of the Northern Great Plains** is
Montana's state agricultural museum, with exhibits that trace a
century of farm history as well as a veritable outdoor park of antique machinery. The Smithsonian's collection of mounted Horna-
day buffalo is a permanent feature here. Open summers only. Admission. ~ 1205 20th Street; 406-622-5316; www.ftbenton.com.

Fort Benton's position on the Missouri River has not been
forgotten in modern times: It is the primary departure point for
commercial boat tours and float trips down the **Upper Missouri**

National Wild and Scenic River. There are also canoe rentals and all varieties of non-motorized boating. Contact the Bureau of Land Management for information. ~ P.O. Box 1160, Lewistown, MT 59457; 406-538-7461, fax 406-538-1904.

From Fort Benton to the James Kipp Recreation Area northeast of Lewistown, the broad, slow-flowing Missouri winds through the scenic White Cliffs, Citadel Rock State Monument, Hole-in-the-Wall and other geological curiosities, offering sightings of abandoned homesteads and a great deal of wildlife. The **Upper Missouri River Visitors Center** has full information for prospective river travelers. Closed in winter. ~ 1718 Front Street, Fort Benton; 406-622-5185.

Tiny **Loma**, 14 miles northeast of Fort Benton up Route 87 where the Marias River enters the Missouri, is of note for a small but excellent museum. The **House of a Thousand Dolls** displays numerous playthings dating back to the 1830s. Open by appointment only; closed October through May. Admission. ~ 106 1st Street, Loma; 406-739-4338. The little town also features a picturesque trail along the banks of the Missouri, with interpretive signs describing the steamboat era.

There's a shuttle service for floaters and canoeists 28 miles northeast of Fort Benton at Virgelle's Coal Bank Landing, a primary put-in point for floats of the Missouri River Breaks. After Virgelle, the Missouri turns east while Route 87 proceeds north.

Southeast of Fort Benton via Route 80 is the community of **Square Butte**, a gateway to the BLM-administered **Square Butte Natural Area**, noted for its geology, its raptor colony and population of wild goats. Public access is across private property and can be variable. ~ 406-538-1900. Also nearby is the **Highwood Mountains** national forest region, popular among hikers and campers.

LODGING   There are two small motels in Fort Benton. Neither is anything spectacular, but both are adequate. The 11-room **Fort Motel** is located on Route 87. ~ 1809 St. Charles Street, Fort Benton; 406-622-3312. BUDGET.

Pioneer Lodge is housed in the former T. C. Power & Co. store facing the levee. Historical themes flavor each room. Continental breakfast. ~ 1700 Front Street, Fort Benton; 406-622-5441, 800-622-6088, fax 406-622-5413; www.pioneerlodge mt.com, e-mail pioldgmt@aol.com. MODERATE.

DINING   The **Banque Club** occupies the premises of the former Stockman's National Bank on the levee opposite the Grand Union Hotel. The days of the open range may be gone, but the cuts of homegrown Montana beef served up at this supper club perpetuate the memory. Dinner only. ~ 1318 Front Street, Fort Benton; 406-622-5272. BUDGET TO DELUXE.

The Kings Hill area south of Great Falls, an alternate and
more direct route from the city to Yellowstone National
Park, is known for its rural pleasures and scenic vistas in
the Little Belt Mountains. The interesting old spa and mining
town of White Sulphur Springs are en route.

Kings Hill

For 23 miles east from Great Falls, Route 89 runs together with
Routes 87 and 200 across rolling farmland. An interesting detour
en route is **Mehmke's Steam Engine Museum**. This is a large, privately owned collection of steam engines, all of them still operational. A sizeable variety of other antique farm machinery is also
on display. It's a mechanic's dream . . . or nightmare. ~ Route 87,
10 miles east of Route 89; 406-452-6571.

SIGHTS

Near Belt, Route 89 turns south off Route 87/200 as the
Kings Hill Scenic Byway, crossing the Little Belt Mountains to
White Sulphur Springs. ~ 406-547-3361.

This 71-mile Lewis and Clark National Forest highway follows
Belt Creek past **Sluice Boxes State Park,** located at an abandoned
railroad grade. ~ Evans-Riceville Road, Belt; 406-454-5840, fax
406-761-8477. The highway rolls on through the historic mining
and ranching communities of Neihart and Monarch to 7393-foot
Kings Hill Pass. On the south side of the pass is the **Showdown
Ski Area,** Montana's oldest. ~ Route 89, Neihart; 406-236-5522,
800-433-0022; www.showdownmontana.com.

On the east side of the Big Belt Mountains, about 28 miles
south of Showdown, is the town of **White Sulphur Springs**. The
namesake hot springs here have high levels of chloride, sulfate,
sodium, potassium and bicarbonate, as well as calcium, silica
and magnesium. Known for centuries by Ameri-
can Indians, today the 135° springs are enclosed
by (and cooled at) the **Spa Hot Springs Motel.** Two
pools are open year-round to the public. Admission.
~ 202 West Main Street, White Sulphur Springs; 406-
547-3366, fax 406-547-3378; www.spahotsprings.
com, e-mail spabear59645@yahoo.com.

The hot springs from
which the town of White
Sulphur Springs takes its
name have been com-
pared to Germany's
famed Baden-Baden
spa.

The casual visitor to White Sulphur Springs is more
likely to spot the cut-sandstone Victorian mansion, looming high on a hill over the town, than the springs themselves.
This is **The Castle,** built in 1892 as a private home and now hous-
ing the **Meagher County Museum.** Open summers, the museum
displays period furnishings and memorabilia of regional history; an
adjacent carriage house exhibits antique buggies. Admission. ~ 310
2nd Avenue Northeast, White Sulphur Springs; 406-547-2324.

The White Sulphur Springs area was once awash in mineral
wealth. An 1864 gold strike in Confederate Gulch yielded $16
million worth of ore in a half-dozen years, but few ruins remain
at the site of Diamond City, the hub of the boom.

A few original log buildings survive at **Fort Logan**, 18 miles northwest of White Sulphur Springs via Route 360. Listed on the National Register of Historic Places, the 1870 army post was constructed to protect miners from hostile Indians. A blockhouse, a stable and officers quarters remain at the site, now a ranch headquarters. Five miles beyond Fort Logan is **Camp Baker**, launch point for rafting and float-fishing trips down the Smith River.

LODGING

Right on the Kings Hill Byway, ten miles south of Showdown, the **Montana Mountain Lodge** offers five rooms with private baths. In winter, cross-country skiers can head out on extensive trail systems that begin at the front door. In summer there's hiking and fishing. The lodge provides a hot tub, of course. A full breakfast is included, and dinner is available. ~ 1780 Route 89 North, White Sulphur Springs; 406-547-3773; www.montanamountain lodge.com, e-mail mtlodge@ttc-cmc.net. MODERATE.

American Indians called them "wampum waters." Today, two year-round pools at the **Spa Hot Springs Motel** contain the healing mineral waters of White Sulphur Springs. The motel's 21 rooms have private baths and offer free access to the pools (nonguests pay an admission fee). ~ 202 West Main Street, White Sulphur Springs; 406-547-3366, fax 406-547-3378. MODERATE.

The **Bonanza Creek Country** is an all-inclusive guest ranch, 40 miles east of White Sulphur Springs off Route 12, that keeps an intimate feeling by restricting itself to just 12 guests at any one time. There's a variety of lodging: an 1880s duplex, a Plains Indian tepee, a cowboy's cabin, even an American Indian–themed cabin. Horseback riding, hiking and fishing are favored activities here. Six-night minimum. Closed mid-September through May. ~ Lennep Route, Martinsdale; 406-572-3366, 800-476-6045, fax 406-572-3366; www.bonanzacreekcountry.com, e-mail bonanza@3rivers.net. ULTRA-DELUXE.

DINING

For mouth-watering goodness, locals recommend the **Mint Bar's** broasted chicken. The rest of its menu (chicken, fish, shrimp— everything except its burgers) is prepared in a pressure cooker. ~ 27 East Main Street; White Sulphur Springs; 406-547-9986. BUDGET.

Slide into a booth at **Happy Days Cafe**, a mom-and-pop diner that whips up three square meals a day. Omelettes and pancakes are the usual breakfast fare; sandwiches, burgers and salads make up the lunch menu; and steaks, fish-and-chips, and pork chops are some of the dinner items. ~ 307 3rd Avenue Southwest, White Sulphur Springs; 406-547-2223. BUDGET TO MODERATE.

PARKS

SLUICE BOXES STATE PARK 🏃 ⏝ Deep in the gold-rush country of the Little Belt Mountains, this park incorporates a trail that leads along an abandoned railroad grade to impressive geological features. Restrooms are available at the trailhead. ~ Take Route 89 eight miles south from Belt off Route 200; the park trailhead is about half a mile down the Evans-Riceville Road; 406-454-5840, fax 406-761-8477.

SMITH RIVER STATE PARK 🛶 🚣 At this unique state park, a 59-mile stretch of the remote Smith River canyon is set aside for rafters and fishermen on float trips. River enthusiasts put in at Camp Baker, 26 miles northwest of White Sulphur Springs, and take out at Eden Bridge, about 20 miles south of Great Falls. Permits are required, and are distributed by lottery. The lottery deadline is approximately February 15th every year. Facilities include picnic tables, toilets and hand-launch access. ~ To the put-in, take Route 360 northwest from White Sulphur Springs 16 miles toward Fort Logan, then follow signs north eight miles on Smith River Road to Camp Baker; 406-454-5840, fax 406-761-8477.

Visitors must cross a river to get to Sluice Boxes State Park, limiting hiking to low-water season (mid-July to October).

▲ There are 27 primitive camps for boaters and rafters.

North central Montana spans the extremes of cold-water and warm-water fishing in the northern Rockies. At higher elevations, the

Outdoor Adventures

FISHING

Teton River and other streams flowing from the Rocky Mountain Front are excellent for several species of trout. The Milk and Marias rivers carry trout, catfish and perch. Warm-water species like bass, walleye, northern pike, catfish and perch do well in the Missouri River, especially below Fort Benton.

A good bet is **Wolverton's Fly Shop.** They can provide you with fly-fishing gear and guides. Closed Sunday and Monday. ~ 210 5th Street South, Great Falls; 406-454-0254.

Contact **Montana River Outfitters** for trips on the Smith, the south fork of the Flathead, and the Missouri rivers. Trips may last up to seven days. Closed weekends in winter. ~ 923 10th Avenue North, Great Falls; 406-761-1677; www.mountainriver outfitters.com.

BOATING

Ask about commercial boat tours, or get information about renting a vessel and navigating downstream, at the **Upper Missouri River Visitors Center.** Closed in winter. ~ 1718 Front Street, Fort Benton; 406-622-5185. You can also obtain information at the wild and scenic river headquarters north of Lewistown. ~ Route 191; 406-538-7461. Among the leading commercial operators is **Missouri River Outfitters.** ~ P.O. Box 762, Fort Benton, MT 59442; 406-622-3295; www.mroutfitters.com.

Elsewhere in the region, the Tiber Marina on Lake Elwell, southwest of Chester, offers boat rentals, and such lakes as Gibson Reservoir (west of Choteau) and Lake Frances (at Valier) have boat launches and other facilities.

RIVER RUNNING

Most of the rivers of eastern Montana are too slow for whitewater rafting, and many of them are quite muddy. An exception is the Smith River south of Great Falls, a 61-mile stretch administered by the Montana Department of Fish, Wildlife & Parks. ~ 406-454-5840. **Montana River Outfitters** rents rafts and offers guided voyages on the Smith and Flathead rivers, and to the white cliffs of the Missouri. Closed weekends in winter. ~ 923 10th Avenue North, Great Falls; 406-761-1677. **Missouri River Canoe Company** also offers guided trips, rents canoes and kayaks and operates a shuttle for independent Missouri River floaters at the Virgelle river-ferry landing about 30 miles northeast of Fort Benton. Closed November through April. ~ 406-378-3110; www. paddlemontana.com.

DOWNHILL SKIING

None of the ski areas in eastern Montana has on-site lodging, but there are several excellent day resorts.

Showdown Ski Area, established in 1936 on the Kings Hill Scenic Byway 60 miles south of Great Falls, is Montana's oldest ski area. The resort in the Little Belt Mountains has two chairlifts and two tows serving 34 runs and 1400 feet of vertical from an 8200-foot summit. ~ Route 89, Neihart; 406-236-5522, 800-433-0022; www.showdownmontana.com.

Teton Pass Ski Area is in Lewis and Clark National Forest on the fringe of the Bob Marshall Wilderness, 35 miles west of Choteau. The area boasts 25 trails served by a chairlift and a rope tow; vertical drop is 1010 feet from a 7200-foot summit. ~ West Fork Teton River Road, Choteau; 406-466-2209, 406-466-3666; ski tetonpass.com.

Bear Paw Ski Bowl draws its clientele from the Havre area. It has one chairlift, one tow and 25 runs on a 900-foot vertical drop from a summit elevation of 5280 feet. ~ Rocky Boy's Indian Reservation, Box Elder; 406-265-8404; www.skibearpaw.com.

Ski Rentals The large, well-stocked **Scheels All Sports** rents downhill skis. ~ 3 Holiday Village Mall, 1200 10th Avenue South, Great Falls; 406-453-7666.

CROSS-COUNTRY SKIING

The **Kings Hill Winter Sports Complex** has 18 kilometers of groomed trails for all abilities in Lewis and Clark National Forest. ~ Route 89, Neihart; 406-236-5511.

Ski Rentals **Bighorn Wilderness** specializes in telemark skis. Closed Sunday. ~ 600 Central Avenue, Great Falls; 406-453-2841.

GOLF

Among the leading 18-hole public courses is the **Eagle Falls Golf Course**. ~ River Road, Great Falls; 406-761-1078. Tee off at the

Marias Valley Golf & Country Club. This medium-to-difficult 18-hole course is built around the Marias River. There's a pro shop and snack bar. ~ Route 417 South, Shelby; 406-434-5940; www.mvgc.com. The nine-hole **Beaver Creek Golf Course** crosses Beaver Creek twice. The course has a pro shop, equipment rentals and a driving range. ~ Route 2 West, Havre; 406-265-7861.

In Great Falls, **Montana Park** has four courts. ~ 18th Street Southwest and Fox Farm Road. Contact Great Falls Recreation & Park Activities for more information. ~ 1700 River Drive North; 406-771-1265.

TENNIS

Bonanza Creek Country, a guest ranch east of White Sulphur Springs, offers rides into the Crazy and Castle mountains. ~ Lennep Route, Martinsdale; 800-476-6045.

RIDING STABLES

For trips into the Bob Marshall Wilderness and Two Medicine, take a five- to eight-day trip with the reputable **A Lazy H Outfitters**. ~ P.O. Box 1079, Choteau, MT 59422; 406-466-5564, 800-893-1155; www.alazyh.com. There's also the **JJJ Wilderness Ranch** for five- to ten-day treks through the Bob Marshall Wilderness. ~ P.O. Box 310, Augusta, MT 59410; 406-562-3653; www.triplejranch.com.

PACK TRIPS

National Forest roads and trails are generally open to mountain biking, but wheeled vehicles—motorized or not—are not allowed in designated wilderness areas. Local bicycle shops have information on planned activities and mountain-biking routes.

BIKING

Among the most popular areas for mountain bikers is Kings Hill, with 212 miles of trails from the Showdown Ski Area. The 12-mile **Kings Hill Loop Trail**, at about 7500 feet elevation, is a favorite of many. ~ Route 89, Neihart; 406-547-3361. In the **Highwood Mountains**, where there are 16 miles of trails, novices like the two-and-a-half-mile **Thain Creek Loop Trail** at 4600 feet elevation. ~ Highwood Road, Highwood; 406-791-7700.

> Great Falls' River Road, which follows the Missouri River downstream for five miles from downtown's 10th Avenue Bridge to Giant Springs/ Heritage State Park, is paralleled by the River's Edge Trail, an immensely popular urban bike route.

Bike Rentals Knicker Biker offers rentals, repairs and information. Closed Sunday. ~ 1123 Central Avenue, Great Falls; 406-454-2912.

All distances listed for hiking trails are one way unless otherwise noted.

HIKING

GREAT FALLS River's Edge Trail (5 miles) follows an abandoned railway bed through Great Falls, along the east and south shores of the Missouri River. The trail begins at Oddfellows Park, just under the Warden Street Bridge, and continues to Giant Springs/Heritage State Park. Along the way, you'll encounter Crooked Falls. The trail connects with several other parks, and draws bicyclists, in-line skaters and runners as well as day hikers. ~ 406-444-2535.

Located within Giant Springs/Heritage State Park, the **North Shore Trail** (11 miles) follows Lewis and Clark's route as they discovered the great falls of the Missouri. Pristine and nearly untouched, it's a wonderful near-wilderness experience.

ROCKY MOUNTAIN FRONT Mill Falls Trail (.1 mile) is a short stroll from the Mill Falls Campground to a cascade surrounded by fir and spruce trees. It begins about 30 miles west of Choteau off Forest Road 109.

Clary Coulee Trail (6 miles), which begins 26 miles west of Choteau off Canyon Road, climbs more than 1200 feet above the North Fork of the Teton River and along the eastern ridge of Choteau Mountain, yielding far-reaching, panoramic views of the Great Plains.

Mortimer Gulch National Recreation Trail (5 miles) zigzags up a 550-foot ridge above Gibson Reservoir; deer, elk and bighorn sheep are often seen in spring, and the views are wonderful year-round. It begins 35 miles west of Augusta via Sun River Road.

WESTERN HI-LINE The **Sweet Grass Hills**, northeast of Shelby and just south of the Canadian border, are administered by the BLM as a special recreation management area; from the north side of East Butte, try the scenic, undeveloped 3-mile ascent to the 6958-foot East Butte. This area, which is of great spiritual importance to American Indians, hosts an impressive herd of elk.

FORT BENTON AREA Windy Mountain/Briggs Creek Trail (7 miles) is a loop trek through the Highwood Mountains, 42 miles east of Great Falls in Lewis and Clark National Forest. The trail climbs gradually up a creek bed and descends a mountain slope.

KINGS HILL The **Porphyry Peak-Ranch Creek Trail** (10 miles) climbs 1.2 miles from Kings Hill Pass to the fire lookout (manned in summer) above the Showdown Ski Area, then descends Mizpah Ridge, circumventing a steep cirque to Ranch Creek. Follow the blue diamond signs designating it as a winter cross-country trail.

Equipment **Big Horn Wilderness** is the best place to fill your hiking needs before hitting the trail. ~ 600 Central Avenue, Great Falls; 406-453-2841.

Transportation

CAR

Four principal highways provide the thread that binds north central Montana. Great Falls is at the easternmost point of **Route 15**, which extends north from Helena to the Canadian border. **Route 87**, though not a freeway, directly connects Great Falls with Billings, 230 miles southeast, and with Havre, 112 miles northeast. **Route 89** runs north from Yellowstone National Park through White Sulphur Springs and Great Falls en route to Glacier National Park. Finally, **Route 2**, the Hi-Line, extends east from Glacier National Park through Havre and on to North Dakota.

Great Falls International Airport, the region's principal terminal, is served by Big Sky, Delta, Northwest, Skywest and Horizon Airlines. ~ 406-727-3404; www.gtfairport.com. **Havre City County Airport** is a regional airport served by Big Sky Airlines from Billings. ~ 406-265-4671.

AIR

Rimrock Trailways serves all of Montana's major cities and many of its smaller ones. ~ 800-255-7655. In Great Falls, it arrives and departs from the Union Bus Depot. ~ 1st Avenue South and 4th Street; 406-453-1541.

BUS

Amtrak's (800-872-7245; www.amtrak.com) Seattle–Chicago "Empire Builder" makes several stops on the Hi-Line east of Glacier National Park. They are in Cut Bank at 4 Route 2 and Central Avenue; in Shelby at 198½ B.N. Right of Way, 406-434-5031; in Havre at 235 Main Street, 406-265-5381; and in Malta at 51 South 1st Street.

TRAIN

Great Falls International Airport has the following rental agencies: **Avis Rent A Car** (800-331-1212), **Enterprise Rent A Car** (800-325-8007), **Hertz Rent A Car** (800-654-3131) and **National Car Rental** (800-328-4567). At the Havre Airport you'll also find **Budget Rent A Car** (800-527-0700).

CAR RENTALS

Great Falls Transit, known by the acronym GFT, has extensive bus networks throughout the city and its suburbs. Adult fares are less than $1. Buses run from 6 a.m. to 6:30 p.m. Monday through Friday and from 9:30 a.m. to 5:30 p.m. on Saturday. ~ 406-727-0382.

PUBLIC TRANSIT

In Great Falls, dial **Diamond Cab**, which also operates wheelchair-accessible vans. ~ 1000 11th Street North; 406-453-3241.

TAXIS

FIVE

Southwest Montana

Mining discoveries near the crest of the Continental Divide provided the initial impetus for Montana's growth. More than a
century and a quarter later, that mining heritage remains the
unifying theme throughout southwest Montana.

The Montana Territory was established in 1862 after major
gold discoveries at Bannack and Virginia City—the former now
a ghost town, the latter saved from that fate by tourism. Statehood was granted in 1889; the capitol has remained for more than 100 years in
another gold-boom town, Helena. Its main street is still called Last Chance Gulch,
and nearby Victorian mansions attest to its former affluence.

Soon after Montana became a state, world demand for copper turned Butte into
"the richest hill on earth." At the turn of the 20th century, more than 100,000
people lived in the city. Today, its population is barely a third that large. But Butte's
stately and historic downtown (referred to as "Uptown" for its hillside location)
is more reminiscent of 19th-century San Francisco than of any other town in the
Rockies. Butte's copper mines continue to be America's most productive.

If you want to see what *might* have happened to Butte, pay a visit to one or
more of the myriad ghost towns on either side of the Continental Divide. Some,
like the former territorial capitals of Bannack (now a state park) and Virginia
City (a bustling tourist mecca), are well preserved. Many others are no more than
names on maps and perhaps a foundation or two.

In addition to the historical value of the region's cities, ghost towns and bat-
tlefields, southwest Montana offers sterling natural features (such as the Gates of
the Mountains on the Missouri River near Helena), manmade attractions (including Butte's World Museum of Mining), wildlife viewing and outdoor-sports
opportunities throughout its national forests and wilderness areas.

▼▼▼▼▼▼▼▼▼▼
Helena Area

An 1864 gold strike in Last Chance Gulch led to the founding of Helena, nestled between the Continental Divide and
the Missouri River. Dubbed the "Queen City of the Rockies"

because of its grand architecture and cultural sophistication, Helena became the capital of the Montana Territory within a year of its founding and ultimately was chosen as the state capital.

Aside from its urban enticements, the city is an access point to numerous ghost towns and scenic attractions, including Helena National Forest and the Gates of the Mountains Wilderness, where the Missouri River leaves the mountains and heads into the northeastern plains.

Helena's gold rush lasted for about two decades, a period during which, in today's dollars, an estimated $3.6 billion worth of the mineral was taken from Last Chance Gulch. Today, Last Chance Gulch is the historic main street of this colorful town of 28,000, and the three-block stretch from 6th Avenue to Wong Street is a pedestrian mall. Markers describe statues and buildings of historical and architectural significance, including an old bordello.

Self-guided walks of **Last Chance Gulch** and the surrounding **Capital City Historic District** are described in brochures available from the Helena Chamber of Commerce. ~ 225 Cruse Avenue, Suite A, Helena; 406-442-4120. Or take the **Last Chance Tour Train**, a four-car trolley that offers one-hour city tours from mid-May through September. Trips begin more or less hourly from outside the Montana Historical Society, opposite the State Capitol. Closed mid-September through April. Fare. ~ 6th Avenue and Roberts Street, Helena; 406-442-1023, 888-423-1023, fax 406-442-1003; www.lctours.com, e-mail lholmes@lctours.com.

SIGHTS

Within the historic district, more distinctive even than the capitol is the **St. Helena Cathedral**, its two gothic spires towering high above Last Chance Gulch. Modeled after the famous cathedral of Cologne, Germany, and the Votive Church of Vienna, Austria, the cathedral was completed in 1913. Its multimillion dollar stained-glass windows (by F. X. Zettler of Munich) are reputed to be the finest series ever produced by Zettler. The breathtaking interior includes hand-carved oak pews, an altar and stations of the Cross in Italian marble, and bronze light fixtures. ~ 530 North Ewing Street, Helena; 406-442-5825.

The **Montana State Capitol** and the surrounding capital district lie about a mile east of Last Chance Gulch. Completed in 1902 and expanded ten years later, the imposing neoclassical capitol building features a copper-faced dome that rises 165 feet above its 14-acre grounds. Its exterior is of Montana sandstone and granite; the interior is decorated in French Renaissance style. Of particular note are panels by noted painters depicting themes from the state's past. A mural by Charles M. Russell is among the artist's masterpieces: *Lewis and Clark Meeting Indians at Ross' Hole* covers the wall above the rostrum of the House of Representatives. Check with the Montana Historical Society (406-444-2694; www.montanahistoricalsociety.org) for up-to-date tour information. ~ 6th Avenue at Montana Avenue, Helena.

Opposite the capitol is the excellent museum of the **Montana Historical Society**. Its largest permanent gallery traces the history of the state, from prehistory through World War II; there are also galleries of Russell's art. The state archives are also housed here, and there's a museum store. Closed Sunday. Admission. ~ 225 North Roberts Street, Helena; 406-444-2694; www.montanahis toricalsociety.org.

The official residence of Montana's governor has moved, but the **Original Governor's Mansion** is open for guided tours. Built in 1888, the Victorian mansion three blocks above Last Chance Gulch was the home of nine governors between 1913 and 1959. Other impressive late-19th-century mansions can be glimpsed on a driving or walking tour of the **mansion district**, located northwest of Last Chance Gulch, mainly west of Benton Avenue and south of Hauser Boulevard. Call ahead for tour schedule. Admission. ~ 304 North Ewing Street, Helena; 406-444-4789, 800-243-9900; www.montanahistoricalsociety.org.

Other historic attractions in downtown Helena include the **Helena Civic Center**, a former Shrine temple built in exotic Moorish style with a needle-slim minaret, now the home of a large auditorium and a multi-purpose room used for community activities. ~ 340 Neill Avenue; 406-447-8481, fax 406-447-8480; www.ci.helena.mt.us, e-mail dstavnes@ci.helena.mt.us. The **Old Fire Tower**, erected in 1876, is one of five of its type still standing in the United States. ~ Congress and Pine streets. The **Pioneer Cabin**, Helena's oldest structure, was built in 1864 and still houses many original furnishings. It's recently been restored. Open summer weekdays or by appointment. ~ 200 South Park Street; 406-443-7641. Just off Last Chance Gulch, the **Holter Museum of Art** features changing exhibits of contemporary and historical art. Closed Monday in winter. ~ 12 East Lawrence Street; 406-442-6400, fax 406-442-2404; www.holtermuseum.org, e-mail pheld@holtermuseum.org.

Looming 1300 feet above Last Chance Gulch is **Mount Helena**, which offers seven separate hiking trails to its peak. For more information see the "Hiking" section in this chapter.

A series of Missouri River reservoirs, created by early-20th-century dams, provide wide recreational opportunities east of Helena. **Holter Lake**, **Hauser Lake** and **Canyon Ferry Lake** attract walleye, trout, kokanee salmon and perch anglers, as well as boaters, waterskiers and board sailors.

If you've never been bitten by the rockhounding bug, you should discover for yourself what the fuss is all about and screen

Text continued on page 142.

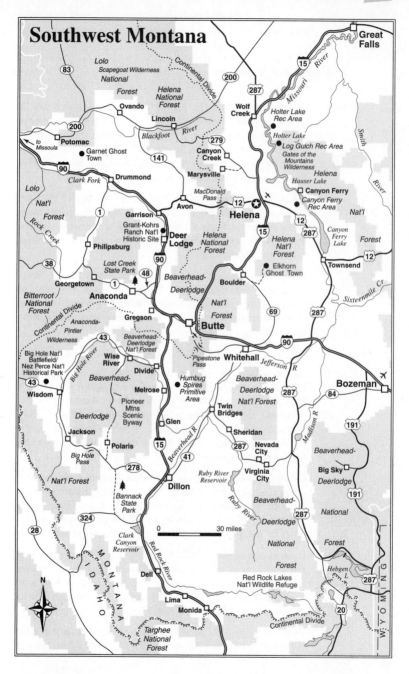

Southwest Montana

Great Falls

83
Lolo
Scapegoat Wilderness
Helena National Forest
National
Forest
Continental Divide
200
287
15
Missouri River
Smith River

Ovando
Lincoln
Wolf Creek
Holter Lake Rec Area

200
Potomac
to Missoula
Blackfoot River
279
Holter Lake
Log Gulch Rec Area
Gates of the Mountains Wilderness
Hauser Lake
Helena

Garnet Ghost Town
Canyon Creek
141
90
Clark Fork
Drummond
Marysville
MacDonald Pass
Canyon Ferry
Canyon Ferry Rec Area

Lolo Nat'l Forest
Avon
12
Helena
Nat'l Forest

1
Garrison
Grant-Kohrs Ranch Nat'l Historic Site
Deer Lodge
Helena National Forest
15
287
12
Canyon Ferry Lake

Philipsburg
Rock Creek
90
Helena Nat'l Forest
12

38
Lost Creek State Park
48
Beaverhead-Deerlodge
Boulder
Elkhorn Ghost Town
Townsend

Georgetown
1
Anaconda
Nat'l
Forest
69
287

Bitterroot National Forest
Gregson
Butte
90

Continental Divide
Anaconda-Pintler Wilderness
43
Beaverhead-Deerlodge Nat'l Forest
Pipestone Pass
Whitehall
Jefferson R.
Bozeman

Big Hole Nat'l Battlefield/Nez Perce Nat'l Historical Park
43
Wise River
Divide
Humbug Spires Primitive Area
Beaverhead-Deerlodge Nat'l Forest
287
84

Wisdom
Big Hole River
Beaverhead-
Melrose
Twin Bridges
191

Jackson
Deerlodge
Pioneer Mtns Scenic Byway
Glen
Sheridan
Beaverhead-

Polaris
15
287
Nevada City
Big Sky
Deerlodge

Big Hole Pass
278
Beaverhead R.
41
Virginia City
191

28
Nat'l Forest
Dillon
Ruby River Reservoir
Beaverhead-
287
National

324
Bannack State Park
0   30 miles
Ruby River
Deerlodge
Forest

Clark Canyon Reservoir
Red Rock River
National

M O N T A N A
I D A H O
Dell
Forest
Red Rock Lakes Nat'l Wildlife Refuge
Hebgen L.
287
W Y O M I N G

N
Lima
Monida
Continental Divide
20

Targhee National Forest

Helena to Jackson

Day 1 • Leaving **Helena** (page 136) early, drive 20 miles north on Route 15 to **Gates of the Mountains** (page 142). Take the narrated boat tour to this appealing Lewis and Clark site. Browse through the visitor exhibits before or after your tour. Return to Helena for lunch at the **Windbag Saloon** (page 145). Check into luxurious **The Sanders—Helena's Bed & Breakfast** (page 144).

• For an introduction to Montana's capital city, hop aboard the **Last Chance Tour Train** (page 137). Then join one of the guided tours of the **Montana State Capitol** (page 137). Afterward, visit the nearby **Montana Historical Society** (page 138) with its excellent museum and bookstore.

• Before dinner, peruse the titles at the **Main News Smoke Shop** (page 146) then head to **On Broadway** (page 145), one of Helena's finest restaurants. If you're still feeling perky, see if the **Myrna Loy Center for the Performing and Media Arts** (page 147) has a film or concert scheduled.

Day 2 • Continue your tour of Helena by visiting the twin-spired **St. Helena Cathedral** (page 137) and the **Original Governor's Mansion** (page 138), where you can take a guided tour. At this point, you can either drive straight to **Deer Lodge** (page 151), Montana's museum capital, or linger in Helena before hitting the highway with a detour to the **Archie Bray Foundation for the Ceramic Arts** (page 146).

• Follow Route 12 west then pick up Route 90 south, exiting at Deer Lodge (56 miles total). Make your first stop **Grant-Kohrs Ranch National Historic Site** (page 151), where costumed interpreters re-enact and describe the open-range cattle era. Plan on at least two hours for seeing the fabulous 23-room ranch home and outbuildings.

• If you passed on the Archie Bray tour in Helena, spend the rest of the afternoon at one or more of Deer Lodge's six downtown museums. One ticket gains you entry into all of them. If time or energy is running short, go for the biggies—the **Montana Auto Museum** (page 151) and the **Old Montana Prison** (page 151).

• Treat yourself to a double-dip ice cream cone at the stand outside the prison then follow Route 90 east (30 miles) to Exit 211 and drive three miles to **Fairmont Hot Springs Resort** (page 152). Dine at the resort (where you'll also spend the night). Be sure to take along a swimsuit to relax in those soothing mineral pools.

Day 3
• You can pass a leisurely morning playing at the Fairmont. Choose between golfing, horseback riding and water sliding. Or aim directly for **Big Hole National Battlefield** (page 165), 81 miles away via Routes 90, 15 and 43.

• Before entering this National Historic Park, stop in **Wisdom** (page 164) for lunch or to grab a sandwich to go. Reserve the afternoon for learning about the tragic 1877 conflict between the Nez Perce Indians and the U.S. Infantry. There's a superb visitors center and interesting selfguided walking tours on the hauntingly beautiful battlefield grounds.

• When you're ready to call it a day, drive 28 miles along Routes 43 and 278 to **Jackson** (page 165). Stay the night at **Jackson Hot Springs Lodge** (page 166), where you can also eat dinner and soak those well-traveled muscles. From Jackson, it's just 30 more miles to Dillon and Route 15.

for sapphires at the **Spokane Bar Sapphire Mine,** beside Hauser Lake. Here, there's a dig option available, or you could purchase gravel for screening. Call ahead in winter. ~ 5360 Castles Road; 406-227-8989, 877-344-4367; www.sapphiremine.com.

Holter Lake offers access to one of the Helena area's preeminent attractions: the **Gates of the Mountains.** Narrated commercial **tour boats** that depart from the Upper Holter Lake marina, 20 miles north of Helena, ply a steep canyon whose quarter-mile-high limestone walls seemed to open and close before the eyes of the advancing Lewis and Clark expedition in 1805. Beyond these "gates," as the explorers dubbed them, were the Missouri River headwaters and the crest of the Rockies. Tours operate from Memorial Day through September. Fare. ~ Route 15 Exit 209; 406-458-5241; www.gatesofthemountains.com.

The canyon's western slopes make up the **Gates of the Mountains Game Preserve;** to the east lies the **Gates of the Mountains Wilderness.** Both are vehicle-free parcels of **Helena National Forest.** ~ 2800 Skyway Drive, Helena; 406-449-5201. Rocky Mountain goats, deer, bighorn sheep, osprey, eagles and occasional bear—as well as ancient American Indian petroglyphs—can be seen from the tour boat.

Due east of Helena is 25-mile-long, 4-mile-wide Canyon Ferry Lake, whose **Canyon Ferry Recreation Area** is the state's most popular for water-sports enthusiasts. Admission. ~ Canyon Ferry Road. Located at the lake's southern head is **Townsend,** 32 miles from Helena via Route 12. The highway turns east here across the Big Belt Mountains to the town of White Sulphur Springs.

South of Helena, a half-hour's drive in the direction of Butte on Route 15, is the town of **Boulder.** Worth a look is the **Jefferson County Courthouse,** built in 1889 and on the National Register of Historic Places: It features gargoyles perched on 24-inch-thick stone walls above its three-story entrance.

Just east are the **Boulder Hot Springs,** located near a mine noted for its high content of radon, a mining byproduct considered helpful by sufferers of arthritis, emphysema and other ailments. Hot (104°F) and cold soaking pools and therapeutic massages are featured at the health resort here, built in 1888 and currently undergoing restoration. ~ Route 69; 406-225-4339; www.boulderhotsprings.com.

HIDDEN ▶   One of Montana's finest ghost towns is **Elkhorn,** reached by traveling seven miles southeast of Boulder on Route 69, then following signs north another eleven miles. ~ Forest Road 258; www.ghosttowngallery.com.

A real-life frontier town is **Marysville,** about 22 miles northwest of Helena off Route 279. At its zenith, this boom town near the Drumlummon Mine (said to have produced as much as $50

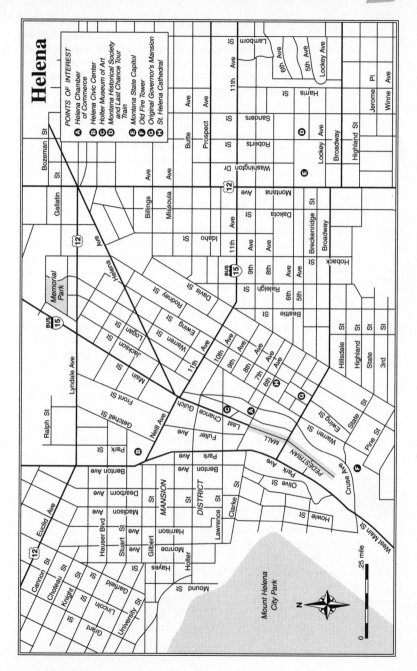

Helena

POINTS OF INTEREST

- **A** Helena Chamber of Commerce
- **B** Helena Civic Center
- **C** Holter Museum of Art
- **D** Montana Historical Society and Last Chance Tour Train
- **E** Montana State Capitol
- **F** Old Fire Tower
- **G** Original Governor's Mansion
- **H** St. Helena Cathedral

million in gold) supported a population of 3000 with six hotels, four general stores, two churches and a school. Today, only the presence of the nearby Great Divide ski area and other sports options in the surrounding Helena National Forest preserve it as a "living" ghost town. A bar/restaurant complex is the only functioning business. ~ Marysville Road.

Route 279 crosses the Continental Divide at Flesher Pass, then follows the upper reaches of the Blackfoot River into **Lincoln**. The ranching community is the gateway to National Forest recreation at several small lakes as well as the **Scapegoat Wilderness Area**, which borders the south end of the famed Bob Marshall Wilderness. No road, in fact, crosses the Divide between Lincoln and Route 2, which traces the southern boundary of Glacier National Park 100 miles to the north.

LODGING

The **Barrister Bed & Breakfast** offers five rooms in a three-story 1874 Victorian estate. All rooms have private baths and televisions, with phones available on request. Full breakfast is served each morning, and in the evening complimentary wine and hors d'oeuvres are available. ~ 416 North Ewing Street, Helena; 406-443-7330, 800-823-1148, fax 406-442-7964; www.thebarris termt.tripod.com, e-mail barrister1@qwest.net. DELUXE.

For sheer elegance, you'd have to search far and wide to find a more genteel place to spend the evening than **The Sanders— Helena's Bed & Breakfast**. This antique-filled B&B occupies a three-story 1875 mansion overlooking Last Chance Gulch and the cathedral, just a block from the Original Governor's Mansion. The home has seven restored bedrooms, all with private baths, phones, modems, TVs and air conditioning. Gourmet breakfasts are served in a lovely dining room and complimentary sherry, fruit and homemade cookies are available to guests. ~ 328 North Ewing Street, Helena; 406-442-3309, fax 406-443-2361; www. sandersbb.com, e-mail thefolks@sandersbb.com. DELUXE.

AUTHOR FAVORITE

West of Helena's Mansion District, the **Appleton Inn** is an 1890 Victorian home that boasts original cherry and oak woodwork, two parlors, a porch and fragrant gardens. Six charming, antique-filled rooms may feature clawfoot tubs and pencil-post beds; the whimsical Attic Room is filled with books and toys. If you check into the Family Suite, you'll get the entire third floor to yourself. Full breakfast. Closed November through March. ~ 1999 Euclid Avenue, Helena; 406-449-7492, 800-956-1999, fax 406-449-1261; www.appletoninn.com, e-mail appleton@ixi.net. MODERATE TO DELUXE.

The **Holiday Inn—Helena Downtown** is in the heart of historic downtown. It has an indoor pool, a restaurant, a nightclub and a lounge. Its 71 guest rooms are standard issue with queen-size beds and air conditioning. ~ 22 North Last Chance Gulch, Helena; 406-443-2200, 800-332-2290, fax 406-442-4030; www.holidayinnhelena.com. DELUXE.

The three-story **Mountain Valley Inn & Suites** offers 74 clean, comfortable standard rooms as well as four suites with sitting areas, microwaves and refrigerators (a big draw for families). Amenities include a pool, hot tub, high-speed internet connection and an adjoining casino and lounge. A full breakfast is included in the price. ~ 2101 11th Avenue, Helena; 406-443-2300, 800-541-2743, fax 406-442-7057; www.mvishelena.com, e-mail info@mvishelena.com. MODERATE.

Helena's largest and most luxurious lodging is the **Red Lion Colonial Hotel**, just off Route 15. This two-story hotel's 149 spacious rooms have just what you would expect from an upscale property, including king- or queen-size beds and air conditioning: some have microwaves and refrigerators. A restaurant and lounge are located off the elegant atrium lobby, and the hotel offers two swimming pools, a hot tub and a coin laundry. ~ 2301 Colonial Drive, Helena; 406-443-2100, 800-733-5466, fax 406-442-0301; www.redlion.com. MODERATE.

An hour's drive west of Helena, surrounded by ponderosa pines and within view of the Scapegoat Wilderness, is **Leeper's Motel**. This clean little bargain has private baths, cable TV and coffeemakers in all 15 rooms, kitchenettes in four. A spa and sauna are available for guest use. ~ Route 200 West, Lincoln; 406-362-4333, fax 406-362-4261; e-mail leepersmotel@linctel.net. BUDGET.

DINING

Northern Italian cuisine is the menu mainstay at **On Broadway**, lodged in an 1889 grocery store refurbished in art deco style. A wide choice of chicken, seafood and vegetarian dishes—as well as a handful of meat dishes—share the spotlight with one of the city's best wine lists. Dinner only. Closed Sunday. ~ 106 Broadway, Helena; 406-443-1929; www.onbroadwayhelena.com. DELUXE.

You can get two pounds of beef ribs for $21.95 at the **Windbag Saloon**. This is steak-lover's paradise, but there are lots of chicken and fish dishes as well. The desserts are worthy of a legend. The rustic building, it is claimed, was "one of the cleanest, most respected bordellos in all of Montana" until "Big Dorothy" was closed down in 1973. Closed Sunday. ~ 19 South Last Chance Gulch, Helena; 406-443-9669; www.windbag.com. DELUXE.

Bert & Ernie's Dining Saloon and Grill offers a wide variety of sandwiches and salads, and a handful of nightly dinners including a seafood special. The best things here are the eclectic antique decor and the extensive list of microbrews and wines by the glass.

Closed Sunday. ~ 361 North Last Chance Gulch, Helena; 406-443-5680; www.bertanderniesofhelena.com. BUDGET TO DELUXE.

Asian cuisine in Helena? You bet. The tantalizing aroma of simmering coconut-milk curry draws diners by the droves to **Toi Thai**. Among the fiery (or mild—your choice) fare are satays, *pad thai* and *pad see ew*. Reservations recommended. Dinner only. Closed Sunday and Monday. ~ 423 North Last Chance Gulch, Helena; 406-443-6656. MODERATE TO DELUXE.

Overland Express, off the freeway between the Best Western Colonial Hotel and the Super 8 Motel, offers generous steaks, chicken and seafood in a modern rustic atmosphere that families enjoy. ~ 2250 11th Avenue, Helena; 406-449-2635. MODERATE TO ULTRA-DELUXE.

Just five miles south of Helena, the **Montana City Grill & Saloon** draws a local clientele that's addicted to its famous huckleberry barbecue sauce. In addition to ribs and steaks, the menu features pasta, seafood and sandwiches. On weekends, chef Steve Vincelli creates special theme menus featuring a variety of cuisines, such as Southwestern, Cajun and Italian. Breakfast, lunch and dinner on Sunday; otherwise, dinner only. ~ 1 Jackson Creek, Montana City; 406-449-8890; www.montanacitygrill.com, e-mail pvincelli@montana.com. MODERATE TO ULTRA-DELUXE.

SHOPPING

HIDDEN ►

Potters from all over the world come to work and study at the **Archie Bray Foundation for the Ceramic Arts**. The public gallery offers outstanding traditional and contemporary pottery, sculpture and ceramics. A self-guided walking tour is available year-round. ~ 2915 Country Club Avenue, Helena; 406-443-3502; www.archiebray.org.

State legislators peruse the racks at the **Main News Smoke Shop**. Local and regional newspapers and more than 500 magazine titles are sold here. Closed Sunday. ~ 9 North Last Chance Gulch, Helena; 406-442-6424.

The **Montana Book Company** specializes in books about Montana and works by local authors; occasionally you can listen in on a reading. Closed Sunday except in November and December. ~ 331 North Last Chance Gulch, Helena; 406-443-0260, fax 406-443-9213; www.mtbookco.com, e-mail staff@mtbookco.com.

The **Leather Store and More** carries a wide assortment of goods in leather and suede: Western wear, motorcycle gear, casual pieces, boots, chaps and vests. If you don't see what you like, the in-house craftsmen can customize your vision. Closed Sunday. ~ 438 North Last Chance Gulch, Helena; 406-443-2007; www.leathermontana.com.

HIDDEN ►

Certainly one of the Helena area's most intriguing stores is **The Prospector's Shop**, five miles west on the MacDonald Pass highway. On display are all manner of mining equipment and supplies, from metal detectors to sluice boxes and gold dredges to actual gold nuggets. It's fascinating just to stop and browse a while. Call ahead for hours. ~ 6312 Route 12 West, Helena; 406-442-1872.

The **Capital Hill Mall** is Helena's largest shopping mall. Anchored by the **JC Penney** and **Dillard's** department stores, shops here include **Waldenbooks** and **Footlocker**. ~ 1600 11th Avenue, Helena; 406-442-0183; www.capitalhillmall.com.

Since its earliest days of gold-rush affluence, Helena has been a magnet for performing artists of national renown.

NIGHTLIFE

The **Myrna Loy Center for the Performing and Media Arts**, occupying the renovated Lewis and Clark County Jail, showcases music, theater and dance, as well as films, conferences and festivals. ~ 15 North Ewing Street, Helena; 406-443-0287, fax 406-443-6620; www.myrnaloycenter.com.

> Local firefighters used to rappel down Helena Civic Center's 17-story minaret for practice exercises.

Local thespians perform Friday through Sunday nights in the historic brownstone **Grandstreet Theatre**, close to Last Chance Gulch. ~ 325 North Park Avenue, Helena; 406-447-1574; www.grandstreet.net. And the **Helena Symphony Orchestra and Chorale** makes its home beneath the exotic minaret of the Moorish-style Helena Civic Center. ~ Benton and Neill avenues, Helena; 406-442-1860; www.helenasymphony.org.

For late-night revelers in Helena, **Bullwhackers** is a disco-nightclub in the Holiday Inn—Helena Downtown that attracts a mostly mid-to-late-20s crowd. Open Monday through Sunday until 2 a.m. Cover. ~ 22 North Last Chance Gulch, Helena; 406-443-2200.

Like other Montana cities, Helena has numerous casinos with low-stakes poker and keno machines. Among the more popular is the **Last Chance Casino**, which also features live keno and serves three square meals a day. ~ 1001 North Last Chance Gulch, Helena; 406-442-4474.

MOUNT HELENA CITY PARK 🚶 🚲 This small mountain is noteworthy not for its elevation (only 5468 feet), but for its proximity to the State Capitol. Several trails rise to the summit, a quarter-mile above Last Chance Gulch. Easiest is the gradually ascending 1906 Trail. The Prairie Trail is especially attractive during the spring and early summer wildflower season; the winding Prospect Shafts Trail passes old mining sites. Many visitors climb one path and descend on another. ~ Go south on Park Avenue, then make a right on Reeders Village Drive; 406-447-8463, fax 406-447-8460; www.ci.helena.mt.us.

PARKS

HOLTER LAKE RECREATION AREA

Located at the lower (north) end of the Missouri River reservoir that flows between the lofty limestone cliffs of the Gates of the Mountains, this area is especially popular with boating and fishing enthusiasts. Facilities include picnic areas and restrooms. Day-use fee, $2. ~ Take Route 15 north from Helena for 33 miles to Wolf Creek Exit 226, go east three miles on Recreation Road to the Wolf Creek Bridge, then drive south three miles on Beartooth Road; 406-494-5059, fax 406-533-7660; www.mt.blm.gov, e-mail dfoinfo@mt.blm.gov.

▲ There are 50 RV/tent sites (no hookups), $10 per night; 14-day maximum stay. Nearby Log Gulch, administered by the Bureau of Land Management, has 100 RV/tent sites available on the same basis.

GATES OF THE MOUNTAINS WILDERNESS AREA

A handful of trails traverse the rugged backcountry east of the Missouri River between Elkhorn and Beaver creeks, providing spectacular views of the Gates of the Mountains canyon, especially from the sheer slopes of 7190-foot Willow Mountain. This 28,500-acre preserve is rich in wildlife, including bighorn sheep and mountain goats. ~ There are several trailheads on Beaver Creek Road, 20 miles northeast of Helena via York Road and York-Nelson Road. The Meriwether picnic area on the Missouri River also offers trail access; the Gates of the Mountains tour boat will drop hikers at that spot; 406-449-5201, fax 406-449-5436.

▲ Primitive only.

CANYON FERRY RECREATION AREA

The most popular and largest of Montana's federal recreation areas consists of 24 units around the 76-mile shoreline of Canyon Ferry Lake. All but six of the sites are within a few miles of the Canyon Ferry Dam at the reservoir's north end; the park visitors center is located in adjacent Canyon Ferry Village, along with lodging and RV resorts, restaurants, a grocery store and other facilities. Facilities include picnic areas, restrooms, showers, and three marinas with boat rentals and concessions. ~ For park headquarters, take Route 12/287 ten miles east from Helena, then turn north on Route 284 (Canyon Ferry Road) and continue eight miles to Canyon Ferry Village; 406-475-3310, fax 406-475-9147.

> Wildlife viewing around the shore of Canyon Ferry Lake is excellent, especially from November to January, when several hundred bald eagles make their winter homes here.

▲ There are 383 RV/tent sites (no hookups) in seven developed and three group-use (available by reservation only; 406-475-3310) campgrounds; the largest is *Hellgate* (130 RV/tent sites), nine miles southeast of Canyon Ferry Village on Hellgate Gulch Road. No charge to $10 per night.

HELENA NATIONAL FOREST 🏃 🚴 🏇 🏕 ⛵ 🛶 ⛷ 🚣
Three principal units make up this 975,000-acre national forest,
one of ten in the state. The largest segment takes in both sides of
the Continental Divide west of Helena, from the Scapegoat
Wilderness nearly to Boulder. Smaller parcels include the Big Belt
Mountains, east of Canyon Ferry Lake, and the Elkhorn Mountains, south of the capital. The forest includes 1000 miles of trails
and 1600 miles of backroads. Facilities include picnic areas and
restrooms. ~ Principal highways are Route 200, through Lincoln;
Route 12, west of Helena and east of Townsend; and Route 15,
between Great Falls and Butte; 406-449-5201, fax 406-449-5436.

▲ There are 143 RV/tent sites plus seven tent-only sites (no
hookups) in nine campgrounds; no charge to $8 per night. Seven
recreational cabins within the forest are available by reservation
for $25 per night.

SCAPEGOAT WILDERNESS AREA 🏃 🏇 🚣 The southernmost
of three contiguous wilderness areas that extend south 100
miles along the crest of the Rockies from Glacier National
Park, the 240,000-acre Scapegoat features striking alpine
scenery, massive limestone cliffs along its eastern front and numerous small lakes and trout-rich streams. ~ Lincoln, on Route
200, is the gateway community. Nearest trail access is from the
Indian Meadows Trailhead in Helena National Forest, on
Copper Creek Road 15 miles northeast of Lincoln; 406-
362-4265, fax 406-362-4253.

▲ Primitive only.

▼▼▼▼▼▼▼▼▼▼▼▼▼▼▼

Pintler Scenic Route

The Pintler Scenic Route, which follows Route
1 through historic mining towns and the
Beaverhead-Deerlodge National Forest, combines with Route 90 through Deer Lodge to make a 150-mile
driving loop that can easily take up a full day. Butte is 41 miles
southeast via Route 90 from Deerlodge. From Helena, the most
direct access is via Route 12 west across MacDonald Pass to
Garrison, a 46-mile drive; from Butte, the loop is accessed 18
miles northwest at the Anaconda exit from Route 90.

SIGHTS

It's nine miles from the interstate into **Anaconda**, a city of 10,000
founded by Marcus Daly when he erected a copper smelter and
reduction works in 1883. Though it ceased operating in 1980,
the 585-foot **Anaconda Smelter Stack**, on a hill south of town,
remains the city's landmark and a state historic park. Once known
as the Washoe Stack, it is one of the world's tallest freestanding
brick structures—taller even than the Washington Monument.
The Jack Nicklaus–designed **Old Works Golf Course**, built around
the smelter, has attracted golfers from all over the world.

The downtown **Anaconda Historic District** is worthy of exploration. Vintage tour buses depart twice daily in summer from the **Anaconda Visitors Center,** housed in a replica of an old train depot that once served the Anaconda Copper Mining Company. Booklets describing a self-guided walking tour are available here. Hour-long bus tours of the area leave at 10 a.m. and 2 p.m. daily from mid-May to mid-September. Admission. ~ 306 East Park Street, Anaconda; phone/fax 406-563-2400; e-mail anachamber @aol.com.

Among the district's significant buildings is the **Hearst Free Library,** built in 1898 and donated to the city by Phoebe Hearst, wife of Anaconda investor George Hearst and mother of San Francisco publisher William Randolph Hearst. Closed Sunday and Tuesday. ~ Main and 4th streets; 406-563-6932, fax 406-563-5393. The **Copper Village Museum and Arts Center** housed the Anaconda City Hall from 1895 to 1982. Now it showcases Montana-based artists. Closed Sunday and Monday. ~ 401 East Commercial Street; 406-563-2422. The copper dome of the **Deer Lodge County Courthouse** towers above Anaconda. ~ 800 South Main Street; 406-563-4025. The **Washoe Theater** is a 978-seat art deco theater built in 1936. The Smithsonian Institution rates the theater's elaborate interior as one of the most beautiful in the nation. ~ 305 Main Street; 406-563-6161.

HIDDEN ►

The 10,000-foot-high peaks of the Anaconda-Pintler Wilderness rise to the south as Route 1 follows Warm Springs Creek west from Anaconda to **Georgetown Lake,** a year-round recreation area in Beaverhead-Deerlodge National Forest. Kokanee salmon and rainbow trout draw anglers in summer; the Discovery Basin ski area, only five miles north of the lake, caters to winter enthusiasts. The lake freezes over in winter to the delight of snowmobilers and ice anglers. ~ 406-859-3211.

At Georgetown Lake, the Pintler Scenic Route turns north and follows Flint Creek to the Clark Fork River. About ten miles north of the lake, it's a short detour into **Philipsburg,** an 1860s silver-mining town and now (in its entirety) a National Historic District. The many circa-1890s brick businesses along Broadway, the town's colorful main street, have been restored and now house a variety of shops and restaurants.

Twenty-one ghost towns lie within 40 miles of Philipsburg, so it's appropriate that the town's **Granite County Museum and Cultural Center** is the home of the Ghost Town Hall of Fame. Here you can find photographs of and information on such lost communities as Granite, Southern Cross, Princeton and Red Lion. Closed January through April. Admission. ~ 135 South Sansome Street, Philipsburg; 406-859-3020.

Philipsburg is still a sapphire-mining center. Learn about the precious gems at the **Sapphire Gallery**. Dig through gravel concentrate to find a few. Closed Saturday. ~ 115 East Broadway, Philipsburg; 406-859-3236, fax 406-859-3631; www.sapphire-gallery.com, e-mail sapphire@sapphire-gallery.com.

Route 1 rejoins the interstate at Drummond, 26 scenic miles north of Philipsburg. Missoula is 48 miles northwest. Turn left here on Route 90 to Bearmouth, the next exit, 15 miles west, and detour to **Garnet,** one of the best-preserved of Montana's myriad ◄ HIDDEN ghost towns. You must travel six miles east on a frontage road and ten miles north on a narrow, steep, decidedly backcountry byway to reach the ruins of this community.

After an 1897 gold strike, Garnet was home to about 1000 men, women and children. Four hotels, 13 saloons and a school were among its buildings. But after the claims were mined out, the population dwindled and disappeared. Today the Bureau of Land Management and the nonprofit Garnet Preservation Association operate a small visitors center and maintain a couple of dozen log structures. Some mining still continues in the area. A trail leads about 300 yards to the townsite from the picnic ground near the parking area. Admission. ~ Bear Creek Road; 406-329-3914, fax 406-329-3721; www.garnet ghosttown.org, e-mail garnetghosttown@yahoo.com.

> Two of Garnet's historic log cabins can be rented in winter by snowmobilers or cross-country skiers.

If you choose to bypass Garnet and turn southeast (right) at Drummond instead, you'll follow Route 90 about 31 miles past Goldcreek and Garrison to **Deer Lodge,** home of several important tourist attractions.

Chief among them is the **Grant-Kohrs Ranch National Historic Site.** For more than a century the headquarters of a cattle empire that once controlled one million acres of the northern Rockies, the ranch was set aside by the federal government in 1972 to illustrate the history of the ranching industry. Half-hour guided tours of the elegant 23-room Kohrs home, built in 1862 and expanded in 1890, begin at the visitors center. Guests may take themselves through interpretive displays in a bunkhouse row and buggy shed, a tack room, a blacksmith shop and more. Cattle graze and draft horses still work the remaining 1500 acres of the ranch. ~ Route 10 North, Deer Lodge; 406-846-2070, fax 406-846-3962; www.nps.gov/grko/home.htm.

Within the walls of the **Montana Territorial Prison** are three separate museums. The foreboding **Old Montana Prison,** with its massive gray stone walls and crenelated guard towers, was in active use for 108 years until 1979. Guided and self-guided tours give glimpses of the cellblocks and maximum-security corridors. The **Montana Auto Museum** features more than 125 perfectly restored automobiles from 1903 to the 1970s; the **Law Enforcement Museum** is a memorial to Montana officers who have died in the line of duty. The Law Enforcement Museum is closed November to mid-May. Admission. ~ 1106 Main Street, Deer Lodge; 406-846-3111, fax 406-846-3156; www.pcmaf.org.

The **Powell County Museum** displays artifacts and photos from local history. Open from Memorial Day to Labor Day. ~ 1193 Main Street, Deer Lodge; 406-846-3111, fax 406-846-3156. **Yesterday's Playthings** exhibits more than a 1000 dolls and a century's worth of toys. Closed October to mid-May. Admission. ~ 1017 Main Street, Deer Lodge; 406-846-1480, fax 406-846-3156.

LODGING   Three miles off Route 90 near Anaconda is the **Fairmont Hot Springs Resort**. Set in picturesque surroundings at the foot of 10,600-foot Mount Haggin, the resort attracts hot-spring soakers and swimmers with four indoor and outdoor pools, one with a twisting, 350-foot waterslide. Golfers are drawn to its 18-hole golf course, one of Montana's best. There's even a zoo for the kids. There are 152 spacious rooms and suites with standard furnishings and amenities, two restaurants and a lounge/casino. ~ 1500 Fairmont Road, Fairmont; 406-797-3241, 800-332-3272, fax 406-797-3337; www.fairmontmontana.com, e-mail fairmontmt@ aol.com. DELUXE TO ULTRA-DELUXE.

Situated atop the Harp Pub in an 1890 Victorian-style building, the **Celtic House Inn** offers ten antique-decorated rooms that exude a British country air. All have private baths; some have kitchenettes. ~ 23 Main Street, Anaconda; 406-563-2372. MODERATE.

Scharf's Motor Inn meets basic requirements for travelers who want to spend a night near the Grant-Kohrs Ranch and Montana Territorial Prison. Rooms are clean and comfortable if nothing fancy, and the motel has its own family restaurant. A couple of kitchens are available for families. ~ 819 Main Street, Deer Lodge; 406-846-2810. MODERATE.

DINING   If you're in Anaconda anytime before mid-afternoon, drop by **Rose's Tea Room** for Scottish scones and traditional black or herbal teas. Also available are continental breakfasts, light lunches and dessert specials. Closed weekends. ~ 303 East Park Street, Anaconda; 406-563-5060. BUDGET.

For steak, chicken and seafood, Anaconda locals head to the **Barclay II Supper Club & Lounge**. This low-lit, informal restaurant has full bar service but a firm no-smoking policy. Dinner only. Closed Monday. ~ 1300 East Commercial Street, Anaconda; 406-563-5541. MODERATE TO ULTRA-DELUXE.

The place to go in Deer Lodge is the **Broken Arrow Casino & Steakhouse**. This candlelit steakhouse in the heart of downtown, between the Territorial Prison and the Grant-Kohrs Ranch, serves up dinners in a rustic ambience. There's an adjoining casino lounge. ~ 317 Main Street, Deer Lodge; 406-846-3400. MODERATE TO DELUXE.

Ghost Towns

The thing about mining-boom towns is, as soon as the ore is worked out of the hills or streams, there's nothing left to hold a town there. Thus it has been throughout the Rocky Mountain foothills of southern Montana, where settlements that thrived with thousands of people in the latter half of the 19th century dwindled to nearly nothing by the early 20th. A visit to one of these abandoned communities can be a poignant experience. You can almost see the miners carrying their gold dust to the assay office, almost hear the rowdy shouts and raucous music as you stroll by the old saloon.

The two most accessible ghost towns are Bannack and Nevada City, both gold-mining communities dating from the 1860s. They are very different. **Bannack**, a Montana state park, has been left mostly unrestored, except to prevent the ravages of time and nature from taking their course too quickly. **Nevada City**, a privately owned museum, has been fully and carefully restored as it probably appeared in its heyday, right down to the interior furnishings of its 100-or-so buildings. (For more details, see Chapter Six.)

Hidden treasures await backroad explorers with time and perhaps a four-wheel-drive vehicle.

Elkhorn was an 1880s silver-mining town whose smelter produced as much as $30,000 worth of ore in a single month. Its ruins, some still scarred with bullet holes, contain fine examples of frontier architecture. To get there, take Route 69 seven miles southeast from Boulder; then follow signs east and north another eleven miles. ~ Forest Road 258, south of Helena.

Situated east of Missoula, **Garnet** was home to about 1000 men, women and children after an 1897 gold strike. Four hotels, 13 saloons and a school were among its buildings. A couple dozen of the town's vacated log structures are preserved today ~ Exit Route 90 at Bearmouth; follow the frontage road about six miles east; then turn north on steep and narrow Bear Creek Road.

For an overview of Montana's ghost towns, stop to see the **Ghost Town Hall of Fame** at the Granite County Museum and Cultural Center on the Pintler Scenic Route west of Butte. ~ 135 South Sansome Street, Philipsburg; 406-859-3020. In the Sapphire, Flint Creek and other ranges surrounding Philipsburg are no fewer than 21 ghost towns with names like Granite, Princeton, Red Lion and Southern Cross.

SHOPPING Anaconda is a good place to look for hard-to-find antiques. One of Montana's largest antique shops is located here. **Brewery Antiques** is a great spot to find Western paraphernalia. ~ 125 West Commercial Street, Anaconda; 406-563-7926.

HIDDEN ► Farther up the Pintler Scenic Route, the **Sapphire Gallery** is a natural stop for gems. But the shop also displays and sells an intriguing variety of international artworks, as well as framed fossils-as-art. Closed Saturday. ~ 115 East Broadway, Philipsburg; 406-859-3236.

NIGHTLIFE Wet your whistle at the **Harp Pub**, which has—among others—McEwan's Scottish lager, Guinness, Harp and Bass on tap. In fact, it boasts the largest selection of beers and single-malt scotches in the area. ~ 23 Main Street, Anaconda; 406-563-2372.

In Deer Lodge, the **Deer Lodge Players** perform musical comedies and melodramas year-round; 406-846-3455.

PARKS **LOST CREEK STATE PARK** 🚶 ⛵ A short nature trail leads to the base of Lost Creek Falls, which makes a spectacular drop from the

HIDDEN ► 1200-foot-high limestone cliffs of the Flint Creek Range north of Anaconda. Rocky Mountain goats and bighorn sheep are frequently seen here; bring binoculars. Facilities include picnic areas and restrooms. ~ From Anaconda, take Route 1 east for one and a half miles, Route 273 north for two miles, then Forest Road 635 west for six miles; 406-542-5500.

▲ Twenty-five primitive sites; free; 14-day maximum stay.

ANACONDA-PINTLER WILDERNESS AREA 🚶 🐎 ⛵ High rocky peaks, several of them over 10,000 feet, speckled with alpine lakes, meadows and forests, are the feature of this 159,000-acre wilderness. It extends for some 40 miles on both sides of the Continental Divide southwest of Anaconda and encompasses parts of two national forests: the Beaverhead-Deerlodge and Bitterroot. As in all wilderness areas, no vehicular travel is permitted. ~ Popular access points are East Fork Reservoir and Moose Lake, south of Georgetown Lake; Pintler and Lower Seymour lakes, in the Big Hole Valley on the east slope of the wilderness; and the East Fork of the Bitterroot River near Sula, off Route 93 on the west; 406-832-3178, fax 406-832-3311.

▲ Primitive only; 14- to 16-day maximum stay..

▼▼▼▼▼▼▼▼
Butte At the turn of the 20th century, few cities in western North America were larger than Butte, which stretches down a long slope on the west side of the Continental Divide. Urbane and cosmopolitan, "the richest hill on earth" had a population of more than 100,000, a powerful position in the national labor movement and a cast of millionaires.

Though the city was founded on gold in the 1860s and thrived on silver in the 1870s, copper was king. During the 1880s, Butte became the world's greatest copper producer. In succeeding decades, some 19 *billion* pounds of the ore were taken from underground by hard-rock miners, and state-of-the-art smelters extracted the metal for shipment around the nation and overseas.

"Copper kings" like Marcus Daly and William Andrews Clark fought for control of the city's wealth. (Daly's Anaconda Copper Mining Company amalgamated with John Rockefeller's Standard Oil and dominated Butte into the 1970s.) Irish and Cornish miners, followed by dozens of other nationalities—among them Italians, Finns, Serbians, Croatians, Germans, Chinese and Mexicans—came to Butte and created their own distinct ethnic communities.

After the First World War, demand for copper decreased and an exodus from Butte began. The population declined further after 1955, when labor-intensive hard-rock mining was abandoned in

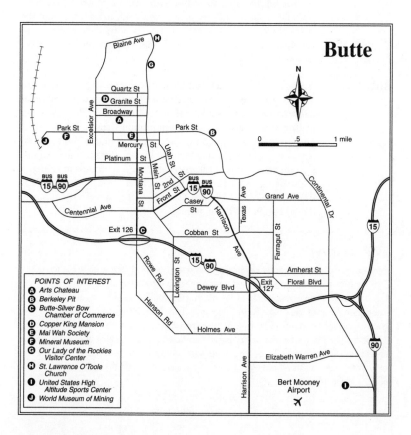

Butte

POINTS OF INTEREST
A Arts Chateau
B Berkeley Pit
C Butte-Silver Bow
   Chamber of Commerce
D Copper King Mansion
E Mai Wah Society
F Mineral Museum
G Our Lady of the Rockies
   Visitor Center
H St. Lawrence O'Toole
   Church
I United States High
   Altitude Sports Center
J World Museum of Mining

favor of more cost-efficient open-pit mining, changing the face of Butte forever. Whole neighborhoods on the city's east side were evacuated and razed to allow the hillside to be excavated. The first hole, the Berkeley Pit, was exhausted and closed in 1982; other adjacent mines are currently being worked.

Today, Butte is a city in transition. Though only about 30,000 people live here, its history is evident everywhere.

Uptown Butte is the city's downtown. It is reminiscent of parts of San Francisco without its cable cars; built on a hillside at about 5700 feet, it has preserved an eclectic turn-of-the-20th-century architecture and clings to a big-city ambience in a small-town environment. Black headframes that once towered over the entrances to hard-rock mines are a unique accent on the city skyline. About six square miles, encompassing 4500 buildings, have been designated a National Historic Landmark District—one of the largest such districts in the United States.

The hillsides that surround Butte, wasted of vegetation in an era when copper smelters spewed toxic sulfurous fumes into the atmosphere, are finally recovering. The city, meanwhile, is diversifying its economy to include medical and energy research, education and tourism.

SIGHTS   A 90-minute introductory tour of the city on **Old No. 1**, a motorized replica of an open electric trolley, is offered several times daily throughout the summer from the **Butte–Silver Bow Chamber of Commerce, Visitor and Transportation Center.** The chamber also provides free brochures on a walking tour of Butte's business district, as well as contacts for historic district tours. Admission for trolley ride. Visitors center closed weekends in winter. ~ 1000 George Street at the Montana Street exit, Butte; 406-723-3177, 800-735-6814, fax 406-723-1215; www.butteinfo.org, e-mail butteinfo@butteinfo.org.

EVEL KNIEVEL

Perhaps Butte's most famous celebrated native son of the 1960s and 1970s is Evel Knievel, a motorcycle daredevil who leaped to international fame and faded from view nearly as quickly. One of his most famous stunts was an attempted jump of the Snake River Canyon at Twin Falls, Idaho, on a rocket-powered cycle in 1974. Knievel was traveling up a launch ramp at 350 miles per hour when his safety parachute flew open, propelling him upward 1000 feet before he drifted downward almost 1500 feet to the canyon floor. He suffered only facial cuts and bruises. Knievel currently resides in Florida.

Start a self-guided tour of Butte at the **Berkeley Pit**, 7000 feet wide, more than a mile long and 1800 feet deep. The pit has been filling with ground water since its pumping system was shut down with the mining operation; it is the deepest body of water in Montana, but its chemical content is an ecological hell for the Environmental Protection Agency and the mine's owner, the Atlantic Richfield Company (ARCO). A public tunnel leads to a viewing stand (closed December through February) with taped narrations; a visitors center/gift shop outside the tunnel is open daily in summer. ~ 200 Shields Street; 406-723-3117, fax 406-723-1215.

For a more thorough look at Butte's mining history, head west two miles on Park Street to the **World Museum of Mining**. The 33-acre museum, located on the site of the Orphan Girl Mine, re-creates an 1880s mining camp. The museum highlights Butte and its surrounding areas' mining heritage with extensive exhibits, a mine yard filled with artifacts, an underground mine and "Hell Roarin' Gulch"—a three-square-block mining village with more than 50 replicas of town buildings. Closed November through March. ~ At the end of Museum Way; 406-723-7211; www.miningmuseum.org, e-mail rurban@miningmuseum.org.

On the nearby campus of Montana Tech, the **Mineral Museum** displays more than 1300 mineral specimens, including a 27.5-ounce gold nugget found in the surrounding mountains. A statue of Marcus Daly stands in the middle of Park Street at the entrance to the campus. Closed weekends November through April. ~ Next to Main Hall, off West Park Street; 406-496-4414, fax 406-496-4451.

Daly's archrival, William A. Clark, is likewise commemorated by the **Copper King Mansion**. His elegant former home—a three-story, 34-room manor in the heart of Uptown Butte—has been preserved, inside and out, as it was in the 1880s. Though in use year-round as a bed and breakfast, the mansion is open daily for tours from May through September and other times by appointment. Admission. ~ 219 West Granite Street; 406-782-7580; e-mail esigl@in-tch.com.

Two blocks away, another mansion, this one built in 1898 for William Clark's son Charles, has been converted to a heritage museum. The four-story **Arts Chateau**, designed in the style of France's Loire River castles, houses permanent and changing exhibits of regional art. Admission. ~ 321 West Broadway; 406-723-7600, fax 406-723-5083; www.artschateau.org, e-mail glenb@in-tch.com.

◄ *HIDDEN*

High above Butte, overlooking the city from an elevation of 8000 feet on the crest of the Continental Divide, a 90-foot statue of **Our Lady of the Rockies** is said to represent all women "regardless of nationality or belief." It was built by volunteers in 1985 and is maintained by a nonprofit organization. Daily summer bus

Text continued on page 160.

Historic Butte

With over 4500 buildings listed on the National Register of Historic Places, Butte has the second largest historic district in America. Strolling the hilly streets is the best way to experience it. This Uptown walking tour introduces you to several distinctive homes and civic structures (circa 1870s–1920s) that adorn "The Richest Hill on Earth." Read the plaques posted outside each building for more information. The route takes one to three hours, depending on whether or not you take the individual building tours.

GETTING STARTED Make **Butte–Silver Bow Chamber of Commerce, Visitor and Transportation Center** (page 156) your first stop. After combing through the brochures and maps, take 20 minutes to peruse the displays and learn about Butte's mineral-rich geology and early-day settlement. ~ 1000 George Street; 406-723-3177, 800-735-6814, fax 406-723-1215; www.butteinfo.org, e-mail butteinfo@butteinfo.org. From here, drive north on Montana Street to Quartz Street, turn right and park in the second block.

QUARTZ STREET FIRE STATION For much of the 20th century, firefighters set forth from this 1920s-era brick fire hall to douse Uptown blazes. Today, it serves as Butte–Silver Bow Public Archives. Step inside (the entrance is in the alley) and look around. Note the tower where firemen kept watch over Butte. Closed weekends. ~ 17 West Quartz Street; 406-497-6226; www.co.silverbowmt.us.

SILVER BOW CLUB Head west (left) on Quartz to the end of the block. Turn south (left) onto Alaska and walk to the corner. This Renaissance Revival–style building originally served as the Silver Bow Club, an elite men's club for mining and banking barons. When J. P. Morgan came to town, Butte's power brokers wined and dined him here. From the 1940s to 1980s the club housed Butte's Miner's Union. Today it's an office building. ~ 123 West Granite Street.

BUTTE WATER COMPANY Cross West Granite Street to examine number 124. With its Ionic columns and balconies, this Beaux Arts–style structure initially headquartered the Montana Independent Telephone Company. Since 1918, it's housed Butte's water utility. ~ 124 West Granite Street.

SILVER BOW COUNTY COURTHOUSE Cross West Granite again and go west (left) to the corner. Statesmen William Jennings Bryan and

Franklin D. Roosevelt addressed Butte's citizens from the steps of the Silver Bow County Courthouse, a four-story Beaux Arts–style structure. The building reflects the wealth and power of early-day Butte when it was the center of Montana politics and commerce. Inside, note the marble staircases and stained-glass dome. Closed weekends. ~ 155 West Granite Street.

COPPER KING MANSION   Head west (left) on West Granite, crossing Montana. Stop outside the Copper King Mansion (page 157), the home of Butte's first mayor, a German-Jewish immigrant named Henry Jacobs. This building was also the town's first brick residence. At the end of the block stands the ornate Victorian mansion owned by multimillionaire William Andrews Clark. For up-close views of the copper magnate's 34-room extravaganza, take a guided tour (fee). Better yet, stay as a B&B guest and relive Butte's glory days. ~ 219 West Granite Street; 406-782-7580; e-mail esigl@in-tch.com.

DR. CAMPBELL'S HOUSE   Turn south (left) on Idaho Street. Walk a block to West Broadway then veer west (left). Stop outside number 307 (a private home) and admire its stone and stucco façade, decorated arched entrance, and bay windows. The flared roof design brings to mind Spanish cathedrals and adds a whimsical touch. The house prompted locals to dub this stretch of West Broadway the Mediterranean Block. ~ 307 West Broadway.

ARTS CHATEAU   Walk west (left) to the corner. The Arts Chateau (page 157), a turreted French Chateau–style mansion, was built for Clark's son, Charles. Today, this four-story museum showcases Montana art and international exhibits. Take the self-guided tour of the lavish 26-room house with its turn-of-the-20th-century furnishings, stained-glass windows and hand-painted wallpaper. Admission. ~ 321 West Broadway; 406-723-7600; www.artschateau.org.

FOX THEATER   Go one block south (left) on Washington and cross West Park Street to the columned Fox Theater, with its Masonic detail. Renamed the Mother Lode to celebrate the region's mining heritage, this 1200-seat theater is now a performing-arts center, home of the Butte Symphony and Butte Community Concerts. Peek inside if it's open. ~ 316 West Park Street.

tours begin from the gift shop in the Butte Plaza Mall. Admission. ~ 434 North Main Street; 406-782-1221, 800-800-5239, fax 406-782-7314; www.ourladyoftherockies.org, e-mail ourlady@in-tch.com.

Farther up Main toward the Butte hilltop is the **St. Lawrence O'Toole Church**. The miners' church, built in 1897, features hand-carved altars with marble and brass handrails, and 40 frescoes. Open Friday and Sunday from June through August. ~ 1308 North Main Street; 406-782-9220.

HIDDEN ▶   The **Mai Wah Society**, in the heart of the historic district, dis-plays artifacts and photographs from Butte's once-bustling Chinese community. Closed Sunday and Monday; closed October through May. Admission. ~ 17 West Mercury Street; 406-732-3231; www.maiwah.org, e-mail info@maiwah.org.

On the plains at the southeast edge of Butte is the **United States High Altitude Sports Center**, an Olympic training facility and the site of world-class speed-skating competitions. In the audience you might even run into Butte's best-known native son of the 1960s and 1970s: motorcycle daredevil Evel Knievel. Closed October through April. ~ 1 Olympic Way, off Continental Drive; 406-497-2832, fax 406-497-2054.

LODGING

HIDDEN ▶   For a taste of Victorian luxury without modern amenities, William A. Clark's **Copper King Mansion** is a real find. Five ex-quisite bedrooms (two with private baths, the others with shared baths) display the likes of hand-painted fresco ceilings, sycamore and walnut woodwork and other turn-of-the-20th-century touches. A gourmet breakfast is served in a dining room whose cupboards brim with the finest crystal and silver. The mansion is entirely deserving of its listing as a National Historic Site. ~ 219 West Granite Street; 406-782-7580; e-mail esigl@in-tch.com. MODERATE TO DELUXE.

The ten-story **Finlen Hotel and Motor Inn**, with its mansard roof, is a massive presence in the Uptown skyline. Modeled after New York's Astor, it opened in 1924 and was long the favored hotel in this mining city. The Finlen fell on hard times but has undergone renovation and is now a registered historic landmark. The 16 cozy rooms on the tower's second and third floors have been reopened to travelers. Another 34 are in an adjoining two-story motor inn. ~ 100 East Broadway; phone/fax 406-723-5461, 800-729-5461; www.finlen.com. BUDGET.

The **Capri Motel**, like the Copper King and Finlen, is in Up-town Butte, within walking distance of many of the city's attrac-tions and better restaurants. This well-kept, two-story lodge has 68 rooms with TVs; a continental breakfast is included. Within the motel are a guest laundry and hot tub. ~ 220 North Wyo-ming Street; phone/fax 406-723-4391. BUDGET.

The **Red Lion Inn** may be more distant, but it's also more up-scale.Facilities at this 131-unit motor inn include a full-service restaurant and lounge, a heated indoor pool, a hot tub, a sauna and a workout room. A park across the street has tennis courts and a running track. Breakfast is included. ~ 2100 Cornell Avenue; 406-494-7800, 800-443-1806 (outside Montana), fax 406-494-2875; www.redlionbutte.com, e-mail reservations@ redlionbutte.com. MODERATE.

Butte's finest is the **Copper King Ramada Inn**. Though its 146 rooms are four miles south of the Uptown historic district, oppo-site the airport on Route 2, they are spacious and tastefully fur-nished. There are separate restaurants for fine dining and casual meals. Beneath a two-story atrium roof are a swimming pool, a hot tub, a sauna and an exercise room that is under construction. Ad-joining is the CopperDome, a 24,000-square-foot facility beneath an inflated roof used for indoor tennis, trade shows and confer-ences. ~ 4655 Harrison Avenue; 406-494-6666, 800-332-8600, fax 406-494-3274; www.ramadainncopperking.com, e-mail info@ramadainncopperking.com. MODERATE TO DELUXE.

DINING

Creative Continental dining in an old mining town? That's what you get at the **Uptown Café**. There's a heavy emphasis on sea-food (from *cioppino* to coquilles Saint-Jacques) at this elegant gallery-style eatery, but look for chicken, beef and pasta dishes as well. The wine list is enlightened. No lunch on Saturday and Sunday. ~ 47 East Broadway; 406-723-4735, fax 406-723-3724; www.uptowncafe.com. DELUXE TO ULTRA-DELUXE.

When Cornish miners came to Butte during the 1800s, they brought their love of pasties (pronounced PAST-ees), hearty meat-and-potato fillings wrapped in dough and baked. Soon all the other European immigrants adapted this traditional meal (known by the Cornish as "a letter from 'ome") for their very own. Today, this flaky, turnover-like treat continues to enjoy star status as a Butte specialty. It's passed around at weddings and funerals, sold in fundraisers and featured at many restaurants throughout the city. One place to try them is **Gamer's**, set in a century-old soda

AUTHOR FAVORITE

At the **Metals Banque Grill**, you can actually eat in the vault of a restored bank tower. In an atmosphere of Italian marble, African ma-hogany and solid copper window frames, choose from steak, seafood, pasta or Mexican specialties. Closed Sunday. ~ 8 West Park Street; 406-723-6160. MODERATE.

fountain with the original counter, high ceilings and mezzanine seating. Its standard steak-and-potato pasties, covered in gravy, are big enough for two meals. Breakfast and lunch only. ~ 15 West Park Street; 406-723-5453. BUDGET.

HIDDEN ► If the **Pekin Noodle Parlor** isn't Butte's oldest restaurant, it's close. Established a century ago in what was then a bustling Chinatown, it remains a "hole in the wall." Guests are served heaping helpings of chow mein, chop suey and egg foo yung. ~ 117 South Main Street; 406-782-2217. BUDGET TO MODERATE.

HIDDEN ► Just around the corner is a veritable Butte institution, **Pork Chop John's**. Though John's has since extended its little empire to Billings and Bozeman, this tiny chop shop—a streetside takeout window and a half-dozen counter stools inside—is the original. (There's another outlet at 2400 Harrison Avenue.) Try the pork nuggets or the porkchop sandwich. Closed Sunday. ~ 8 West Mercury Street; 406-782-0812; www.porkchopjohns.com. BUDGET.

Four miles farther south—indeed, at the edge of town—is **Lydia's Supper Club**, which has a distinctly Italian flavor. Antipasto appetizers precede, and pasta accompanies, each entrée; cappuccinos follow. Lydia's is fully licensed, but a smoke-free policy helps preserve the restaurant's beautiful collection of antique stained-glass windows, illumined by candlelight. ~ 4915 Harrison Avenue; 406-494-2000, fax 406-494-3332. DELUXE TO ULTRA-DELUXE.

SHOPPING Art lovers are well served at the gift shop and sales gallery at the **Arts Chateau**, the focus of arts in Butte and the home of the Butte–Silver Bow Arts Foundation. Paintings, prints, crafts and books are among the items available for purchase. ~ 321 West Broadway; 406-723-7600.

In addition to being a multimillionaire, copper magnate William A. Clark was a Montana state senator.

Butte's premier bookstore is **Books and Books**, which offers an extensive selection of current and classic literature and occasional appearances by authors. Closed Sunday. ~ 206 West Park Street; 406-782-9520.

Whitehead's Cutlery Store is worth a visit if only to view its vast collection of weaponry. This is the place to buy home and commercial cutlery, pocket and hunting knives. Closed Sunday. ~ 73 East Park Street; 406-723-9188.

For collector's editions and used books of all types (the children's and Western Americana sections are fairly large), **Second Edition Used Books** is your best bet. Assorted benches and stuffed chairs accommodate browsers. Closed Sunday. ~ 112 South Montana Street; 406-723-5108, 800-298-5108; e-mail secondedition @in-tch.com.

Right in the Copper City itself, the **Butte Copper Co.** boasts that it has "anything and everything in copper." Its stock includes copper jewelry, other semiprecious metals and gems, and various less pricey souvenirs. ~ 3015 Harrison Avenue; 406-494-2070.

Butte Plaza is the region's only full-size shopping mall, with some 40 stores and a six-plex cinema. ~ 3100 Harrison Avenue; 406-494-3362.

The **Butte Center for the Performing Arts** sponsors classical per-   **NIGHTLIFE**
forming artists at the magnificent art deco Fox Theater in the heart of Uptown Butte. ~ 316 West Park Street; 406-723-3602; www.buttecenter.tripod.com.

In the adjoining Copper King Ramada Inn, **Miss T's** has established itself as the city's most upscale nightclub with live rock bands on weekends, and comedy nights on Thursday. Occasional cover. ~ 4655 Harrison Avenue; 406-494-1616.

Check out the live performances at the **Silver Dollar Saloon**, a comfortable, friendly bar with an open atmosphere. Occasional cover. ~ 133 South Main Street; 406-782-7367.

You'll find Irish and non-Irish alike nursing pints of Guinness and Harp (both on tap) at **Irish Times Pub**. Local and touring rock-and-roll bands take the stage on Friday and Saturday, but you can retreat to the pool and dart room if you prefer your nights quieter. Closed Sunday through Thursday. Cover for live music and special events. ~ 2 East Galena Street; 406-782-8142. You'll know **Mulroney's Bar** by the Irish flag out front. ~ 112 North Main Street; 406-723-8016.

Butte's largest casino is the **Gold Rush Casino**. It boasts casino machines, live poker and keno games. ~ 22 West Galena Street; 406-723-3211; www.goldrushcasinobutte.com.

BEAVERHEAD-DEERLODGE NATIONAL FOREST 🏃 🚴 🐎 🎣   **PARKS**
🛶 ⛵ 🎿 Up until 1996, the Beaverhead and Deerlodge national forests were separate entities. Today, the more than three million acres comprising the Beaverhead-Deerlodge National Forest contain 370 lakes, 60 campgrounds, two ski areas and 2800 miles of trails. The forest is readily explored on the Pioneer Mountains National Scenic Byway and on the Gravelly Range Road, which climbs to elevations of nearly 10,000 feet south of Virginia City. The Sheepshead Mountain Recreation Area, on Maney Lake 19 miles north of Butte via Route 15 and Forest Road 442, has a campground, a picnic area, a fishing pier and sports fields designed specifically for the disabled. Facilities include picnic areas and restrooms. ~ Forest areas can be reached from interstate freeway exits in all directions from Butte, as well as Route 2 (Harrison Avenue South) through Pipestone Pass and Route 1 (the Pintler Scenic Route) to Georgetown Lake. Routes 43 (through the Big Hole Valley), 278 (Dillon to Wisdom) and 287 (through Virginia City), as well as the Pioneer Mountains and

Gravelly Range roads, provide the most direct access to the areas south of Butte; 406-683-3900, fax 406-683-3855; e-mail jdego lia@fs.fed.us.

▲ There are 850 sites: 680 tent/RV sites for tents and trailers, and 85 sites ideal for pickups with campers; no hookups; no charge to $8 per night. Recreational cabins may also be rented for $15 to $30 per night.

▼▼▼▼▼▼▼▼▼▼▼
Big Hole Valley

Southwest of Butte, Route 43 is the principal thoroughfare to the remote, often-snowbound Big Hole Valley. Best known for its hay-fattened cattle, the Big Hole is rarely visited except by trout anglers, hunters and travelers following the most direct route between Boise and Butte.

SIGHTS

The valley is reached by traveling on Route 15 west and south from Butte some 25 miles to the town of Divide. A series of country roads follow the lower Big Hole River some 50 miles around McCartney Mountain to its confluence with the Jefferson River near Twin Bridges; for tourists, the main point of interest on this route is the **Humbug Spires Primitive Area**, reached from a freeway interchange about three miles south of Divide. The Humbug Spires—ancient, 600-foot granite towers—are much loved by rock climbers. ~ Moose Creek Road, Divide; 406-533-7600, fax 406-533-7660.

Route 43 begins at Divide and proceeds westerly 77 miles to its junction with Route 93 at Lost Trail Pass on the Idaho border. En route, the highway transits but two villages: **Wise River** (12 miles from Divide), junction point of the Pioneer Mountains Scenic Byway through Beaverhead-Deerlodge National Forest, and **Wisdom** (51 miles from Divide), the Big Hole Valley's largest community with a whopping 115 citizens.

The **Pioneer Mountains Scenic Byway** (Forest Road 484) runs 40 miles south from Wise River to Route 278 west of Dillon. Most of the road (gravel for all but its last ten miles) is open for car travel only from June or July to October, as snow comes early and stays late after that, it remains open to snowmobiles. But during the peak summer season, it provides access to outstanding landscapes and outdoor recreational activities.

There are several attractions along the Pioneer Mountains Scenic Byway. Visitors may dig for quartz, garnets and amethysts at **Crystal Park**. ~ Route 484, Polaris; 406-683-3900. An abandoned narrow-gauge railroad can still be seen in the ghost town of **Coolidge**, a 1920s silver-mining community. In winter, access is by snowmobile only. ~ Forest Road 2465. Also in the area are the **Canyon Creek Charcoal Kilns**, which demonstrate how dependent miners were upon wood to fuel their smelters and steam engines, and prehistoric Indian sites and Depression-era campgrounds built by the Civilian Conservation Corps. ~ Forest Road 7401. On the paved route, open year-round, are two resorts. **Elk Horn Hot Springs** offers a mineral pool, a res-taurant and a rustic lodge. ~ Route 484, Polaris; phone/fax 406-834-3434. **Maverick Mountain** is a popular local ski resort. ~ Route 484, Polaris; 406-834-3454.

Rockhounds at Crystal Park are limited to hand tools only.

At **Wisdom**, Route 43 meets Route 278, leaving you two options. Turn west toward Idaho (it's just 26 miles to Lost Trail Pass, at the head of the Bitterroot Valley south of Missoula), or continue south and east across Big Hole Pass to Dillon, 65 miles east.

If you choose the westbound route, you're 11 miles from **Big Hole National Battlefield**, just beneath 7264-foot Chief Joseph Pass. The pass was named for the Nez Perce Indian leader who in 1877 led his people on an ill-fated exodus from their tribal lands in northeastern Oregon and central Idaho. The party of about 800 was camped at what is now the national battlefield site when U.S. infantrymen attacked before dawn on August 9. The tribe fought back valiantly, gaining the upper-hand before withdrawing and continuing their long march. But Nez Perce casualties were high and their spirit was broken. Less than two months later—at Bear's Paw, Montana, near Chinook—they surrendered and were either forced onto a reservation or exiled, as in the case of Chief Joseph.

The tragedy of the Nez Perce is related in displays and a video program at the national battlefield's visitors center and museum. Several trails begin at a picnic area and wind through the battle-ground, which is one of Montana's three units of the Nez Perce National Historical Park. Admission in summer. ~ Route 43, Wisdom; 406-689-3155, fax 406-689-3151; www.nps.gov/biho.

Proceed south on Route 278 toward the headwaters of the Big Hole River and you'll pass through **Jackson**, another tiny vil-lage, and cross 7360-foot Big Hole Pass. A junction on your left turns north toward Polaris and Wise River (the Pioneer Moun-tains Scenic Byway); it's 30 miles more from here to Dillon.

LODGING

Built in 1922, the **Elk Horn Hot Springs Lodge** offers ten lodge rooms and ten log cabins in very rustic environs. The Elk Horn has two outdoor hot-spring pools, a sauna heated by the springs, and a restaurant; there are no individual phones here, but the lodge has a pay phone! ~ P.O. Box 514, Polaris, MT 59746; phone/fax 406-834-3434, 800-722-8978; www.elkhornhotsprings.com, e-mail jkn3434@montana.com. MODERATE.

The **Sundance Lodge** has two modern duplexes, both of them with fireplaces, and one pondside homestead with cooking facil-ities. There's also a home-cooking restaurant, and despite temperatures that are sometimes the coldest in the United States, it's open year-round. ~ Route 43, Wise River; 406-689-3611, fax 406-689-3605. MODERATE.

DINING

There are plenty of small cafés in the Big Hole Valley. The **Wise River Club** serves three meals a day every day, with locally grown steaks its specialty. ~ Route 43, Wise River; 406-832-3258. MODERATE TO DELUXE. **Fetty's Bar & Cafe** offers country-style breakfasts all day long for late risers. ~ Route 43, Wisdom; 406-689-3260. BUDGET. **Rose's Cantina** serves hearty enchiladas in a most unlikely location. Closed Monday. ~ Route 278, Jackson; 406-834-3100. MODERATE.

PARKS

HUMBUG SPIRES PRIMITIVE AREA 🚶 🚲 White granite outcroppings, 70 million years old, rise like steeples 600 feet into the sky at this 8000-acre Bureau of Land Management preserve. Backpackers and rock climbers are drawn to the scenic location. ~ Take Route 15 south from Butte 28 miles or north from Dillon 37 miles to Exit 99 at Moose Creek; then drive three miles northeast on Moose Creek Road to the Humbug Spires trailhead; 406-533-7600, fax 406-533-7660.

▲ Primitive only at Humbug Spires. There are 20 RV/tent sites (no hookups) at the BLM's Divide Bridge campground, two miles west off Route 15 Exit 99; $6 per night; 14-day maximum stay.

BIG HOLE NATIONAL BATTLEFIELD 🚶 🏛 💧 One of three Montana parcels of the widespread Nez Perce National Historical Park, the Big Hole battlefield was the site of an August 1877 fray between Chief Joseph's Nez Perce and the U.S. infantry. Facilities include picnic areas, restrooms and a visitors center, all wheelchair accessible. ~ On Route 43, 11 miles west of Wisdom; 406-689-3155, fax 406-689-3151; www.nps.gov/biho.

AUTHOR FAVORITE

From the welcoming wood-paneled lobby to the relaxing mineral pool, **Jackson Hot Springs Lodge** offers Montana-style comfort. Cabins (most with fireplaces) and hotel rooms are available; there are also two-bedroom suites suitable for families. If you prefer to camp, you'll find a number of tent sites and RV spaces with full hookups. A restaurant and lounge round out the amenities. ~ P.O. Box 808, Jackson, MT 59736; 406-834-3151; www.jacksonhotsprings.com, e-mail hotresort@jacksonhot springs.com. MODERATE.

The southernmost reach of Montana is focused around Dillon, an old Union Pacific railroad town of about 9000 people that has become a center for ranching and summer recreation. An hour's drive south of Butte and a similar distance north of the Idaho border on Route 15, Dillon is located on the Beaverhead River, a short drive from Montana's most authentic ghost town, Bannack, and not far from the laidback scenery of the Red Rock River Valley.

▼▼▼▼▼▼▼▼▼▼▼▼

Dillon & the Red Rock River Valley

SIGHTS

The **Dillon Visitors Information Center**, housed in an old train depot, offers a brochure on a walking tour of Dillon's historic late-19th-century downtown. The center also has an impressive Lewis and Clark display and an extensive wetlands bird exhibit. ~ 125 South Montana Street, Dillon; 406-683-5511; www.beaver headchamber.com, e-mail chamber@bmt.net. The most intriguing building is the **Beaverhead County Courthouse**, whose four-faced Seth Thomas clock looks in all directions from a 60-foot tower. ~ Pacific and Bannack streets, Dillon; 406-683-3750.

Next door to the visitors center is the **Beaverhead County Museum**, a log building that boasts an impressive and well-organized collection of artifacts and memorabilia from American Indian (mainly Shoshone) and pioneer history. There's a one-room schoolhouse and lots of information on the ghost town of Bannack—drop by here before visiting the real thing. A quarter-mile-long boardwalk leads past a homesteader's cabin and Dillon's first flush toilet (in an outhouse, of course). Closed weekends in winter.~ 15 South Montana Street, Dillon; phone/fax 406-683-5027.

The University of Montana—Western has a Victorian main hall built in 1896. ~ 710 South Atlantic Street; 406-683-7011. Don't miss the campus art gallery/museum, featuring the Seidensticker Wildlife Collection of trophy game from Africa, Asia and North America. Closed weekends. ~ 406-683-7232; www.um western.edu.

No visit to Dillon would be complete without a sidetrip to **Bannack State Park**, 25 miles southwest via Route 278. The town was founded in 1862 on Grasshopper Creek, site of the first major gold strike in the future Montana. Bannack was briefly the territory's first capital (before Virginia City) and claimed its first school, first hotel and first jail.

As Bannack grew to 3000, so did its reputation for lawlessness. But one of the West's most remarkable chapters was written here and in Virginia City by a league of vigilantes in 1864. When the vigilantes realized that their sheriff, Henry Plummer, was secretly the leader of a gang of murderous "road agents" known as The Innocents, they hunted the gang down, denied them legal trials and hanged them on gallows built by Plummer himself.

The gallows can still be seen on a walking tour of Bannack, as well as the imposing Meade Hotel and courthouse, Skinner's Saloon, the Methodist church, the Masonic temple, Bachelor's Row and other sites. Rings for leg irons remain in the floor of the Bannack jail. Guided tours are offered three times daily, on weekends and holidays during summer. Admission. ~ 4200 Bannack Road, Dillon; 406-834-3413, fax 406-834-3548; www.bannack.org, e-mail bannack@montana.com.

From Bannack State Park, you can loop through **Clark Canyon Recreation Area**. Clark Canyon Reservoir, which attracts anglers from miles around for its excellent trout fishing, was formed by the damming of the Red Rock River and Horse Prairie Creek. Traces of Lewis and Clark's Camp Fortunate can be found on its northwest shore. Dillon is 20 miles north of the dam. ~ Routes 15 and 324; 406-683-6472, fax 406-683-0065.

South of Clark Canyon, Route 15 follows the gently rising Red Rock River Valley through the communities of **Dell** and **Lima**. Both are old railroad towns with a number of historic buildings.

HIDDEN ►   At Monida, on the Idaho border, turn east onto Centennial Valley Road for 28 miles to reach the remote **Red Rock Lakes National Wildlife Refuge**. Established in 1935 to protect nesting grounds of the rare trumpeter swan, it is also home to sandhill cranes, great blue herons and striking waterfowl, as well as raptors, moose, elk and antelope. Today it is estimated that between 400 and 500 swans make this Montana–Idaho–Wyoming border area their home. ~ Centennial Valley Road, Lakeview; 406-276-3536, fax 406-276-3538; www.redrocks.fws.gov, e-mail redrocks@fws.gov.

LODGING   Tucked alongside the Beaverhead River, the **Hidden Valley Guest Ranch** offers guests a variety of activities, from tubing and fly-fishing to hiking and mountain biking. The adventurous will find waterfalls, ponds and naturally warm springs throughout the ranch's hundreds of acres, while comfort-seekers won't stray far

sights

AUTHOR FAVORITE

You can smell the sagebrush and almost hear the gunshots ring out as you meander the deserted main street of **Bannack State Park**. This is an 1860s ghost town at its authentic best: preserved but mostly unrestored, except to ward off Mother Nature and Father Time. Its 60-odd hand-fashioned buildings of rough-hewn logs and brick masonry contain little more than the memories and shattered dreams of their former owners. (For more information on Bannack State Park, see "Parks" section below.)

from their private outdoor hot tub. Accommodations here are in three spacious cabins with fully equipped kitchens. You can also opt to stay in one of the two tepees—both are comfortably furnished and even have bathrooms. ~ 10135 Route 91 South, Dillon; 800-250-8802; www.hvgr.com, e-mail david@hvgr.com. DELUXE TO ULTRA-DELUXE.

The **Metlen Hotel** may be on "the other side of the tracks," and it has definitely seen better days, but it's a magnet for the true low-fare traveler. Built in 1897, this three-story white elephant has survived nearly a century as a residential hotel. Most of the 20-some rooms share down-the-hall bathrooms; a handful of rooms have private baths but minimal furnishings. Check out their historic back bar, lifted from the ghost town of Bannack. ~ 5 South Railroad Avenue, Dillon; 406-683-2335. BUDGET.

The **Sundowner Motel** is a friendly property at the edge of downtown Dillon with 32 spacious rooms, queen-size beds and a playground. Refrigerators are available by request. ~ 500 North Montana Street, Dillon; 406-683-2375, 800-524-9746, fax 406-683-6505. BUDGET.

The **Best Western Paradise Inn** is located at Dillon's north end at Route 15 Exit 63. The two-story motel has 65 rooms with king- or queen-size beds and air conditioning. A restaurant serves three meals daily, and there's a lounge and casino, an indoor swimming pool and a whirlpool. ~ 650 North Montana Street, Dillon; 406-683-4214, fax 406-683-4216. MODERATE.

DINING

Dillon was never a mining town per se, but **Blacktail Station** has captured a smidgen of that atmosphere, with antique mining equipment displayed on rough-hewn walls in the basement of a historic building opposite the Beaverhead County Museum. White tablecloths and linens deck the tables. Choose from a menu that includes prime rib and chicken. Every week there's a seafood special and a pasta feast. Upstairs is a lounge featuring live weekend entertainment. No lunch on weekends. ~ 26 South Montana Street, Dillon; 406-683-6611, fax 406-683-4514; www.beaverhead.com/blacktail. MODERATE TO ULTRA-DELUXE.

Twenty miles south of Dillon near Clark Canyon Reservoir is the **Buffalo Lodge**. The rural getaway, popular among hunters and anglers, is known locally for its steaks and burgers. Closed Monday except in summer. ~ 19975 Route 15 South, Dillon; 406-683-5535. MODERATE TO ULTRA-DELUXE.

SHOPPING

Plop down in the overstuffed chair and peruse a few titles before making your purchase at **The Bookstore**. In addition to new and used books, this tiny shop carries a selection of music, greeting cards and guitar accessories. ~ 26 North Idaho Street, Dillon; 406-683-6807.

PARKS

BANNACK STATE PARK 👤🚤 This true ghost town preserves the main street and more than 60 buildings of Montana's first territorial capital. Picnic areas, restrooms and a visitors center round out the amenities. Day-use fee, $3. ~ Take Route 278 west from Dillon 21 miles, then turn south on Route 5 and continue for four miles on Bannack Road; 406-834-3413, fax 406-834-3548; www.fwp.state.mt.us, e-mail bannack@montana.com.

▲ There are 28 RV/tent sites (no hookups); $12 per night; 14-day maximum stay.

CLARK CANYON RECREATION AREA 🚣🛶🎣🚤🚤🚤 🚤 Waterskiing and fishing (in the winter, ice fishing) are the most popular pursuits on 6600-acre Clark Canyon Reservoir. Numerous campgrounds make this area readily accessible. Facilities include picnic areas and restrooms. ~ Routes 15 and 324, 20 miles south of Dillon; 406-683-6472, fax 406-683-0065.

▲ There are nine campgrounds (no hookups), most without designated sites, no charge.

HIDDEN ►   **RED ROCK LAKES NATIONAL WILDLIFE REFUGE** 👤🚲🏇 🏕️🚤 🚤 Framed on two sides by the Continental Divide, this remote refuge is a crucial nesting area for the rare trumpeter swan. Located more than 25 miles in any direction from paved roads, it is also an ideal haven for waterfowl, songbirds, raptors, moose, elk and antelope. About three-quarters of the preserve's 45,000 acres is designated wilderness. You'll find restrooms here. Be sure to fill your gas tank in town. ~ From Dillon, take Route 15 south 63 miles to Monida on the Idaho state border, then turn east for 28 miles on gravel Centennial Valley Road (formerly Red Rock Pass Road); 406-276-3536, fax 406-276-3538; www.r6.fws.gov/redrocks.

▲ Primitive only.

▼▼▼▼▼▼▼▼▼▼▼▼▼
Outdoor Adventures

FISHING

Cold-water species such as trout, whitefish and arctic grayling thrive in the high-elevation streams and lakes on either side of the Continental Divide in southern Montana. In nationally famous streams like the Big Hole and Beaverhead, anglers cast for three species of trout—brook, brown and rainbow—as well as mountain whitefish. Many rivers also have the rarer cutthroat trout; a few may have bull trout. Georgetown Lake, west of Anaconda, offers kokanee salmon. A few high-elevation lakes, such as Holter, have walleye and yellow perch, but these are mainly low-elevation species.

For fishing tackle or information on guided expeditions, try **Fran Johnson's Sport Shop**. Closed Sunday. ~ 1957 Harrison Avenue, Butte; 406-782-3322. Or try **Montana Troutfitters**, with a

fully operational guide staff and a fly-fishing school. ~ 1716 West
Main Street, Bozeman; 406-587-4707; www.troutfitters.com.
One regional fly-fishing specialist is **Fish-On Fly**
& Tackle. ~ 3346 Harrison Avenue, Butte; 406-
494-4218. For more information, contact the **Mon-**
tana Department of Fish, Wildlife & Parks. ~ 1420
East 6th Avenue, Helena, MT 59620; 406-444-2535.

Fishing is not just a sport
in Montana. To many, it's
a religion.

Lodges throughout western and southern Montana
provide fly-fishing guides and instruction. For visitors
with money to burn and a powerful passion to catch tro-
phy-size cutthroat, rainbow and German brown trout, it's
hard to top the facilities operated by **Craig Fellin Outfitters.**
From June through September, experienced guides take visitors
out for dry fly-fishing. ~ 8205 Wise River, Elkhorn Road; 406-
832-3252; www.flyfishinglodge.com.

Because southwest Montana is mainly a high plateau on the eastern flank of the Bitterroot Range, its rivers don't offer the same
level of whitewater rapids as some in other parts of the state. But
flatwater paddlers, especially canoeists, appreciate the tranquil-
ity and wildlife-watching opportunities of the region. The Big Hole
River (from Wisdom to Wise River) and Jefferson River (from
Twin Bridges to Three Forks), as well as the remote Red Rock
Lakes, are among the most appealing stretches.

**RIVER
RUNNING**

For cutthroat and brookies on the Big Hole River, contact
Pioneer Outfitters. ~ 400 Alder Creek Road, Wise River; 406-
832-3128; www.pioneeroutfitters.com. Rafts and other river
equipment are available for rent from **Montana Outdoor Sports.**
~ 708 North Main Street, Helena; 406-443-4119.

HELENA AREA   Great Divide, 22 miles northwest of Helena off
Route 279, is a midsize area with140 runs and a 1503-foot vertical drop from the rim of the Continental Divide. Facilities include
five chairlifts and a surface tow. There's also night skiing on
Friday. ~ Marysville Road, Marysville; 406-449-3746, 406-447-
1310 (snow report); www.greatdividemontana.com.

**DOWNHILL
SKIING**

BUTTE AREA   For sheer scenic beauty, it's hard to top **Discovery**
Basin. Looking across Georgetown Lake toward the Anaconda
Range, 20 miles west of Anaconda and 45 miles from Butte, it
has six chairlifts running from just below the summit of 8187-
foot Rumsey Mountain. There are 52 runs with a 1670-foot vertical. ~ Discovery Basin Road, Georgetown; 406-563-2184;
www.skidiscovery.com.

DILLON AREA   **Maverick Mountain** is among the most isolated
of Montana's ski areas. Located in Beaverhead-Deerlodge Na-

tional Forest near Elk Horn Hot Springs on the Pioneer Mountains National Scenic Byway, 35 miles west of Dillon and about 100 miles southwest of Butte, it appeals to committed skiers with 18 trails, averaging more than a mile in length, and a 2120-foot vertical drop. There's one chairlift; a surface tow serves a beginner's bowl. ~ Pioneer Mountain Scenic Byway, Polaris; 406-834-3454; www.wintermt.com.

Ski Rentals Many stores throughout the region offer equipment rentals and information. **The Outdoorsman** offers downhill ski rentals. Closed Sunday. ~ 2700 Harrison Avenue, Butte; 406-494-7700. A shop specializing in cross-country equipment is **Montana Outdoor Sports**. ~ 708 North Main Street, Helena; 406-443-4119. In Missoula, contact **Pipestone Mountaineering** for cross-country, backcountry and telemark ski rentals. ~ 129 West Front Street; 406-721-1670; www.pipestonemtng.com.

CROSS-COUNTRY SKIING

West of Butte, the **Mt. Haggin Nordic Ski Area**, created by the Mile High Nordic Ski Club, offers groomed cross-country trails at the foot of the Anaconda Pintlers; it operates by donation and volunteer energy. ~ 11 miles south of Anaconda toward Wisdom; 406-782-0316.

For information on renting equipment, see the ski-rental section in "Downhill Skiing" above.

GOLF

Public courses in southwest Montana include **Bill Roberts Municipal Golf Course**, featuring a fairly challenging 18 holes, a club house and a pro shop. ~ Benton and Cole avenues, Helena; 406-442-2191. **Deer Park Golf Course** is a beginner-friendly yet challenging nine-hole course complete with putting green, driving range and equipment rentals. ~ 295 Golf Course Road, Deer Lodge; 406-846-1625; www.dearparkgolf.com. In Dillon, play at **Beaverhead Golf Club**, a public, nine-hole course. Call for tee times. ~ 1200 Route 41, Dillon; 406-683-9933; www.beaverheadgolf.com. *Golf Digest* and *Golf Magazine* gave their Best New Course awards to the **Old Works Golf Course**, a Jack Nicklaus–designed wonder incorporating Warm Springs Creek and Anaconda's historic copper smelters. This extremely challenging 18-hole course also features a one-and-a-half-mile walking trail for non-golfers. ~ 1205 Pizzini Way, Anaconda; 406-563-5989; www.oldworks.org.

Vehicles (including bikes) are not permitted in wilderness areas, but some highway loops—including the Pintler Scenic Route and the Big Hole Valley road—make excellent bike trips.

Wild elk can be a hazard when they graze on the greens at **Fairmont Hot Springs Resort**, an 18-hole, par-72 public course. The 649-yard fifth hole of this course is regarded as one of the most challenging in the state. ~ 1500 Fairmont Road, Gregson; 406-797-3241; www.fairmontmontana.com.

Perhaps the most intriguing place to charge a Montana net is within **The CopperDome Racquet Club**. The inflated Copper-Dome is attached to the Copper King Ramada Inn opposite the Butte airport. Reservations are accepted daily; rentals are also available. ~ 4655 Harrison Avenue, Butte; 406-494-6666.

Elsewhere, city parks and recreation offices have exhaustive listings of municipal courts. In Helena, call 406-447-8463.

TENNIS

Horses go with Montana like salsa with nachos, like Bogie with Bacall, like dogma with religion. It's hard to imagine having one without the other.

RIDING STABLES

Rides are as diverse as the stables, ranches and outfitters that offer them. Rides may be available by the hour or the day, as breakfast trips at sunrise or dinner steak grills around a campfire.

For daytrippers, **Peterson's Fairmont Corral**, located a mile south of the Fairmont Hot Springs Resort outside of Butte, emphasizes guided breakfast and dinner trail trips. ~ Star Route East, Anaconda; 406-797-3377.

Diamond Hitch Outfitters leads a variety of trail rides, from hourly to day-long to multi-day trips. ~ 3405 Ten Mile Road, Dillon; 406-683-5494, 800-368-5494; diamondhitchoutfitters. com.

Mountain bikers enjoy roads and trails in national forests throughout southwest Montana. Guided mountain-bike tours through the backcountry byways of Horse Prairie and Medicine Lodge are offered by **Dave Willborn Outfitter**. ~ 775 Medicine Lodge Road, Dillon; 406-681-3117.

BIKING

Bike Rentals **Montana Outdoor Sports** rents full-suspension and ten-speed mountain bikes. ~ 708 North Main Street, Helena; 406-443-4119. One of the region's best bike shops is **Thin Air Bikes and Boards**, which offers rentals and repair service as well as retail sales. ~ 827 South Montana Street, Butte; 406-782-4726.

The national forests, wilderness areas and other public lands of southwest Montana contain literally thousands of miles of trails that offer an astounding range of choices for hikers of all experience and ability levels.

HIKING

Following are a few of the region's more popular trails. All distances listed are one way unless otherwise noted.

HELENA AREA Mount Helena is a 900-acre city park with seven separate trails to its 5468-foot peak. The reward for climbers is a bird's-eye view of the capital's Last Chance Gulch, a quarter-mile below the summit. Many hikers take the easy **1906 Trail** (2 miles) to the summit and descend on a steeper path, like the **Prospect Shafts Trail** (1.5 miles) past old mining sites, or the **Prairie Trail** (2.5 miles), which is especially colorful during the spring and early summer wildflower seasons. Nearest trailhead to downtown Helena is at the end of Mount Helena Drive.

Refrigerator Canyon Trail (2 miles) offers access into the eastern part of the Gates of the Mountains Wilderness. After climbing dramatically through a narrow limestone canyon, the moderate trail levels out to several excellent viewing points. The trailhead is on Beaver Creek Road north of Hauser Lake.

Hanging Valley (6 miles) in Helena National Forest northeast of Hauser Lake climbs rapidly through limestone cliffs on the west side of the Big Belt Mountains before dropping into a valley of giant Douglas fir. The trail, which involves a 1460-foot elevation gain, begins at the Vigilante campground near York.

PINTLER SCENIC ROUTE The **Continental Divide National Scenic Trail** (45 miles) is actually part of a 3100-mile Canada-to-Mexico trek; the segment through the Anaconda-Pintler Wilderness from Storm Lake, south of Georgetown Lake, to East Fork Road, east of Sula, offers a challenging backpack and spectacular views along the boundaries of Beaverhead-Deerlodge and Bitterroot national forests.

BUTTE The **Sheepshead Trail System** (4.5 miles) is a system of paved paths that provide handicapped access to the outdoors. These Beaverhead-Deerlodge National Forest trails traverse meadows and wooded hills, and loop around a small lake. Trails begin at the Sheepshead Mountain Recreation Area, 19 miles north of Butte via Route 15 to Elk Park.

The **Bear Gulch Trail** (4 miles), which begins about 22 miles north of Butte off Route 15 Exit 151, is an easy hike through an alpine meadow at about 6500 feet elevation. Beginning at the end of Forest Road 8481, it follows a small creek to the wildflower-rich grassland between Sullivan and Bear mountains in Beaverhead-Deerlodge National Forest.

Louise Lake National Recreation Trail (3.5 miles) leads up to a shimmering lake cradled between the 10,000-foot peaks of the Tobacco Root Mountains. Wildlife viewers often spot mountain goats. The trailhead is in Beaverhead-Deerlodge National Forest. From Route 90 take the Cardwell exit east of Whitehall, then Route 359 south to South Boulder Road and continue to the trailhead at Bismark Reservoir. The trail is closed from mid-October through June.

BIG HOLE VALLEY **Humbug Spires Trail** (2 miles) is an easy trail entering a fascinating geological preserve of 600-foot Mesozoic granite columns. Rock climbers often gather at this Bureau of Land Management sanctuary, 40 miles north of Dillon.

The moderately strenuous **Pioneer Loop National Recreation Trail** (35 miles) follows the spine of the West Pioneer Mountains, with spectacular views across the upper Big Hole Valley. There

are many alpine tarns and small creeks en route. You can walk
the entire trail between trailheads at Lacy Creek Road #1289
(west of the Wise River) and Sting Creek on the Pioneer Mountains National Scenic Byway (south of Wise River).

DILLON AND THE RED ROCK RIVER VALLEY Lion Creek Trail
(9 miles) is one of the most attractive routes into the Pioneer
Mountains. The path winds through meadows and forests to al-
pine lakes surrounded by 9800-foot peaks. The trailhead is in the
Beaverhead-Deerlodge National Forest west of
Melrose, 30 miles north of Dillon.

The **Upper Rattlesnake Trail** (5.5 miles) is a
relatively short but rugged track through a district
of at least a dozen small lakes in the East Pioneer
Mountains. Reach it via the Birch Creek Road (Forest
Road 192 off Route 801) at Route 15 Exit 74, about
12 miles north of Dillon.

The 3.8 mile-long Nez
Perce National Historical
Trail traces the route by
which Chief Joseph led
his Nez Perce war-
riors after they fled
their 1877 battle-
ground.

Equipment For backpacking gear—tents, backpacks,
sleeping bags, camping stoves and the like—visit **The
Base Camp.** Closed Sunday. ~ 333 North Last Chance Gulch,
Helena; 406-443-5360. In Butte, **Pipestone Mountaineering**
rents much of the same equipment. ~ 829 South Montana
Street, Butte; 406-721-1670.

Montana's two principal interstate highways, **Route
15** and **Route 90**, cross and briefly converge at Butte,
making this area, in a sense, Montana's transportation
hub. Route 90 runs 548 miles east and west across Montana,
connecting many of its largest cities (Missoula, Butte, Bozeman
and Billings) with points west (Seattle) and east (Chicago and Boston). Route 15 runs 385 miles north and south, from the
Canadian border through Great Falls, Helena and Butte to Poca-
tello, Idaho, and points south (Salt Lake City and San Diego).

For road reports, call 800-226-7623 statewide, or call for local
information (406-494-9646).

Transportation

CAR

Butte's **Bert Mooney Airport** is served by Horizon and SkyWest.
Delta, Horizon, Big Sky and SkyWest fly to the **Helena Municipal
Airport.** ~ 406-442-2821; www.butteairport.com.

AIR

Greyhound Bus Lines offers service to the larger towns along the
Route 90/94 corridor, including Butte and Deer Lodge. ~ 800-
231-2222; www.greyhound.com. **Rimrock Trailways** connects
Helena, Butte, Dillon and other towns of southwestern Montana.
~ 406-442-5860.

The central bus terminal in Helena is in the High Country. ~
406-442-5860. In Butte, it is at 101 East Front Street. ~ 406-723-
3287.

BUS

**CAR
RENTALS**

Helena has nine agencies and Butte has eight. At Helena Regional Airport there are **Avis Rent A Car** (800-331-1212), **Hertz Rent A Car** (800-654-3131) and **National Car Rental** (800-328-4567). At Butte's Bert Mooney Airport, you will find **Avis Rent A Car** (800-331-1212), **Hertz Rent A Car** (800-654-3131) and **Budget Rent A Car** (800-527-0700).

**PUBLIC
TRANSIT**

The **Butte–Silver Bow Transit System** runs an extensive route system through Butte and surrounding areas, with nominal fares. ~ 406-497-6200.

TAXIS

Old Trapper Cab Co. covers a 50-mile radius around Helena. ~ 406-449-5525. **City Taxi** serves Anaconda and Butte. ~ 406-723-6511.

SIX

South Central Montana

Southwest Montana grew around mining, southeast Montana around ranching. South central Montana evolved from both economies, but from early in its development, it had something even more important: Tourism.

Credit the Northern Pacific Railroad with opening this section of the state to settlement in 1882. Its major towns, Bozeman and Livingston, were established by rail construction crews, as were other communities like Three Forks, Big Timber and Columbus. More importantly, credit the U.S. Congress with establishing Yellowstone as the nation's first national park a full decade earlier. As soon as the railroad was completed, a spur line from Livingston to Gardiner began carrying tourists to the new park, and the future of south central Montana as a center for outdoor recreationists was assured.

All four of Montana's access routes to Yellowstone originate in this part of the state. Three of them extend up river valleys: the Madison from Three Forks, the Gallatin from Bozeman and the Yellowstone from Livingston. A fourth, from Red Lodge, circles the spectacular Absaroka-Beartooth Wilderness Area on the Wyoming border. Many tourists combine a visit to Yellowstone with a loop trip on any two of these highway routes, which they can extend from 200 to 450 miles or even more.

Apart from the river canyons and wilderness mountains that abut Yellowstone, south central Montana has other attractions worthy of note. Bozeman, home of Montana State University (MSU) and its impressive Museum of the Rockies is only a 45-minute drive from the spectacular Lewis and Clark Caverns and from Three Forks, where the Jefferson, Madison and Gallatin rivers join to form the Missouri River headwaters. Livingston, once the home of "Calamity Jane" Canary, has preserved the historical integrity of its late-19th-century downtown. Red Lodge retains the feel of a cosmopolitan coal-mining town of 100 years ago, while Big Timber is best known for the Greycliff Prairie Dog Town to its east. Many of the region's streams draw anglers and rafters from far reaches of the country. Skiers, meanwhile, delight in the Big Sky, Bridger Bowl and Red Lodge Mountain resorts.

▼▼▼▼▼▼
...man Area

Bozeman is an oasis of sophistication in the center of a thriving agricultural area. Located at the foot of the Bridger Range in the Gallatin River Valley, this city of 34,000 has become a darling of affluent young (or young-at-heart) visitors.

Named for John Bozeman, a 19th-century wagon master, this is Montana's "yuppie" city. A hangout for such Hollywood luminaries as actress Meryl Streep and actor Steven Seagal, its prices are higher than those in other Montana cities.

SIGHTS

The one attraction in Bozeman that no visitor should miss is the **Museum of the Rockies** at the edge of the MSU campus. The museum's dinosaur exhibit is world-class, depicting the site where the first known dinosaur eggs were discovered in North America. Programs at the Taylor Planetarium are comparable to those in much larger cities. Exhibits focus on American Indian culture, contemporary Western art, American history with a Rockies perspective and scientific discoveries. The museum operates a pioneer homestead, features artifacts from a Lewis and Clark expedition campsite and has an excellent gift shop. Admission. ~ 600 West Kagy Boulevard, Bozeman; 406-994-2251, fax 406-994-2682; www.museumoftherockies.org, e-mail wwwmor@montana.edu.

Montana State University, with an enrollment of more than 12,000, is a national leader in agricultural research and education, physical science and technology. Visitors can attend any of the university's cultural and sporting events. ~ South of College Street and west of South 7th Avenue, Bozeman; 406-994-0211, fax 406-994-1756; www.montana.edu, e-mail publicaffairs@montana.edu.

East of the campus is the **South Willson Historic District**. Four dozen houses, from small cottages to large mansions, may be viewed in this residential area. Some of the large homes, which date back to the 1880s, are now fraternity and sorority houses. ~ South Willson Avenue, Bozeman.

A walking-tour guide to the South Willson Historic District is available from the Museum of the Rockies or the **Bozeman Area Chamber of Commerce**. ~ 2000 Commerce Way, Bozeman; 406-586-5421, 800-228-4224, fax 406-586-8286; www.bozeman chamber.com, e-mail info@bozemanchamber.com.

There's more early Bozeman history at the **Gallatin County Pioneer Museum**. A county jail from 1911 to 1982, the building now holds audiences captive with displays of agricultural implements, American Indian artifacts and the jail's original gallows room (complete with noose and drop floor). Closed Monday in fall and winter and Sunday year-round. ~ 317 West Main Street, Bozeman; 406-522-8122, fax 406-522-0367; www.pioneermu seum.org, e-mail pioneermuseum@montana.com.

Text continued on page 182.

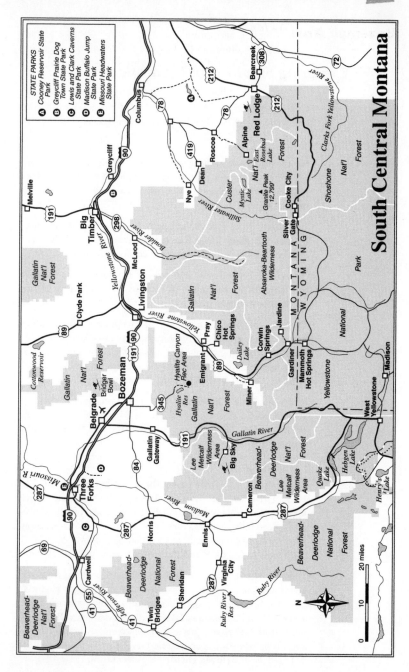

STATE PARKS
Ⓐ Cooney Reservoir State Park
Ⓑ Greycliff Prairie Dog Town State Park
Ⓒ Lewis and Clark Caverns State Park
Ⓓ Madison Buffalo Jump State Park
Ⓔ Missouri Headwaters State Park

South Central Montana

Three-day Weekend

Exploring Small-town Montana

This three-day itinerary offers a sampling of Montana's small-town flavor. It also serves up some intriguing history lessons along the way.

Day 1
- For the big picture of the area, catch an early morning scenic flight over the headwaters region with **Bridger Aviation Services** (page 216) at Pogreba Field, just half a mile south of Three Forks on Old Route 2.

- Take Route 90 to Exit 283 at Logan. Drive seven miles south to **Madison Buffalo Jump State Park** (page 190), where Plains Indians once hunted buffalo and laid up stores of meat.

- Return to Three Forks and browse the folksy **Headwaters Heritage Museum** (page 190). Eat lunch at the **Historic Headwaters Restaurant** (page 192).

- Drive five miles north on Route 90 to **Missouri Headwaters State Park** (pages 190), a National Historic Landmark. Stop at old Gallatin City, then drive another mile to the sod-roofed interpretation area with its walk-through tour of regional history. Explore some of the trails before revisiting Three Forks.

- Dinnertime, grab a downhome meal at the **Longhorn Cafe** (page 192) or go Continental at the upscale **Sacajawea Hotel** (page 191). Spend the night at the Sacajawea or the **Broken Spur Motel** (page 191).

Day 2
- Buy a picnic lunch before leaving Three Forks or plan to eat in La Hood. Drive 18 miles west on Route 2 to **Lewis and Clark Caverns State Park** (page 190). Take the splendid two-hour, two-mile guided tour into these three-million-year-old limestone caves. Afterward, stake out a picnic table for lunch or follow Route 2 four miles west to the **La Hood Park Restaurant** (page 192).

- From La Hood, follow Route 2 to Whitehall. Pick up Route 55 south, which joins Route 41, and drive to **Twin Bridges** (about 34 miles total), where the Ruby, Beaverhead and Big Hole rivers converge to form the Jefferson. Take the 45-minute tour at **R.L. Winston Rod Company** (page 194), which makes world-class fly rods. They offer one tour weekdays at 2 p.m. Then visit the tin-ceilinged **Twin Bridges Historical Association** (page 194).

- Feel like shopping? Drop by **Montana Mad Hatter** (page 197), for a handmade cowboy hat. Nearby, sip on a latte and admire the hand-spun, hand-woven wool rugs and saddle blankets at **The Weaver's Studio** (page 197)

- Dine sumptuously at **The Old Hotel** (page 196), where you can also spend the night. This handsomely restored 1879 bed and breakfast has a dynamite dinner menu. Reservations advised.

Day 3
- After breakfast, drive 29 miles south on Route 287 to **Alder Gulch** (page 193) and **Nevada City** (page 194). Take a self-guided tour through this rambling ghost-town museum, which offers a glimpse of frontier life in the 1860s.

- Drive a mile or hop aboard the **Alder Gulch Shortline** (page 195) to another heritage attraction, **Virginia City** (page 195). Roam the streets of this former territorial capital, which preserves Montana's early gold mining and Vigilante history. Don't miss **Boot Hill Cemetery** (page 195).

- Come evening, join the locals at the **Blue Anchor Restaurant** (page 196) or head to the upscale **Banditos** (page 197). Then watch a 19th-century melodrama performed by the **Virginia City Players** (page 198) or a musical revue at the **Brewery Follies** (page 198). Stay overnight at the **Fairweather Inn** (page 196) or the **Bennett House Country Inn** (page 196).

The **American Computer Museum** claims to be the "world's oldest museum of its type." Visitors can trace the computer's history from the abacus and early mechanical calculators through the development of the microchip. Guided tours and videos are geared for all ages and levels of computer knowledge. (That Bozeman should have a museum devoted to the evolution of the computer may be more an ode to the reach of the modem than to any particular role the city has played in the history of technology.) Closed Sunday, Monday and Thursday from September through May. Admission. ~ 2304 North 7th Avenue, Bozeman; 406-582-1288; e-mail director@compustory.org.

At the **Fish Technology Center**, visitors can observe U.S. Fish and Wildlife Service research the health, nutrition, reproduction and management of fish in hatcheries and in the wild. The center, established in 1965, also works with threatened species such as the pallid sturgeon and the Big Hole arctic grayling. Other species can also be seen. ~ 4050 Bridger Canyon Road, Bozeman; 406-994-9900; http://bozemanfishtech.fws.gov, e-mail bozeman fishtech@fws.gov.

Beyond the Fish Center northeast of Bozeman, Bridger Canyon Road (Route 86) climbs gradually through a short, rocky canyon to a mountain valley surrounded by the peaks of the Bridger Range. A smattering of ranches and new homes have been built in this valley, reminiscent of some in Switzerland. En route, look for directional signs to **Coffrin's Old West Gallery**, which displays a remarkable set of photographs of Sioux and early settler life taken by pioneer cameraman L. A. Huffman between 1878 and 1920. Call for hours; individual appointments welcomed. ~ 8118 Rolling Hills Drive, Bozeman; 406-586-0170, fax 406-586-9339; www.coffrinsoldwestgallery.com.

Sixteen miles from Bozeman at the head of the valley is **Bridger Bowl,** a popular local ski resort within Gallatin National Forest. ~ 15795 Bridger Canyon Road; 406-587-2111, 800-223-9609, fax 406-586-1518; www.bridgerbowl.com, e-mail skitrip@bridgerbowl.com.

GALLATIN VALLEY HIGHWAY Gallatin National Forest dominates Gallatin County south of Bozeman. Route 191 follows the Gallatin River, one of the three headwater streams of the Missouri, upstream nearly to its source in Yellowstone National Park. Through much of its course, the Gallatin, a favorite of whitewater rafters and kayakers, follows a narrow gorge between the Spanish Peaks on its west and the Gallatin Range on its east. The magnificent 82-mile drive to West Yellowstone passes two parcels of the **Lee Metcalf Wilderness Area** and a turnoff to the Big Sky resort before entering the northwest corner of Yellowstone Park.

See Chapter Seven for more information. ~ 3710 Fallon Street, Bozeman; 406-522-2520; www.fs.fed.us/r1/gallatin.

Below the head of the canyon, 13 miles southwest of Bozeman, is the old railroad town of Gallatin Gateway and its famous **Gallatin Gateway Inn**. The imposing, mission-style hotel, which is listed on the National Register of Historic Places, was built in 1927 by the Chicago, Milwaukee & St. Paul Railroad. ~ 76405 Route 191, Gallatin Gateway; 406-763-4672, 800-676-3522; www.gallatingatewayinn.com, e-mail gatewayinn@gallatingate wayinn.com.

On the south side of the 10,000-foot Spanish Peaks, 48 miles from Bozeman, is the **Big Sky Resort**. Established in the 1970s by a group of investors, Big Sky has grown into two separate year-round villages. Both Meadow Village and Mountain Village, nine miles apart, have lodging and dining facilities as well as shopping. Recreational activities range from skiing and snowmobiling in winter to golf, tennis, horseback riding, mountain bik-

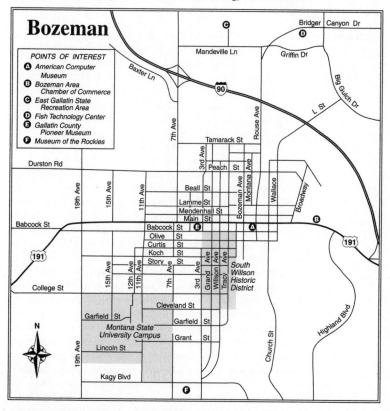

Bozeman

POINTS OF INTEREST
Ⓐ American Computer Museum
Ⓑ Bozeman Area Chamber of Commerce
Ⓒ East Gallatin State Recreation Area
Ⓓ Fish Technology Center
Ⓔ Gallatin County Pioneer Museum
Ⓕ Museum of the Rockies

ing, hiking, rafting and fishing in summer. ~ 1 Lone Mountain Trail, Big Sky; 406-995-5000, 800-548-4486, fax 406-995-5001; www.bigskyresort.com, e-mail info@bigskyresort.com.

In 1955, before Big Sky was even so much as a brainstorm, a **Soldier's Chapel** was built as a Second World War memorial just south of today's road junction. The nondenominational chapel offers a striking view of 11,188-foot Lone Mountain. Closed October through April. ~ Route 191, Big Sky; 406-995-4089.

Late network newscaster and Montana native Chet Huntley was one of the founders of Big Sky Resort.

If you want to get a closer look, you can take a **gondola** from Mountain Village to the 9500-foot level of the mountain. Operating summers as well as winters, the gondola affords memorable panoramas of the surrounding terrain. Admission.

From Big Sky, you can continue up the Gallatin River on Route 191, skirting the corner of Yellowstone National Park. The park's west entrance is at West Yellowstone, 39 miles south of Big Sky.

LODGING

Built in 1889, the **Lindley House Bed & Breakfast** is a lovely Victorian on the National Historic Register. Eight elegant and charming rooms (two with shared bath) are appointed with antiques and rugs; the Marie Antoinette suite has a fireplace, balcony and clawfoot bathtub. Outside, you can soak in the hot tub or wander through the English garden. A full gourmet breakfast is served in the dining room. Reservations recommended; two-night minimum required. ~ 202 Lindley Place, Bozeman; 406-587-8403, 866-587-8403, fax 406-582-8112; www.lindley-house.com, e-mail steve@lindley-house.com. MODERATE TO ULTRA-DELUXE.

In the heart of the South Willson Historic District, three blocks from downtown Bozeman, is the **Voss Inn**, a restored 1883 Victorian with elegant hardwood floors. Its six rooms all have private baths and contain such period antiques as clawfoot tubs, carved armoires, and brass or iron beds. Rooms are air-conditioned or have fans. Gourmet breakfasts can be delivered to the rooms or eaten family style in the parlor; afternoon tea is served in the parlor, which has a piano and small library. Each room also comes with sherry for the guests. ~ 319 South Willson Avenue, Bozeman; 406-587-0982, fax 406-585-2964; www.bozeman-vossinn.com, e-mail vossinn@bridgeband.com. DELUXE.

The **Bozeman Backpacker's Hostel** is a find. It has a dozen bunk beds in three dorm rooms; hostelers share toilets, showers and kitchen facilities. There is also a private room. Unlike many hostels, this one is open year-round and doesn't have a curfew. ~ 405 West Olive Street, Bozeman; 406-586-4659. BUDGET.

The chateau-like tower of the **Best Western GranTree Inn** is a landmark for visitors arriving off Route 90. This pleasant two-story property has a restaurant and coffee shop, a lounge and casino, an indoor pool, a jacuzzi and a coin laundry. Its 119 rooms, all reached from inside corridors, are spacious and well lit, with wood furniture. ~ 1325 North 7th Avenue, Bozeman; 406-587-5261, 800-624-5865, fax 406-587-9437. DELUXE.

Bozeman's largest motel, and one of its best bargains, is the **Holiday Inn**. Located north of the interstate off of 7th Avenue, this two-story lodging has an art deco appeal that extends from its restaurant and lounge to its 179 rooms, all with standard furnishings. The motel has an indoor pool, a jacuzzi, a Nautilus exercise area, a coin laundry and a game room. The hotel offers free lodging to children under 12 accompanied by a parent. Kids eat free in the restaurant, too. ~ 5 Baxter Lane, Bozeman; 406-587-4561, 800-366-5101, fax 406-587-4413; www.holidayinnbozeman.com. DELUXE.

For a taste of old-time luxury, visit the **Gallatin Gateway Inn**, a restored railroad hotel listed on the National Register of Historic Places. Built in Spanish Colonial style in 1927, the inn has a cavernous lobby with a huge fireplace and a grand piano beneath mahogany ceiling beams. Its 34 rooms are cozy but comfortable; most have full private baths. The 15-acre grounds include an outdoor swimming pool, a hot tub, a fly-casting pond and mountain-bike rentals. The inn's gourmet restaurant draws dinner guests from Bozeman, 13 miles north. ~ 76405 Route 191 South, Gallatin Gateway; 406-763-4672, 800-676-3522, fax 406-763-4672; www.gallatingatewayinn.com, e-mail gatewayinn@gallatingatewayinn.com. DELUXE TO ULTRA-DELUXE.

The most prestigious place to stay at the Big Sky resort complex is **The Huntley Lodge at Big Sky**, which also has a fine restaurant and a lounge with live entertainment. A three-story granite fireplace greets guests in the lobby. The 200 rooms are modern and spacious. On-site recreation includes golf, tennis, horseback riding, mountain biking and fishing; the lodge has two swimming pools, two saunas, whirlpools, a steam room and two exercise rooms. There are children's programs and a playground, a coin laundry and ski and sports shops. Closed mid-April to Memorial Day and from October to Thanksgiving ~ 1 Lone Mountain Trail, Big Sky; 406-995-5000, 800-548-4486, fax 406-995-5001; www.bigskyresort.com, e-mail info@bigsky.com. DELUXE TO ULTRA-DELUXE.

Montana's Yellowstone country has many friendly guest ranches. One of the longest established is the **Lone Mountain Ranch**, homesteaded as a cattle ranch in 1915 and attracting paying guests since the 1940s. Guests stay in 24 one- to four-bedroom log cabins with full baths and fireplaces; gourmet meals are served in an elaborate log-and-stone dining hall. Activities on the 250-acre ranch include horseback riding, trout fishing and hiking in summer, cross-country skiing and sleigh rides in winter. Closed in May and November. ~ P.O. Box 60069, Big Sky, MT 59716; 406-995-4644, 800-514-4644, fax 406-995-4670; www. lmranch.com, e-mail lmr@lmranch.com. ULTRA-DELUXE.

DINING

Noted for its excellent wine list and seafood chowder chockfull of scallops, shrimp and salmon, **Boodles** has earned a reputation as one of Bozeman's most popular eateries. Expect to find regional-international fare such as Angus beef tenderloins, hand-cut steaks, and grilled ahi tuna. Exposed brick walls, an antique back bar, and friendly service add to the warm atmosphere, and it's conveniently located in the heart of the historic downtown. Once the kitchen closes, the bar scene swings into action. Reservations recommended. Brunch is served on Sunday. ~ 215 East Main Street, Bozeman; 406-587-2901. MODERATE TO DELUXE.

John Bozeman's Bistro boasts "world cuisine with Montana style," and it delivers on that promise. It offers up innovative preparations of steak, seafood and other popular dishes, often with Asian culinary twists. Lunch and dinner are served Tuesday through Saturday. Closed Sunday and Monday. ~ 125 West Main Street, Bozeman; 406-587-4100, fax 406-587-0875. DELUXE TO ULTRA-DELUXE.

The Garage Restaurant Soup Shack and Mesquite Grill is just what its name implies: a small downtown diner with a mesquite charcoal grill. The result: steak, chicken, ribs and other foods with gourmet taste and low price tags. The patio is a great place for people watching. ~ 451 East Main Street, Bozeman; 406-585-8558. MODERATE.

HIDDEN ►

Order hearty soups and healthy salads at **Community Food Co-op**. This casual natural-foods deli also features a menu board of sandwiches and entrées, as well as daily ethnic specials such as sweet-potato quesadillas, Anasazi eggplant stew and tempeh stir-fry. A great deal at a low price. ~ 908 West Main Street, Bozeman; 406-587-4039, fax 406-587-7955; www.bozo.coop, e-mail huh@bozo.coop. BUDGET.

South of Bozeman (a mile south of the Big Sky junction) in a Best Western motel, **Buck's T-4** offers two attractive alternatives to resort restaurants. Buck's dining room specializes in wild game, from pheasant to wild boar, moose and antelope, at exotic prices. Steaks and seafood are also available. In the same location, the **Gameroom Grill** serves pizzas and other lighter, low-priced fare. Both restaurants are closed from late October to Thanksgiving. ~ Route 191, Big Sky; 406-995-4111, fax 406-995-2191; www. buckst4.com, e-mail dining@buckst4.com. ULTRA-DELUXE.

SHOPPING

Among Bozeman's shopping meccas is the **Emerson Center for the Arts and Culture**, a nonprofit arts center whose tenants include craftspeople (jewelers, ceramicists, woodworkers and cloth-iers) and cultural organizations. Some three dozen artisans have their studios in this former school built in 1919; many of them welcome visitors. Studios and gal-leries are closed Sunday and Monday. ~ 111 South Grand Avenue, Bozeman; 406-587-9797, fax 406-587-5998; www.theemerson.org.

It's fun to browse down-town Bozeman's 100 or so retail stores, including eight galleries and five antique shops.

To see the work of noted contemporary regional artists such as Gary Bates, Gennie DeWeese or Jerome Rankin, check out the **Beall Park Art Center**, four blocks north of Main Street. Closed Sunday and Monday. ~ 409 North Bozeman Street, Bozeman; 406-586-3970.

For true 19th- and 20th-century Western classics, you can't beat the top-of-the-line selection (with prices to match) at **Thomas Nygard Inc.** If you've ever had a hankering for a Charles Russell or an Albert Bierstadt, Nygard can help you out. Closed Sunday. ~ 135 East Main Street, Bozeman; 406-586-3636; www.nygardgallery.com.

Located in the Old Red Barn on Main Street, **The Antique Mall** claims to be one of Montana's largest antique malls. It boasts furniture, glassware, art and memorabilia. Closed Sunday. ~ 1530 West Main Street, Bozeman; 406-587-5281.

Readings by celebrated authors are regular features of **The Country Bookshelf**, an excellent, comprehensive bookstore in Bozeman. ~ 28 West Main Street, Bozeman; 406-587-0166.

Bozeman's largest enclosed shopping center is **Gallatin Valley Mall**, located about a mile west of downtown. Among its five dozen retailers are **Macy's**, **Zales**, **JC Penney** and **The Bay**. ~ 2825 West Main Street, Bozeman; 406-586-4565; www.gallatinvalleymall.com.

Check out the **farmers market** on summer Saturdays from about 9 a.m. to noon. Everything sold is made or grown in Mon-tana. ~ Gallatin County Fairgrounds (Haynes Pavilion), corner of Tamarack and Black streets, Bozeman; 406-388-6701; www.montanafarmersmarket.com.

The **Bozeman Symphony Orchestra and Symphonic Choir** has a fall-through-spring season. ~ 104 East Main Street, Bozeman; 406-585-9774; www.symphony.gomontana.com. **The Inter-mountain Opera Association** mounts one or two productions each year. ~ 104 East Main Street, Bozeman; 406-587-2889; www.operabozeman.org. In addition to regular year-round per-formances the **Montana Ballet Company** performs Tchaikov-sky's Nutcracker every Christmas season. ~ 221 East Main Street, Bozeman; 406-582-8702; www.montanaballet.com. All three or-ganizations perform at the Willson School auditorium. ~ 404 West Main Street, Bozeman.

NIGHTLIFE

Summer also brings **Shakespeare in the Parks** to Bozeman. The company presents two plays—typically Shakespearean or classical—almost nightly in a ten-week tour, late June to Labor Day, of 50 Montana communities. The tour begins and ends in Bozeman and plays its home stage (the MSU Campus Grove) several times. ~ 406-994-3901; www.montana.edu/shakespeare.

The spring-to-fall **Vigilante Theatre Company** produces several shows throughout the year, including dramas, comedies and musicals. The company is based in the Emerson Center for the Arts and Culture. ~ 111 South Grand Avenue, Bozeman; 406-586-3897; www.vigilantetheatrecompany.com.

There's a variety of popular nightlife hot spots in Bozeman. **Zebra Cocktail Lounge** features rock, jazz, funk, reggae or rhythm-and-blues bands most nights. Occasional cover. ~ 321 East Main Street, Bozeman; 406-585-8851; www.zebracocktail lounge.com.

At **Mixers** you can often see country bands; other nights they have a deejay spinning hip hop, techno and alternative rock. Occasional cover. ~ 515 West Aspen Street, Bozeman; 406-587-1652.

The **Cat's Paw** is a casino bar with a restaurant on the premises. ~ 721 North 7th Avenue, Bozeman; 406-586-3542.

Coffeehouses have gotten big among nondrinkers here; the **Leaf and Bean** often hosts acoustic musicians, poets and other throwbacks to the Beat days of Greenwich Village. The live music happens Thursday, Friday and Saturday nights, with bluegrass jams every Tuesday night. ~ 35 West Main Street, Bozeman; 406-587-1580.

PARKS

EAST GALLATIN STATE RECREATION AREA 🎣 🛶 A local park that surrounds little Glen Lake near the confluence of Bridger and Bozeman creeks, East Gallatin owes its existence to community volunteers. The canyon's reservoir, created in the 1940s, has a "no-wake" rule that restricts motorboaters to low speeds. Watersports lovers of all kinds appreciate their efforts. Facilities include picnic areas, a playground and restrooms. ~ Located on Manley Road, off Griffin Drive (between 7th and Rouse avenues) north of the Bozeman city limits; 406-587-4724, fax 406-587-9551.

HYALITE CANYON RECREATION AREA 🚶 🚲 🐎 🛶 🛶 Covering 34,000 acres of Gallatin National Forest southeast of Bozeman, this wheelchair-accessible park area is popular among hikers, mountain bikers and anglers seeking cutthroat trout and arctic grayling. Trails include a half-mile hard-surfaced track to Palisade Falls, a one-and-a-quarter-mile gravel track to Grotto Falls, and a strenuous five-and-a-half-mile ascent of 10,299-foot Hyalite Peak. There are picnic areas and restrooms. ~ From downtown Bozeman, take South 19th Avenue seven miles south to Hyalite Canyon Road (Route 62). It's ten miles from here to Hyalite Reservoir, twelve to the Palisade Falls trailhead; 406-522-2520, fax 406-522-2528; www.fs.fed.us/r1/gallatin.

▲ There are 37 RV/tent sites (no hookups) at three campgrounds; $10 per night in the summer; 16-day maximum stay.

GALLATIN NATIONAL FOREST 🏃🚴🏇 🎿🏠⛷🛶 ⛴⛴🎣 Stretching east and west across the Absaroka, Gallatin, Bridger and Madison ranges, this 1.7-million-acre forest includes large parts of two wilderness areas (the Absaroka-Beartooth and the Lee Metcalf), the upper reaches of four important trout rivers (the Yellowstone, Gallatin, Madison and Boulder), and the Bridger Bowl ski resort. Picnic areas and restrooms round out the amenities. ~ Route 191, south of Bozeman, and Route 89, south of Livingston, traverse the forest, and Route 287 northeast of West Yellowstone follows the Madison River to the Earthquake Lake Visitors Center (open summer). Numerous other spur roads provide access; 406-522-2520, fax 406-587-6758.

The stretch of the Madison River cutting through Lee Metcalf Wilderness Area's Bear Trap Canyon is some of the most challenging whitewater in the state. The run is for experienced rafters only.

▲ There are 650 RV/tent sites (no hookups) at 34 campgrounds; no charge to $12 per night; 16-day maximum stay. Reservations (877-444-6777) are accepted for campgrounds near Bozeman. Also, 24 recreational cabins can be reserved for $20 to $35 per night.

LEE METCALF WILDERNESS AREA 🏃🏇🏠🛶 Four parcels, totaling nearly a quarter million acres, include the spectacular Spanish Peaks area rising to more than 11,000 feet north of Big Sky; the crest of the Madison Range southwest of Big Sky as far as Quake Lake; the Monument Mountain region adjoining the northwest corner of Yellowstone National Park; and steep Bear Trap Canyon on the Madison River downstream from Ennis Lake. There's fine hiking and horseback riding, as well as rafting on the Madison. ~ Access from Big Sky, off Route 191 south of Bozeman; from Routes 191 and 287, north of West Yellowstone; and from Beartrap Canyon on the Madison River, off Route 84 west of Bozeman; 406-682-4253, 406-683-2337, fax 406-683-2970; e-mail mtinfo@mt.blm.gov.

▲ Primitive only.

Traveling west from Bozeman, Route 90 bypasses a series of small Gallatin Valley towns whose names speak of founders from a variety of backgrounds: Belgrade (Serbian), Churchill (British), Amsterdam (Dutch), Manhattan (New Yorker!).

Three Forks Area

SIGHTS   At Route 90 Exit 283, 25 miles west of Bozeman, a secondary road leads seven miles south to **Madison Buffalo Jump State Park**. This site preserves a cliff over which American Indians stampeded bison as long as 2000 years ago. Interpretive displays describe how buffalo meat and hides were thus obtained on a mass scale before the mid-16th century, when horses altered the Plains Indians' hunting practices. Admission. ~ Buffalo Jump Road, Logan; 406-994-4042, fax 406-994-4090.

At the valley's west end, located near the point where three rivers come together to form the Missouri River about 30 miles from Bozeman, is the intriguing town of **Three Forks**. Three Forks has a colorful history as a tribal crossroads, trading post and rail center.

Once the site of an 1810 trading post, the **Headwaters Heritage Museum** now contains a friendly jumble of artifacts and curiosities, including the largest brown trout ever caught in Montana. Displays include detailed re-creations of an old-fashioned dental office, a pioneer kitchen, a schoolroom, a blacksmith's shop and more. Closed in winter. ~ 202 South Main Street, Three Forks; 406-285-4778, 406-285-3644.

The **Sacajawea Hotel** was constructed in 1910. Recently restored, the handsome rail-junction hotel is on the National Register of Historic Places. ~ 5 North Main Street, Three Forks; 406-285-6515, fax 406-285-4210.

Five miles from town, **Missouri Headwaters State Park** is located at the convergence of the Gallatin, Madison and Jefferson rivers. "All of them run with great velocity and throw out large bodies of water," wrote Captain Meriwether Lewis in 1805. Admission. ~ Trident Road, Three Forks; 406-994-4042, fax 406-994-4090.

Lewis and Clark Caverns State Park, 18 miles west of Three Forks, houses the most impressive limestone caves in the northwestern United States. A fairyland of ancient stalactites, stalagmites and other wonders of the underground, created over millions of years, highlights the two-hour guided tour (offered May through September). Visitors should be modestly fit: They climb

AUTHOR FAVORITE

Who could resist a stop at a Montana fast-food establishment called **Custer's Last Root Beer Stand**? Located at a fork in westbound Route 2 as it heads out of Three Forks toward Lewis and Clark Caverns, this small but jumpin' joint has good burgers and great root beer. ~ 23 West Date Street, Three Forks; 406-285-6713. BUDGET.

a gradually sloping three-quarter-mile paved trail to the cavern entrance; descend another three-quarters of a mile through the fascinating subterranean chamber; then return one-half mile to the visitors center. The route includes more than 600 steps leading through low tunnels, narrow rock slides and cathedral-size chambers inhabited by bats. The cave's interior is a constant 50°F. Closed October through April. Admission. ~ Route 2, Cardwell; 406-287-3541 or 406-287-5424 (summer), fax 406-287-3034.

MADISON VALLEY HIGHWAY From Route 2 between Three Forks and Cardwell, Route 287 cuts south through Norris and Ennis to West Yellowstone and Yellowstone National Park. It's 107 miles from the Route 2 junction to the park entrance, most of it up the scenic valley of the Madison River. Flanked on the east by the 11,000-foot peaks of the Madison Range and on the west by the 10,000-foot Tobacco Root and Gravelly ranges, the route offers ready access to the Beaverhead-Deerlodge National Forest and several parcels of the Metcalf Wilderness.

At Norris, 19 miles from the route's start, Route 84 from Bozeman (38 miles east) joins the Madison Valley highway. Six miles east from McCallister is the **Trail Creek Access Recreational Area**, which provides access to the Metcalf Wilderness where the Madison River emerges from Beartrap Canyon. There's fishing, picnicking, whitewater rafting and hiking. ~ Route 84, Norris; 406-682-4082.

Ennis is in the heart of the Madison Valley, on the east side of the Tobacco Root Mountains, just 13 miles from the historic mining town of Virginia City (see "Alder Gulch," below). Ennis (pop. 800) is a hunting and fishing center whose three blocks of downtown businesses boast Old West–style facades.

Twelve miles south, visitors are welcome at the **Ennis National Fish Hatchery**, at the foot of the Gravelly Range. The hatchery breeds 23 million rainbow trout eggs each year to stock streams throughout the U.S. ~ 180 Fish Hatchery Road; 406-682-4847; e-mail ennis@fws.gov.

LODGING

A historic railroad hotel built in 1910, the three-story **Sacajawea Hotel** is a pleasant place to lay one's head on the road west from Bozeman. Its 30 restored guest rooms are small but clean, each with a private bath. The hotel has a romantic restaurant and small espresso bar; smoking is not permitted. ~ 5 North Main Street, Three Forks; 406-285-6515, 888-722-2529, fax 406-285-4210; www.sacajaweahotel.com, e-mail info@sacajaweahotel.com. DELUXE.

A simple lodging is the **Broken Spur Motel**. The two-story motel has 21 neat, clean rooms with TVs and phones. There are also a suite and two kitchenettes. Continental breakfast, com-

plete with homemade muffins and rolls, is included in the rate. ~
Route 2, Three Forks; 406-285-3237, 888-354-3048, fax 406-
285-3237; www.brokenspurmotel.com, e-mail webmaster@bro
kenspurmotel.com. MODERATE.

In the heart of the Madison River Valley is the **Rainbow
Valley Lodge**. Its 24 guest rooms have log-cabin decor; several
are two-bedroom units with efficiency kitchens. Facilities include
a swimming pool, a barbecue area and a coin laundry; there are
even horse corrals for those intending backcountry excursions. ~
Route 287 South, Ennis; 406-682-4264, 800-452-8254, fax 406-
682-5012; www.rainbowvalley.com, e-mail rnbwvlly@3rivers.
net. MODERATE.

DINING

If you're craving a homestyle meal, head to the **Longhorn Cafe**.
Breakfast offers are omelettes and pancakes; hot meatloaf sand-
wiches, pork chops and burgers pop up at lunch. No dinner.
Closed Sunday. ~ Route 10 West, Three Forks; 406-285-4106.
BUDGET TO MODERATE.

The **Historic Headwaters Restaurant** was first established in
1908, and the decor retains the charm of that bygone era. Fortunately, the food is completely up to date. Dinner entrées include
applewood-smoked pork chops, parmesan-encrusted halibut filet
and fresh salmon cakes. For vegetarians there are pasta and stir-
fry dishes. Closed Monday and Tuesday. ~ 105 South Main Street,
Three Forks; 406-285-4511; www.headwatersrestaurant.com.

Just down the road from Lewis and Clark Caverns State Park,
La Hood Park Restaurant makes an easy stop for a quick meal.
An extensive menu features Montana standbys like steak, chicken
and fresh fish. The homemade *sopapillas*, on the other hand, are
a welcome surprise. ~ Route 2, Cardwell; 406-287-3281.

Perhaps the fine French, Cajun and Creole cuisine dished up
at the **Continental Divide Restaurant** is a legacy of the Louisiana
Purchase. Otherwise, it's hard to explain how a place this good
could have found itself behind an Old West facade in an area that
caters mainly to outdoor sportsmen and tourists. If you're staying in Virginia City, it's worth driving the 13 miles to dine here. The
Sunday jazz brunch is a special treat. Closed in winter. ~ Yellowstone Highway, Ennis; 406-682-7600. DELUXE TO ULTRA-DELUXE.

The **Schoolhouse** near the Route 84 junction is housed in,
you guessed it, an old schoolhouse. The fare here is authentic
Mexican, prepared in delectable homemade fashion. They also
have barbecue and burgers. Closed Monday through Thursday
and January through February. ~ Route 287, Norris; 406-685-
3200. BUDGET TO MODERATE.

SHOPPING

If you're looking for something to read on those long car rides,
look no further than **Magpie Books**, a general new and used book-

store that specializes in Western Americana. Closed Sunday and
Monday. ~ 101 South Main Street, Three Forks; 406-285-4654.

MADISON BUFFALO JUMP STATE PARK 🚶🚴 Using a primitive but highly efficient hunting method, American Indians
stampeded herds of bison over this cliff for some 1500 years—until
they obtained horses and guns in the mid-16th century. Interpretive displays describe the buffalo's importance to the Plains
Indians' way of life. There are picnic areas and restrooms. ~
From Logan Exit 283 off Route 90, five miles east of Three
Forks, take Buffalo Jump Road south for seven miles; 406-994-
4042, fax 406-994-4090.

PARKS

MISSOURI HEADWATERS STATE PARK 🚶⛴🚤⚓ Located
where the Gallatin, Madison and Jefferson rivers flow together
to create the Missouri River, this park offers fishing and hiking,
wildlife viewing, camping and picnicking. Exhibits discuss the
site's importance as a gathering place for American Indians long
before the Lewis and Clark expedition found it
in 1805. Facilities include picnic areas and restrooms. Day-use fee, $5 per vehicle. ~ Take Exit
278 from Route 90 at Three Forks; follow Route
205 east for two miles and then Route 286 (Trident
Road) north for two miles; 406-994-4042, fax 406-
994-4090.

Don't be spooked by the
bats at Lewis and Clark
Caverns State Park—
these nocturnal crea-
tures will be sleeping
when you visit and
will most likely be
startled by *you*.

▲ There are 23 primitive sites (no hookups); $12;
7-day maximum stay.

LEWIS AND CLARK CAVERNS STATE PARK 🚶🏕⚓
Deep limestone caves, some of the most impressive in North
America, are the highlight of Montana's first state park. The park
is open year-round, but cavern tours operate from May through
September only. Bats inhabit the caves, while deer and other animals live on the nearby slopes. Picnic areas, restrooms, showers,
a visitors center, a restaurant and an amphitheater round out the
amenities. Day-use fee, $5 per vehicle. ~ Take Route 2 (off Route
90) from Three Forks (18 miles east to the park) or from Cardwell (seven miles west); 406-287-3541 or 406-287-5424 (summer), fax 406-287-3034; www.fwp.state.mt.us.

▲ There are 40 RV/tent sites (no hookups); $15 per night;
14-day maximum stay. Three primitive cabins are available for $25
to $39 per night depending upon season.

The discovery of the richest deposit of placer gold on earth
took place in the valley of a tiny creek mid-way between
Three Forks and Butte. The Alder Gulch mining district
yielded some $130 million in gold nuggets, gold flakes and gold
dust in the decades that followed the original strike in 1863. After

Alder Gulch

the gold ran out, Virginia City persisted, first as Montana's territorial capital, today as the tourism-oriented seat of Madison
County. Nearly 100 buildings in nearby Nevada City have been
completely restored, while the roads surrounding Alder Gulch
offer myriad reminders of the boom era.

SIGHTS

HIDDEN ►

Blink and you'll miss it—**Twin Bridges** is a tiny town about 65
miles from Three Forks, situated where the Ruby, Beaverhead and
Big Hole rivers converge to form the Jefferson. It's prime fly-fishing country, but that's not the only reason to visit this refreshingly
unaffected rural hamlet. With its old-time buildings, Western craft
shops and quietly stunning mountain scenery, Twin Bridges offers
a taste of the pre-celebrity invasion of Montana. Be sure to check
out the Twin Bridges' Floating Flotillas and Fish Fantasies celebration if you're in town the fourth weekend in July. You can see
parade floats that really do float—down the river that is.

Start your explorations at the **Twin Bridges Historical
Association**, which holds a collection of mining artifacts, farm
equipment and turn-of-the-20th-century photos. ~ 203 South
Main Street, Twin Bridges.

HIDDEN ►

R.L. Winston Rod Company has been hand-crafting fly-fishing rods since 1929. Originally based in San Francisco, the business moved to Twin Bridges in 1976. Tours of the operation are
available every weekday at 11 a.m. A must for fly-fishing enthusiasts. Closed on the weekends. ~ 500 South Main Street, Twin
Bridges; 406-684-5674; www.winstonrods.com, e-mail info@win
stonrods.com.

On the banks of Ram's Horn Creek halfway between Twin
Bridges and Nevada City, look for a large log building with a historical marker sign nearby. **Robber's Roost** was a
roadhouse (read *saloon/bordello*) where villains
and ne'er-do-wells gathered in the 1860s and 1870s
when stagecoaches that ran between Virginia City
and Bannack were subject to regular holdups. ~ 2841
Route 287, Sheridan.

Not surprisingly, Nevada
City is a favorite of movie
companies; such films as
Little Big Man and *Return
to Lonesome Dove*
were shot here.

Nevada City, 29 miles from Twin Bridges, and Virginia City, little more than another mile up Alder Gulch,
grew up around the 1863 gold strike in the Tobacco Root
Mountains. When President Abraham Lincoln created the
Montana Territory the following year, Virginia City was chosen
as its capital and remained so until Helena wrested that status
away in 1875. But long after other mining towns were abandoned, Alder Gulch continued to produce gold.

By World War II, though, Nevada City was a ghost town and
Virginia City was getting decidedly long in the tooth. A team of
historic preservationists headed by Charles and Sue Bovey restored and furnished original buildings wherever possible; in the

case of Nevada City, they moved several complete structures in from other areas.

Today, Nevada City has the authentic flavor of an early-day mining camp. Officially known as the **Nevada City Museum**, it consists of several streets with cabins, an old piano store and the pioneer-era Star Bakery. There are also a cozy hotel and a restaurant. Closed October through March. Admission. ~ Route 287; 406-843-5555.

Across the highway from the open-air museum, the **Alder Gulch River of Gold** allows visitors to try their hands at gold panning, rocking and sluicing. The business also has a gift shop and mining museum, including a historic dredge. Closed in winter. Admission. ~ Route 287, Nevada City; 406-843-5526.

The Nevada City music hall contains a remarkable collection of machines that produce music ranging from the harmonic to the cacophonic.

While Nevada City is a re-creation, **Virginia City**, a National Historic Landmark district, remains very much alive. Every building along the three-block stretch of Wallace Street west of Broadway is of original construction. No other main street in the American West can make that claim.

Walking-tour brochures are available from numerous merchants as well as the **Virginia City Area Chamber of Commerce**. ~ 302 West Wallace Street, Virginia City; 406-843-5555, 800-829-2969; www.virginiacitychamber.com, e-mail info@virginiacitychamber.com.

Wallace Street is the main drag; in addition to several restaurants and numerous fine shops worth a browse, its buildings of special note include the 1864 **Montana Post** print shop, whose old typesetting equipment is a reminder that the territory's first newspaper was printed here; **Ranks Mercantile** (1865), Montana's oldest continuously operating business; **Stonewall Hall** and **Content Corner** (both 1865), once original territorial government buildings; the **E. L. Smith General Store** (1863); the **Sauebier Blacksmith Shop** (1863); and the **McGovern Store** (1864), featuring original 19th-century women's wear.

Pioneer artifacts and historical photographs and documents are displayed at the **Thompson-Hickman Memorial Museum**. Closed October through April. ~ 218 East Wallace Street, Virginia City; 406-843-5238. Other events of historical significance are recorded at the **Spencer Watkins Museum**. Closed in winter. ~ 219 West Wallace Street, Virginia City; 406-843-5500. Admission. Atmospheric **Boot Hill Cemetery** is just two blocks north of Wallace Street. ~ Jackson and Jefferson streets, Virginia City.

The **Alder Gulch Shortline** narrow-gauge railroad, located at West Wallace and Main streets in Virginia City, runs all summer long between the 1901 Northern Pacific Depot at Virginia City's west end and the **Steam Railroad Museum** (Route 287, Nevada City), lodged in railcars in Nevada City and displaying outstanding steam cars of the time. ~ 406-843-5247.

LODGING

HIDDEN ►

A variety of lodgings are available in the Alder Gulch area. **The Old Hotel**, occupying a restored 1879 hostelry, is a cozy bed-and-breakfast inn. The two suites are tastefully decorated with antiques and have separate entrances. The sitting room in each suite features a double futon, easily accommodating children or extra guests. Breakfast is included in the rate; a fisherman's lunch can be packed upon request. Limited opening mid-October to February, closed in March. ~ 101 East 5th Avenue, Twin Bridges; 406-684-5959; www.theoldhotel.com, e-mail oldhotel@3rivers.net. DELUXE.

A stately 1879 Queen Anne Victorian, the **Bennett House Country Inn** offers six eclectically decorated rooms, all with shared bath, and a small log cabin complete with kitchenette. Ask ahead to see if the hot tub is available. Breakfast is included in the rate. ~ 115 East Idaho Street, Virginia City; 406-843-5220, 877-843-5220; www.bennetthouseinn.com, e-mail stay@bennetthouse inn.com. MODERATE TO DELUXE.

When you book with the **Fairweather Inn**, you can opt for Victorian hotel rooms with private or shared baths, upscale suites with period antiques or rustic mining cabins in Nevada City whose interiors have been restored but whose exteriors have hardly been touched. Closed late September to mid-May. ~ 305 West Wallace Street, Virginia City; 406-843-5377, 800-829-2969, fax 406-843-5237; www.virginiacity.com/fair.htm, e-mail rogako@3rivers.net. MODERATE.

DINING

HIDDEN ►

En route to Alder Gulch, the family-oriented **Blue Anchor Restaurant** offers three meals a day, seven days a week. Home-style breakfasts are of the egg-and-potato variety. For lunch you can get soup and sandwiches, and for dinner hearty steak and prime rib. No dinner on Tuesday or Wednesday. ~ 102 North Main Street, Twin Bridges; 406-684-5655. BUDGET TO DELUXE.

The inventive cuisine at **The Old Hotel** makes it popular with locals and visitors alike. Fresh local ingredients combine in tasty concoctions: asparagus crêpes, rack of lamb with raspberry chipotle sauce, chili honey–glazed pork medallions. Vegetarians will find dishes such as stuffed eggplant and spinach lasagna. Reservations are strongly recommended. Closed Monday and from mid-October to late November. Check out the Sunday brunch. ~ 101 East 5th Avenue, Twin Bridges; 406-684-5959; www.theoldhotel.com, e-mail oldhotel@3rivers.net. DELUXE TO ULTRA-DELUXE.

Built in 1863 and considered to be the oldest surviving eating establishment in Montana, the **Star Bakery** is open for breakfast, lunch and dinner. No dinner on Monday. Closed Labor Day to Memorial Day. ~ Route 287, Nevada City; 406-843-5525. BUDGET TO MODERATE.

Locals flock to the **City Bakery** for homemade goodies like scones, croissants and turnovers. A special savory treat is the prosciutto roll. Closed mid-September to mid-May. ~ 325 West Wallace Street, Virginia City; 406-843-5227; e-mail jarvismail@yahoo.com. BUDGET.

City Bakery is famous for its Vigilante Bread— the first sliced bread in the region.

Located in the old Wells Fargo Building, **Banditos** serves up excellent southwestern fare. Along with chimichangas, fajitas and *carne asada*, they also serve a variety of fresh fish dishes. The word is definitely out about this place, so reservations are strongly advised. No lunch. Closed October to late May. ~ 320 Wallace Street, Virginia City; 406-843-5556. DELUXE.

In the summer, the **Copper Palace/Roadmaster Grill** adds an element of fun to your dining experience. The Copper Palace is an old-time pub that features Montana microbrews. A 1950 Roadmaster stands as the centerpiece for the Roadmaster Grill. It's not the only car in the lot, though: the bed of a 1947 Chevy pick-up serves as the salad bar, while both the front and rear of a 1949 Cadillac and a 1957 Chevy Bel Aire have been converted into seating areas (reservations recommended for car seating). Specialties are barbecue and rotisserie chicken. Closed October through May. ~ 126 West Wallace Street, Virginia City; 406-843-5234, fax 406-843-5273; www.roadmastergrille.com. MODERATE.

SHOPPING

Design your own cowboy hat at the **Montana Mad Hatter**, specialists in handmade headgear. Be sure to check out the beadwork and other fine details that adorn their carefully crafted creations. Closed weekends, except Saturday by appointment.~ 100 West 4th Avenue, Twin Bridges; 406-684-5869; www.montanahats.com.

◄ *HIDDEN*

The Weaver's Studio offers more hand-crafted wonders, displaying a variety of wool rugs and saddle blankets. There's also a small espresso bar on the premises. Call for hours. ~ 108 South Main Street, Twin Bridges; 406-684-5744.

There are plenty of souvenir shops in the restored mining towns of Alder Gulch, but the **Vigilante Gift Shop** may be the biggest and friendliest of the bunch. ~ 109 West Wallace Street, Virginia City; 406-843-5263.

NIGHTLIFE

Virginia City's **Bale of Hay Saloon** was used to store hay for the livery next door during the town's boom years, but it was restored as this saloon in 1945. Always rustic and often lively, the saloon features occasional live music and antique music machines. Closed mid-September to mid-May. ~ 330 West Wallace Street, Virginia City; 406-843-5700.

From June to mid-September, the **Virginia City Players**—Montana's oldest summer-stock troupe—act out 19th-century melodramas and vaudeville shows nightly except Monday at the Virginia City Opera House. ~ 338 West Wallace Street, Virginia City; 406-843-5314; www.vcplayers.com. The **Brewery Follies** offer cabaret-style follies every night but Tuesday at the Gilbert Brewery. ~ Hamilton and Jefferson streets, Virginia City; 406-843-5218; www.breweryfollies.com.

Livingston Area

East of Bozeman, interstate Route 90 crosses a low pass in the Bridger Range and descends to the Yellowstone River Valley, where it enters the historic rail town of Livingston. The hub of the upper Yellowstone Valley, Livingston is a place where wilderness meets the Wild West. Founded in 1882 by the Northern Pacific Railroad and named for a director of that line, the town was the original gateway to Yellowstone National Park. Tourists changed trains here from the main east–west line to a spur line that followed the Yellowstone River upstream to Gardiner at the park's north entrance.

The community quickly became a trading center for farmers, ranchers and miners of the Yellowstone Valley, and by 1905 a thriving city of about 5000 people had emerged. Modern Livingston's population hovers around 16,000. But 436 buildings from that turn-of-the-20th-century boom era are preserved; its downtown historic district and three residential districts are on the National Register of Historic Places. Among them is a log cabin that once was the home of notorious frontierswoman Martha "Calamity Jane" Canary. (When a public disturbance led to her being jailed, she became disenchanted with Livingston and left town.)

SIGHTS

The place to begin a walking tour, or to gather information on area attractions, is the **Livingston Chamber of Commerce.** Closed weekends September through April. ~ 303 East Park Street, Livingston; 406-222-0850, fax 406-222-0852; www.yellowstone-chamber.com, e-mail info@livingston-chamber.com.

The **Livingston Depot Center** is located in the 1902 Northern Pacific station, designed in Italianate style by an architectural firm that created New York's Grand Central Station. Exhibits include rail history, Yellowstone exploration, blues shows and special events. It's open daily from the end of May to the end of September and doubles as a performing-arts center in the winter. Admission. ~ 200 West Park Street, Livingston; 406-222-2300; www.livingstondepot.org, e-mail depot@ycsi.net.

There are more history exhibits across the tracks and two blocks north at the **Yellowstone Gateway Museum of Park County.** Located in an early-20th-century schoolhouse, it's open daily in summer and closed weekends the rest of the year. Admission. ~ 118 West Chinook Street, Livingston; 406-222-4184; www.livingston museums.org, e-mail museum@ycsi.net.

The **International Fly Fishing Museum** is a must-see for avid anglers. Closed weekends September through May. Admission. ~ 215 East Lewis Street, Livingston; 406-222-9369.

PARADISE VALLEY   The Route 89 corridor upriver to Yellowstone Park, 53 driving miles south of Livingston, follows the scenic **Paradise Valley** beneath the constant gaze of the Absaroka Range. The Yellowstone River—the longest undammed river in the United States—is considered a blue-ribbon trout stream through this portion, which is also popular among whitewater rafters.

Twenty miles south, near the small towns of Emigrant and Pray, are the **Chico Hot Springs**. A resort here provides access to natural mineral hot springs and other health therapies. ~ Chico Road, Pray; 406-333-4933, 800-468-9232; www.chicohotsprings.com, e-mail chico@chicohotsprings.com.

In winter, Absaroka Dogsled Treks takes couples or small groups on canine-powered trips into the Emigrant Peak area. ~ Chico Hot Springs; 406-333-4933.

Farther south, via Sixmile Creek Road, **Dailey Lake** is as popular among board-sailing enthusiasts as with trout and walleye fishermen. Trailheads above the lake lead into the Absaroka-Beartooth Wilderness Area.

Climbing the Yellowstone valley from Emigrant, Route 89 circles 8600-foot Dome Mountain, home of a historic winter elk range. West of the hamlet of Miner (38 miles from Livingston), Rock Creek Road extends nine miles to a trailhead for the **Gallatin Petrified Forest**, whose fossilized specimens include still-upright tree trunks estimated to be between 35 and 55 million years old. Another nine miles past Miner, near the small tourist center of **Corwin Springs**, bright-red **Devils Slide** is an unmistakable geological feature: The exposed sedimentary rocks at the base of Cinnabar Mountain are about 200 million years old.

It seems only natural to stay in historic hotels throughout historic communities. The **Murray Hotel**, in the heart of town, has 28 suites with individual theme decor, private baths, wet bars and standard amenities. There's also a restaurant and bar. ~ 201 West Park Street, Livingston; 406-222-1350, fax 406-222-2752; www. murrayhotel.com, e-mail info@murrayhotel.com. MODERATE TO DELUXE.

LODGING

For a relaxing getaway complete with soothing mineral springs and elegantly prepared meals you should pay a visit to the grande dame of Montana resorts, the turn-of-the-20th-century **Chico Hot Springs**. Accommodations range from guest rooms in the original main lodge to contemporary hotel rooms, condominiums and cab-

Text continued on page 202.

Choosing a
Guest Ranch

Only two states, Colorado and Wyoming, have more guest ranches than does Montana, and perhaps no one region in either of those states boasts more of these rural resorts than south central Montana.

The bible of the guest-ranch genre, *Gene Kilgore's Ranch Vacations*, lists 15 of them in this part of Montana, and official state tourism rolls triple the figure.

The earliest guest ranches (then better known as "dude ranches") were established around the turn of the century in Montana, Wyoming and Colorado for easterners enthralled by the idea of Buffalo Bill–style adventure and romance.

With railroads traversing the continent and the hostile Indian tribes subjugated, working cattle ranchers often found themselves besieged by requests from friends and relatives who wanted to come and visit for weeks at a time. Some of these ranchers saw an opportunity to increase their revenues, and so began advertising accommodations and charging guests.

By the 1920s, 35 of them in the greater Yellowstone National Park area banded together to form **The Dude Ranchers' Association**, which today remains the most respected of all guest-ranch coalitions. In recent years, membership in the association has more than tripled to 118 ranches in 12 Western states and two Canadian provinces. That figure represents only a fraction of the total number of guest ranches. ~ P.O. Box 2307, Cody, WY 82414; 307-587-2339, fax 307-587-2776; www.duderanch.org, e-mail info@duderanch.org.

In 1994, according to the Tourism Works for America Council in Washington, D.C., visitors spent $31 million for U.S. guest-ranch vacations, paying anywhere from $550 to $1895 per week for the privilege. A 1994 survey by the council indicated that five percent of the adult U.S. population had at some time visited a dude or cattle ranch.

In the text of this chapter, you may already have read about the Boulder River, Lone Mountain, Lost Fork and Mountain Sky ranches. But there are many others.

The **C-B Cattle and Guest Ranch**, 20 miles southeast of Ennis, has no planned activities but attracts scores of anglers each summer to fly-fish the renowned waters of the Madison River. Closed late August to late June. ~ Box 148, Cameron, MT 59720; 406-682-4608 (summer), 951-676-5646 (winter); www.cbranch.com.

There's the **Diamond J Ranch**, surrounded by the Lee Metcalf Wilderness, whose family orientation is clear in the number and variety of children's programs it offers: from horseback riding and fishing to skeet shooting, swimming and tennis. A one-week minimum stay is required. Closed mid-September to mid-June. ~ Box 577, Ennis, MT 59729; 406-682-4867, 877-929-4867, fax 406-682-4106; www. diamondjranch.com, e-mail totalmgt@3rivers.net.

In the foothills northeast of Bozeman is the **G Bar M Ranch**, a working cattle ranch that has welcomed guests since the 1930s. Guests spend most of their week herding cattle, repairing fences and basically paying for the chance to be ranch hands.~ Box 29, Clyde Park, MT 59018; 406-686-4423; www.gbarm.com, e-mail gbarmranch@mcn.net.

That's just a sampling of the options available. But how do you, as a first-time potential guest, determine which ranch experience is best for you and your family?

Not the least factor is price range. You can expect to pay anywhere from $75 to $275 per person per night. At the low end, your accommodation will be quite rustic and you may be cooking your own meals. At the top end, you will live in luxury and dine on gourmet cuisine. Many ranches require a one-week minimum stay for their guests, especially during summer; others may allow guests to stay on a nightly basis.

Also consider the range and choice of activities, the existence of children's programs, the level of staff involvement, the number of other guests with whom you'll be sharing your visit, and the accessibility of the ranch.

ins. Besides the famed pools, the resort offers dogsled rides in winter and fishing and horsebackriding in summer. No phones or TVs in the rooms guarantee peace and quiet. ~ Chico Road, Pray; 406-333-4933, fax 406-333-4694; www.chicohotsprings.com, e-mail chico@chicohotsprings.com. MODERATE.

DINING

For a simple yet hearty meal, the **Pickle Barrel** makes hot and cold sandwiches to order; the cheesesteak is a popular choice, as is the bobcat special. If you're more in the mood for soup, there are three to choose from, including the daily chili with steak. ~ 131 South Main Street, Livingston; 406-222-5469. BUDGET.

Dim lighting and white tablecloths set the tone for a romantic meal at the **Livingston Bar & Grille**. A 1900s-era mahogany bar adds to the elegant ambiance. The French-inspired menu of steak, lobster, veal and pasta is complemented by a selection of Spanish and French wines. Dinner only. ~ 130 North Main Street, Livingston; 406-222-7909, fax 406-222-0663. DELUXE TO ULTRA-DELUXE.

Crazy Coyote Mexican Food serves up south-of-the-border standbys, including fajitas, enchiladas and burritos. Salsas range from mild to fiery hot. Vegetarian options are available upon request. Closed Sunday. ~ 206 South 11th Street, Livingston; 406-222-1548. BUDGET.

For a touch of culinary class served on colorful antique dishes, pay **Rumours** in downtown Livingston a visit. The owner describes the fare at her cheerful restaurant as French comfort food. And rightly so, though offerings aren't limited to Gallic classics. You're as likely to find portobello mushroom pasta and daily risotto specials on the menu as you are *boeuf bourguignon* or *coq au vin*. Homemade chicken pot pie ranks as the hands-down lunch favorite at this sunny inviting eatery. For breakfast, don't miss the oatmeal brûlée—crème brûlée baked over old-fashioned slow-cooked oats and crowned with fresh berries. And yes, it is

AUTHOR FAVORITE

The **Mountain Sky Guest Ranch** is one of the grand old dude ranches of Montana. Located 32 miles southwest of Livingston, five miles west of Route 89 in the Paradise Valley, it has 30 cabins—some rustic, some modern—and a rebuilt lodge with three stone fireplaces and a grand piano. Guests must book a full week's stay (in summer, at least), during which they get three gourmet meals daily, evening entertainment, top-class horseback riding and fly-fishing. Closed October through May. ~ Big Creek Road, Emigrant; 406-333-4911, 800-548-3392, fax 406-333-4537; www.mtnsky.com, e-mail mountainsky@mcn.net. ULTRA-DELUXE.

worth every calorie. ~ 102 North 2nd Street, Livingston; 406-222-5154. BUDGET TO DELUXE.

Among Livingston's art galleries is the **Paradise Gallery**, where the art of Carol Newbury Howe and other wildlife artists is presented. Open by appointment only. ~ East River Road, Livingston; 406-222-6297. **Books and Music Etc.** is the leading book dealer. Closed Sunday January through May. ~ 106 South Main Street, Livingston; 406-222-7766.

SHOPPING

Livingston has a pair of noteworthy stage groups. The **Firehouse 5 Playhouse** presents a variety of community musicals and holiday specials throughout the year, summer vaudeville from July 4th to July 10th, as well as a children's workshop in early summer. ~ Sleeping Giant Trade Center, Route 89, Livingston; 406-222-1420. The **Blue Slipper Theatre**, now in its fourth decade, serves up comedies, mysteries, dramas and other more serious productions year-round. ~ 113 East Callender Street, Livingston; 406-222-7720.

NIGHTLIFE

You know you're in hunting country when you walk into **The Sport**—the walls are hung with various animal-head trophies. It's a friendly place if you don't happen to be a four-legged creature. ~ 114 South Main Street, Livingston; 406-222-9500.

SACAJAWEA PARK Located beside the Yellowstone River, this Livingston municipal park is one of the nicest in Montana. At its broad riverine lagoon, children can fish or feed ducks and geese. Within the park is Livingston Civic Center, where indoor scenes from Robert Redford's 1992 *A River Runs Through It* were filmed. Picnic areas, restrooms, a band shell, tennis courts, a playground and a wading pool round out the amenities. ~ From downtown Livingston, follow South Yellowstone Street to its south end; 406-222-8155, fax 406-222-3260.

PARKS

Big Timber—33 miles east of Livingston and an hour's drive from Bozeman at the foot of the Crazy Mountains—is at a geographical transition point. West of the town, the Absaroka Range rises to lofty heights, while east stretch the vast Great Plains. A livestock-producing and recreational center surrounded by Gallatin National Forest, Big Timber has several sites of interest.

▼▼▼▼▼▼▼▼▼▼▼▼
Big Timber Area

A historical museum, the **Crazy Mountain Museum**, features a miniature reproduction of Big Timber as it appeared in 1907, when it was known as Cobblestone City. Exact down to the finest architectural details, it covers more than 12 blocks of the old town at a scale of $^1/_{16}$ inch to one foot. Fewer than 20 percent of the

SIGHTS

184 buildings represented in the model still stand in downtown Big Timber. Open summer and by appointment. Closed Monday. ~ Frontage Road, Route 90 Exit 367, Big Timber; 406-932-5126.

Also in Big Timber, firearms aficionados enjoy informal tours of the **Shiloh Rifle Manufacturing Co.** Closed Saturday and Sunday. ~ 201 Centennial Drive, Big Timber; 406-932-4454; www.shilohrifle.com. Sharps and Winchester rifles and accessories circa 1870 are on display at the **C. Sharps Arms** showroom. Closed Sunday. ~ 100 Centennial Drive, Big Timber; 406-932-4353; www.csharpsarms.com, e-mail csharps@ptc-cmc.net. The **Yellowstone River Trout Hatchery** is open for visits. ~ Fairgrounds Road, Big Timber; 406-932-4434.

The **Crazy Mountains**, a small but rugged Rockies subrange whose jagged summits rise to more than 11,000 feet, are located to the north of Big Timber. The range is mostly contained within Gallatin National Forest. The most direct access is via Big Timber Canyon Road, which begins 11 miles north of Big Timber off Route 191.

South of Big Timber, Route 298 (Boulder Road) follows the **Boulder River** more than 40 miles upstream from its confluence with the Yellowstone River to near its source in the Absaroka-Beartooth Wilderness. A good number of national-forest campgrounds are located along this corridor; more than a dozen trails extend into the wilderness, where vehicular travel is forbidden. A highlight along this route is the **Boulder River Falls**, 27 miles south of Big Timber. The impressive 90-foot falls once cascaded through a natural stone bridge at low water, but the arch collapsed in 1988 after centuries of erosion.

Columbus is the home of Montana Silversmiths, the world's largest manufacturer of silver jewelry, belt buckles and other cowboy-style trappings.

Sheep and cattle ranchers have waged a successful war against prairie dogs, which compete with stock for grasses and forage, and whose burrowing creates holes that often cause leg injuries to livestock. The prairie dog's range is now less than 20 percent its original size. The **Greycliff Prairie Dog Town State Park**, nine miles east of Big Timber, is a 98-acre park that preserves a traditional prairie-dog colony, albeit tiny compared to the huge cities of these ground squirrels that once spread across the plains. Admission. ~ Route 90 Exit 377, Greycliff; 406-247-2940, fax 406-248-5026; e-mail twalters@state.mt.us.

The town of **Columbus,** an old stage and rail station on Route 90 where the Stillwater River joins the Yellowstone, lies about halfway between Big Timber and Billings. Aside from being the junction of Route 78, which threads its way 48 miles through the foothills of the Beartooth Range to Red Lodge, Columbus is the gateway to the Stillwater Mining Company, largest platinum mine in the United States, 35 miles west near Nye.

The **Museum of the Beartooths** has one of the finest collections of homestead-era farm and household machinery you'll ever find. Closed Monday and from October through May. ~ 440 East 5th Avenue North, Columbus; 406-322-4588.

You definitely feel like you've time-warped backwards a century when you spend the night at the historic **Grand Hotel**. Built in 1890, this beautifully restored brick hotel now functions as a B&B as well as a community gathering place. Victorian-decorated rooms come furnished with oak-framed mirrors, highboy dressers, comfy beds and plush terry robes. Most rooms have private baths. ~ 139 McLeod Street, Big Timber; 406-932-4459; www.thegrand-hotel.com, e-mail thegrandhotel@mcn.net. MODERATE TO ULTRA-DELUXE.

LODGING

One of Montana's longest established guest ranches is the **Boulder River Ranch**. Situated at 5000 feet in an Absaroka Mountain canyon, the ranch—which is open only from June to mid-September, and accepts payment by cash or check only—first opened to guests in 1918. Today it's run by the third- and fourth-generation Aller family, and boasts 15 rustic cabins, family-style meals and a wide range of riding and fishing activities. Closed mid-September to mid-June. ~ 2815 Boulder Road, McLeod; 406-932-5926, fax 406-932-6411; www.boulderriverranch.com, e-mail boulderriver@mcn.net. DELUXE TO ULTRA-DELUXE.

The best place to dine in Big Timber is the two-story, red-brick **Grand Hotel**. Built in 1890, the historic hotel's Victorian restaurant serves outstanding steak, lamb and pan-roasted salmon. Their Sunday brunch and holiday buffets are quite popular. Perhaps because of the fire danger, smoking is permitted only in the adjacent bar. ~ 139 McLeod Street, Big Timber; 406-932-4459, fax 406-932-4248; www.thegrand-hotel.com, e-mail thegrandhotel@mcn.net. DELUXE TO ULTRA-DELUXE.

DINING

Silver works fashioned by Montana Silversmiths are on display at **River Bend Trading**. The shop features an extensive collection of belt buckles. ~ 549 North 9th Street, Columbus; 406-322-4753, 800-803-4753; www.riverbendtrading.com.

SHOPPING

GREYCLIFF PRAIRIE DOG TOWN STATE PARK Located just off the freeway, this park preserves a traditional colony of common black-tailed prairie dogs. Visitors can stroll among the burrows and observe the animals' behavior, especially their community warning system, but they are actively discouraged from feeding the squirrel-like rodents, who remain wary of intrusions. Picnic areas, restrooms and interpretive displays are among the

PARKS

facilities. Day-use fee, $1 per person. ~ From Big Timber, take Route 90 east nine miles to Exit 377; 406-247-2940.

▼▼▼▼▼▼▼▼▼▼▼▼

Red Lodge Area

An hour's drive southwest from Billings on Route 212, or two hours southeast from Livingston via Routes 90 and 78, brings travelers to the foot of Montana's loftiest mountains. Granite Peak, at 12,799 feet the highest of the high, crowns the plateau that towers above the historic mining town of Red Lodge. It and numerous smaller communities provide access to the lakes and streams of Custer National Forest and the Absaroka-Beartooth Wilderness.

Red Lodge, which lists its elevation as 5555 feet, is the logical portal to the region. Its 2000 residents live in a lovely town whose appearance may not be a lot different from what it was during its coal-mining boom of 1890–1910.

SIGHTS

Stop by the **Red Lodge Area Chamber of Commerce & Visitor Center** for maps, brochures and advice from the helpful staff. ~ 601 North Broadway, Red Lodge; 406-446-1718, 888-281-0625; www.redlodge.com, e-mail information@redlodge.com.

Six blocks of Broadway (the main street) from 8th to 14th streets and numerous side streets make up the **Red Lodge Historic District**. Nearly all the buildings date from the boom period. Among them are the Theatorium, decorated with imported Italian marble statues; the 1889 railroad station; the 1893 Spofford (now Pollard) Hotel, which hosted such historical figures as "Buffalo Bill" Cody, "Calamity Jane" Canary and John "Liver Eatin'" Johnston; the 1899 Carbon County Courthouse; and the 1897 Finnish Opera House, now the Mountain People Shop.

The Finns were one of many European groups who settled in their own small enclaves near the banks of Rock Creek. Others included Irish, Scots, Italians, Germans and Slavs. Today, those roots are celebrated each August during the three-day Festival of Nations.

Much of the region's history is retold through artifacts and memorabilia south of town at the **Carbon County Historical Museum**. Closed Sunday and Monday from Labor Day to Memorial Day. Admission. ~ 224 North Broadway Avenue, Red Lodge; 406-446-3667. The old homestead cabin of "Liver Eatin'" Johnston, upon whose life the Robert Redford movie *Jeremiah Johnson* was based, stands intact a few blocks away.

Also in Red Lodge, the **Beartooth Nature Center & Children's Petting Zoo** exhibits native Montana animals in their natural habitats. The park also has a playground, picnic area and concessions. Open daily in summer. Admission. ~ Coal Miners' Memorial Park, Route 212, Red Lodge; 406-446-1133; www.beartoothnaturecenter.org, e-mail info@beartoothnaturecenter.org.

The hills around Red Lodge were always rich in coal, but perhaps none more so than those flanking **Bearcreek**, over the hill to the east. In 1943, though, the mining industry—already on the wane—heard its death knell. An underground explosion in the Smith Mine killed 74 men near Washoe, four miles from Red Lodge. A tipple and several outbuildings still stand as sober reminders of Montana's worst coal-mining disaster.

Red Lodge's coal industry never recovered from the Smith Mine tragedy. Since World War II, tourism has been the economic mainstay of the area. In summer, Red Lodge is a northeastern gateway to Yellowstone National Park; in winter, the **Red Lodge Mountain Ski Area**, with 2000 feet of vertical terrain just six miles west of town, is a popular destination. ~ 305 Ski Run Road; 406-446-2610, 800-444-8977; www.redlodgemountain.com.

Spectacular mountain scenery lies west of Red Lodge off Route 78 via Roscoe. Particularly sterling is **East Rosebud Lake**, about 32 miles from Red Lodge. Above this small alpine lake, accessible by foot or horseback, East Rosebud Creek has carved a canyon reminiscent of Yosemite's glacial grandeur.

Numerous trails leave the Beartooth Highway (Route 212) to enter the Beartooth Plateau portion of the **Absaroka-Beartooth Wilderness Area**. Nearly a million acres in size, this wilderness area includes some two dozen mountains over 12,000 feet in elevation. Traveling around the rim and over the top of the Beartooth Plateau, visitors get spectacular vistas across magnificent glaciated peaks and pristine alpine lakes. (*Note*: Because snow stays late and returns early, the Beartooth Highway normally is open only from Memorial Day weekend to mid-October.)

Cooke City is perhaps best regarded as a stepping-off point for wilderness excursions. There's fishing, hunting and mountain climbing in the adjacent mountains, as well as horseback and backpacking trips.

Sixty-six miles across the Beartooth Plateau from Red Lodge, and accessible only after a 35-mile passage through a corner of Wyoming, is the Montana town of **Cooke City**. Located just four miles from Yellowstone's northeast entrance, the village goes about life in peaceful seclusion. The town also has a **Yellowstone Wildlife Museum** that displays more than 100 animals and birds in lifelike dioramas. Closed October through Memorial Day. Admission. ~ Route 212; 406-646-7814. Only a few hundred people live here and in the hamlet of **Silver Gate**, three miles west.

Of particular note is the 14-mile trail to **Grasshopper Glacier**   ◄ HIDDEN
in the Absaroka-Beartooth Wilderness Area. The glacier, one of the largest ice fields in the continental United States, takes its name from the millions of grasshoppers (of a now-extinct species) frozen in a sheer 80-foot cliff of glacial ice. Nearby is **Granite Peak**, at 12,799 feet Montana's tallest.

Beartooth Highway

The **Beartooth Highway** (Route 212) is a two-lane national scenic mountain byway beginning eight miles southwest of Red Lodge. Set your odometer so you'll know when to pull over for recommended stops. If you want to hike during the slow-paced drive across the top of Montana and Wyoming, pack along a picnic lunch. Otherwise, plan to eat in Cooke City. You can take this spectacular 65-mile drive between Red Lodge and Cooke City from either direction. Set aside at least three hours to savor the memorable high-elevation vistas.

RED LODGE   Spend the day before your road tour strolling the downtown streets and shops of Red Lodge, a historic mining community with a charm all its own. Stay overnight at the **Pollard Hotel** (page 209) or **Rock Creek Resort** (page 208).

ROCK CREEK VISTA   The road gets off to a fingernail-biting start with a series of switchbacks leading up a steep mountain slope. About 20 miles into your journey, stop at Rock Creek Vista. Walk to the promontory for views of Rock Creek Canyon.

BEARTOOTH PLATEAU   In another two miles you'll reach the 10,000-foot Beartooth Plateau. For the next 20 miles, the highway winds through the same kind of alpine landscape found in the Arctic where tundra, sedges and small flowering plants eke out an existence. Wildlife watchers often spot eagles or hawks in this rugged landscape above timberline. The lucky traveler may also be rewarded with glimpses of bears, mountain goats and bighorn sheep.

LODGING   One of the region's classiest resorts is undoubtedly the **Rock Creek Resort,** five miles south of Red Lodge at the foot of the Beartooth Highway. The handsome Beartooth Lodge, adjacent Grizzly Condos and the Twin Elk building have 87 guest rooms (34 with kitchens) designed in contemporary rustic style with balconies. There are also two three-bedroom townhouses available. The Old Piney Dell restaurant serves exquisite American and Continental cuisine. The resort offers tennis and mountain biking, as well as an indoor swimming pool, a sauna, a jacuzzi and a fitness club; golf, horseback riding, snowmobiling and skiing are available nearby. Kids will enjoy a playground. ~ Route 212 South, Red Lodge; 406-446-1111, 800-667-1119, fax 406-446-3688; www.rock creekresort.com, e-mail info@rcresort.com. MODERATE TO DELUXE.

TWIN LAKES   At Mile 27, stop at Twin Lakes parking area. Twin Lakes is a double cirque above Rock Creek Canyon. In another half mile, you can spot in the distance the distinctive glacially carved spire known as the Bear's Tooth.

AT THE TOP   Three miles down the road, you'll cross 10,947-foot Bear-tooth Pass, the highest stretch of highway you'll travel on this trip. Drive another 8.3 miles to **Top of the World** store, a 1934 log general store where you can buy snacks, groceries or a fishing license.

CLAY BUTTE FIRE LOOKOUT   At 42.2 miles, turn right onto three-mile-long Clay Butte Road. Drive to Clay Butte Fire Lookout. From the outside walkway you'll have excellent views of Beartooth Butte, the Beartooth Mountains, the Clarks Fork valley, and the Absaroka Range's volcanic peaks. Take time to see the exhibits, memorabilia and interpretation. You can also trek along the ridge for more panoramas.

OVER AND ACROSS   Drive another mile, stop at the **Pilot-Index overlook** for a glimpse of the upper Clarks Fork valley. At 48.1 miles, stop at the scenic **Clark Fork overlook** turnout. In another 4.5 miles, pull over at the **Bridge across Crazy Creek** and walk along the cascading stream if you want to stretch your legs. Continue driving until you reach Cooke City, where you'll spend the night.

COOKE CITY   Formerly a booming mine town, this remote mountain resort community lies just outside Yellowstone National Park. You can try your hand at fishing, go hiking, or mount a horse or mountain bike. Soak up the vibes of Western small-town life and banter with the locals at the red-brick **Cooke City Store** (page 211). For dinner, try the restaurant at **Soda Butte Lodge** (page 210), which specializes in pan-fried walleye.

Red Lodge's **Pollard Hotel**, built in 1893, once hosted the likes of "Buffalo Bill" Cody and William Jennings Bryan. In 1897, the bank at the Pollard Hotel was robbed by Harry Longworth—the Sundance Kid himself. It's the only hotel in the northern Rockies to be accepted as a member of the select Historic Hotels of America. Entirely nonsmoking, the Pollard has 39 rooms and suites, some with indoor balconies, others with parlors and hot tubs; all have private bathrooms. Fare in the upscale restaurant is creative Continental; a full fitness club has saunas, a weight room and racquetball courts. ~ 2 North Broadway, Red Lodge; 406-446-0001, 800-765-5273, fax 406-446-0002; www.thepollard.net, e-mail pollard@pollardhotel.com. DELUXE TO ULTRA-DELUXE.

For economical lodging in Red Lodge, check out the **Yodeler Motel**. The Yodeler's Scandinavian-style decor and its willingness to take in dogs as well as people make it a travelers' favorite. There are 23 rooms with coffeemakers and cable TV; rooms with steam baths or jacuzzis (and one kitchen) are available on request. ~ 601 South Broadway, Red Lodge; 406-446-1435, 866-466-1435; www.yodelerhotel.com, e-mail yodeler@wtp.net. BUDGET TO MODERATE.

In Cooke City, **Soda Butte Lodge** has a little of everything. Most of the 32 guest rooms have queen-size or double beds; all have full baths and Western-style decor. Family suites are also available. The lodge restaurant is open for three meals daily, and there's a casino, hot tub and heated indoor pool. ~ Route 212, Cooke City; 406-838-2251, 800-527-6462, fax 406-838-2253; www.cookecity.com, e-mail sodabutte@imt.net. MODERATE TO DELUXE.

DINING

Carbon County Steak House serves up a variety of pastas and steaks at reasonable prices. They also feature a number of chicken and seafood dishes such as fresh mussels flown in every Friday. There's a pleasant bar as well. Dinner only. Closed Monday and Tuesday. ~ 121 South Broadway, Red Lodge; 406-446-4025. DELUXE.

With a menu that encompasses Mexican, Italian and American dishes, **Bogart's Restaurant** has something for everyone. Slip into a booth at this family-style eatery and choose from spinach enchiladas and chicken tamales to pizza and pasta to steaks, burgers and gardenburgers. ~ 11 South Broadway, Red Lodge; 406-446-1784. MODERATE.

Two miles north, **The Round Barn** is a bargain for big eaters. On weekends it offers a smorgasbord of salads, main courses and desserts to hungry families. The 64-foot-diameter brick barn was once a milking parlor for a dairy farm; today, the upper story is a dinner theater where vaudeville, family musicals and visiting instrumentalists appear throughout the year. Closed Monday through Thursday. ~ Route 212, Red Lodge; 406-446-1197; www.roundbarnrestaurantandtheater.com. MODERATE.

SHOPPING

Outdoor recreationists should definitely pay a visit to **Sylvan Peak**. The owner is an ace seamstress known for her well-designed swimwear, fleece and skiwear creations. ~ 9 South Broadway, Red Lodge; 406-446-1770; www.sylvanpeak.com.

Batteries are not included—and certainly not needed—at **Magpie Toymakers**, where its wonderfully whimsical creations appeal to both children and adults. Alongside original wooden toys are traditional diversions such as tops, yo-yos and paper dolls. ~ 115 North Broadway, Red Lodge; 406-446-3044.

Don't miss the vintage 1886 **Cooke City Store**, a landmark community hub and typical small-town mercantile. Open from mid-May to mid-September. ~ 101 Main Street, Cooke City; 406-838-2234.

Red Lodge locals spend a lot of time at the **Snow Creek Saloon**. ~ 124 South Broadway, Red Lodge; 406-446-2542. On weekends, they often travel eight miles east to the **Bear Creek Saloon and Steakhouse**, where pig races are the big events on hot summer nights. Closed Monday through Wednesday. ~ Route 308, Bearcreek; 406-446-3481.

NIGHTLIFE

ABSAROKA-BEARTOOTH WILDERNESS AREA 🚶🏇🛶🎣

PARKS

Abutting Yellowstone National Park's northern edge, and nearly half as large as the park itself, this 944,000-acre wilderness comprises two distinctly different mountain ranges: in its western half, the rugged, forested Absarokas; in the east, near Red Lodge, the alpine meadows and plateaus of the Beartooths. Several Absaroka peaks top 11,000 feet, but more than two dozen Beartooth summits exceed 12,000, including Granite Peak, Montana's highest mountain at 12,799 feet. Seven species of trout inhabit the small lakes of the Beartooth Plateau. The wilderness features nearly 1000 alpine lakes and more than 700 miles of hiking trails. Horseback riders are welcome; motorized vehicles are not. ~ The Absaroka-Beartooth has many gateways, including Mill Creek Road, off Route 89 south of Livingston; the Boulder River road from McLeod, south of Big Timber; East and West Rosebud roads, off Route 78 south of Absarokee; and Route 212 (the Beartooth Highway) southwest of Red Lodge; 406-522-2520.

From mid-October to May, when the Beartooth Highway (Route 212) is closed, the area's towns are virtually isolated, reachable by only a 113-mile one-way road from Livingston, via Mammoth Hot Springs and Tower Junction.

▲ Primitive only.

COONEY RESERVOIR STATE PARK 🎣🚿🛶🚤🐟 Fishing, boating, swimming and wildlife watching are the hobbies of choice at this irrigation reservoir, south of the Yellowstone River in the shadow of the Beartooth Range. Facilities include picnic areas, showers and restrooms. Day-use fee, $5. ~ From Red Lodge, head north 21 miles on Route 212 to Boyd, then go west eight miles on Cooney Dam Road; 406-445-2326, fax 406-444-4952; www.fwp.state.mt.us.

▲ There are 75 RV/tent sites (no hookups); $15 per night; seven-day maximum stay.

Outdoor Adventures

FISHING

The whitewater streams that flow northward from the Yellowstone caldera—the Madison, Gallatin, Yellowstone, Boulder and Stillwater rivers, as well as Rosebud and Rock creeks and other rivulets—are all internationally renowned, blue-ribbon trout streams. No fewer than seven species of trout, including rainbow, brook, brown, cutthroat, bull, lake and golden, are taken from their waters, as well as arctic grayling and mountain whitefish. At lower elevations, Dailey and some other lakes offer walleye pike, yellow perch and other species. Each August, Livingston hosts the International Federation of Fly Fishers Conclave, largest of its kind on the continent.

There are two good places to purchase tackle and inquire about guided expeditions. **Montana Troutfitters** is one. Guided trips explore the Madison, Gallatin, Yellowstone and surrounding rivers. Closed Sunday in winter. ~ 1716 West Main Street, Bozeman; 406-587-4707; www.troutfitters. com. The other is one of the oldest stores in the West—**Bud Lilly's Trout Shop**, in business since 1950. Fly-fishing outings visit the Yellowstone River, Madison River and Henry's Fork. ~ 39 Madison Avenue, West Yellowstone; 406-646-7801, 800-854-9559; www.budlillys.com. Fly-fishing specialists include **The Rivers Edge**. ~ 2012 North 7th Avenue, Bozeman; 406-586-5373; www. theriversedge.com. Also try **Jacklin's Outfitters for the World of Fly-Fishing**. ~ 105 Yellowstone Avenue, West Yellowstone; 406-646-7336.

Keep in mind that rivers are higher in June, when snow is still melting in the summits, than in August. That means the water is usually colder and wilder in spring, but rocks pose more of a hazard in late summer.

Dan Bailey's Fly Shop, in the south-central part of the state, was established in 1938. Today it is one of the largest wholesalers of fishing tackle on earth, producing more than a half-million trout flies annually. ~ 209 West Park Street, Livingston; 406-222-1673.

RIVER RUNNING

There's outstanding whitewater rafting and kayaking in the upper reaches of the Madison, Gallatin, Yellowstone, Boulder and Stillwater rivers, south of Bozeman. The Madison boasts Beartrap Canyon, with alternating calm water and rapids through the Lee Metcalf Wilderness below Ennis Lake. The Gallatin, squeezed into a narrow canyon above Big Sky, has the region's most challenging whitewater. The Yellowstone, above Emigrant, appeals to families with wildlife viewing, hot springs and a handful of exciting-but-not-too-exciting rapids.

Flatwater paddlers enjoy the gentler stretches of the Jefferson River (Twin Bridges to Three Forks) and Yellowstone River (Pray to Livingston).

Leading outfitters in the region include **Montana Whitewater**. ~ P.O. Box 1552, Bozeman, MT 59771; 406-763-4465, 800-799-4465; www.montanawhitewater.com. Also try **Yellowstone Raft Company**. ~ P.O. Box 160262, Big Sky, MT 59716; 406-995-4613, 800-348-4376; www.yellowstoneraft.com. In Red Lodge, contact **Beartooth Whitewater**, which runs the Stillwater. ~ 601 North Broadway, Red Lodge; 406-446-3142, 800-799-3142. Many outfitters also offer guided kayaking expeditions.

DOWNHILL SKIING

BOZEMAN AREA   Just 16 miles from Bozeman, an easy distance for a day destination, is **Bridger Bowl**. The resort's "mogul-cutter" grooming equipment and its steep Bridger Ridge—looming 500 feet above the upper lifts, for those willing to hike a bit—make it a favorite mountain for expert skiers and snowboarders. But there are plenty of groomed bowls and powder glades for novice and intermediate skiers. The Gallatin National Forest resort has 2000 acres of terrain and a 2000-foot vertical drop from its 8100-foot summit. Sixty-nine runs are served by seven chairlifts and one surface tow. ~ 15795 Bridger Canyon Road, Bozeman; for conditions call 406-586-2389, for reservations call 800-223-9609, fax 406-586-1069; www.bridgerbowl.com, e-mail skitrip@bridger bowl.com.

The **Big Sky Resort**, in the Madison Range less than an hour's drive south of Bozeman, is beginning to get its due as a major national destination for winter-sports lovers. Established in the 1970s by the late newscaster Chet Huntley, the ski resort boasts a vertical drop of more than 4300 feet (the state's longest) from the over-11,000-foot level of Lone Mountain to the Mountain Village complex at its base. One gondola, one 15-person tram and 16 other lifts serving 150 runs weave across 3600 acres of skiable terrain. All levels of skiing ability are well served. ~ Big Sky Road, Big Sky; 406-995-5000, 800-548-4486, fax 406-995-5001; www.bigskyresort.com, e-mail info@bigskyresort.com.

RED LODGE AREA   **Red Lodge Mountain**, at the edge of the Beartooth Plateau just outside the old coal-mining town of Red Lodge, is little more than an hour's drive from Billings. Eight chairlifts ascend to the summit of 9416-foot Grizzly Peak, from which 70 runs drop 2400 feet to the base lodge. The ski resort is in Custer National Forest. Lodging is in Red Lodge. ~ 305 Ski Run Road; 406-446-2610, 800-444-8977; www.redlodgemountain.com.

Ski Rentals   For downhill and cross-country equipment rentals or purchases and information, visit **Chalet Sports**. ~ 108 West Main Street, Bozeman; 406-587-4595. **World Boards Inc.** is the place for snowboarders. Closed Sunday. ~ 601 West Main Street, Bozeman; 406-587-1707. You can also try **The Ski Station** for snowboard or downhill ski rentals. ~ 412 North Broadway, Red Lodge; 406-446-1086, 406-245-5559.

CROSS-COUNTRY SKIING

The region's leading Nordic center is the **Bohart Ranch Cross-Country Ski Center**, just up the road from the Bridger Bowl downhill area. Bohart Ranch has 25 kilometers of groomed and tracked trails, as well as a year-round biathlon training range and a warming cabin. ~ 16621 Bridger Canyon Road, Bozeman; 406-586-9070; www.bohartranchxcski.com. At Big Sky, the **Lone Mountain Ranch** caters to cross-country skiers with 75 kilometers of groomed and tracked trails for all ability levels. ~ Big Sky; 406-995-4644, 800-514-4644; www.lmranch.com. If you're in the Red Lodge area, head to **Red Lodge Nordic** for 17 kilometers of groomed trails. Located barely three miles west of town off Route 78, Red Lodge Nordic offers ski and snowshoe rentals in addition to lessons. ~ Fox Lane, Red Lodge; 406-446-9191 or 406-446-1770.

For information on renting equipment, see the ski-rental section in "Downhill Skiing" above.

GOLF

All courses listed close in winter. Call ahead to find out spring opening dates. Eighteen-hole public golf courses include **Bridger Creek Golf Club**. ~ 2710 McIlhattan Road, Bozeman; 406-586-2333. Arnold Palmer designed the **Big Sky Golf Course**. ~ Meadow Village, Big Sky; 406-995-5780, www.bigskyresort.com. Also try the **Red Lodge Mountain Golf Course**. ~ 828 Upper Continental Drive, Red Lodge; 406-446-3344; www.redlodgemountain.com.

TENNIS

City parks and recreation offices have exhaustive listings of municipal courts. In Bozeman, try **Bogart Park**. ~ 325 South Church Avenue. Or for more information, call 406-582-3200; www.bozeman.net.

RIDING STABLES

Beartooth Wagon and Sleigh Rides offers free wagon rides through the town of Red Lodge from Memorial Day to Labor Day. When snow falls, they have sleigh rides. ~ P.O. Box 63, Red Lodge, MT 59068; 406-446-2179.

AUTHOR FAVORITE

Mountain bikers enjoy roads and trails in national forests throughout southern Montana. I almost hate to let the secret out, but some of the best areas are the seasonal alpine and Nordic ski trails at the **Big Sky Ski & Summer Resort**, south of Bozeman. ~ 1 Lone Mountain Trail, Big Sky; 406-995-4211; www.bigskyresort.com.

Overnight pack trips from a night to a week or longer can be set up for fishermen, hunters, photographers or nature lovers. Most trips are guided, but some outfitters can arrange "wilderness drop trips": They'll pack you in and out, but you're on your own during the interim.

There are dozens of outfitters in the region. **Jake's Horses** climbs into the Madison Range near the Big Sky resort complex, Yellowstone's northwest corner and the Gallatin Range. Jake offers hourly trail rides year-round and extended pack trips in the summer. ~ 5645 Ram's Horn, Big Sky; 406-995-4630, 800-352-5956; www.jakeshorses.com. **Medicine Lake Outfitters** offers much of the same. ~ 3246 Linney Road, Bozeman; 406-388-4938; www.packtrips.com.

The Absaroka-Beartooth and Lee Metcalf wildernesses—between Bozeman/Livingston and Yellowstone National Park—are extremely popular for pack trips. Visitors centers can offer extensive lists of outfitters.

Bozeman is the biking center of the southern Montana region. Bicyclists and runners share numerous urban trails, chief among them the one-and-a-half-mile **Gallagator Linear**, which connects the Museum of the Rockies, on Kagy Boulevard near South 3rd Avenue, with Bogart Park, at South Church Avenue and Story Street. An extension of the Gallagator is under construction at this writing. Also popular is the **Painted Hills Trail**, off Kagy Boulevard in the southeast corner of Bozeman. (In winter, cross-country skiers enjoy the same trails that bikers do when there's no snow.) Inquire locally for the "Bozeman Area Bike Trail Map."

Bike Rentals The region has several leading bike shops. Check out **Bangtail Bikes** for sales, rentals and repairs. Closed Sunday. ~ 508 West Main Street, Bozeman; 406-587-4905; www.bangtailbikes.com. In Livingston, contact **Timber Trails** for mountain bike rentals. (Wintertime, they also rent snowshoes and cross-country skis.) The folks who work here are knowledgeable about the area and willingly share their expertise with visitors. Closed Sunday. ~ 309 West Park Street, Livingston; 406-222-9550.

The greater Yellowstone ecosystem is one of the most environmentally remarkable in North America, with its mountains and river canyons, hot springs and alpine meadows, and its vast array of wildlife. Hikers can explore the backcountry in a way that drivers never will. And they have the opportunity to take advantage of several dozen recreational cabins available (by reservation) from the U.S. Forest Service at a cost of $15 to $30 per night. Contact specific National Forest offices. ~ www.fs.fed.us/recreation/reservations.

Following are a few of the region's more popular trails. All distances listed are one way unless otherwise noted.

BOZEMAN AREA Bridger Foothills National Recreation Trail (20.8 miles) begins at the foot of Montana State University's hillside "M" at Bozeman's northern city limits, and follows the rim of the Bridger Range through Gallatin National Forest. It ends after a 2640-foot elevation gain at Fairy Lake campground, at the foot of 9665-foot Sacajawea Peak, highest summit in the Bridgers.

Palisades Falls National Recreation Trail (.6 mile) is designed for visually impaired hikers. Beginning about 20 miles south of Bozeman off East Fork Road, above Hyalite Canyon, the hard-surfaced Gallatin National Forest trail climbs just over 500 feet to the 900-foot waterfall. There are descriptive signs in both English and Braille.

Hyalite Peak Trail (7.2 miles) ascends to the peak of 10,299-foot Hyalite Peak, high point of the Gallatin Range south of Bozeman. The trailhead for this strenuous climb is at 7000 feet, three miles south of Hyalite Reservoir at the end of Hyalite Canyon Road.

THREE FORKS AREA Potosi Trail (3 miles) begins at the Beaverhead-Deerlodge National Forest's Potosi Campground, on South Willow Creek Road 13 miles southwest of Harrison off Route 287. Moderately difficult, it climbs a couple of steep ridges to an alpine plateau with wonderful views over a series of small lakes and streams.

Indian Creek Trail (17 miles) links the Madison and Gallatin river valleys with a route across the Madison Range through the Lee Metcalf Wilderness Area. The best entrance is from Taylor Fork Road (at 7000 feet) off Route 191 between Big Sky and West Yellowstone; the path ascends Taylor Creek, transits an 8500-foot saddle just past the Cache Creek Ranger Station, then descends Indian Creek to Bear Creek Road (at 6000 feet) southeast of Cameron off Route 287.

LIVINGSTON AREA Pine Creek Trail (5 miles) follows steep, rocky Pine Creek from the Pine Creek campground, 14 miles

FLYING HIGH

You'll find no better way to gain an eye-opening perspective on the Headwaters region, than by seeing the confluence of the Madison, Jefferson, and Gallatin rivers from the air, courtesy of **Bridger Aviation Services** in Three Fork. While you're cruising over the countryside you can also spot ancient tipi rings and herds of grazing antelope and elk. ~ 1680 Airport Road, Three Forks; 406-285-4264, fax 406-285-3954; www.bridgeravia tion.com, e-mail fly@bridgeraviation.com.

south of Livingston, past Pine Creek Falls to glacial Jewell Lake. The alpine gem lies at 9032 feet in the Absaroka-Beartooth Wilderness. There's a 3400-foot elevation gain on this trail.

Rock Creek North Trail (4 miles) climbs 2000 feet into the Crazy Mountains from a Gallatin National Forest trailhead off Rock Creek Road North, northeast of Livingston. It ends at Rock Lake, resting in a saddle between 11,214-foot Crazy Mountain and 10,737-foot Conical Peak, the highest points in the stark, craggy range.

BIG TIMBER AREA Elk Mountain Trail (14 miles) begins in the Boulder River watershed off Forest Road 31A, nine miles south of McLeod; follows Elk Creek to the ruins of an abandoned mining community on the flank of Elk Mountain; then crosses more Gallatin National Forest highlands before descending Lodgepole Creek to Limestone Road, near the huge platinum mine eight miles west of Nye.

RED LODGE AREA Lake Fork Trail (18 miles) offers a good glimpse of the Absaroka-Beartooth Wilderness. The trail begins at about 8000-foot elevation, one and a half miles west of Route 212, 14 miles south of Red Lodge; proceeds upstream past alpine lakes to Sundance Pass, at about 10,500 feet; then drops rapidly to the West Fork of Rock Creek, ending at about 7600 feet at the end of Route 71.

Granite Peak Trail (12 miles) is one of the three most often used routes to the summit of Montana's highest mountain, 12,799-foot Granite Peak in the Absaroka-Beartooth Wilderness. The trail begins at East Rosebud Lake and circles Froze to Death Mountain; from there, narrow rock ledges, glacial snow bridges and vertical climbs make this one for experienced mountaineers.

Transportation

Route 90 is the east–west interstate artery through south-central Montana. Three Forks, Bozeman, Livingston, Big Timber and Columbus are all about a half-hour's drive, each from the last, along this route, which continues west to Butte and beyond, and east to Billings (and, ultimately Chicago and Boston). North–south **Route 287** (through Three Forks), **Route 191** (Bozeman), **Route 89** (Livingston) and **Route 212** (Red Lodge) tie the region's main towns to Yellowstone National Park.

CAR

Bozeman's **Gallatin Field Airport** is served year-round by Delta, Horizon, Northwest, United Express and SkyWest by charters. ~ 406-388-8321; www.gallatinfield.com.

AIR

Greyhound Bus Lines offers service to the all of the larger towns along the Route 90/94 corridor. In summer, it also stops at West Yellowstone, on a spur route south from Bozeman to Idaho Falls. ~ 800-231-2222; www.greyhound.com. The central bus terminal

BUS

in Bozeman is located at 1205 East Main Street. ~ 406-587-3110. In Livingston, it's at 1404 East Park Street. ~ 406-222-2231.

TRAIN

While Amtrak operates normal passenger service across the Hi-Line, there's another option for aficionados of rail travel. The *Montana Daylight*, owned by **Montana Rockies Rail Tours**, runs between Sandpoint, Idaho, and Livingston, Montana, at the northern gateway to Yellowstone National Park, between Memorial Day and Labor Day. The three-day, two-night, 478-mile excursion—passengers travel by day, sleep in Missoula and Bozeman at night—can be extended by more than a week with optional bus tours into Yellowstone, Glacier and other national parks. The train trip itself recalls the halcyon days of rail travel with its restored late '40s and early '50s streamliner cars, including domeliner-lounge carriages, and impeccable service. It's not cheap, but for this mode of transportation, it's a wonderful experience. ~ 4100 McGhee Road, Sandpoint, ID; 800-519-7245; www.montanarail tours.com.

CAR RENTALS

Bozeman has 12 car-rental agencies. At Gallatin Field Airport, you'll find **Avis Rent A Car** (800-331-1212), **Budget Rent A Car** (800-527-0700), **Hertz Rent A Car** (800-654-3131) and **Alamo/ National Car Rental** (800-227-7368).

Outside the airport, rentals can also be found in Livingston at **Yellowstone Country Auto Rentals**. ~ 207 South 2nd Street; 406-222-8600.

TAXIS

For cab service, consult Bozeman's **All Valley Cab** (406-388-9999), Big Sky's **Mountain Taxi** (406-995-4895) or Livingston's **VIP Taxi** (406-222-0200).

SEVEN

Yellowstone National Park

Yellowstone, the world's first national park, which overlaps Montana's southern border, remains first on nearly every visitor's list of Most Remarkable Places.

Nowhere else on earth is there as large and varied a collection of hydrothermal features—erupting geysers, bubbling mud caldrons, hissing fumaroles, gurgling mineral springs. The park is estimated to contain 10,000 thermal features, including more than 200 active geysers. Sites like Old Faithful Geyser and Mammoth Hot Springs have become part of the American lexicon, if not the American identity.

No other place in the contiguous 48 states has as great a concentration of mammals as does Yellowstone, or as extensive an interactive ecosystem. The park is home to an amazing five dozen species of mammals, including eight hoofed animals (bighorn sheep, pronghorn antelope, mountain goat, bison, elk, moose, mule deer and white-tailed deer) and two bear (black and grizzly).

Then there's the magnificent Grand Canyon of the Yellowstone, with its spectacular waterfalls: 136-square-mile Yellowstone Lake, the largest lake in North America at so high an elevation; rugged mountains reaching above 10,000 feet in all directions. It's no wonder folks didn't believe the first stories they heard coming out of the West.

The park's 2.2 million acres were set aside by Congress as a national park on March 1, 1872. But convincing Washington had not been easy.

The heart of Yellowstone was once a giant volcanic caldera, 28 miles wide, 47 miles long and thousands of feet deep. Some geologists think the explosion that created this crater 600,000 years ago may have been 2000 times greater than that of Mount St. Helens in 1980. Three ice ages sculpted the modern landscape, but they couldn't quiet the earth beneath. Nomadic tribes, who lived and hunted in the area for thousands of years thereafter, apparently avoided the most active geothermal areas, as did the Lewis and Clark expedition of 1804. Ever respectful of native superstition, William Clark noted that Indians who visited the region had "frequently heard a loud noise like thunder, which makes the earth tremble. . . . They conceive it possessed of spirits, who were adverse that men should be near them."

John Colter, a wayward member of the Lewis and Clark party, spent the winter of 1807 trapping and wandering throughout the area; he apparently was the first white man to observe the natural wonders of Yellowstone. But no one back East believed him. It didn't help when Jim Bridger, a mountain man as famous for his tall tales as for his knowledge of wilderness survival, claimed that "a fellow can catch a fish in an icy river, pull it into a boiling pool, and cook his fish without ever taking it off the hook."

Finally, in 1870, a group of respected Montana citizens set out to explore the area and put an end to rumor. Astonished by their discoveries (including Old Faithful), the Washburn-Langford-Doane party convinced Dr. Ferdinand Hayden, U.S. Geological Survey director, to investigate. In June 1871, Hayden took a survey party of 34 men, including painter Thomas Moran and photographer William Henry Jackson, to northwestern Wyoming. Their visuals and Hayden's 500-page report helped convince Congress to set aside this remarkable wilderness the following year. By the early 20th century, when rail access to the north entrance became possible, tourists were flooding in.

With 3472 square miles of terrain, Yellowstone measures 54 miles east to west and 63 miles north to south, making it bigger than the state of Delaware. Its elevation ranges from 11,358 feet, atop Eagle Peak in the Absarokas, to 5314 feet, at the north entrance. The park has 370 miles of paved roads and more than 1200 miles of marked backcountry trails. In summer, when tourists descend, its population is greater than that of St. Louis or Cleveland. Its rainfall varies from 80 inches a year, in the southwestern Falls River Basin, to 10 inches at Mammoth Hot Springs. Snow can fall in any month of the year.

Generally speaking, the park is open only from May through October, and many of its lodges and campgrounds have shorter seasons than that. But a second, the winter season—running from mid-December to mid-March—attracts snowmobilers and cross-country skiers to the Old Faithful and Mammoth Hot Springs areas. Ironically, although 96 percent of the park is in Wyoming, only two of its five entrances—from Jackson (south) and Cody (east)—are in this state. Three entrances—West Yellowstone (west), Gardiner (north) and Cooke City (northeast)—are in Montana, which contains only 3 percent of the park. Idaho has the other 1 percent.

▼▼▼▼▼▼▼▼▼▼▼▼▼▼▼
Yellowstone Gateway Communities

Just outside the three entrances to Yellowstone National Park are a handful of small towns that serve a year-round coterie of tourists and outdoor-sports lovers. The most popular are West Yellowstone, at the park's west entrance, and Gardiner, at the north entrance. Cooke City and Silver Gate, at the northeast entrance, are more remote. For further details on these two towns, see Chapter Six.

SIGHTS   **WEST YELLOWSTONE**   With about 1200 full-time residents, West Yellowstone is the primary "suburb" of Yellowstone National Park. Founded in 1909 as a Union Pacific railroad terminus where

Yellowstone visitors could transfer to stagecoaches for their tour of the national park, it gradually grew into the tourism- and outdoor recreation–focused community it is today.

The train stopped running to West Yellowstone as private automobiles came into common use after World War II. The imposing stone Union Pacific Depot, damaged by the massive 7.1-magnitude 1959 earthquake but restored in 1972, is now the **Yellowstone Historic Center**. Permanent displays on regional history and wildlife are complemented by special features on the earth-

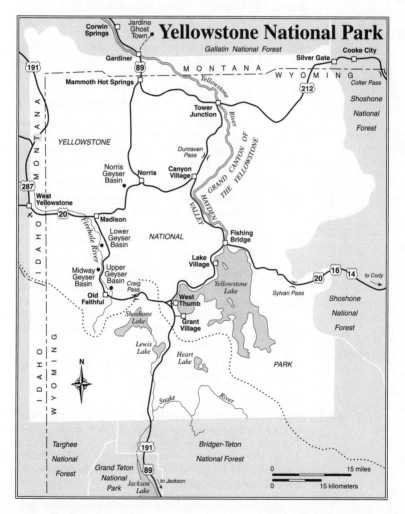

Text continued on page 224.

Yellowstone National Park

This itinerary begins at the remote **Cooke City** (page 207) entrance to the park, facilitating access through the spectacular and less-traveled Lamar Valley. But it can also be followed from the **Mammoth Hot Springs** (page 229) entrance. In that case, follow **Grand Loop Road** east to Tower Junction to pick up this tour.

Day 1
- Buy a backpacker's to-go lunch then drive 12 miles to Yellowstone's Northeast Entrance. Follow Northeast Entrance Road for about 15 miles until you enter the **Lamar Valley**, prime wolf territory. Watch for elusive gray wolves as well as moose and water fowl as you cover the remaining 14 miles to **Tower Junction** (page 231).

- Park by the general store at Tower and take an easy walk to **Tower Fall** (page 231) overlook. Trek another half mile downhill on the footpath for a closer peek. Before heading back to Grand Loop Road, treat yourself to ice cream at the general store.

- Drive south 12 miles to **Dunraven Pass** (page 232) and park. Pack along lunch and some warm clothes then hike three miles up **Mount Washburn** (page 232) for excellent 360-degree vistas. Look for bighorn sheep as you gain an elevation of 1400 feet. You can eat lunch at the summit or Dunraven Pass picnic area. Allow at least four hours for this hike.

- Travel south 7 miles to **Canyon Village** (page 232). Stop at the visitors center for trail guides. To see the **Grand Canyon of the Yellowstone** (page 232) at sunset, take South Rim Drive to the end of the road and park at Artist Point. Stroll to both overlooks. Backtrack to the brink of Upper Falls. Walk a quarter mile to the overlook. Return to Canyon Village.

- Dine at the **Canyon Lodge Dining Room** (page 244), where you'll spend the night. Attend the evening interpretive program.

Day 2
- The canyon looks most spectacular by morning light so take North Rim Drive to **Inspiration Point** (page 233). Walk to the overlook then head to **Grandview Point** (page 233) to spot eagles and ospreys. Drive to the brink of **Lower Falls** (page 233), the southernmost parking lot on the North Rim. Take a short hike to the overlook. See any rainbows?

- Go south on Grand Loop Drive through **Hayden Valley** (page 233). Look for bison, elk and pelicans along the way. Stop ten miles later at **Mud Volcano** (page 234). Buy a guide and take the 20-minute boardwalk tour past sputtering mud pots.

- Drive six miles south to **Lake Village** (page 235) and have lunch at the **Lake Yellowstone Hotel Dining Room** (page 244). Backtrack to **Fishing Bridge** (page 234) and allow an hour to walk around the area and see the rustic museum/visitors center. Return to Grand Loop Road and drive to **West Thumb** (page 236).

- Buy a trail guide at the West Thumb Ranger Station and note eruption predictions. Then tour the **West Thumb Geyser Basin** (page 236). A half-mile boardwalk loops through this active hot spot, which also happens to be a haunt of bison and bears.

- Look for huge pond lilies floating atop Isa Lake as you drive over Craig Pass on the 17-mile ride to **Old Faithful** (page 237). At Old Faithful, stop in the visitors center to buy trail guides, learn eruption predictions, and watch a film explaining geothermal activity.

- Stay at the **Old Faithful Inn** (page 243). After dinner there, follow the 1.5-mile-loop trail circling Old Faithful Geyser. Attend the evening program at the visitors center auditorium.

Day 3
- Before breakfast, take an early morning three-mile round trip hike along the **Firehole River** (page 238) to Morning Glory Pool. Don't miss the Castle or Grand geysers. Grab a picnic lunch after breakfast, then hit the road.

- Drive north about 8 miles to **Midway Geyser Basin** (page 240). Stop to look at rainbow-hued Grand Prismatic Spring and the steamy crater of Excelsior Geyser. Head north another couple miles to **Fountain Paint Pots** (page 240). Stroll the half-mile boardwalk around bubbling hot springs, fumaroles and mud pots.

- Head north to Madison, then go east on Grand Loop Road. Stop at **Gibbon Falls** (page 241) to enjoy the view and have lunch. Drive north to **Norris junction** (page 241), where you can easily spend two hours. After buying a trail guide at the visitors center, find out eruption predictions. Focus on the thermal features of Porcelain Basin. If time permits, catch eruptions later on the Back Basin.

- Push on to **Mammoth** (page 229). See the exhibits at the Horace M. Albright Visitors Center, pick up trail guides, and watch the 12-minute film on artist Thomas Moran. After dinner at the **Mammoth Hot Springs Hotel** (page 242), where you'll spend the night, wander along the boardwalk to Mammoth Hot Springs Terraces. Catch the evening program at Mammoth Campground Amphitheater.

quake of 1959 and the 1988 Yellowstone fires; there's also a bookstore and a theater showing documentary videos. Tours of the entire historic district are also available. Closed mid-October to mid-May. Admission. ~ Yellowstone Avenue and Canyon Street, West Yellowstone; 406-646-1100, fax 406-646-7461; www.yellowstonehistoriccenter.com, e-mail museum@wyellowstone.com.

Located almost across the street, the **Yellowstone IMAX Theatre** presents *Yellowstone* on its six-story screen with digital stereo sound. The films, which change from year to year, are shown hourly between 9 a.m. and 9 p.m. from June through September; times vary the rest of the year. Admission. ~ 101 South Canyon Street, West Yellowstone; phone/fax 406-646-4100.

The great earthquake of August 17, 1959, had its epicenter just northeast of Hebgen Lake. The tremor dropped Hebgen's north shore 19 feet and caused a landslide that blocked the Madison River canyon, forging adjacent Quake Lake. Twenty-eight campers died. The **Madison Canyon Earthquake Area and Visitor Center**, at the west end of Quake Lake, overlooks the area of the slide caused by the earthquake. Closed September to Memorial Day. Admission. ~ Route 287; 406-682-7620, fax 406-823-6990; www.fs.fed.us/r1/gallatino.

The **West Yellowstone Chamber of Commerce**, open year-round, is one of the most comprehensive you'll find. Besides providing basic information on the town and the national park, forest and park rangers advise on nearby camping when "Full" signs cover the campground board at Yellowstone's west entrance. ~ 30 Yellowstone Avenue, West Yellowstone; 406-646-7701, fax 406-646-9691; www.westyellowstonechamber.com, e-mail wycc@wyellowstone.com.

North of West Yellowstone, two miles up Route 287, is the **West Yellowstone Interagency Fire Center**, where summer visitors can take a facility tour, including a closer look at smoke-

---

GRIZZLIES

Next door to the IMAX Theatre, on the south side, is the **Grizzly & Wolf Discovery Center** where visitors can observe the natural behavior of grizzly bears in an outdoor viewing area constructed with minimal barriers. Several bears reside here; they have been orphaned or taken in as habitual "problem bears." There is also a pack of gray wolves living in their own habitat. In addition, the center has museum displays and a gift shop. Admission. ~ South Canyon Avenue, West Yellowstone; 406-646-7001, 800-257-2570, fax 406-646-7004; www.grizzlydiscoveryctr.com, e-mail info@grizzlydiscoveryctr.com.

jumping techniques. Closed October through May. ~ Route 287 at the Yellowstone Airport; 406-646-7691, fax 406-646-9598.

One of the most popular places to send campers is **Hebgen Lake**, less than five miles northwest of the town. Numerous recreation areas and campgrounds speckle the south and west shores of the 15-mile-long lake. Hebgen is especially popular among boaters, fishermen and wildlife watchers, who keep their eyes peeled for moose and trumpeter swans.

GARDINER   Astride the Yellowstone River just five miles north of Mammoth Hot Springs in Yellowstone National Park, Gardiner began life as an entertainment boomtown for soldiers stationed at Mammoth in the late 19th century. By the time the Army turned over its responsibilities to the National Park Service during World War I, the saloons, gambling halls and cigar factory were less important to Gardiner than its position as a terminus for the Yellowstone rail spur from Livingston. As at West Yellowstone, tourists changed from train coaches to stagecoaches at Gardiner to explore the park.

Today, more than one million visitors a year stream through the Roosevelt Arch to the North Entrance, the only park entrance open year-round. The town, while retaining some of its Wild West flavor, has a tidy tourist infrastructure of motels, restaurants, bars and plenty of outfitters. For more information contact the **Gardiner Chamber of Commerce**. ~ P.O. Box 81, Gardiner, MT 59030; 406-848-7971; www.gardinerchamber.com.

Six miles northeast of Gardiner on a rutted dirt road is **Jardine**,   ◄ *HIDDEN* where miners struck gold in 1866. Various century-old mining structures can be seen by ambitious visitors to this not-quite-a-ghost-town: Since 1989, the Mineral Hill Mine has pulled about 42,000 ounces of gold a year from the side of Palmer Mountain. The mine is now defunct. ~ Forest Road 493; 406-848-7971; www. gardinerchamber.com, e-mail gardinerchamber@gomontana.com.

Doing Yellowstone on the cheap? The **Madison Hotel Youth**   **LODGING** **Hostel/Motel** is a good place to start. The hotel can accommodate as many as two dozen backpackers in nonsmoking rooms. The dorm-style units, with three bunk beds, are the least expensive; rooms in the hotel and motel are budget to moderate, depending on amenities and privacy. Shared facilities include toilets and showers, a TV lounge and a coffee bar. There's no kitchen, though a microwave and a small refrigerator are available. Closed mid-October to the end of May. ~ 139 Yellowstone Avenue, West Yellowstone; 406-646-7745, 800-838-7745, fax 406-646-9766; www.wyellowstone.com/madisonhotel. BUDGET TO MODERATE.

West Yellowstone's best bet is the **Travelers Lodge**. This two-story motor hotel has 44 rooms of varying sizes. All have televisions; some have refrigerators. Facilities include a whirlpool, a heated pool and a coin laundry. A continental breakfast is provided. Closed November and the first two weeks of April. ~ 225 Yellowstone Avenue, West Yellowstone; 406-646-9561, 800-831-5741, fax 406-646-4478; www.travelersyellowstone.com, e-mail travelers@montana.com. MODERATE.

The **Stage Coach Inn** is one of the nicest motels around. A shingle-roofed lodging with a rock facade and a balcony that surrounds its large, knotty pine-paneled lobby and stone fireplace, it looks as if it came straight out of a storybook. The 83 guest rooms are cozy and nicely decorated. The inn has an upscale dining room, a casino/lounge, a spa and sauna, and a guest laundry. ~ 209 Madison Avenue, West Yellowstone; 406-646-7381, 800-842-2882, fax 406-646-9575; www.yellowstoneinn.com, e-mail sci@yellowstoneinn.com. MODERATE TO DELUXE.

Sleepy Hollow Lodge serves as the home away from home for countless anglers and vacationing families. Thirteen log cabins are appointed with handmade furniture, refrigerators and coffeemakers; some are equipped with kitchens. Sleepy Hollow offers a continental breakfast. Closed in winter. ~ 134 Electric Street, West Yellowstone; 406-646-7707; www.sleepyhollowlodge.com, e-mail sleepyhollow@wyellowstone.net. MODERATE.

Just outside the entrance to Yellowstone, **The Hibernation Station** is within walking distance to all the local sights. Its individually decorated log cabins are far from rustic—most of them boast whirlpool tubs, fireplaces and kitchenettes. Several family-sized cabins that sleep up to six people are also available. ~ 212 Gray Wolf Avenue, West Yellowstone; 406-646-4200, 800-580-3557; www.hibernationstation.com, e-mail reserve@hibernation station.com. DELUXE TO ULTRA-DELUXE.

Right down the street, the **Yellowstone Lodge** offers a more standard hotel experience. Its rooms and suites are spacious and bright; several have microwaves and refrigerators. Amenities include an indoor pool, a jacuzzi and a guest laundry. A deluxe continental breakfast is included in the rate. ~ 251 South Electric Street, West Yellowstone; 406-646-0020, 877-239-9298, fax 406-646-0110; www.yellowstonelodge.com, e-mail ylodge@yellow stonelodge.com. ULTRA-DELUXE.

Six miles north of Mammoth Hot Springs, the two-story **Yellowstone Village Inn** is all rustic wood on the outside but contemporary inside. The rooms include 43 standard-size units and three family condominium suites with full kitchens. The motel also has an indoor pool, and sauna and a guest laundry. ~ Route 89 North, Gardiner; 406-848-7417, 800-228-8158, fax 406-848-7418; www.yellowstonevinn.com, e-mail elk@yellowstonevinn. com. MODERATE TO ULTRA-DELUXE.

DINING

Regional game dishes—including elk and buffalo—are available outside the park's west entrance at the **Rustler's Roost** in the Best Western Pine Motel. Rainbow trout, chicken and prime rib are also on the menu at this family establishment, which offers a soup-and-salad bar, three meals a day during summer and a children's menu as well. ~ 234 Firehole Avenue, West Yellowstone; 406-646-7622, fax 406-646-9443. MODERATE TO DELUXE.

Yellowstone's name, incidentally, derives from the yellow rock cliffs of the Yellowstone River, which originates in the park.

The **Three Bear Restaurant**, located in a motor lodge of the same name, serves breakfast and dinner daily from mid-May to mid-October and mid-December to mid-March. The nonsmoking, family-style restaurant touts its salad bar, prime rib and homemade pastries. The Grizzly Lounge is attached. ~ 205 Yellowstone Avenue, West Yellowstone; 406-646-7811, fax 406-646-4567; www.threebearlodge. com. DELUXE TO ULTRA-DELUXE.

Seafood and pastas dominate the menu at **Bullwinkle's Saloon & Eatery.** You'll find fresh Idaho trout, Black Angus sirloin, and vegetable primavera here, as well as unusual burger choices such as buffalo and portobello mushroom. If you've had a lucky day out fishing, the chef will prepare your very own catch for you. Closed April and November. ~ 19 Madison Avenue, West Yellowstone; 406-646-7974, fax 406-646-7924; www.wyellowstone. com/bullwinkles, e-mail bullwinkles@wyellowstone.com. MODERATE TO DELUXE.

◄ HIDDEN

Alice's Restaurant is seven and a half miles west of the park entrance on Route 20, but many folks find it worth the drive for its rustic atmosphere and excellent steaks. Grilled rainbow trout also highlights the menu. The restaurant is located at the foot of the Continental Divide just east of the Idaho border. Breakfast, lunch and dinner in winter, breakfast and dinner in summer. ~ 1545 Targhee Pass Highway, seven and a half miles west of West Yellowstone; 406-646-7296. MODERATE.

At the north entrance of the park, the **Yellowstone Mine Restaurant**, adjacent to the Best Western by Mammoth Hot Springs, offers a fine steak-and-seafood menu amid the recreated ambience of a 19th-century mine. There's a kids' menu, and breakfast is served as well. The Rusty Rail lounge is adjacent. No lunch. ~ Route 89 at Hellroaring Street, Gardiner; 406-848-7336, fax 406-848-7120. DELUXE.

SHOPPING

Outside the park's west entrance in West Yellowstone, check out **Eagle's Store** for Western wear, outdoor equipment and American Indian crafts. Closed April and November. ~ 3 Canyon Street, West Yellowstone; 406-646-9300. **Madison Gift Shop** carries a large selection of souvenirs. Closed October through Memorial

Day. ~ 139 Yellowstone Avenue, West Yellowstone; 406-646-7745. **Oak N Pine** is renowned for its custom lodge-style furniture and handmade quilts. Closed mid-October through December. ~ 120 Canyon Street; 208-558-9511. **The Cradleboard Gift Shop** carries jewelry, pottery and American Indian rugs. ~ 104-D Canyon Street, West Yellowstone; 406-646-9577; www.the cradleboard.com.

In Gardiner, **Kellem's Montana Saddlery** may be the most intriguing store outside the north entrance to Yellowstone Park; its inventory runs from handmade saddles and other cowboy gear to clothing, silver jewelry and Montana-made gifts. Closed Sunday. ~ 214 Park Street, Gardiner; 406-848-7776. The **Yellowstone Outpost Mall** puts ten shops and restaurants under one roof at the north end of town. ~ Route 89 at Hellroaring Street. For literature and espresso, try **High Country Trading**, a gift shop and coffee bar. ~ 308 Park Street, Gardiner; 406-848-7707. Across the street in the Yellowstone Mine Restaurant building is **Gold Strike Gifts**, where you'll find many made-in-Montana goods along with cards, books and T-shirts. ~ Route 89 South; 406-848-7132.

NIGHTLIFE   The **Playmill Theatre** has presented a summer season of melodrama and musical comedy since 1964. ~ 29 Madison Avenue, West Yellowstone; 406-646-7757; www.playmill.com.

For pure imbibing, travel nine miles north of West Yellowstone on Route 191 (just past the Route 287 junction) to **Eino's Tavern**, which has a grill alongside Hebgen Lake, big-screen TV and even fuel for snowmobilers. Closed for two weeks after Thanksgiving. ~ 8955 Gallatin Road; 406-646-9344.

The most historic bar in the greater Yellowstone area is Gardiner's **Two-Bit Saloon**, a mining-era relic that remains open 18 hours a day, year-round. ~ Route 89, Gardiner; 406-848-7743.

PARKS   **HENRY'S LAKE STATE PARK** 🏃 🚴 ⛵ 🏕 🚤 🐟 🎣 Henry's Lake is a quiet mountain oasis just 15 miles west of West Yellowstone, on the Idaho side of Targhee Pass. Sheltered on three sides by the Continental Divide, the lake fills an alpine valley of about 12 square miles. The 585-acre park, on the southeast shore near its outlet to Henry's Fork of the Snake River, is ideal for trout-fishing enthusiasts. Facilities include picnic tables and restrooms. Day-use fee, $4. ~ From West Yellowstone, take Route 20 west 13 miles to Goose Bay Road; turn northwest two miles to the park entrance; 208-558-7532, fax 208-558-7045; e-mail hen@idpr.state.id.us.

▲ All 50 RV/tent sites have hookups; $16 per night for RVs, $12 for tents; 14-day maximum stay. Closed October to Memorial Day.

The following touring information assumes that you're entering Yellowstone from Mammoth Hot Springs,

Yellowstone National Park

at its northern boundary. It proceeds clockwise around the park circuit for 141 miles and returns to Mammoth, but it can be easily picked up from any other gateway.

MAMMOTH HOT SPRINGS AREA Where the North Entrance Road enters the park, it passes beneath the 30-foot stone **Roosevelt Arch**, dedicated in 1903 by President Theodore Roosevelt and inscribed "For the Benefit and Enjoyment of the People." It then swings by the steaming, subterranean outlet where the **Boiling River** flows into the Gardiner River and transits 600-foot-deep **Gardiner Canyon**.

SIGHTS

The Grand Loop Road begins its descent to Mammoth Hot Springs and the park's north entrance at **Golden Gate Canyon**, whose rock walls are splashed with yellow lichen. Where Glen Creek tumbles out of Swan Lake Flat, Rustic Falls drop 47 feet into the canyon. To the east, one-way Bunsen Peak Road winds around the base of Bunsen Peak, following the rim of the Gardiner River's 800-foot Sheepeater Canyon. Trails leave this road for the summit of 8564-foot Bunsen Peak and the foot of pretty Osprey Falls, deep in Sheepeater Canyon.

The **Mammoth Hot Springs**, truly one of Yellowstone's highlights, are a spectacular series of steaming travertine terraces in a steady state of metamorphosis. Super-heated ground water rises to the surface as carbonic acid, dissolving great quantities of natural limestone. As it seeps through cracks in the earth, it deposits the limestone, which solidifies again as travertine (calcium carbonate). This white mineral provides a habitat for colorful bacterial algae (cyanobacteria), whose varying pastel hues reflect the temperature of the water they inhabit: White bacteria live in the hottest water, followed, in descending order, by yellow, orange, brown and, in the coolest, green.

The result of this thermal dynamism on the lower slopes of Terrace Mountain is a lopsided wedding cake of a hillside. About

ELK MAGNET

One of the most surprising aspects of Mammoth Hot Springs is their apparent allure to elk. Dozens of the magnificent antlered creatures bed down in the terraces, seemingly oblivious to tourists who pass within a few feet. Keep in mind, however, that these are dangerous animals—it is illegal to approach within 25 yards of an elk.

500 gallons of water flow from the springs per minute; by some estimates, two tons of dissolved limestone are deposited each day. But the springs and terraces are constantly changing, new ones emerging while others become dormant.

Probably the best place to view the entire Mammoth area is from the **Lower Terrace Overlook** off the Upper Terrace Loop Drive. Boardwalk trails lead a half mile downhill through the main terrace region to the village beyond. Features like **Minerva Spring** and **Jupiter Spring** go through cycles of activity and dormancy lasting years at a time. **Opal Terrace**, at the foot of the hill, deposits as much as a foot of travertine per year in its most active periods. **Liberty Cap**, a cone formed by a long-extinct hot spring, marks the north end of the Mammoth Hot Springs; it is 37 feet high and 20 feet in diameter at its base.

At the south end of the Mammoth Hot Springs area is the one-and-a-half-mile **Upper Terrace Loop Drive**, a narrow, one-way route that turns right off the Grand Loop Road about a mile and a half south of Mammoth village. The thermal landscape here is highly varied: Some terraces have been inactive for five centuries, others have come back to life after decades of dormancy, and still others have erupted from verdant forest in relatively recent times—even as park rangers and frequent visitors watched.

Mammoth was the first settlement in Yellowstone National Park. Park headquarters are lodged in the gray stone buildings of the former **Fort Yellowstone**, a cavalry post during the three decades the park was administered by the U.S. Army, from 1886 to 1917. ~ 307-344-7381. Also in the historic fort is the **Horace M. Albright Visitors Center**, whose exhibits explain the Army's role during those early years. There are also excellent wildlife displays and theater programs explaining the evolution of the national park. ~ 307-344-2263.

Other village facilities, open year-round, include restaurants, a general store and other shops, a gas station with repair services, a medical clinic, a post office, a campground and an amphitheater for evening programs. There's even a corral for trail riders.

East of Mammoth Hot Springs, the Grand Loop Road continues 18 miles to Tower Junction. En route, about four miles from Mammoth, it passes **Undine Falls**, which drop 60 feet between perpendicular cliff walls on Lava Creek.

TOWER-ROOSEVELT AREA   The saddle between Mammoth and Tower Junction is known as the **Blacktail Deer Plateau**. Nature lovers may spot the mule deer from which it gets its name on **Blacktail Plateau Drive**, a one-way, six-and-a-half-mile eastbound dirt road that leaves the main road about ten miles east of Mammoth (eight miles west of Tower Junction) to traverse forests of fir, spruce, pine and aspen, and hills covered with sagebrush and wildflowers.

About three and a half miles before Tower Junction you'll pass **Garnet Hill**. The rocks here are Precambrian granite gneiss estimated to be roughly 2.7 billion years old, formed before the first primitive lifeforms even began to appear on the planet. Imperfect garnets can be found in this ancient formation.

A short side road a little over a mile west of Tower Junction leads to a **petrified tree**, enclosed by a tall iron fence to prevent the vandalism that consumed its former neighbors. Petrified trees—like this upright 20-foot redwood stump—were fossilized 50 million years ago after falling volcanic ash covered them. They can be found in isolated locations throughout northern Yellowstone, especially nearby **Specimen Ridge**, where between nine and twelve separate petrified forests—one on top of another—have been identified.

◀ HIDDEN

Tower Junction takes its name from the unusual basalt pinnacles that rise above the Yellowstone River canyon just south of here. They include **Overhanging Cliff**, a columnar formation that actually hangs over the road, and **The Needle**, a 260-foot spire of volcanic breccia. Note: Sections of the road from Tower Junction to Canyon will be closed through 2006.

Tower Fall is about two miles south of the junction off the Grand Loop Road; it plummets 132 feet from the palisades into **The Narrows**, at 500 feet the deepest part of this section of the canyon, and its most confined. A trail that leads to the foot of the waterfall reveals more steam vents and hot springs, including **Calcite Springs**, where the geothermal waters deposit calcite, gypsum and sulfur.

At Tower Junction itself are a ranger station, a service station, horse corrals and the **Roosevelt Lodge**, a rustic 1920s log building (with cabins and a restaurant) named for Teddy Roosevelt. The environmentalist president favored this area's rolling hills for camping around the turn of the 20th century.

There are really two junctions at Tower Junction: that of the Grand Loop Road with the **Northeast Entrance Road,** and that of the **Lamar River** with the Yellowstone River. The Northeast Entrance Road follows the Lamar Valley upstream for the first half of its 29-mile run to the park's Northeast Entrance, closely paralleling an old American Indian route, the Bannock Trail. Bison and elk winter in the broad, open meadows of this glacial valley. **Lamar Buffalo Ranch**, eleven miles east of Tower Junction, was used as a breeding preserve for bison for a half century after its establishment in 1907, during which time it helped Yellowstone's once-rare bison population increase from 25 to a modern estimate of over 3000. It's now home to the **Yellowstone**

Association Institute, a nonprofit field school offering courses year round on the park's wildlife, geology, flora and history. Some courses earn university credit. ~ 307-344-2294, fax 307-344-2485; www.yellowstoneassociation.org, e-mail registrar@yellow stoneassociation.org.

There are two park campgrounds along this route: **Slough Creek campground** and **Pebble Creek campground**. Beyond are the isolated communities of Silver Gate and Cooke City and the rugged Beartooth Plateau.

The Northeast Entrance Road turns away from the Lamar River about three miles past the Lamar Buffalo Ranch and follows **Soda Butte Creek** for the next 20 miles. **Soda Butte** itself, on the south side of the highway about five miles from Buffalo Ranch, is a long-dead travertine terrace not unlike those of Mammoth Hot Springs. The route climbs through the Absaroka Range, cutting a path between 10,928-foot **Abiathar Peak** and 10,404-foot **Barronette Peak**, en route to the Northeast Entrance, just across the Montana state line. Beyond are the isolated communities of Silver Gate and Cooke City (see "Yellowstone Gateway Communities") and the rugged Beartooth Plateau.

South of Tower Junction, the Grand Loop Road passes Tower Fall, then begins a 12-mile ascent into the Washburn Range, a stretch that is Yellowstone's highest road. The area southeast of the highway, between Antelope Creek and the rim of the Yellowstone canyon, is a refuge for grizzly bears. Any human travel (even by foot) is prohibited in the area. Note: Sections of the road from Tower Junction to Canyon will be closed through 2006.

Trails from 8859-foot **Dunraven Pass** lead through groves of gnarled whitebark pine and subalpine fir to the fire lookout atop 10,243-foot **Mount Washburn**, a summer range for bighorn sheep. There are magnificent views from here across the Yellowstone caldera to the Red Mountains, 35 miles away, and on clear days to the Teton Range, 100 miles to the southwest.

CANYON AREA   From Dunraven Pass the Grand Loop Road makes a five-mile descent through dense stands of lodgepole pine to **Canyon Village**.

Visitors will find two lodges here, as well as dining facilities and a lounge, a campground and an amphitheater, riding stables and a general store, service station, post office and ranger station. The **Canyon Visitors Center** features a history of bison called "Where the Buffalo Roam." A future exhibit will portray the creation of the Yellowstone River canyon by lava, glaciers and floods as well as other aspects of park geology. Closed for renovations until 2006. ~ 307-242-2550.

While the **Grand Canyon of the Yellowstone** extends 24 miles to The Narrows, just past Tower Fall at its northern end, the truly "grand" part is its first couple of miles, which include the Upper and Lower Yellowstone Falls. For your first view of the falls (you'll want more than one), take the two-and-a-half-mile, one-way North Rim Drive east and south from Canyon Village.

Your first stop is **Inspiration Point**, where you can park and descend several dozen steps to a lookout. To the southwest (about 1.4 miles) is the **Lower Falls**, at 308 feet Yellowstone's highest waterfall. (Around the corner to the south, out of view from this point, are the 109-foot **Upper Falls**.) The canyon is about 1000 feet deep at this point (it ranges from 800 to 1200), while the distance from here to the South Rim is about 1500 feet. Farther downriver are places where it widens out to about 4000 feet.

Southwest of Inspiration Point, nearer Lower Falls, there are additional viewing points off North Rim Drive at **Grandview Point**, **Lookout Point** and **Red Rock Point**. A parking area just before the drive rejoins the Grand Loop Road signals a three-quarter-mile paved trail that switchbacks 600 feet downhill to the lip of the Lower Falls.

Less than a half mile south, after Grand Loop Road crosses Cascade Creek (whose own **Crystal Falls** empty into the Yellowstone just below this point), look for a turnout to the Upper Falls. The trail to the brink of these falls is almost a stairway, and it's only a couple of hundred yards in either direction.

Just over a half mile from the Upper Falls turnout, and about 2.3 miles south of Canyon Village, cross the Chittenden Bridge to Artist Point Road, which branches northeast along the canyon's South Rim. It ends 1.6 miles beyond at **Artist Point**, directly opposite Grandview Point but with a strikingly different perspective on the canyon. Among them is **Uncle Tom's Trail**, named not for a Harriet Beecher Stowe character but for Tom Richardson, who built the first trail into the canyon in 1898.

The contrast between the reckless river that rushes through the Yellowstone canyon and the quiet, tranquil stream that meanders through the **Hayden Valley** is quite striking. Yet only about three miles separate these two opposite faces of the Yellowstone

INSPIRED HOMES AT INSPIRATION POINT

The vivid hues of Inspiration Point's canyon walls—yellow, red, orange, brown and even blue—are proof of ancient hydrothermal action on rhyolite, a fine-grained volcanic rock heavy in silica, and its mineral oxides. Though the cliffs still exude steam and seem forbidding, they make a fine home for ospreys, which scan for fish from their huge summer nests built on rock porches high above the Yellowstone River.

River. Whereas the canyon is hostile to most wildlife, the lush, six-mile valley between Alum and Trout creeks is a natural sanctuary.

Bison, moose, elk, bear and other large animals wander the former lakebed while trumpeter swans, sandhill cranes, great blue herons, white pelicans and other stately waterfowl abound in the marshes. Fishing is prohibited in the valley.

An intense thermal area beyond Elk Antler Creek marks the south end of the Hayden Valley, about 11 miles from Canyon Village. The varied features here are arguably the park's most foul smelling. The stench of hydrogen sulfide gas emanates from the constantly churning caldron of murky **Mud Volcano**. Rising volcanic gases continually bubble to the surface of **Black Dragon's Caldron**, which erupted in 1948 with such frenzy that it flung pitch-black mud dozens of feet around; **Sour Lake**, whose acid water has killed nearby trees; **Dragon's Mouth**, whose bursts of steam roar and echo within its cavern; and **Sulphur Caldron**, its water yellow with sulfur.

YELLOWSTONE LAKE AREA   Spawning cutthroat trout leap up the cascades at **Le Hardy Rapids** on the Yellowstone River in June and July, making their final approach to nearby Yellowstone Lake. **Lake Junction** is just three miles south from this point.

The first of three communities situated along the lake's northwest shore is **Fishing Bridge**, whose facilities (just east of Lake Junction) include a full-service garage, a general store, an RV park, a ranger station and a park for hard-sided recreational vehicles. A camping restriction was imposed because of the area's popularity among park bears.

Despite its name, the bridge—which spans the Yellowstone River at its outlet from Yellowstone Lake—was closed to fishing in 1973. Visitors now use it primarily for watching the summer spawning spectacular of native cutthroat trout returning to the river to lay their eggs. Pelicans, gulls and even bears are a part of the show. Exhibits at the **Fishing Bridge Visitors Center** focus on the bird life of the Yellowstone Lake area as well as lake ecology and grizzly bears. ~ 307-242-2450.

SAFETY FIRST!

Numerous roadside parking areas have been created to accommodate wildlife viewing in Hayden Valley. Nevertheless, traffic jams are common. Park officials continually warn visitors to view large animals only from a distance, even if they're in their cars. The ferocity of grizzly bears is well documented, but bison, though they may seem docile, can be unpredictable and temperamental as well.

Here also, you'll get your first panoramic view of **Yellowstone Lake**. Measuring 20 miles from north to south, 14 miles from east to west, and with 110 miles of shoreline, this is the highest (7733 feet) large lake in the Western Hemisphere outside of South America's High Andes.

If you want, you can turn off the Grand Loop Road at Lake Junction and take the park's **East Entrance Road** toward Cody, Wyoming, 77 miles distant. It's 26 miles from Fishing Bridge, through the dense evergreen forests surrounding 8530-foot Sylvan Pass in the Absaroka Range, to the East Entrance station.

For its first nine miles, the East Entrance Road traces the north shore of Yellowstone Lake. Moose occasionally browse in the fens and sedge meadows of the **Pelican Creek Flats**, one to three miles east of Fishing Bridge. Although there's no immediate cause for alarm, the earth in this area is rising by as much as an inch per year. This is a warning of future volcanic activity, perhaps along the line of what exists in the Norris Geyser Basin today.

It wasn't long ago, in geological terms, that hydrothermal explosions created the craters now filled by **Mary Bay** and adjacent **Indian Pond**. The bottom sediment in Mary Bay is still very warm, and a fault line that runs along Yellowstone Lake's northeastern shore continues to feed hot springs, among them **Beach Springs** (at Mary Bay), **Steamboat Springs** (at Steamboat Point) and **Butte Springs** (at the foot of Lake Butte). There are picnic areas at each of these thermal locations, which are five, six and seven miles, respectively, from Fishing Bridge.

A short spur road climbs 600 feet to the **Lake Butte Overlook** for one last panoramic glimpse of Yellowstone Lake. Then it's back to the East Entrance Road and up the west side of the Absaroka Range. Look for marmots and pikas on the rocky slopes at higher elevations. Beyond **Sylvan Pass**, 20 miles from Fishing Bridge, the highway descends nearly 1600 feet in seven miles to **East Entrance**.

The turnoff from the Grand Loop Road to **Lake Village** is less than two miles south of Lake Junction. Lake Village is the home of the park's oldest lodging, the **Lake Yellowstone Hotel**, which opened to visitors in 1891. Though renovated, it has kept its historic flavor and is still going strong. Lake Village also has cabins, restaurants, stores, a ranger station and a hospital. Another two miles south is **Bridge Bay**, the lake's primary abode for tent campers and, with 429 sites, the park's largest campground. Besides a ranger station, amphitheater and store, Bridge Bay boasts a marina. You will need permits both to fish and to operate your boat; obtain them at ranger stations. You can swim without a permit, but be cautious: The average lake surface temperature, even in mid-August, is about 60°.

As you follow the lakeshore south and west from Bridge Bay to West Thumb, a distance of about 17 miles, passing a half-dozen picnic sites en route, you'll get a feeling for the breadth of this huge mountain lake: It covers 136 square miles and has an average depth of 139 feet, though at its deepest point it's 390 feet. Of five islands in the lake, three—Stevenson, Dot and Frank—are easily visible from this lakeshore drive.

GRANT VILLAGE–WEST THUMB AREA   Much of southern Yellowstone bears the scars of the dramatic 1988 forest fires that ravaged about 36 percent (783,000 acres) of the park's vegetation and that took 25,000 firefighters about three months and $120 million to quell. But exhibits at the **Grant Village Visitors Center** (307-242-2650; www.travelyellowstone.com) beside the lakeshore amphitheater, explain fire's role not only as a destructive force but also as a creative one. It clears areas for the growth of new vegetation, which in turn serves to nurture a greater diversity of wildlife. Naturalists say major fires such as these occur once or twice a century when nature is allowed to take its course.

After Yellowstone, the world's most active thermal areas are in Iceland, New Zealand, Chile and Russia's Kamchatka Peninsula.

Grant Village, located a mile east of the highway and a couple of miles south of West Thumb junction, lies on Yellowstone Lake's **West Thumb**, a bay so named because early surveyors thought the lake was shaped like a hand. (In our my opinion, it's shaped more like a tired backpacker, and this bay is his or her drooping head.) The southernmost park community was named for Ulysses S. Grant, who as president signed the bill that created Yellowstone National Park in 1872. It has a 299-room hotel, restaurants, campgrounds, boat ramps, several shops, a service station, a post office and other facilities.

The **West Thumb Geyser Basin**, noted for the vivid colors of its springs, is less than two miles north of Grant Village on the lakeshore. A walkway winds past features like the **Thumb Paint Pots**, the intensity and hue of whose colors seem to change seasonally with the light; **Abyss Pool**, with a deep, cobalt blue crater of remarkably clear water; **Fishing Cone**, a spring whose volcanolike mound is surrounded by lake water; and **Lakeshore Geyser**, which spouts up to 60 feet high when it's not submerged by Yellowstone Lake.

If you're heading south toward Grand Teton National Park and Jackson, Wyoming, you'll turn south at West Thumb, past Grant Village, on Route 89/191. Six miles south of Grant you'll find yourself on the east shore of pretty **Lewis Lake**, a three-mile-long, two-mile-wide favorite of fishermen. The lake lies just within the ancient Yellowstone caldera and is the namesake of explorer Meriweather Lewis, although he never set foot within 100 miles of it.

The outflow from Lewis Lake is the **Lewis River**, which flows through a steep-sided canyon with its black lava walls 600 feet high. Look for turnouts for **Lewis Falls**, a 37-foot drop, and **Moose Falls**, a split waterfall that enters the Lewis from Crawfish Creek. The Lewis River joins the Snake River just before the South Entrance ranger station. From here, you can cover the 64 miles to Jackson in about 90 minutes on the **John D. Rockefeller, Jr., Memorial Parkway**, a busy highway with lots of junctions and turnouts.

If you're continuing on the Grand Loop Road, you'll want to take the westbound fork from West Thumb junction. It crosses the Continental Divide twice—the first time at 8391 feet elevation—en route to Old Faithful.

OLD FAITHFUL AREA   In a saddle between the crossings of the Divide, you can turn off at Shoshone Point for a view down Delacy Creek to Shoshone Lake, the park's second-largest body of water, three miles south. This is moose country. In the far distance, on clear days, you can see the towering spires of the Grand Tetons.

At Craig Pass, straddling the Divide, is tiny, spring-fed **Isa Lake**, whose waters drain west (via the Lewis, Snake and Columbia rivers) to the Pacific Ocean and east (via the Firehole, Madison, Missouri and Mississippi rivers) to the Gulf of Mexico and the Atlantic Ocean. Brilliant water lilies cover the lake's surface in midsummer.

About 15 miles from West Thumb is a wooden platform from which you can view the **Keppler Cascades**. This series of falls and rapids near the headwaters of the Firehole River plunges more than 100 feet between nearly vertical canyon walls.

It's only another two miles to the cloverleaf junction for **Old Faithful Geyser**, Yellowstone's best-known sight and the world's most famous geyser. While not the largest, the highest or the most regular geyser in the park, Old Faithful has demonstrated remarkably consistent behavior since its 1870 discovery. It erupts 19 to 21 times per day at intervals averaging about 76 minutes, varying by 45 to 100 minutes on either side. Eruptions, lasting from 90 seconds to five minutes, eject between 4000 and 8000 gallons of boiling water to heights of up to 180 feet. The **Old Faithful Visitors Center**, next to the Old Faithful Inn by the west parking area, can tell you when to expect the next discharge. Normally, the shorter the last eruption, the less time you'll have to wait before for next one.

The park community of Old Faithful is one of Yellowstone's largest villages, with three overnight lodges; several restaurants,

WALKING TOUR

The Norris Geyser Basin

In a walk of less than two miles beginning just a few hundred yards west of the road junction, you can take in dozens of geysers, hot springs, mud pools and silica terraces in "one of the most extreme environments on earth," as it's called by some park publications.

NORRIS GEYSER BASIN MUSEUM   Start your visit at the rustic Norris Geyser Basin Museum, where displays interpret hydrothermal geology. Then set out on the one-and-a-half-mile loop trail through patchily forested Back Basin (to the south) or the half-mile loop around the more open Porcelain Basin (to the north). ~ 307-344-2812.

DARK CAVERN GEYSER   From an overlook northeast of the Norris museum you can get a good panorama of **Porcelain Basin**, which appears as a steaming sheet of whitish rock. Silica and clay are responsible for the milky color characteristic of this area's various springs and geysers; some are rimmed with orange, indicating the presence of iron compounds. This is a very dynamic basin whose features come and go every few years. The Dark Cavern Geyser, which erupts several times an hour to heights of 15 to 20 feet, is among the more constant.

cafeterias and snack bars; numerous stores and shops; a full-service garage; a 24-hour medical clinic; a post office and other community facilities.

HIDDEN ▶   It's also the focal point of Yellowstone's spectacular **Upper Geyser Basin**, the world's single largest concentration of geysers. Weaving from the visitors center through the basin, on either side of the aptly named **Firehole River**, are about four miles of boardwalks and paved, wheelchair-accessible trails as well as many more miles of dirt paths. The geysers of Upper Geyser Basin are a motley group of predictable and unpredictable, large and small gushers.

Directly opposite Old Faithful, overlooking the northeast bank of the river, is the Geyser Hill Group. It includes the **Anemone Geyser**, which bubbles explosively every 7 to 15 minutes; the **Plume Geyser**, which has erupted to 25 feet high every 20 minutes since 1942, when it first became active; the **Beehive Geyser**, which shoots water 150 feet or higher at irregular intervals of one to ten days; the four **Lion Geysers**, connected underground, which gush two or three times a day; and the **Giantess Geyser**, which erupts vio-

EMERALD SPRING   The first thing you'll encounter along the **Back Basin** is the highly acidic Emerald Spring, which has a pH of 4.5—nearly that of tomato juice. Its water, however, is crystal clear and green in color when bright sunlight filters through to its sulfur-coated floor, 27 feet deep. This is an extremely hot pool, normally about 194°, just 5° below the boiling point at this elevation.

STEAMBOAT GEYSER   Next is Back Basin's Steamboat Geyser, the world's tallest active geyser—when it is, indeed, active. Its eruptions, though spectacular, are *highly* unpredictable. After its 1969 eruption, Steamboat lay dormant for nine years. In May 2000 the geyser erupted again, ending another long period of dormancy. When the geyser does blast, it sends a shower of water 300 feet into the air for as long as 40 minutes. It was last active in March 2003.

ECHINUS GEYSER   Echinus Geyser is far more dependable than Steamboat Geyser, though the rate and duration of its eruptions have slowed in recent years. Its explosions come only a few times a day, and they last only up to four minutes. Still, the water rises skyward 40 to 60 feet. Small crowds gather on benches around its cone much as they do (on a larger scale!) around Old Faithful. Echinus is also the largest acid-water geyser known, with a pH level between 3.3 and 3.6—almost as high as vinegar. Acid-water geysers are extremely rare; most of those known to exist on earth are in the Norris Geyser Basin.

lently once or twice an hour, during a half- to two-day period, two to six times a year, and returns to dormancy in between.

Downstream is the **Castle Geyser,** possibly the oldest in the park. Its ancient cone is 120 feet around. Castle's twice-daily explosions rise to 90 feet, last about 20 minutes and are followed by another 30 to 40 minutes of furious steaming. Nearby **Grand Geyser,** the world's tallest predictable geyser, erupts like a fountain up to 200 feet high every seven to fifteen hours.

Farther down the trail, keep your eyes out for the **Giant Geyser,** one of Yellowstone's largest (spurting up to 250 feet for 90 to 120 minutes) and least active (it can be dormant for years at a time); the **Grotto Geyser,** whose weirdly shaped cone has absorbed the tree trunks that once surrounded it; and **Riverside Geyser,** whose 75-foot column of water arches over the Firehole River for 20 minutes every seven hours or so.

Upper Geyser Basin also includes several attractive springs and pools, the best known of which is **Morning Glory Pool,** reached by a one-and-a-half-mile stroll from the visitors center. Labeled in 1880 for its likeness to its namesake flower, the hot spring began to cloud because of vandalism (mainly trash thrown in the pool). The vivid colors of these pools—yellow, orange, brown and green—are due to the presence of photosynthetic algae on the submerged earth. There are several more geyser basins along the Grand Loop Road as it proceeds north from Old Faithful toward the Madison junction.

There are several more geyser basins along the Grand Loop Road as it proceeds north from Old Faithful toward the Madison junction.

Black Sand Basin, on Iron Creek just a mile south of Old Faithful village, is so named for its obsidian sand. It includes the **Emerald Pool**, whose deep-green center is bordered by orange and brown, and **Cliff Geyser**, a wildly unpredictable feature whose frequent eruptions vary in length from minutes to hours.

Biscuit Basin, another 1.7 miles north, got its name from a now-defunct feature of **Sapphire Pool**. Prior to the earthquake of 1959, this pool was a small geyser surrounded by biscuitlike mounds of geyserite, the hardened deposits of mineral water ejected by the geyser. Immediately after the quake, Sapphire Geyser staged a series of huge and violent eruptions, scattering the biscuits far across the basin. It hasn't erupted since. But nearby **Jewel Geyser**, surrounded by gemlike balls of geyserite set in colorful bacteria, erupts four or five times an hour.

The principal features of **Midway Geyser Basin** are **Excelsior Geyser** and **Grand Prismatic Spring**. Excelsior Geyser erupted in 1888 (to a height of 300 feet) and again in 1985 (nonstop for two days, to a height of 55 feet. If you missed it then, don't hold your breath). At all other times, it's like a pot of scalding water that continually boils over—at a rate of five million gallons *per day*. When the air cools at sunset, the geyser's steam fills the entire basin. Grand Prismatic Spring is North America's largest hot spring at 370 feet in diameter; it has azure blue water at its center, colorful bacteria around its edges.

Two miles past Midway, a turnoff down the three-mile, one-way **Firehole Lake Drive** marks the beginning of **Lower Geyser Basin**. This basin covers more ground than some of the others but its geysers are not as striking, with the exception of the **Great Fountain Geyser**, whose hour-long eruptions reach heights of 100 to 230 feet; intervals between eruptions vary from 7 to 15 hours. Where the drive rejoins the Grand Loop Road you'll see the **Fountain Paint Pots**, a multicolored collection of gurgling mud pools that vary in size, color and intensity.

MADISON AREA–WEST ENTRANCE Grand Loop Road follows the Firehole River downstream another six and a half miles to Madison. Two miles before Madison, the river drops into a deep, dark canyon. Coming from the south, you must proceed to a

turnoff for one-way **Firehole Canyon Drive**, about a half mile from Madison, and then backtrack. The two-mile route penetrates the 800-foot, black lava walls of the canyon, reaching its climax where the 40-foot **Firehole Falls** ✦✦✦✦✦✦✦✦✦✦✦✦✦✦✦✦✦✦✦✦✦✦✦
tumble and churn into the **Firehole Cas-**
cades. Madison is one of the park's smaller communities. It doesn't offer overnight lodging (aside from camping), stores or service stations, but it does have a campground, a ranger station, an amphitheater, an information station and a bookstore (seasonal hours). ~ 307-344-7381.

Above Firehole Falls is a big swimming hole; the miles of geothermal activity upstream raise the river's temperature about 30° higher than normally would be expected at this elevation and latitude.

If you're ready for a sidetrip, a left turn at the junction will take you down the **West Entrance Road** 14 miles to the bustling town of West Yellowstone, Montana. The route closely parallels the Madison River and is excellent for wildlife viewing.

To continue your tour, turn right at Madison and remain on the park's Grand Loop Road. About four and a half miles ahead, and right beside the highway, is **Gibbon Falls**, a veil-like 84-foot drop over a rock face. The route continues to ascend through the minor Monument and Gibbon geyser basins to Norris, 14 miles northeast of Madison.

NORRIS AREA   For many visitors, Yellowstone's most intriguing thermal area is not the Upper Geyser Basin around Old Faithful but the **Norris Geyser Basin**, pervaded by the perpetual, pungent smell of hydrogen sulfide. Thermal activity seems to be on the increase here. After a moderate earthquake struck the area in March 1994, long-dormant geysers surged back to life, and geologists monitored dramatic increases in ground temperature in certain parts of the basin. See the "Walking Tour" for more information.

◀ *HIDDEN*

From Norris junction, the **Norris Canyon Road** proceeds 12 miles east to Canyon Village, effectively dividing the Grand Loop Road into two smaller loops. En route, about three miles east of Norris, it passes the pretty **Virginia Cascades**, where the Gibbon River slides through a narrow canyon and drops 60 feet. Most of the route is densely forested.

The **Museum of the National Park Ranger** is housed in a restored log cabin—a former U.S. Army outpost built in 1908. Exhibits here explain how park protection began as a domestic military function and how it evolved into the highly specialized occupation it is today. ~ Located less than a mile north of the junction off of Norris Canyon Road, at the entrance to the Norris campground; 307-344-7353.

The Grand Loop Road north from Norris to Mammoth Hot Springs, a distance of about 21 miles, passes several interesting geothermal features. Vents in the slopes of **Roaring Mountain**, five miles from Norris, hiss and steam at the side of the road. A glossy black volcanic glass from which ancient American Indians made utensils and tools forms 200-foot-high **Obsidian Cliff**, nine miles from Norris. **Sheepeater Cliff**, 14 miles from Norris, is composed of pentagonal and heptagonal columns of basalt, another volcanic byproduct.

This region of low-lying streams and small lakes is a favorite of moose, who feed on willow shrubs and underwater plants, and who often wander through the **Indian Creek campground**, located just to the southwest of Sheepeater Cliff.

The Grand Loop Road begins its descent to Mammoth Hot Springs and the park's north entrance at **Golden Gate Canyon**, so named for the yellow lichen that paints its otherwise-barren rock walls.

LODGING   Yellowstone National Park probably offers more accommodations and more hotels of historic value than any other park. In all, Yellowstone boasts nine properties with 1043 hotel rooms and 1159 cabin units. *Note:* All accommodations must be booked through **Xanterra Parks & Resorts**. Online bookings are generally faster and easier to make. ~ Yellowstone National Park; 307-344-7311, fax 307-344-7456; www.travelyellowstone.com, e-mail info-ynp@xanterra.com

Only two park accommodations are open in both winter and summer. One is at Old Faithful; the other is the **Mammoth Hot Springs Hotel**, built in 1937, which incorporates a wing of an earlier inn from 1911 (during the heyday of Fort Yellowstone). Its 223 rooms and cabin units come either with (deluxe) or without (moderate) private baths; four ultra-deluxe-priced, suite-style cabins have private hot tubs. Facilities include a dining room, a fast-food outlet, a lounge and a gift shop. A decorative highlight is a huge United States map made of 15 woods from nine different countries. Closed mid-March to early May and mid-October to mid-December. ~ Mammoth Hot Springs; 307-344-7311. MODERATE TO ULTRA-DELUXE.

The rustic **Roosevelt Lodge Cabins**, so named because of their proximity to President Teddy Roosevelt's favorite camping areas, have the feel of an earlier era. The cabins are of simple frame construction; some have electric heat and private baths, but most have wood-burning stoves and share a bathhouse. In the main lodge are two stone fireplaces, a family-style restaurant, a lounge and a gift shop. Closed early September to early June. ~ Tower Junction; 307-344-7311. BUDGET TO MODERATE.

Not far from the Grand Canyon of the Yellowstone is the 609-room **Canyon Lodge & Cabins**. The two multi-story lodges have hotel-style rooms with private baths; cabins are single-story four- or six-plex units, all with private toilets and showers, while more modest, single-style cabins are also available. In the main lodge are a dining room, cafeteria, snack shop, lounge and gift shop. Closed late August to early June. ~ Canyon Village; 307-344-7311. BUDGET TO DELUXE.

The grande dame of Yellowstone hostelries is the **Lake Yellowstone Hotel & Cabins**. First opened in 1891 and listed on the National Register of Historic Places, the 296-room hotel has been fully renovated and again boasts its long-sequestered 1920s wicker furniture. The Sun Room, which has great lake views (especially at sunrise!), offers evening cocktail service and frequent piano or chamber-music performances. Other facilities include a lakeside dining room, a deli and a gift shop. Guests choose between ultra-deluxe hotel rooms, less-expensive annex rooms or cabins with private baths. Closed early October to mid-May. ~ Lake Village; 307-344-7311. MODERATE TO ULTRA-DELUXE.

Relax in rocking chairs on the lodge porch of the **Lake Lodge Cabins** to take in a sweeping view of Yellowstone Lake to the east. The Lake Lodge has 186 cabins, some cozy, some spacious, all with private baths. In the classic log lodge are a big fireplace, a cafeteria, a lobby bar and a gift shop. There's also a guest laundry. Closed late September to mid-June. ~ Lake Village; 307-344-7311. BUDGET TO MODERATE.

Grant Village has 299 standard rooms, all with private bathrooms and showers. Facilities include a dining room and separate restaurant, a lounge, a gift shop and a guest laundry. Closed late September to late May. ~ West Thumb; 307-344-7311. MODERATE TO DELUXE.

> Swimming is prohibited in thermal features and discouraged in Yellowstone and other lakes because of the high risk of hypothermia from the freezing waters.

The massive yet rustic **Old Faithful Inn** was acclaimed a National Historic Landmark in 1987. Built of pine logs from the surrounding forests and volcanic rock from a nearby quarry, this 325-room hotel is said to be one of the largest log structures in the world. The gables on its steeply pitched roof were a trademark of architect Robert Reamer. In the enormous lobby are a stone fireplace and a clock handcrafted from copper, wood and wrought iron. The inn has ultra-deluxe suites and rooms with private baths, along with moderate-priced rooms with shared toilets and showers down the hall. There's also a restaurant and deli. Closed mid-October to early May. ~ Old Faithful; 307-344-4600. MODERATE TO ULTRA-DELUXE.

From the **Old Faithful Lodge Cabins**, just a couple of hundred yards south of the famous geyser, it seems as if you can reach out and touch the park landmark. The 97 rustic cabins include "pioneer" and "frontier" units, with private toilets and showers, and "rough rider" units that share a common bathhouse. Closed mid-September to mid-May. ~ Old Faithful; 307-344-7311. BUDGET TO MODERATE.

Winter activities in this thermal basin center around the **Old Faithful Snow Lodge & Cabins**. Most cabins have private baths, as does the lodge. Closed mid-March to early May and mid-October to mid-December. ~ Old Faithful; 307-344-7311, 307-545-4810 ext. 4998. MODERATE TO DELUXE.

DINING

Most restaurants within Yellowstone National Park are in the hotels and lodges themselves. Reservations are required at some hotel dining rooms.

Patrons of the **Mammoth Hot Springs Hotel Dining Room** can enjoy three American-style meals a day amid the steaming travertine terraces for which the area is named. MODERATE. In the same lodge, **The Terrace Grill** dishes up fast food and snacks. BUDGET. Closed mid-March to early May and mid-October to mid-December. ~ Mammoth Hot Springs; 307-344-7311.

The **Canyon Lodge Dining Room** offers nightly steak-and-seafood dinners in a forested setting just a half mile from the north rim of the Grand Canyon of the Yellowstone. Their cafeteria serves three meals daily and the deli offers up sandwiches. Closed early September to early June. ~ Canyon Village; 307-344-7311. DELUXE.

Yellowstone's top-end culinary experience is at the **Lake Yellowstone Hotel Dining Room**. Prime rib, steak, seafood, chicken and vegetarian meals, as well as daily specials, are served in a classic lakeside setting of etched glass and wicker furniture. Breakfast and lunch are also available. Reservations required. Closed mid-October to late May. ~ Lake Yellowstone Hotel, Lake Village; 307-242-3899. DELUXE.

The **Lake House** serves up pizza, pasta and steak entrées along with a sterling view across Yellowstone Lake. Breakfast is served as well as buffets. No lunch. Closed mid-September to early June. ~ Grant Village, West Thumb; 307-344-7311. MODERATE.

AUTHOR FAVORITE

For a taste of how things used to be, look no further than the **Old West Dinner Cookout**. Adventurous diners mount horses or clamber aboard a wagon and ride a short distance to Yancey's Hole, where they are served a hearty chuck-wagon dinner of steak, corn, watermelon, baked beans, corn muffins, cole slaw and more. If old-fashioned fun rings your bell, definitely add this outing to your Yellowstone to-do list. Reservations required. Closed early September to mid-June. ~ Roosevelt Lodge, Tower Junction; 307-344-7311. DELUXE.

The **Old Faithful Inn Dining Room** offers a gourmet menu of prime rib, steak, seafood and poultry beneath the log beams and braces of this immense lodge. Etched glass panels are replicas of carved-wood murals. Three meals a day are served. Reservations are required for dinner. MODERATE. The hotel's **Pony Express** serves a take-out lunch and dinner menu. BUDGET. Closed mid-October to early May. ~ Old Faithful Inn, Old Faithful; 307-344-7311.

You may also dine at the **Old Faithful Snow Lodge Dining Room**, which is just as nice as that at the Old Faithful Inn's **Obsidian**. Standard American fare is served for breakfast, lunch and dinner. MODERATE TO DELUXE. Fast food and other light fare are the specialties of the **Geyser Grill**. BUDGET. Closed mid-March to early May and mid-October to mid-December. ~ Old Faithful Snow Lodge & Cabins, Old Faithful; 307-344-7311.

SHOPPING

Most of Yellowstone's lodging facilities have gift shops for your souvenir needs. In addition, there's **Yellowstone General** Headquartered in Bozeman and West Yellowstone, this company operates all general stores, photography shops and tackle shops within the park. That means prices don't differ from one location to another. They're open year-round at Mammoth Hot Springs (307-344-7702) and seasonally at Grant Village (307-242-7390), Old Faithful (307-545-7282, 307-545-7237), Tower Fall (307-344-7786), Canyon Village (307-242-7377), Fishing Bridge (307-242-7200), Lake Village (307-242-7563) and Bridge Bay (307-242-7326).

NIGHTLIFE

Clearly, no one comes to Yellowstone Park for its nightlife, which is mostly limited to lounging around a lodge fireplace or swapping stories around a campfire. For more social interaction, there are comfortable lounges with full bar service at Grant Village, Old Faithful Inn, Mammoth Hot Springs Hotel, Roosevelt Lodge, Canyon Lodge, Lake Yellowstone Hotel and Lake Lodge.

PARKS

YELLOWSTONE NATIONAL PARK 🚶 🚴 🐎 🏕 ⛵ 🚤 Superlatives rule in Yellowstone's 2.2 million acres: the largest and most varied hydrothermal region on earth, the largest lake in North America at an incredibly high elevation (7700 feet), the greatest diversity of wildlife in the Lower 48—the list goes on. Within the park are 9 overnight lodges, 24 restaurants and snack shops, 11 general stores and numerous other shops, 49 picnic areas, restrooms, 5 visitors centers, 2 museums, 11 amphitheaters, a marina and 1200 miles of hiking and horse trails with 97 trailheads. Park fishing permits ($15 for three days, $20 for seven days or $35 for an annual license) can be obtained at ranger stations, visitors centers, general stores, and most angler shops in neighboring communities; the fishing season is generally from late May through October. Anglers must release all native sport fish; refer to park fishing regulations for further information. Permits are required for boating and float tubes. Motorized boating permits can be obtained at the South Entrance, Lewis Lake Campground, Grant Village Ranger Station, Bridge Bay Marina and the Lake Ranger Station. Non-motorized boating permits are more widely available and can be found at the same location for motorized permits. Cutthroat trout, Arctic grayling and mountain whitefish are native to Yellowstone waters. Entrance fee: $20 weekly vehicle pass, $15 weekly motorcycle pass, $10 hiker and bicyclist pass. ~ There are five different park entrances: South Entrance (via Route 89/191 from Jackson and Route 287 from Dubois); West Entrance (via West Yellowstone, Route 20 from Idaho Falls, Route 191 from Bozeman and Route 287 from Ennis); North Entrance (via Gardiner, Route 89 from Livingston); Northeast Entrance (via Cooke City, Route 212 from Red Lodge and Billings); and the East Entrance (Route 14/16/20 from Cody); 307-344-7381, fax 307-344-2005; www.nps.gov/yell.

▲ There are 2203 units (1863 for tents/RVs, 340 for RVs only) at 12 campgrounds (hookups at Fishing Bridge only), plus 300 backcountry tent sites. Numbers of sites, open dates and fees are listed below. National Park Service campgrounds: *Lewis Lake* (85, mid-June to early November, $12); *Norris* (116, mid-May to late September, $14); *Indian Creek* (75, early June to mid-September, $12); *Mammoth* (85, year-round, $14); *Tower Fall* (32, mid-May to late September, $12); *Slough Creek* (29, late-May to October 31, $12); *Pebble Creek* (36, early June to late September, $12). Xanterra Parks & Resorts campgrounds: *Grant Village* (425, mid-June to early October, $17); *Madison* (280, early May to late October, $17); *Canyon* (271, early June to early September, $17); *Bridge Bay* (429, late May to mid-September, $17); *Fishing Bridge* (340, RVs only, full hookups, mid-May to mid-September, $31). National Park Service campgrounds are available on a first-come, first-served basis only. Campgrounds run by Xanterra may be reserved on a same-day basis by calling 307-344-7901. Advance reservations may be made by calling 307-344-7311; www.xanterra.com, or by writing Yellowstone National Park Lodges, P.O. Box 165, Yellowstone National Park, WY 82190.

GRAND TETON NATIONAL PARK 🚶 🚲 🏇 🏕 🛶 🐟 🚤

Anyone who has ever laid eyes upon the stunning heights of the Teton Range has come away awestruck. Even people whose only glimpse of these dramatic mountains has been in photographs or paintings find themselves haunted by their beauty. Climaxed by the 13,770-foot **Grand Teton**, this commanding range boasts 16 peaks of 11,000 feet or higher in a north–south stretch of less than 20 miles, towering over a string of conifer-shrouded lakes. Despite its close proximity to Yellowstone, the 485-square-mile Teton Park is very different from its famous sister. Teton doesn't have premier attractions like Yellowstone; its allure is scenery that seems so close you can reach out and touch it. But the park demands active effort to fully appreciate it. Mountaineers are challenged by the Grand Teton and other peaks, while water-sports enthusiasts enjoy floating the upper Snake River and scanning its shores for wildlife.

Within the park are lodges, restaurants, stores, picnic tables, restrooms, amphitheaters, visitors centers and marinas. Swimming is permitted everywhere (although it is not recommended in the Snake River); there are designated beaches at Colter Bay and Signal Mountain Lodge. If your aim is to do some fishing, the park's lakes and rivers yield mountain whitefish and brown, cutthroat and lake trout. Fly-fishing for trout in the upper Snake River is an angler's dream. Single-entry weekly pass, $20 per vehicle, $15 per motorcycle, $10 per hiker or bicyclist. A $40 annual pass also includes entry to Yellowstone National Park. ~ Take Route 26/89/191 north from Jackson or west from Dubois, or Route 89/287 north from Jackson or south from Yellowstone National Park; 307-739-3300, fax 307-739-3438; www.nps.gov/grte, e-mail grte_info@nps.gov.

> The highest elevation in Yellowstone Park is Eagle Peak, 11,358 feet, located in the Absaroka Range on the park's southeast boundary.

▲ There are 850 RV/tent sites at five park campgrounds (trailers allowed; no hookups), $12 per night; Jenny Lake has 49 tent sites with a seven-day maximum stay; 14-day maximum stay elsewhere; closed October through April. There are many more units at three privately owned campgrounds; $32 to $43 per night: *Colter Bay RV & Trailer Park* (112 trailer sites with hookups; 307-543-3100); *Colter Bay Tent Village* (72 tent sites; 307-543-3100); *Grand Teton Park KOA* is located 8 miles east of the park (36 tent sites, 114 RV sites with hookups; 307-733-1980). Reservations accepted. Closed September through April.

Outdoor Adventures

FISHING

Within the boundaries of Yellowstone National Park, all anglers regardless of residency must obtain a park license. There are three licenses for adults: three-day ($15), seven-day ($20) and annual ($35): kids 15 and under fish free, but still need a license. Anyone fishing elsewhere in Wyoming, including Grand Teton National Park, must obtain a state license. For more information, call the **Wyoming Game and Fish Division** for a list of licensed outlets. ~ 5400 Bishop Boulevard, Cheyenne, WY 82006; 307-733-2321, 307-777-4600.

Yellowstone Lake is renowned for its cutthroat trout, as is the upper portion of the Yellowstone River between Fishing Bridge and the Hayden Valley. Rainbow and brook trout and grayling are native to waters on the west side of the Continental Divide, including Shoshone and Lewis lakes, the Gallatin and Madison rivers and their tributaries, and Hebgen Lake, outside the park near West Yellowstone, Montana. All native sport fish species in Yellowstone are now under catch-and-release only fishing rules. Cutthroat trout, Montana Greyling and Mountain Whitefish are protected by these rules.

Jackson Lake and other lakes located in Grand Teton National Park have excellent cutthroat and mackinaw (lake trout) fisheries. The Snake River is considered superb for cutthroat and brook trout.

Within Yellowstone National Park, you can buy or rent complete fishing gear at marinas on Yellowstone Lake; guides are generally available at the marinas as well. **Bridge Bay Marina** rents rods and reels. ~ Bridge Bay Marina; 307-344-7381. Or try **Grant Village** for your supplies. ~ West Thumb; 307-242-3400. Tackle is also available at **Yellowstone General Stores** located throughout the park. ~ Mammoth Hot Springs; 307-344-7702.

Outfitters in the gateway communities include **Bud Lilly's Trout Shop,** a full-blown fly shop that offers guide services and organizes trips. ~ 39 Madison Avenue, West Yellowstone; 406-646-7801; www.budlillys.com. Or try **Jacklin's Outfitters for the World of Fly Fishing** for trout guides. ~ 105 Yellowstone Avenue, West Yellowstone; 406-646-7336; www.jacklinsflyshop.com. **Parks' Fly Shop** also has fishing equipment, guides and information. ~ 2nd Street, Gardiner; 406-848-7314.

BOATING   Marinas on Yellowstone and Jackson lakes offer full boat-rental services and guided lake trips. In Yellowstone, 40-passenger excursion boats leave the **Bridge Bay Marina** several times daily on lake cruises. Closed October through May. ~ Bridge Bay; 307-344-7381, 307-242-3876. Trips leave from **Fishing Bridge** from mid-June to mid-September. ~ Meet at Fishing Bridge RV Park or the Lake Hotel. Closed October to May. Ranger stations provide boat-operating permits on request.

In Grand Teton, visit the **Colter Bay Marina,** which is administered by the park and features daily scenic and fishing boat trips, as well as breakfast and evening trips on selected days. ~ Rockefeller Parkway, Moran; 307-739-3300. Or try the privately owned **Signal Mountain Lodge,** which rents deck cruisers and fishing boats May through September. ~ Teton Park Road, Moran; 307-543-2831. Shuttles across little Jenny Lake are operated by **Jenny Lake Boating.** ~ 307-734-9227.

Winter Wonderland

If anything, the natural wonders of Yellowstone National Park are more spectacular in winter than in summer. Imagine, for instance, the steam from hot springs and geysers filling the frigid Rocky Mountain air as snow falls all around.

From mid-December to mid-March, Yellowstone is a paradise for cross-country skiers, snowmobilers and snowshoers. Although the park is accessible by car only at its north entrance, via Gardiner, Montana—this route, through Mammoth Hot Springs to Tower Junction and Cooke City, Montana, on the Beartooth Plateau, is kept open year-round—there are other ways to get there.

Heated, ten-passenger snowcoaches (track vans) run from the south and west entrances as well as from Mammoth Hot Springs. Coaches operated by **Xanterra Parks & Resorts** depart from the south entrance for Old Faithful every afternoon, returning every morning. The journey takes three and a half hours. ~ Mammoth Hot Springs; 307-344-7311; www.travelyellowstone.com. Similar trips connect Old Faithful and Canyon Village with West Yellowstone and Mammoth Hot Springs. Other snowcoaches are run by **Yellowstone Alpen Guides**. ~ 555 Yellowstone Avenue, West Yellowstone; 406-646-9591; www.yellowstoneguides.com.

Mammoth Hot Springs Hotel and Old Faithful Snow Lodge are the only park accommodations open during winter (mid-December to early March), although warming huts throughout the park provide shelter. Old Faithful, like the rest of the park, can be reached only across snow. But like the Mammoth hotel, the Snow Lodge serves three good meals daily and offers both Nordic skiing and snowshoeing equipment rentals and lessons. It's a good base for winter exploration of the park. Ice skaters will enjoy the Mammoth Hot Springs Hotel's outdoor rink, which has skate rentals. ~ Mammoth Hot Springs; 307-344-5400.

Hundreds of miles of cross-country ski trails are marked in Yellowstone, and the most popular are groomed. Those include the geyser basin trails at Old Faithful and the canyon rim trail at the Grand Canyon of the Yellowstone. Trail maps are available at visitors centers.

For guided cross-country skiing expeditions, talk to Yellowstone Alpen Guides (see above) or **Yellowstone Expeditions**. ~ P.O. Box 865, West Yellowstone, MT 59758; 800-728-9333; www.yellowstoneexpeditions.com.

Snowmobiles are restricted to 300 miles of park roads, groomed regularly. Expect a four-foot snowpack beside highways. Xanterra Parks & Resorts rents snowmobiles with helmets and all appropriate clothing.

RIVER RUNNING   The best rivers in the greater Yellowstone area for whitewater rafting and kayaking are the Snake, south of Jackson, and the Gallatin, north of Yellowstone in Montana. For tranquil float trips or easy canoeing with spectacular scenery and abundant wildlife, it is hard to top the upper Snake River through Grand Teton National Park.

Most of the rafting outfitters that operate in the rivers north of Yellowstone National Park are based in Bozeman, Livingston or Big Sky. An exception is the **Yellowstone Raft Company**, which runs the Yellowstone, Gallatin and other rivers on the north side of the park. Day and half-day trips are offered May through October. ~ P.O. Box 46, Gardiner, MT 59030; 406-848-7777.

The **Grand Teton Lodge Company** offers scenic float trips, including lunch and dinner voyages, along a ten-and-a-half-mile stretch of the upper Snake from mid-May to early October. ~ Jackson Lake Lodge, Moran; 307-543-2811. Numerous other outfitters, including **Triangle X Float Trips**, put in at Deadman's Bar, south of Moran, and take out at Moose Visitors Center. ~ Moose; 307-733-6445.

CROSS-COUNTRY SKIING   Yellowstone National Park has hundreds of miles of marked cross-country ski trails, including groomed tracks near Old Faithful and the Grand Canyon of the Yellowstone (see "Winter Wonderland" in this chapter.)

Just outside the park boundaries, **The Rendezvous Ski Trails** offer 26 kilometers of groomed trails, and another eight kilometers ungroomed, from November through April. The U.S. national cross-country and biathlon (skiing and shooting) teams train here each year. ~ West Yellowstone; 406-646-7701. Some 65 kilometers of marked but ungroomed trails are open to cross-country skiers in **Grand Teton National Park**; maps are available at the Moose Visitors Center, open daily in winter. ~ Moose; 307-739-3399.

Ski Rentals   Freeheel & Wheel rents skis, poles and boots. ~ 40 Yellowstone Avenue, West Yellowstone; 406-646-7744. Nordic specialists with rentals include **Skinny Skis**. ~ 65 West Deloney

AUTHOR FAVORITE

The three-mile **Mount Washburn Trail** leads to a panoramic point, but the climb isn't as steep as Avalanche Peak. This would be the hike to tackle if you only have time for one. It's worth every uphill bootstep to see those incredible vistas of Yellowstone and beyond. Bighorn sheep are often seen on top. There are trailheads on the Grand Loop Road (north of Canyon Village) at the Dunraven Pass picnic area and the Chittenden Road parking area.

Street, Jackson; 307-733-6094. **Wilson Backcountry Sports** also has equipment rentals. ~ 1230 Ida Drive, Wilson; 307-733-5228.

The **Mammoth Hot Springs Hotel** has an outdoor rink with skate rentals open throughout the winter. ~ Mammoth Hot Springs; 307-344-5400.

ICE SKATING

Three stables in Yellowstone National Park and two in Grand Teton offer park visitors ample opportunities for one- and two-hour guided rides in off-the-road wilderness. Private outfitters throughout the region provide many more options. Half-day, full-day and extended overnight trips are available. Some outfitters offer riding lessons; more commonly, novice riders will be matched with gentler horses.

RIDING STABLES

One-hour guided trail rides depart from corrals at **Mammoth Hot Springs** (307-344-5400), **Roosevelt Lodge** (307-344-5273) and **Canyon Village** throughout the day. Roosevelt visitors can also ride to Yancey's Hole for an Old West dinner cookout or hop aboard a horse-drawn stagecoach for half-hour rambles around the Tower Junction area. Schedules vary; the summer riding season is longest at lower-lying Mammoth than at the other two sites.

In Grand Teton National Park, the Grand Teton Lodging Company offers all manner of trail rides from the **Colter Bay Village Corral**. ~ Rockefeller Parkway, Moran; 307-543-2811. There is also the **Jackson Bay Lodge Corral**. ~ Rockefeller Parkway, Moran; 307-543-2811.

Guided pack trips through Yellowstone's backcountry and the nearby wilderness area are offered by **Hell's a Roarin' Outfitters**, who have more than 300 horses in their stables. Closed September through May. ~ Route 89 North, Gardiner; 406-848-7578; www.hellsaroarinoutfitters.com. **Adventures Beyond Yellowstone** is another option, with overnight horseback treks to prime fishing spots. Closed Labor Day through June. ~ 21 Shooting Star Road, Gardiner; 406-848-7287; www.abyellowstone.com. **Beartooth Plateau Outfitters** specializes in five-day-long fishing trips from June through September; all supplies and gear are included. ~ 302 Main Street, Cooke City; 406-838-2328, 800-253-8545; www.beartoothoutfitters.com.

PACK TRIPS & LLAMA TREKS

The llama is more a hiking companion than a mode of transportation; it carries all the gear while you proceed on foot. Guided four- to five-day llama treks through Yellowstone Park or the nearby Jedediah Smith Wilderness are the specialty of **Jackson Hole Llamas**. Routes range from easy to strenuous. ~ P.O. Box 12500, Jackson, WY 83002; 307-739-9582, 800-830-7316; www.jhllamas.com.

Yellowstone Llamas offers wilderness llama-trekking expeditions from July through September. ~ P.O. Box 5042, Bozeman, MT 59717; 406-586-6872, 877-864-9672; www.yellowstonellamas.com.

BIKING   Mountain bikes have become a common sight in recent years, joining touring bikes on and off the roads of northwestern Wyoming. Many of the routes here are narrow and dangerous, so helmets and rear-view mirrors, small tool kits, first-aid kits and emergency survival kits are essential accessories.

YELLOWSTONE NATIONAL PARK   Bicycling through Yellowstone can be an exhilarating experience but it is not without peril. There are no bicycle lanes along park roads, and because roads are narrow and winding, high-visibility clothing and helmets are recommended. Keep an eye out for campers and RVs passing you from behind; their projecting mirrors pose a particular safety threat.

Though a few bike paths do exist around park communities, bicycles are not permitted on boardwalks or backcountry trails in Yellowstone National Park.

Grand Teton National Park roads and other valley highways are great for touring; hundreds of miles of trails and dirt roads head into adjacent national forests. Wilderness areas are off-limits. The 15-mile RKO Road in Grand Teton National Park, a dirt road along a bluff on the west side of the Snake River from Signal Mountain to Cottonwood Creek, is a good bet for a moderate day ride.

Bike Rentals   In the Yellowstone area, a good full-service bicycle shop is **Yellowstone Bicycles**. ~ 132 Madison Avenue, West Yellowstone; 406-646-7815. The full-service **Freeheel & Wheel** rents mountain, tour and kids' bikes (helmets included). ~ 40 Yellowstone Avenue, West Yellowstone; 406-646-7744.

HIKING   All distances listed for hiking trails are one way unless otherwise noted.

WEST YELLOWSTONE AREA   The best trails in this vicinity are in Yellowstone National Park itself. **Yellowstone Alpen Guides** offers custom guided walks on many of them. ~ 555 Yellowstone Avenue, West Yellowstone; 406-646-9591, 800-858-3502; www.yellowstoneguides.com. If you're on your own, check out **Skyline Ridge Trail** (21 miles) through the Cabin Creek Recreation and Wildlife Management Area north of Hebgen Lake. This track, which follows the base of a 10,000-foot ridge across an alpine meadow, is reached via Forest Road 986 (off Route 191) or Forest Road 985 (off Route 287).

YELLOWSTONE NATIONAL PARK   Yellowstone contains more than 1200 miles of marked hiking trails and 97 trailheads. Backcountry permits are required for all overnight hikes in Yellowstone Park. They can be obtained from ranger stations and visitors centers within 48 hours before you start your hike. Or you can write the park to reserve permits in advance for a $20 fee. ~ Backcountry Office, P.O. Box 168, Yellowstone National Park, WY 82190; 307-344-2160. Topographic maps are sold at Hamilton Stores.

Trails include the boardwalks and handicapped-accessible trails at **Upper Geyser Basin** (Old Faithful), **Norris Geyser Basin** and **Mammoth Hot Springs**, among others.

For youngsters, the **Fountain Paint Pot Nature Trail** (.5 mile) in the Lower Geyser Basin and the **Children's Fire Trail** (.5 mile) east of Mammoth Hot Springs have several interpretive stations to help teach about thermal activity and forest fires, respectively.

Avalanche Peak Trail (2.5 miles) is a strenuous ascent to a 10,566-foot summit, a mile west of Sylvan Pass on the East Entrance Road. Look for the unsigned trailhead opposite the Eleanor Lake picnic area. The trail transits several eco-zones before achieving the peak, which provides spectacular views across Yellowstone Lake to the Tetons and beyond.

Seven Mile Hole Trail (5.5 miles) offers an impressive way to see the Grand Canyon of the Yellowstone . . . close up. Beginning on the Inspiration Point spur road a mile east of Canyon Village, it clings to the rim of the gorge for the first mile and a half, then swings into the pine forest and drops rapidly for three miles to the canyon floor near Sulphur Creek. Perhaps needless to say, the return climb is harder than the descent.

The moderate **Bechler River Trail** (32 miles) traverses the park's rarely visited southwest corner. It begins at Old Faithful, crosses the Continental Divide three times and then descends steep-sided Bechler Canyon, passing dazzling waterfalls and hot springs. The trail crosses Bechler Meadows, a low-lying haven for moose, black bear and trumpeter swans, and ends at Bechler River Ranger Station, off Cave Falls Road 25 miles east of Ashton, Idaho.

GRAND TETON NATIONAL PARK Hidden Falls Trail (2.5 miles) is an easy walk around the southwest shore of Jenny Lake from the South Jenny ranger station and a strenuous half-mile uphill scramble to the secluded cascade. If you want to continue, there's another half-mile climb to Inspiration Point and then six and a half more through Cascade Canyon to lovely Lake Solitude. From early June to mid-September, boat shuttles across Jenny Lake are available to return tired hikers from near Hidden Falls to the South Jenny ranger station.

Two Ocean Lake Trail (12.2 miles) circles the three-mile-long lake in the park's northeastern corner, skirts adjacent Emma

Matilda Lake and climbs to a panoramic outlook toward Jackson Lake at Grand View Point. It's of moderate difficulty.

Teton Crest Trail (27 miles) has many feeder trails and many spurs. One popular if strenuous circuit of the Grand Teton begins at Jenny Lake Lodge (6900 feet), climbs west on the Paintbrush Canyon Trail to Lake Solitude, then turns south along the upper slopes of Mount Owen and the high Tetons. The trail crests at about 11,000 feet before descending again on switchbacks through Death Canyon to Phelps Lake and Teton Village (6300 feet).

All overnight backcountry camping requires a permit, which can be obtained for a nominal fee at ranger stations.

MOUNTAIN CLIMBING   The Teton Range is considered one of the world's finest tests for experienced climbers. Yet even first-timers can master the apparently insurmountable 13,770-foot Grand Teton itself, given that they have good physical strength, determination and expert instruction.

The latter element can be provided by Jackson Hole's two internationally renowned climbing schools. One is **Exum Mountain Guides** with headquarters at South Jenny Lake. ~ P.O. Box 56 Moose, WY 83012; 307-733-2297. Another highly respected school is **Jackson Hole Mountain Guides**, who take climbers up the Grand Teton, into the Beartooth Wilderness and various locations throughout the West. ~ 165 North Glenwood Street, Jackson, WY; 307-733-4979.

Teton Mountaineering has the largest inventory of equipment and clothing in the area. ~ 170 North Cache Street, Jackson, WY; 307-733-3595.

▼▼▼▼▼▼▼▼▼▼▼

Transportation

CAR   To reach Yellowstone, take **Route 89/191** north from Jackson; **Route 14/16/20** west from Cody; **Route 212** southwest off Route 90 near Billings, Montana; **Route 89** south at Livingston, Montana, or **Route 191** south at Bozeman, Montana, off 90; **Route 287** southeast off 90 near Butte, Montana; or **Route 20** northeast off **Route 15** at Idaho Falls.

AIR   The **West Yellowstone Airport** in West Yellowstone, at the west entrance to Yellowstone National Park, is served by regular SkyWest commuter flights and by charters. The airport closes from mid-October to mid-May.

Jackson Hole Airport has regular daily nonstop arrivals from and departures to Denver and Salt Lake City, with connecting flights from many other cities. It is served by American Airlines, SkyWest Airlines, United and United Express. Regional charters and scenic flights are available at the aviation center adjacent to the airport. ~ 307-733-7695.

Limousines and taxis take visitors to and from the airport. Try calling **The 4 by 4 Stage** (406-388-6404, 800-517-8243) in West Yellowstone, or in Jackson, call **Buckboard Cab.** ~ 307-733-1112.

Greyhound Bus Lines serves West Yellowstone, Montana (between Idaho Falls, Idaho, and Bozeman, Montana), in summer. ~ 800-231-2222; www.greyhound.com.   **BUS**

    Gray Line (800-443-6133) offers seasonal charter service and guided tours through Yellowstone Park. There's an office in Jackson Hole. ~ 1680 Martin Lane, Jackson, WY; 307-733-4325.

    Karst Stage (406-586-8567) and the **Montana Motor Coach Ltd.** (406-586-6121) offer seasonal charter service between Bozeman and West Yellowstone, Livingston and Gardiner, and Yellowstone National Park.

In West Yellowstone, you'll find **Avis Rent A Car** at the Yellowstone Airport. ~ 800-331-1212. **Big Sky** rents cars in town. ~ 429 Yellowstone Avenue; 406-646-9564. **Budget Rent A Car** also has rentals available in town. ~ 131 Dunraven Street; 800-527-0700 are in town.   **CAR RENTALS**

    Rental agencies at the Jackson Hole Airport are **Alamo** (800-327-9633), **Avis Rent A Car** (800-331-1212), **Budget Rent A Car** (800-527-0700) and **Hertz Rent A Car** (800-654-3131).

A variety of guided all-day motorcoach tours of Yellowstone National Park are offered from various park lodgings by **Xanterra Parks & Resorts.** ~ 307-344-7311; www.xanterra.com.   **PUBLIC TRANSIT**

EIGHT

Southeast Montana

Southeast Montanans truly have a home "where the buffalo roam, where the deer and the antelope play."

It was once that way, at least. Two centuries ago, tens of millions of American bison, in herds of thousands, cavorted through these mountains and prairies and down the Yellowstone River valley. Deer and pronghorn antelope remain in large numbers, but the bison were hunted to near-extinction in the 19th century and have made only a modest comeback in the 20th and 21st centuries.

The bison nearly met the same fate as their Jurassic predecessors, whose bones and other fossil remains have been found en masse from the Rockies' eastern slope to the Makoshika Badlands near Montana's boundary with North Dakota. In fact, more skeletons of *Tyrannosaurus rex*, believed to have been the largest dinosaur ever to walk the earth, have been found in Montana than in all other discovery areas put together.

As far as human habitation goes, this has always been a land more suited to outdoors lovers and implacable individualists than to genteel urbanites. The American Indians—primarily Crow (Sioux) and Cheyenne—who lived in this region before the arrival of whites were horsemen and hunters who relied heavily on bison to provide food and hides for clothing and shelter.

When the white man arrived in the 19th century, relations with the American Indians were at first mutually tolerant, if not cordial. But as settlers' demands for land increased—for railroads, for ranches, for riches promised by gold, silver and copper strikes in the nearby mountains—hostilities flared. Tribes stepped up a campaign of raids against white settlements to protect their traditional hunting grounds.

The U.S. cavalry tried to suppress the uprisings and restrict the native people to reservations. At first, they were unsuccessful. In 1876, American Indians scored their greatest triumph at the Battle of the Little Bighorn (southeast of modern Billings), where a combined force of Sioux and Cheyenne annihilated more than 200 soldiers under the command of Lieutenant Colonel George Custer.

It was to be their last hurrah, as they were soon overwhelmed and subjugated. Today the Crow and Northern Cheyenne indian reservations stretch side by side from the Pryor Mountains to the Tongue River.

Modern Billings is a thriving community of 90,000 that dominates the region; it owes its existence to railroads and ranching. Through Billings flows the Yellowstone River, the longest undammed river in the contiguous 48 states. Only one other community in the region—Miles City, with a population of 8500—has more than 6000 people.

Billings Area

Montana's largest city nestles between sandstone cliffs in the valley of the Yellowstone River, within the shadow of the Rockies but with an outlook toward the Great Plains. Billings is the urban hub for a vast and sparsely populated region that includes eastern Montana, northern Wyoming and the western Dakotas.

Called "The Magic City" because it sprang up almost overnight after its founding as a railroad town in 1882, Billings grew as an agricultural, trade and transportation center. Now oil and medicine are major industries as well, and two colleges (Montana State University–Billings and Rocky Mountain College) attract a young population and enliven the city's cultural life.

For Rocky Mountain travelers, Billings is a gateway to such attractions as Little Bighorn Battlefield National Monument, the Bighorn Canyon National Recreation Area, the mountain town of Red Lodge and its spectacular Beartooth Highway, which travels past Montana's highest peaks to Yellowstone National Park. The Yellowstone, Musselshell and Bighorn rivers are acclaimed fishing streams, and there are unique geological and cultural features throughout southeastern Montana's "Custer Country."

SIGHTS

Many visitors get their first impression of Billings at the **Visitors Center and Cattle Drive Monument**, a few blocks off Route 90 Exit 450. The bronze sculpture in front of the modern building was commissioned to commemorate Montana's centennial cattle drive of 1989 to Billings from Roundup, 50 miles north. Closed weekends from September to mid-May. ~ 815 South 27th Street, Billings; 406-252-4016, 800-711-2630; www.billingschamber. com, e-mail info@billingschamber.com.

Perhaps the most notable of Billings' downtown attractions is the **Moss Mansion**. Built in 1901 by famed architect Henry Janeway Hardenbergh for bank president Preston B. Moss, this elegant three-story mansion features a Moorish entryway (inspired by Spain's Alhambra), a formal French parlor and an English Tudor dining room. Elaborate original furnishings provide a glimpse of the Mosses' Victorian lifestyle. Guided tours are offered year-round. Admission. ~ 914 Division Street, Billings; 406-256-5100, fax 406-252-0091; www.mossmansion.com, e-mail mossmansion@mossmansion.com.

Two museums are worth a visit. The **Western Heritage Center**, in an imposing Romanesque sandstone structure at the corner of 29th Street, focuses on American Indian and pioneer history throughout the Yellowstone valley region. The center also offers a continuing calendar of educational programs. Closed Monday and in January. ~ 2822 Montana Avenue, Billings; 406-256-6809; www.ywhc.org. The **Yellowstone Art Museum** has a permanent collection of work by regional artists, from the days of exploration to modern times. Changing exhibits (about six a year) showcase leading contemporary artists. There's a gift shop here as well. Closed Monday. Admission. ~ 401 North 27th Street, Billings; 406-256-6804, fax 406-256-6817; yellowstone.art museum.org, e-mail artinfo@artmuseum.org.

You can get a good feel for Billings' layout by driving or, even better, biking the **Black Otter Trail** along the rim of its overlooking sandstone cliffs—"The Rimrocks"—north of downtown. The route begins just west of Main Street (Route 87) in the Billings Heights area, above the grounds of the MetraPark exhibition center.

Boothill Cemetery is all that remains of the short-lived town of Coulson (1877–85). Among the graves is that of H. M. "Muggins" Taylor, who as an Army scout first carried the news of Custer's defeat at Little Bighorn to the outside world. He was later gunned down while serving as Coulson's sheriff.

A short distance farther west along the Black Otter Trail is the **grave of Yellowstone Kelly**, a famed frontier scout whose lifespan (1849–1928) paralleled the pioneering and development of the American West. On a clear day, five Rocky Mountain spur ranges (the Big Horn, Pryor, Beartooth, Crazy and Snowy) can be seen from the gravesite.

The Black Otter Trail rejoins Airport Road just before busy Billings-Logan International Airport. Facing the terminal from the city side of the parking area is the **Peter Yegen, Jr., Yellowstone County Museum**. Its displays include the last switch steam engine used in Yellowstone, an authentic roundup wagon and, outside, a life-size statue, *The Range Rider of the Yellowstone*, facing the metropolis at the foot of the Rimrocks. Closed Sunday. ~ 1950 Terminal Circle, Billings; 406-256-6811, fax 406-254-6031; www.pyycm.org.

If the *Range Rider* could see far enough into the bluffs on the far side of the valley, he might spot **Pictograph Cave State Park** just southeast of Billings. An estimated 4500 years ago, prehistoric hunters lived in three different caves at this site; some 30,000 artifacts, including distinctive rock paintings (petroglyphs), have told archaeologists a great deal about the hunters' way of life. Short

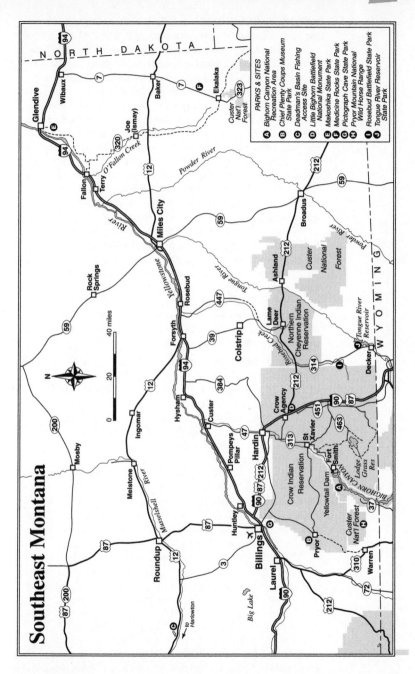

Southeast Montana

PARKS & SITES

- Ⓐ Bighorn Canyon National Recreation Area
- Ⓑ Chief Plenty Coups Museum State Park
- Ⓒ Deadman's Basin Fishing Access Site
- Ⓓ Little Bighorn Battlefield National Monument
- Ⓔ Makoshika State Park
- Ⓕ Medicine Rocks State Park
- Ⓖ Pictograph Cave State Park
- Ⓗ Pryor Mountain National Wild Horse Range
- Ⓘ Rosebud Battlefield State Park
- Ⓙ Tongue River Reservoir State Park

NORTH DAKOTA

WYOMING

trails lead to the caves; there are also interpretive signs and a pic-nic area. Take Exit 452 (Lockwood) from Route 90 and follow Coburn Road four miles south. Closed October through April. Admission. ~ Coburn Road, Billings; 406-247-2940, fax 406-248-5026; www.pictographcave.org, e-mail twalters@mt.gov.

ZooMontana features plants and animals from around the world that are naturally adapted to live in Montana's rigorous climate. Canyon Creek runs through the 70-acre park, which opened in 1993 as Montana's first big zoo. Waterfowl, river ot-ters and other native North American animals are joined by Siberian tigers and other cold climate species. A sensory garden features fragrant flowers, and domesticated animals inhabit a turn-of-the-20th-century homestead. Admission. ~ 2100 South Shiloh Road, Billings; 406-652-8100, fax 406-652-9281; www.zoomontana.org, e-mail zoomont@zoomontana.org.

In Laurel is the **Chief Joseph Statue and Canyon Creek Battle-field Marker**. Chief Joseph and his band of Nez Perce fled before the U.S. Cavalry near here in 1877, in the penultimate skirmish before their subsequent surrender at Bear's Paw, near Havre. (The actual Canyon Creek battleground is seven and a half miles north on Route 532.) There is a self-guided display of the Canyon Creek battle and a covered picnic area. ~ Firemen's Park, Laurel; 406-628-8105, fax 406-628-2041; www.laurelmontana.org, e-mail secretary@laurelmontana.org.

THE MUSSELSHELL VALLEY   North of Billings, the **Musselshell River** parallels the Yellowstone for about 150 miles, at a distance of about 35 to 40 miles, from its sources in the Crazy and Little Belt mountains until it turns abruptly north to flow into the Mis-souri. Route 12 follows the famed trout and catfish stream east from White Sulphur Springs downstream to Melstone, where it makes its northerly bend; then Route 12 crosses the prairies to join Route 94 at Forsyth.

Harlowton, 92 miles northwest of Billings, was once the ter-minus of the world's longest electrified rail line, connecting it with the silver-mining town of Castle (now a ghost town) in the Castle Mountains to the west. The last E-57B engine to run on that line is now the centerpiece of **Electric Engine Park** in the heart of this small town. ~ Route 12 and Central Avenue, Harlowton.

The **Upper Musselshell Museum** recalls some of the boom times in its early-1900s re-creations of a general store, schoolroom and homestead. Other displays include dinosaur bones, American Indian artifacts, farm tools and vintage clothing. Closed Monday and from mid-September to mid-May; open by appointment the rest of the year. Admission. ~ 11 South Central Avenue, Harlow-ton; 406-632-5519; www.harlowtonmuseum.com.

From Harlowton, the Musselshell River flows past **Deadman's Basin Fishing Access Site** and through the Golden Valley, so named for the autumn colors that line the river. ~ Deadman's Basin Road, Shawmut; 406-247-2940.

Pause in **Roundup**, another small town 66 miles east of Harlowton and 50 miles north of Billings, at the crossroads of Routes 12 and 87, to see the **Musselshell Valley Historical Museum**. Open summers, it has 7000 square feet of exhibits including a five-room pioneer home and a simulated coal-mine shaft. Closed October through April. ~ 524 1st Street West, Roundup; 406-323-1525; www.mvhm.com.

Every year since Montana's 1989 statehood centennial, when 3500 riders and 250 wagons herded 3000 head of cattle to Billings, the **Roundup Cattle Drive** has attracted would-be cowpokes on a six-day, five-night mid-August adventure with hands-on experience assured. ~ Roundup; phone/fax 406-358-2454, 800-257-9775; www.roundupcattledrive.com.

Route 12 pursues the course of the Musselshell as far as tiny Melstone, then cuts southeasterly across the plains to Forsyth, 100 miles from Roundup on the Yellowstone River. The Musselshell

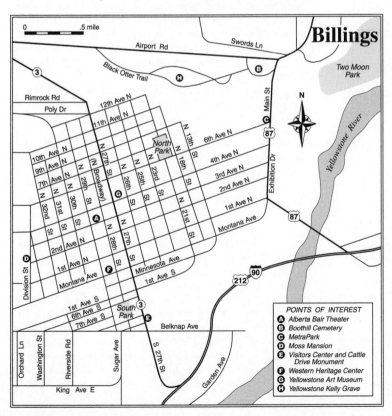

POINTS OF INTEREST
- **A** Alberta Bair Theater
- **B** Boothill Cemetery
- **C** MetraPark
- **D** Moss Mansion
- **E** Visitors Center and Cattle Drive Monument
- **F** Western Heritage Center
- **G** Yellowstone Art Museum
- **H** Yellowstone Kelly Grave

turns due north at Melstone; Route 500, a backcountry road, follows the river in the direction of Fort Peck Lake.

LODGING   The **Josephine Bed & Breakfast**, the only B&B in downtown Billings, offers six bright, antique-filled bedrooms (four with private baths) in a 1912 home a short walk from the downtown hub. All rooms have private baths and one has a jacuzzi for two. Non-smoking; no infants allowed. ~ 514 North 29th Street, Billings; 406-248-5898, 800-552-5898; www.thejosephine.com, e-mail info@thejosephine.com. MODERATE TO ULTRA-DELUXE.

North of downtown en route to the airport and MSU-Billings, the **Rimrock Inn** has all the basics and more, such as a free continental breakfast, a fitness area with a hot tub and a restaurant and lounge. The guest rooms are no-frills. ~ 1203 North 27th Street, Billings; phone/fax 406-252-7107, 800-624-9770; www.billingsrimrockinn.com, e-mail info@billingsrimrockinn.com. BUDGET TO MODERATE.

Downtown Billings' finest accommodations are at the **Historic Northern Hotel**. More than five decades old, the ten-story, 160-room hotel has been fully remodeled with a contemporary Western flair. Some rooms have refrigerators. There's a restaurant, a lounge, an exercise room and a casino. ~ 19 North Broadway, Billings; 406-245-5121, 800-542-5121, fax 406-259-9862; www.thenorthernhotel.com. DELUXE.

Also downtown, and a step down in price, is the **Best Western Ponderosa Inn**. This motel has 130 guest rooms in a pair of two-story buildings. One building faces an outdoor courtyard with a swimming pool; the other looks toward a restaurant. Standard rooms have a range of bed sizes (from double to king), a full bathroom, a desk, air conditioning and complimentary coffee. In addition to the pool, the Ponderosa has a sauna, fitness room and coin laundry. ~ 2511 1st Avenue North, Billings; 406-259-5511, 800-628-9081, fax 406-238-1797; www.ponderosainn.com, e-mail bwpi@180com.net. MODERATE.

Conveniently located off Route 90 for travelers arriving from the west, the **Holiday Inn Grand Montana** is the region's largest. With 317 guest rooms in seven stories adjoining the biggest exposition hall in the northern Great Plains, it has everything you'd expect a convention hotel to have, such as a full-service restaurant, room service and a pub featuring local microbrews. A waterfall tumbles past twin glass elevators in the atrium; there's an indoor pool, a spa, a sauna, an exercise room and a video-game parlor for the children. Softly lit, tastefully decorated rooms come with all the amenities. ~ 5500 Midland Road, Billings; 406-248-7701, 877-554-7263, fax 406-248-8954; www.chotelsgroup.com, e-mail higrandresv@montana.net. MODERATE.

There's adequate lodging in the Musselshell Valley at the **Corral Motel.** This is an older ma-and-pa establishment with 18 small rooms; four are two-bedroom units, three have kitchens, and the entire place is kept neat and clean. ~ Routes 12 and 191, Harlowton; 406-632-4331, fax 406-632-4748. BUDGET TO MODERATE.

DINING

Top of the line in southeastern Montana is **Juliano's,** which serves up generous portions of contemporary American cuisine in a converted turn-of-the-20th-century livery stable behind The Castle, a medieval-looking sandstone manor, and on an outdoor patio. The menu changes monthly and emphasizes seafood dishes like Tasmanian salmon dumplings or ancho chile–dusted prawns. The restaurant does its own baking and has an extensive wine list. ~ 2912 7th Avenue North, Billings; 406-248-6400. DELUXE TO ULTRA-DELUXE.

Also atmospheric, but in a more uptown, contemporary American sort of way, is **Walkers Grill & Tapas Bar,** strewn with barbed wire, cattle guards and other Montana artifacts. Dinner is a creative affair, with bistro-style and Cajun influences in various seafood and meat dishes. Dinner only. Closed Sunday. ~ 2700 1st Avenue North, Billings; 406-245-929, fax 406-248-7607; www.walkersgrill.com, e-mail walkersgrill@bresnan.net. MODERATE TO DELUXE.

For straight beef and seafood, it's hard to top **Jake's Steaks** in the heart of downtown Billings. Try the white bean chili verde for lunch or the coconut crunchy shrimp for dinner, served amid the garden decor of the main restaurant or in the wood-and-brass Good Time Bar. Closed Sunday. ~ 2701 1st Avenue North, Billings; 406-259-9375; www.jakes.tv. DELUXE.

The Granary serves prime rib and Alaskan king crab in a building constructed as a mill by the former Billings Polytechnic Institute in 1935. Students enjoy the outdoor patio lounge. Dinner only. ~ 1500 Poly Drive, Billings; 406-259-3488. ULTRA-DELUXE.

Billings' first brewpub is the **Montana Brewing Company.** This downtown establishment has taken over the first floor of an old power company building, retaining and restoring the original century-old architecture. Besides designer beers, the pub offers

AUTHOR FAVORITE
I know **Jersey Lilly Bar & Cafe** is in the middle of nowhere but I think that just adds to its appeal. You can't miss it: it's the only business in town. People drive many miles to eat its famous Jersey Lilly beans. ~ Route 12, Ingomar; 406-358-2278. MODERATE.

salads, sandwiches and pizzas in a friendly, casual atmosphere. ~ 113 North Broadway, Billings; 406-252-9200; e-mail mbc@wtp. net. BUDGET TO MODERATE.

Bruno's Italian Specialties is a longtime Billings favorite for its pizza and homemade Italian sausage. The spacious restaurant on the north side of downtown is right next door to a casino. ~ 2658 Grand Avenue, Billings; 406-652-4416. MODERATE.

As anyone who travels the highways of Montana will tell you, Roundup's **Busy Bee** has something for everyone. Located on the west side of town on routes 12 and 87, the Bee serves a wide-ranging country-style menu in a pair of homey dining rooms. There's a big salad bar; beer and wine are served, but no spirits. Check out the gift shop, too. ~ 317 1st Avenue West, Roundup; 406-323-2204. BUDGET TO DELUXE.

SHOPPING As the commercial center of a four-state region, Billings is a magnet for shoppers. **Rimrock Mall** has more than 100 shops, anchored by three major department stores. ~ 300 South 24th Street West, Billings; 406-656-3205; www.rimrockmall.com. Somewhat nearer to downtown is **West Park Plaza**, Montana's first mall when it opened in the early 1960s; it has approximately 35 stores. ~ 1603 Grand Avenue, Billings; 406-252-8684.

A fine place to find gifts and crafts is at the **Yellowstone Art Museum.** ~ 401 North 27th Street, Billings; 406-256-6804. **Billings Army/Navy Surplus** is the largest of its kind in the northwestern United States. ~ 15 North 29th Street; 406-259-8528.

NIGHTLIFE The **Alberta Bair Theater for the Performing Arts,** a renovated former Fox theater on the corner of Broadway and 3rd, has been acoustically redesigned and is now in use more than 110 nights a

The Alberta Bair Theater for the Performing Arts is Montana's largest concert hall.

year. Touring professional ballet, opera, theater and symphony companies appear here. ~ 2801 3rd Avenue North, Billings; 406-256-6052; www.alberta bairtheater.org. The **Billings Symphony Orchestra and Chorale** presents concerts at the Bair in September-through-November and February-through-April seasons. ~ 201 North Broadway, Suite 350, Billings; 406-252-3610; www.billingssymphony.org.

Big-name concerts of country and popular musical artists usually are held at **MetraPark Arena**. The greatest concentrations take place in mid-August during the Montana Fair. ~ 308 6th Avenue North, Billings; 406-256-2400; www.metrapark.com.

The **Billings Studio Theatre** stages eight plays of different genres, often including dramas, comedies and musicals. The season runs from September to May. ~ 1500 Rimrock Road, Billings; 406-248-1141; www.billingsstudiotheatre.org.

Casey's Golden Pheasant brings blues, bluegrass and jazz to downtown Billings Monday and Tuesday nights. The rest of the week is deejay dance music. Closed Sunday. Occasional cover. ~ 222 North Broadway; 406-256-5200; www.caseys.net.

Casino lovers can check out **Doc & Eddy's** at two locations: west of downtown at 711 15th Street West, 406-259-0887; and in Billings Heights at 1403 Main Street, 406-248-4336.

LAKE ELMO STATE PARK A 64-acre irrigation reservoir on Billings' northern city limits, Lake Elmo attracts city residents for swimming, fishing (for panfish) and nonmotorized boating. There are restrooms. Day-use fee, $2. ~ Head north on Main Street (Route 87) through Billings Heights; turn left on Pemberton Lane, then right after one-half mile, to Lake Elmo Drive; 406-247-2940, fax 406-248-5026; e-mail twalters@mt.gov.

PARKS

CUSTER NATIONAL FOREST Montana's most diverse national forest extends across nearly 2.5 million acres of the southern part of the state, in six different parcels reaching from the Stillwater River, west of Red Lodge, to Capitol Rock, southeast of Ekalaka on the border of South Dakota. In between, it includes a large chunk of the Absaroka-Beartooth Wilderness as well as the Pryor Mountains, west of Bighorn Canyon, and the Ashland District lands, east of the Tongue River. Picnic tables and restrooms are among the facilities. ~ Main approach roads for the Beartooth region are Routes 212 and 78 from Red Lodge, or Route 419 from Absarokee. Enter the Pryor Mountains via Crow Reservation Road 11, off Route 5 between Pryor and Warren; the Ashland District from Route 212 or Otter Creek Road; and the Ekalaka District from county roads south and east of Ekalaka, at the end of Route 7; 406-657-6200, fax 406-657-6222.

▲ There are 277 RV/tent sites (no hookups), plus 91 for tents only at 20 campgrounds; no charge to $10 per night; up to 14-day maximum stay. A recreational cabin, available at $30 per night, is located at Beaver Creek in the Ashland District. Another in the Beartooth District can be rented for $40 per night.

DEADMAN'S BASIN FISHING ACCESS SITE Trout fishing and other water sports are widely pursued at this prairie irrigation reservoir, located just north of the Musselshell River. There are picnic tables and restrooms. ~ Twenty miles east from Harlowton on Route 12, then one mile north on Deadman's Basin Road; 406-247-2940, fax 406-248-5026; fwp.state.mt.us/fishing/guide.

▲ Primitive only.

▼▼▼▼▼▼▼▼▼▼
**The Big Horns
and Beyond**

Route 90 connecting Billings with Sheridan, Wyoming, 130 miles southeast, is an avenue to many of the leading attractions of southeastern Montana. Traversing the Crow Indian Reservation, it passes directly by the Little Bighorn Battlefield of "Custer's Last Stand" fame and comes within a short drive of Bighorn Canyon National Recreation Area.

SIGHTS

HIDDEN ►

At the northern boundary corner of the Crow Indian Reservation is **Hardin**, a farming and ranching center of 3000 people. The best reason to visit Hardin is to see its **Big Horn County Historical Museum and State Visitors Center**. Located at the east end of town, the free museum carefully preserves more than a dozen homestead-era buildings from all over Big Horn County. Picnic grounds surround the 24-acre "village," which includes a farm home and outbuildings, railroad depot, service station, mercantile shop, school and church (still used for services on summer Sundays). Antique farm implements and machinery are on display. Closed weekends in winter. ~ Route 90 Exit 497, Hardin; 406-665-1671, fax 406-665-3068; www.museumonthebighorn.org.

Hardin lives hard by its memories of Little Bighorn. While the battlefield is 18 miles southeast of here, the **Custer's Last Stand Reenactment** takes place four times each year, in a field six miles west of Hardin, during Little Big Horn Days, the weekend nearest June 25. Thousands attend the hour-long spectacle; advance tickets can be purchased from the Hardin Area Chamber of Commerce (10 East Railway Street, Hardin; 406-665-1672). ~ www.custerslaststand.org.

Located outside Little Bighorn Battlefield National Monument but on the site where the battle first began, **Custer Battlefield Museum** showcases objects found at the Battle of the Little Bighorn plus period military, American Indian and frontier artifacts. Of special note are the historic portraits taken by photographer David F. Barry. His many subjects included General George Armstrong Custer and his wife Elizabeth, as well as Sitting Bull. At the museum store, you'll find books detailing the battle and its major players. Admission. ~ Route 90 Exit 514, Garryowen; 406-638-2000, fax 406-638-2019; www.custer museum.org, e-mail info@custermuseum.org.

Little Bighorn Battlefield National Monument is where the *real* action took place, however, and there's no better way to understand the maneuvers and tactics of the best known of all American Indian battles than to spend some time here. The clash, which took place on June 25 and 26, 1876, memorializes one of the Plains Indians' last armed attempts to defend their life against the white conquest. Admission. ~ Route 90, Exit 510, Junction 212, Crow Agency; 406-638-3217; www.custerslaststand.org.

land administered by the Bureau of Land Management. Back-country roads penetrate the range from Route 310 east of Warren. A four-wheel-drive vehicle is recommended for these rugged roads. ~ Gyp Springs Road via Lovell, Wyoming; 406-896-5013.

Just inside the Crow Indian Reservation's western boundary is **Chief Plenty Coups Museum State Park**, which preserves the log home, medicinal spring and grave of the last Crow chief. Plenty Coups deeded the land, 33 miles south of Billings, "to all people" in 1928. It is now an interpretive center for Crow tribal history as well as a memorial to the chief himself. Open May through September, and by appointment the rest of the year. Admission. ~ Three-quarters of a mile west on Edgar Road, Pryor; 406-252-1289; www.plentycoups.org.

The Crow Indian Reservation is bordered on the east by the wooded mesas and creek beds of the **Northern Cheyenne Indian Reservation**. Covering 442,000 acres west of the Tongue River, the reservation is home to 10,000 Northern Cheyenne, who call themselves the "People of the Morning Star." Visitors are especially welcome for the reservation's annual 4th of July celebration. ~ Little Wolf Capitol Building, 600 Cheyenne Avenue, Lame Deer; 406-477-6284; www.ncheyenne.net.

More impressive is the **Plains Indian Museum at St. Labre Indian School**, on the reservation's eastern frontier 21 miles from Lame Deer. The modern museum has a colorful and varied collection of clothing and artifacts from Cheyenne, Sioux and other plains tribes. The school, founded as a mission in 1884, is notable for its stylized stone church, built in the shape of a tepee but with a wooden cross protruding in place of the center supporting pole. Closed weekends fall through spring; call for hours. ~ Tongue River Road, Ashland; 406-784-4500; www.stlabre.org, e-mail webmaster@stlabre.org.

Rosebud Battlefield State Park, 44 miles southwest of Lame Deer, marks the spot where a confederation of Plains Indian warriors took on a cavalry division in June 1876, setting the stage for the Battle of the Little Bighorn eight days later. ~ Route 314, 18 miles north of Decker; 406-234-0900.

It's an hour's drive north from Lame Deer to Route 94 west of Forsyth. Not quite halfway, Route 39 passes through the town of **Colstrip**, a modern coal-mining town that bills itself as the "Energy Center of Montana." The **Schoolhouse History and Art Center** will show you photos of the town's history, the operation of a coal-fired power plant, and a video about the workings of an open-pit mine. ~ 400 Wood Rose, Colstrip; phone 406-748-4822, www.schoolhouseartcenter.com, e-mail shac@tgrsolution.net.

The little town of **Broadus**, a 44-mile drive east from Ashland on Route 212, has one of the most memorable local museums to be found in the northern Rockies. The **Powder River Historical**

Museum displays and dioramas in the visitors center and summertime ranger-led talks and tours describe the chain of events that led Sioux and Cheyenne warriors to vanquish a corps of 260 U.S. Army cavalrymen. Three-hundred and fifty soldiers survived the massacre, but among the dead was their leader, Lieutenant Colonel George Armstrong Custer.

The national monument, reached off Route 212 at Exit 510 from Route 90, includes the **Custer National Cemetery** (for veterans of the armed services) and a four-and-a-half-mile tour road that winds through the sage-covered hills overlooking the Little Bighorn River.

Given that the Indians were fighting for their ultimate freedom, it's ironic that the national monument is now within the **Crow Indian Reservation**. The vast (2.2-million-acre) reservation is home to about 11,000 Apsaalooké (pronounced ab-SAW-loogay, meaning "Children of the Large-Beaked Bird"), or Crow. It stretches 80 miles north and south, from Billings to the Wyoming border, and 83 miles east and west, from West Pryor Mountain to Rosebud Creek. ~ Crow Agency; 406-638-3700, fax 406-638-3881; www.crownation.net.

After Little Bighorn Battlefield, the Crow Indian Reservation's second ace-in-the-tourism-hole is the **Bighorn Canyon National Recreation Area**. The park spans two states, stretching south well into Wyoming, but it is from Hardin that most Montana visitors reach it. Its central feature is 60-mile-long Bighorn Lake, which fills a dramatic desert canyon whose limestone walls rise a half mile high on either side, revealing millions of years of geologic history. The numerous outdoor stores in tiny **Fort Smith**, at the north entrance to the park 43 miles south of Hardin, make the area's recreational focus abundantly clear. See "Parks" section below for more information. ~ Fort Smith; 406-666-2412.

Bighorn Lake was created in 1965 by 525-foot-high Yellowtail Dam. Today, the **Yellowtail Dam Visitors Center** describes the construction and operation of the dam. Open Memorial Day through Labor Day weekends. ~ Route 313, Fort Smith; 406-666-3218, 406-666-2452.

The best vista of the meandering reservoir and gorge is from the **Devil Canyon Overlook**, a course that requires drivers to backtrack more than 100 miles through Lovell, Wyoming. Those who do are rewarded with a magnificent view where Bighorn Canyon cuts through the Pryor Mountains. ~ Route 37.

Those same Pryor Mountains, on the west side of Bighorn Canyon, are the site of the 38,000-acre **Pryor Mountain National Wild Horse Range**. About 140 mustangs freely roam this rugged desert

The mustangs roaming the Pryor Mountain National Wild Horse Range are believed to be descendants of a herd that has lived in this area for more than two hundred years.

Text continued on page 270.

Custer's Last Stand

By the 1870s, U.S. government policy toward the proud native peoples of the Great Plains had changed from aggressive domination to pseudo-accommodation. Deciding it "cheaper to feed than to fight the Indians," Congress had pledged in 1868 to defend them from further hostility, designating a large part of the Wyoming territory, including the Black Hills, as a permanent reservation for Sioux (Crow), Cheyenne and other tribes.

It seemed that treaties were made to be broken. Following an 1874 gold strike in the Black Hills, thousands of anxious argonauts poured onto reservation lands despite the cavalry's feeble efforts to keep them out. The Indians, who still wished to honor the treaty, refused to cede this portion of their sacred hunting grounds, and the Sioux and Cheyenne stepped up a campaign of hostile raids against mining settlements, pioneer homesteads and ill-fated travelers.

When the renegade clans, led by chiefs Sitting Bull and Crazy Horse, defied a direct order from the Commissioner of Indian Affairs to restrict themselves to reservation lands, the U.S. Army launched a three-pronged campaign against them in the spring of 1876. (Since the order was issued in the dead of winter, it is unlikely that many families could have made it back to the reservation by the end of January, as specified, under any circumstances.)

The first of the three expeditions, from Fort Fetterman, Wyoming Territory, was turned back June 17 on Rosebud Creek, about 40 miles southeast of Sitting Bull's encampment on the Little Bighorn River. A joint Sioux-Cheyenne force sent General George Crook retreating after substantial losses; this Rosebud Battlefield site is now a Montana state park.

The other two prongs of the attack—Colonel John Gibbon's troops from Fort Ellis, Montana Territory, and General Alfred Terry's column from Fort Abraham Lincoln, Dakota Territory—met on the banks of the Yellowstone River. Unaware of Crook's failure, Terry designated Lieutenant Colonel George Armstrong Custer, a Civil War hero, to lead the 600 men of the 7th Cavalry up Rosebud Creek, then cross a saddle of land and slip into the Little Bighorn from the southeast. Terry and Gibbon, meanwhile, would circle in from the Bighorn River to the northwest.

Custer arrived at least 36 hours earlier than Terry and Gibbon, and located Sitting Bull's camp at about dawn June 25. Probably underestimating the tribes' strength, Custer put five 45-man battalions under his direct command and assigned three each to Major Marcus Reno and Captain Frederick Benteen. (A twelfth was assigned to guard the pack train.)

Benteen was charged with scouting the bluffs south of the Indian camp a Custer and Reno headed toward the village. Custer intended to invade t camp from its lower, northern end, while Reno was to strike at the high end of the camp. But the Sioux detected Reno's approach and sent a larg force to stop his advance. Outflanked and overwhelmed, Reno's men retreated in disorder and took up defensive positions in the bluffs with Benteen.

Where had the impetuous Custer gone? When heavy gunfire began sounding from the north, Reno and Benteen concluded that the colone too, had come under attack. By the time they had distributed ammuniti to their troops and moved them northward, however, all activity had ceased. Further Indian attacks caused them to withdraw once again to the bluffs, where they held their defenses until the columns under Terr and Gibson arrived on the afternoon of the following day, June 26.

Custer's precise movements, after he separated from Benteen and Rer will forever be conjecture. But not a man among the 225 who followe Custer into battle survived the skirmish with the Cheyenne and Sioux (A single horse, Comanche, was left standing; for years thereafter, he was saddled but left riderless as he marched in military parades to commemorate the massacre.) Battle accounts rendered by Indians wl participated told how Custer's battalions were surrounded and exterminated.

Said Chief Two Moon of the Northern Cheyenne: "The shooting was quick. Pop-pop-pop very fast. Some of the soldiers were down on th knees, some standing.... The smoke was like a great cloud, and every the Sioux went the dust rose like smoke. We circled all around him— swirling like water around a stone. We shoot, we ride fast, we shoot Soldiers drop, and horses fall on them."

Of the men under the command of Reno and Benteen, 47 were kill 52 wounded, bringing total fatalities probably to 272. No more than Sioux and Cheyenne were killed. After the Indians removed their d the battlefield, the village broke up, with tribes scattering in differen directions.

Little Bighorn Battlefield National Monument and Custer National C are today surrounded by the expansive Crow Indian Reservation. O eastern border is the Northern Cheyenne reservation. Together, the reservations stretch well over 100 miles from the Pryor Mountains Tongue River.

Society Museum is actually two museums in one. The main building, located two blocks off the highway, displays a well-organized homestead-era collection including a complete general store, a ranch's chuckwagon, the original Powder River jail and many antique vehicles.

If those don't grab you, ask to see **Mac's Museum** in a rear   ◀ HIDDEN
building. Until his death in 1986, pioneer resident R. D. "Mac" McCurdy devoted most of his waking hours to his personal collection of arrowheads, fossils, rocks, insects, birds' eggs and more. But those pale in comparison to his 22,000 seashells from throughout the world. Many of them are no larger than pinheads, but McCurdy identified all by their exact genera and species. Scientists visit from all over North America to study McCurdy's collection. Closed Sunday and from October to Memorial Day, except by appointment. ~ Corner of Park Avenue and Wilbur Street at the town square, Broadus; 406-436-2977, 406-436-2753 in the off season.

Also in Broadus, the **Powder River Taxidermy Wildlife Museum** has assembled some 150 wildlife trophies—"everything from a mouse to a moose"—along with antique guns and local art. There's not much more to see east of here until Route 212 leaves Montana for Wyoming's Devils Tower and South Dakota's Black Hills. ~ 708 South Park Street, Broadus; 406-436-2538.

Near the Little Bighorn Battlefield, in downtown Hardin, an early-   **LODGING**
20th-century boarding house has been restored as a bed-and-breakfast home. The **Kendrick House Inn** is a handsome Georgian with five guest rooms decorated in late-Victorian style. Each room has a pedestal sink, but the bathrooms (two of them) must be shared. There are full breakfasts in the dining room, two porches,

AUTHOR FAVORITE

Ever wanted to be a cowboy? The **Schively Ranch** will give you your chance. There are actually two ranches here, an "upper" and a "lower," located in Montana's Pryor Mountains; the Upper Ranch has small cabins with electric heat and central bath facilities, while the lower Dry Head Ranch merely has a bunkhouse. This is a real ranching experience, with lots of horseback riding and trailside, chuckwagon meals. Because the ranch's winter feed-lot is in Wyoming, early-season (April–May) or late-season (October–November) guests can join in cattle drives. ~ 1062 Road 15, Lovell, WY 82431; 406-259-8866 (summer), 307-548-6688 (winter), fax 307-548-2322; www.schivelyranch.com, e-mail schively@tctwest.net. DELUXE TO ULTRA-DELUXE.

and a TV in the library. Closed November through April. ~ 206 North Custer Avenue, Hardin; 406-665-3035, fax 406-665-9090; e-mail stevesmith@msn.net. MODERATE.

The rather plain cinderblock **Lariat Motel** is another cost-conscious choice. Eighteen basic rooms in Western style come with queen or double beds. ~ 709 North Center Avenue, Hardin; 406-665-2683, fax 406-665-3036; e-mail lariat_motel@msn.com. BUDGET TO MODERATE.

Lodging options are scarce in the southeasternmost part of the state, but the **Broadus Motel** will do in a pinch. Kitchen units are available in this modest lodging; all rooms have air conditioning as well as phones and TV. ~ Route 212 West, Broadus; 406-436-2671, fax 406-436-2674. MODERATE.

DINING

Once you get away from Billings, culinary choices are pretty much limited to steak and potatoes. **The Merry Mixer Restaurant & Lounge** is a prime example. You can get a good steak or a big slab of prime rib accompanied by a baked potato, a basic iceberg-lettuce salad and a hearty cup of coffee. The atmosphere is strictly red vinyl and low lights, but the service is friendly. ~ 317 North Center Avenue, Hardin; 406-665-3735. MODERATE.

A longtime favorite here is the **Purple Cow**, a family restaurant open for three meals daily. The Cow offers hearty breakfasts and generous homemade buffets for lunch and dinner, including a large salad bar. Soups and pies are also popular. Closed Monday in winter. ~ Rural Route 1, off Route 90, Hardin; 406-665-3601. MODERATE.

For American Indian fast food, the **Shake & Burger Hut** is worth a visit. Ask for an American Indian taco and you'll get ground beef, cheese and other fixings folded within tasty, pan-fried bread. There are also homemade Mexican specialties.The decor of this tiny establishment is strictly Formica-top tables. Closed Sunday. ~ Crow Agency on Main Street; 406-638-2921. BUDGET.

SHOPPING

American Indian culture vultures might seek out the **Jailhouse Gallery** for modern Indian paintings and craftwork. Closed Sunday. ~ 218 North Center Avenue, Hardin; 406-665-3239. The **St. Labre Indian Museum and Gift Shop**, adjacent to the Northern Cheyenne Reservation, offers beadwork and silver jewelry by local American Indians and Southwestern tribes. ~ St. Labre Indian School, Tongue River Road, Ashland; 406-784-4511; www.stlabre.org.

NIGHTLIFE

Montana's largest gambling establishment is the **Little Bighorn Casino**, a stone's throw from the Little Bighorn Battlefield at the same exit off Route 90. ~ Route 212, Crow Agency; 406-638-4000.

The hangout in the prairies is the **Montana Bar**, where locals gather to knock back a few and play pool, darts or video poker. The mounted wildlife on the walls remind you this is hunting territory. ~ 111 East Wilson Street, Broadus; 406-436-2454.

Nearly on the Wyoming border is the **Stoneville Saloon**, which boasts "cheap drinks, lousy food." Its handcarved bar, dating from 1865, is worth a look in itself. This is a popular spot for motorcyclists, as it's a mere hour's drive down the highway from Sturgis, South Dakota, the late-summer biker capital of America. ~ Route 212, Alzada; 406-828-4404.

LITTLE BIGHORN BATTLEFIELD NATIONAL MONUMENT 𝕏   **PARKS**
Formerly known as Custer Battlefield, this national parkland commemorates one of the final efforts by American Indians to defend their homelands. The monument, surrounded by the Crow Indian Reservation, comprises two parcels, three miles apart, that overlook the Little Bighorn River where Sioux, Cheyenne and other warriors camped prior to their June 1876 massacre of Lieutenant Colonel George Custer and his corps of 260 American soldiers. Visitors center displays and films, guided tours and ranger-led programs explain the background, events and aftermath of that battle. Custer National Cemetery is also on the site. Several self-guided auto and pedestrian tours are available; pick up information at the visitors center. Facilities include a visitors center and restrooms, both of which are wheelchair-accessible. Day-use fee from April to November is $10 per vehicle, $5 for walk-ins. ~ From Route 90, take Exit 510, two miles south of Crow Agency; Battlefield Road enters the national monument about one mile east of the exit off Route 212; 406-638-2621.

For a spectacular view of Bighorn Canyon, stop by Devil Canyon Overlook in the park's southern section.

BIGHORN CANYON NATIONAL RECREATION AREA 𝕏 🚴 🏇
🛶 🎣 🥾 🚤 ⛴ 🎿 Prior to 1965 the Bighorn River cut a deep gorge through the Pryor and Big Horn mountain ranges. Since the construction of 525-foot-high Yellowtail Dam in 1965, Bighorn Lake has stretched 71 miles through the canyon. But the half-mile-high cliffs remain, and boating and fishing enthusiasts have a new playground, and there's a swimming beach at Horseshoe Bend and Ok-a-beh Marina. Fishing is outstanding for trout, walleye, catfish and other species. Visitors centers at Fort Smith, Montana, and Lovell, Wyoming, relate the canyon's geological and natural history. Since no direct route connects Fort Smith with Lovell, a meander of more than 100 miles is required to see both ends of Bighorn Canyon's Bighorn Lake. Picnic tables, restrooms, an amphitheater and two marinas round out the amenities. Day-use fee, $5.~ From Hardin, take Route 313 south 43 miles to the visitors center at Fort Smith. From the visitors cen-

ter at Lovell, Wyoming, on Route 14A east of Cody, take Route 37 north to Devil Canyon and Barry's Landing; 406-666-2412.

▲ There are 30 RV/tent sites (no hookups), plus 27 for tents only at four campgrounds; two campgrounds are accessible only by boat; no charge; 14-day maximum stay.

CHIEF PLENTY COUPS MUSEUM STATE PARK ⌐ Plenty Coups, the last Crow chief, used peaceful means to promote understanding and cooperation between American Indian and white cultures. This park—an interpretive center for Crow tribal history—includes the chief's log home, his grave, a sweat lodge, an old store and a spring of medicinal water. Picnic tables, restrooms and a visitors center round out the amenities. Open May through September, and by appointment the rest of the year. Day-use fee, $2 per person. ~ From Pryor, which is 35 miles south of Billings on the western edge of the Crow Indian Reservation, take Route 416 west one mile; 406-252-1289, fax 406-252-6668.

TONGUE RIVER RESERVOIR STATE PARK ⌐ This 12-mile-long reservoir, set in the uplands amid red shale cliffs and juniper canyons just north of the Wyoming border, is a popular place for camping and water sports. Walleye and bass are the most highly sought fish here. There are picnic tables, restrooms, concession stands (in the summer) and groceries. Day-use fee, $4. ~ From Decker, 20 miles north of Sheridan, Wyoming, take Route 314 six miles north, then Route 382 (the Tongue River Dam Road) one mile northeast; 406-231-0900, fax 406-234-4368.

▲ There are 106 RV/tent sites (no hookups); $15 per night; 14-day maximum stay.

▼▼▼▼▼▼▼▼▼▼▼▼▼▼▼▼▼
Lower Yellowstone Valley

Northeast from Billings, Route 94 follows the Yellowstone River downstream some 223 miles to Glendive, not far from the river's confluence with the Missouri, before turning abruptly east through North Dakota toward Minneapolis and Chicago.

The longest undammed river in the lower 48 states, the Yellowstone—which runs 671 miles from its source in Wyoming's Absaroka Range to the Missouri—in its lower portion is a broad, gently flowing stream. Along with its principal tributaries, the northward flowing Bighorn, Tongue and Powder rivers, it irrigates tens of thousands of square miles of ranchland used in livestock and grain production.

Numerous communities exist along the river's banks, none of them large. This stretch of the Yellowstone may be better known as the home of the paddlefish (see "Outdoor Adventures" at the end of this chapter), a 100-pound-plus living fossil that is basically the same creature it was in the Paleocene era, 70 million years ago.

Along the south bank of the Yellowstone, stretching 27 miles from Huntley (11 miles east of Billings) to Bull Mountain, the Huntley Irrigation Project embraces four small communities and 35,000 acres of lush cropland set aside as a federal homesteading project in 1907. The townsite of Osborn, three miles east of Huntley, is now the location of the **Huntley Project Museum of Irrigated Agriculture**, which preserves 18 buildings and more than 5000 agricultural and household items from the early 20th century. Closed Monday and Sunday. Open Memorial Day through Labor Day, and by appointment the rest of the year. ~ Route 312, Highway Road, Osborn; 406-348-2533; www.huntleyprojectmuseum.org, e-mail hpmia@huntleyprojectmuseum.org.

Near the east end of the Huntley project is **Pompeys Pillar**, a sandstone butte on whose face Captain William Clark carved his name in 1806. That signature is the only direct physical evidence remaining along the trail from the Lewis and Clark expedition of 1803–1806, making the 117-foot-high butte a National Monument. A boardwalk/stairway leads from a picnic area at the base to Clark's signature and a lookout point atop the butte. A visitors center, operated by the Bureau of Land Management, offers interpretive programs through the summer. Take Exit 23 off Route 94. ~ Route 312, Pompeys Pillar; 406-896-5013; www.mt.blm.gov/pillarmon/index.

The village of **Custer**, 52 miles from Billings, is a popular gathering point for fishermen and rockhounds. The anglers come to cast their lines where the Bighorn River meets the Yellowstone, especially during the winter run of eel-like ling. Rockhounds scour the river banks downstream from Custer in search of Montana agates, also called plume or moss agates; geologists remark on the variety of designs sealed inside these stones.

Cut and polished Montana agates, which can be found along the Bighorn River, make stunning jewelry creations.

The towns of Hysham and Forsyth are 22 and 45 miles (respectively) northeast of Custer. Each boasts a small pioneer museum; **Hysham** has a wildlife management area in a nearby bend of the Yellowstone River, while **Forsyth** has the neoclassical **Rosebud County Courthouse**. An ornate copper dome caps the two-story building, listed on the National Register of Historic Places; murals and stained glass adorn the top floor and courtroom. Closed weekends. ~1200 Main Street, Forsyth; 406-346-7318.

Other than Billings, **Miles City** is the largest community in eastern Montana. Located 145 miles east of the "Magic City," and 94 miles west of the North Dakota border, the town of 8500 people lays claim to the moniker "Montana's Cowboy Capital."

Founded in 1877 near old Fort Keogh at the confluence of the Tongue and Yellowstone rivers, and named (as so many Montana towns were) for an Army officer, Miles City became headquarters for the Montana Stockgrowers' Association within three years after the arrival of the Northern Pacific Railroad in 1881. It remains a major ranching and farming center.

Although the open rangeland has long since been fenced, Miles City pays tribute to its cowboy heritage with its annual Breeders Show in February, world-famous Bucking Horse Sale in May and Cattlewomen's Convention in June. The horseracing and rodeo seasons attract tremendous attendance.

Fort Keogh, once the largest Army post in Montana, opened in 1877 following the Little Bighorn uprising and remained of major importance through 1908, when it closed. Several of its original buildings have been incorporated into the Livestock and Range Research Laboratory at Fort Keogh, an applied agricultural science facility two miles from downtown that focuses on genetics, reproduction and nutrition of beef cattle. Closed weekends. ~ Main Street West, Miles City; 406-874-8200, fax 406-874-8289; www.larrl.ars.usda.gov, e-mail diona@larrl.ars.usda.gov.

Give yourself plenty of time at the splendid **Range Rider Museum**, where you'll get a tremendous education in Wild West lore. A miniature replica of old Fort Keogh is displayed in this impressive 12-building complex whose collection also includes a re-creation of the main street of 19th-century Miles City, the Charles M. Russell Art Gallery and a Memorial Hall with hundreds of portraits and plaques remembering pioneer community residents. There's also the Heritage Center, with early photography and American Indian artifacts (including many arrowheads); a one-room school and log house; and displays of manifold antique vehicles, guns and hats. The museum is located just across the Tongue River Bridge from downtown. Closed November through March. Admission. ~ Main Street West, Miles City; 406-232-6146.

Custer County Art Center, upriver from the Range Riders Museum where the Tongue enters the Yellowstone, may be the world's only gallery housed in historic water storage tanks. It fea-

TICKET-FREE ZONE

Miles City got rid of parking meters years ago. It's a lot more fun to browse the quaint downtown historic district without them. Besides, quarters are essential to poker machines—and like every Montana town, Miles City has its quotient of casinos.

tures exhibitions of local and regional works, a collection of vintage frontier photographs and a gift shop stocked with a wide range of art and books. Closed Monday and the month of January. ~ Water Plant Road, Miles City; 406-234-0635, fax 406-234-0637; www.ccac.milescity.org, e-mail ccartc@midrivers.com.

Terry, equidistant from Miles City and Glendive, boasts the dubious distinction of having "the tallest sign in eastern Montana" at a beside-the-interstate convenience store. Certainly more important, it was the home of British photographer Lady Evelyn Cameron, who moved to Terry in 1894 with her naturalist husband and her 5x7 Graflex camera and recorded the lifestyle of eastern Montana homesteaders for the next 34 years. When a Time-Life editor discovered a stash of thousands of Cameron's photos in the basement of a private home, her previously unknown work quickly rocketed to fame. The Cameron Gallery in the Prairie County Museum has an extensive collection of her work. The museum, located in a historic bank building, also displays antique household, farm and business artifacts. Open Memorial Day through Labor Day, and by appointment the rest of the year. Closed Tuesday. ~ Terry; 406-635-4040.

A few miles northwest of town via Scenic View Road (impassable during wet weather) are the Terry Badlands Wilderness Study Area, a 43,000-acre Bureau of Land Management tract containing steep canyons, sparse vegetation and unique geological erosion. There's a scenic overlook, and a few hiking trails. Expect rustic wilderness, no facilities, and plenty of wildlife. ~ 406-233-2800, fax 406-233-2921; e-mail mcfoinfo@mt.blm.gov.

But badlands lovers will be yet more impressed by the pine-and-juniper-studded terrain at the 11,531-acre Makoshika State Park, located southeast of Glendive, 78 miles northeast of Miles City. In Lakota, *makoshika* means "bad earth"; but to paleontologists, this rippled earth has been very good, yielding the complete fossil remains of such great dinosaurs as triceratops and tyrannosaurus. There's a visitors center on the premises. Admission. ~ Snyder Avenue, Glendive; 406-377-6256, fax 406-377-8043; www.be.quick.com/makopark, e-mail makoshika@state.mt.us.

A mile east of downtown Glendive is the Frontier Gateway Museum. Open summers or by appointment, it displays various fossils, Indian and pioneer artifacts, and a re-created 19th-century downtown business district street scene. ~ Belle Prairie Frontage Road, Exit 215, Glendive; 406-377-8168 (summer), 406-365-4123 (winter).

Anglers call Glendive "the paddlefishing capital of the world." Found only in the Yellowstone and Missouri rivers and in China's Yangtze River, paddlefish are prehistoric bottom feeders with two-foot-long, paddle-shaped snouts. See the fishing section in "Outdoor Adventures" at the end of this chapter.

Route 90 turns away from the Yellowstone River at Glendive and makes a beeline for the North Dakota border. Eight miles from the frontier is the small community of **Wibaux**, founded in 1883 by French-born cattle baron Pierre Wibaux. The town office building he constructed in 1892 has been restored and is now the **Pierre Wibaux House Museum**. Besides memorabilia of the cattleman himself, there's a wide variety of turn-of-the-20th-century pioneer items and American Indian artifacts. In the same complex you'll also find an antiquated barbershop, livery stable, railway car, and caboose. Closed October through April. ~ East Orgain and Wibaux streets, Wibaux; 406-796-9969 (summer), 406-796-2381 (winter), fax 406-796-2625.

A twice-life-size statue of Pierre Wibaux stands atop a hill at the west end of Orgain Street, overlooking **St. Peter's Catholic Church**, which Wibaux built in 1885 with money donated by his father in France. The church has beautiful stained-glass windows and a lava-rock exterior that is covered in summer by climbing vines. ~ West end of Orgain Street, Wibaux.

Baker is 45 miles south of Wibaux via Route 7. This pleasant town of 1800 sits at the crossroads of Route 12 and Route 7, 80 miles east of Miles City. Baker Lake, surrounded by parks and recreational facilities, is right in town. Baker also boasts the **O'Fallon Historical Museum**, which displays the "world's largest steer"—almost six feet high and just under two tons in weight—and a variety of vintage clothing and homestead-era items. Call for hours. ~ 723 South Main, behind the courthouse complex, Baker; 406-778-3265.

Started in 1936, the Carter County Museum is Montana's first chartered county museum.

Medicine Rocks State Park, 25 miles south of Baker, commemorates a place of unusual sandstone rock formations that Plains Indian hunting parties once visited to conjure sacred spirits and other "big medicine." ~ Route 7, Ekalaka; 406-234-0900, fax 406-234-4368.

The town of **Ekalaka** (pronounced EEK-a-lack-a), ten miles south of Medicine Rocks at the end of Route 7, is at the end of the line as far as paved highway is concerned. Livestock production and outdoor sports, mainly deer and bird hunting, provide its economic subsistence. The **Carter County Museum** displays a complete skeleton of an *Anatotitan copei*, or duck-billed dinosaur, as well as other prehistoric specimens found in the region. This historic museum also features an extensive collection of American Indian and homestead artifacts. ~ 306 North Main Street, Ekalaka; 406-775-6886, fax 406-775-8785.

LODGING   The **Westwind Motor Inn** is a likely stop for travelers headed east from Billings. With 32 rooms, the twin-story hostelry has all essential amenities, including phones and TVs; refrigerators may be available on request. ~ 225 Westwind Lane, Forsyth; 406-346-2038, 888-356-2038, fax 406-346-2909. MODERATE.

The **Budget Inn Miles City** is located in the heart of the Yellowstone valley. The motel's 32 cozy ground-floor guest rooms have queen-size beds, and morning coffee and doughnuts may be had in the lobby. ~ 1006 South Haynes Avenue, Miles City; phone/fax 406-874-3550. BUDGET.

Miles City's best is the **Best Western War Bonnet Inn**. The 54 rooms are modern and spacious, and facilities at the two-story motel include a sauna, a whirlpool and a small heated pool. Rooms with microwaves and refrigerators may be reserved in advance. A complimentary expanded continental breakfast is included with the room rates. ~ 1015 South Haynes Avenue, Miles City; 406-234-4560, 800-528-1234, fax 406-234-0363. MODERATE.

Approaching the Dakotas, the three-story **Best Western Jordan Inn** is an upscale property that offers respite from summer heat in an indoor swimming pool and warm haven from winter's chill in a sauna. All rooms have combination baths; there's also a dining room, separate coffee shop and full lounge and casino. The hotel features seven original J. K. Ralston artworks and an extensive agate collection. ~ 223 North Merrill Avenue, Glendive; 406-377-5555, 888-453-6348, fax 406-377-6233. MODERATE.

If you find yourself in Baker for the night, you'll find comfortable lodging at the **Sagebrush Inn**. Most rooms have queen-size beds, cable TV and direct-dial phones. ~ 518 West Montana Avenue, Baker; 406-778-3341, 800-638-3708, fax 406-778-2753. MODERATE.

DINING

A popular local hangout on the eastern plains for more than a century has been Miles City's **Hole in the Wall**. An Old West atmosphere still pervades this steak-and-seafood house; prime rib is a house specialty while a salad bar is a concession to changing tastes. Closed Sunday and Monday. ~ 602 Main Street, Miles City; 406-234-9887. MODERATE.

The owners of **Sakelaris' Kitchen** are rightfully proud of the collection of country antiques they've assembled at their restaurant. They're also proud of their home cooking. Open most days at 5:30 a.m., and remaining open for early dinners, this is a great spot for homemade morning cinnamon rolls ("the best you ever sunk your choppers into") and midday soups. ~ Lake City Shopping Center, Baker; 406-778-2202. BUDGET.

SHOPPING

Gear up with Western wear, boots and hats, as well as Montana silver, at **Miles City Saddlery**. Needless to say, there are also plenty of saddles, bridles and tack to win a horse's favor. Closed Sunday. ~ 808 Main Street, Miles City; 406-232-2512; www.miles citysaddlery.com.

Whether you're looking for a Montana memory to take home for yourself or someone else, you'll find plenty of tempting gifts that won't bust your budget at **Pleasantries**. Housed in an 1800s-era brick building with gingerbread trim, 3000-square-foot Pleasantries overflows with Montana-made candles and candies, jams and jellies as well as Western-motifed and Victoriana home accessories. If you've never tasted the likes of huckleberry white-chocolate popcorn or chokecherry syrup, stop by and poke around awhile. Closed Sunday. ~ 506 Main Street, Miles City; 406-234-5644.

PARKS   **MAKOSHIKA STATE PARK** 🚶 🚴 🏕 Skeletons of the greatest dinosaurs to walk the earth have been discovered amid the deep coulees of these badlands, a quarter of a mile southeast of Glendive near the North Dakota border. Grotesquely eroded shale and sandstone columns are other geological features. There are picnic areas, restrooms, visitors center and shooting and archery ranges. Day-use fee, $5. ~ From Glendive, travel southeast on Snyder Avenue; 406-377-6256, fax 406-377-8043; www.be.quick.com/makopark, e-mail makoshika@state.mt.us.

▲ There are 16 RV/tent sites (no hookups); $12 per night; 14-day maximum stay.

MEDICINE ROCKS STATE PARK 🚶 🚴 🏇 🏕 Ancient Sioux believed these pockmarked sandstone rocks to be the home of sacred spirits; they often stopped and prayed for "good medicine." Wind and water erosion created the Swiss-cheese landscape that provides many species of wildlife a haven. The park is largely undeveloped. Picnic areas and restrooms are available. ~ Off Route 7, 25 miles south of Baker and ten miles north of Ekalaka; 406-234-0900, fax 406-234-4368.

▲ There are 15 nondesignated primitive sites; no charge; 14-day maximum stay.

▼ ▼ ▼ ▼ ▼ ▼ ▼ ▼ ▼ ▼ ▼ ▼ ▼ ▼

Outdoor Adventures

FISHING

Warmwater fish like bass, walleye, northern pike, catfish and perch do well in the Yellowstone River below Billings; the Musselshell River is famous for both trout and catfish; and Bighorn Lake is home to walleye, catfish and perch as well as brown and rainbow trout and burbot.

A good tackle source in Billings is the **Rainbow Run Fly Shop**, which is open year-round. ~ 2244 Grand Avenue, Billings; 406-656-3455. **Bighorn Trout Shop** also rents and sells tackle, and provides guides in season. Closed December through February. ~ 313 Parkdale Court, Fort Smith; 406-666-2375. In Miles City, you can get your tackle at **Red Rock Sporting Goods**. ~ 700 South Haynes Avenue, Miles City; 406-232-2716.

With shops in Fort Smith and Billings, **Bighorn Fly & Tackle** has become one of the biggest outfitters and tackle suppliers in the region. You can buy licenses and gear through them and also rent lodging for fly-fishing vacations. They offer year-round guide service on the Bighorn, Stillwater and Yellowstone rivers. ~ 485 South 24th Street West, Billings, 406-656-8257; Main Street, Fort Smith, 406-666-2253, 888-665-1321; www.bighornfly.com.

The most popular place for boating in southeastern Montana is unquestionably Bighorn Lake, in Bighorn Canyon National Recreation Area. There are two marinas on the 71-mile-long reservoir, each offering boat rentals, fuel, and watersports opportunities. **Ok-A-Beh Marina** is below Yellowtail Dam near Fort Smith. Closed Labor Day to Memorial Day. ~ 406-665-3670. **Horseshoe Bend Marina,** north of Lovell, Wyoming, has been mostly closed since 2000 because of insufficient water. Call for more information. Closed Labor Day to Memorial Day. ~ 307-548-7230.

BOATING

East of Red Lodge, you'll find no formal downhill resorts, and cross-country skiing is largely on a choose-your-own-terrain basis. Makoshika and Medicine Rocks state parks are two popular choices with the Nordic types. There are two short cross-country loops in **Custer National Forest**, on Route 212 east of Ashland. ~ 406-784-2344. For rentals in Billings and more information, visit **Reiter's Ski Outfit** for downhill skis. ~ 450 Main Street; 406-252-9341. Or try **The Base Camp** for cross-country skis and special rental packages. ~ 1730 Grand Avenue; 406-248-4555.

SKIING

Billings' **Briarwood Country Club** was acclaimed by *USA Today* as one of Montana's best. ~ 3429 Briarwood Boulevard, Billings; 406-245-2966. **Lake Hills Golf Club** also has 18 holes and is open year-round. ~ 1930 Club House Way, Billings Heights; 406-

GOLF

◆◆

PADDLEFISH FEVER

The lower Yellowstone River's most unusual species is the paddlefish, an enormous bottom feeder with a two-foot snout that hasn't changed much during 70 million years of evolution. Sought for their delicious meat and caviar-like roe, these fish, which weigh well over 100 pounds at full maturity, must be snagged with huge treble hooks and stout casting gear. The paddlefish season extends from May to July; a popular fishing hole is the Yellowstone Intake Diversion Dam, 17 miles north of Glendive via Route 16.

252-9244. **Pryor Creek Golf Club and Estates** has 27 holes, open to the public by invitation only. ~ Route 94, Huntley; 406-348-3900. Roundup, Hardin, Colstrip, Broadus, Forsyth, Miles City, Glendive and Baker have nine-hole courses.

TENNIS   In Billings, look for a municipal court at **North Park**. ~ 6th Avenue North and North 21st Street. Also, there are nine asphalt courts at **Pioneer Park**. ~ 3rd Street West and Avenue D. In winter, try the three indoor courts at **Yellowstone Racquet**; there are also five outdoor courts here. ~ 3440 Rimrock Road; 406-656-8040. MSU has three lighted outdoor courts on its campus. ~ 1500 North 30th Street. The Billings Parks Division has a full listing of city courts. ~ 390 North 23rd Street; 406-657-8372. In Great Falls, **Montana Park** has two unlit courts. ~ 18th Street Southwest and Fox Farm Road. Contact **Great Falls Park & Recreation Department** for more information. ~ 1700 River Drive North; 406-771-1265.

RIDING STABLES   The best way for horse lovers to get into the Montana prairies is to join a cattle drive. This normally involves a full week on the trail with real-life cowboys: riding, caring for horses and performing camp chores, as well as sightseeing and enjoying campfire entertainment.

Operators include **Double Rafter Cattle Drives** ~ P.O. Box 490, Ranchester, WY 82839, 307-655-9539, 800-704-9268, www.doublerafter.com; and **Powder River Wagon Train and Cattle Drive** ~ P.O. Box 483, Broadus, MT 59016, 406-436-2404, 800-492-8835; www.powderrivercattledrive.com. For a complete listing of cattle drive outfitters, contact the **Custer Country Tourism Region**. ~ P.O. Box 904, Forsyth, MT 59327; 406-346-1876.

BIKING   National Forest roads and trails are generally open to mountain biking, but wheeled vehicles—motorized or not—are not allowed in designated wilderness areas. Local bicycle shops have information on planned activities and mountain-biking routes. A popular trail is the 12-mile route through the badlands of **Makoshika State Park**. ~ Makoshika Park Road, Glendive; 406-377-6256, fax 406-377-8043.

HIKING   While the rolling prairies of Montana's southeast don't excite many hikers, there are interesting trails in mountains, state parks (especially Makoshika and Medicine Rocks) and riverfront areas. Trails at Little Bighorn Battlefield National Monument lead past numerous historical markers, while the three-mile Om-Ne-A Trail descending to Bighorn Lake from the rim of Yellowtail Dam can provide a steep challenge. The Ashland Ranger District of Custer National Forest offers three hiking and riding areas: Cook

Mountain, King Mountain and Tongue River Breaks. Call 406-784-2344 for more information.

Billings is immediately west of the junction of two interstate highways: **Route 90**, which runs southeast 98 miles to the Wyoming border, continuing east to Chicago and Boston; and **Route 94**, a spur that follows the Yellowstone River northeast (via Miles City) 247 miles to the North Dakota border at Wibaux, and on to Chicago.

▼▼▼▼▼▼▼▼▼▼
Transportation

CAR

Other major east–west routes are **Route 2**, the Hi-Line, from Glacier National Park through Havre and Glasgow to North Dakota, and **Route 212**, which approaches Billings from the west via Yellowstone National Park and Red Lodge, then travels east off Route 94 at Little Bighorn Battlefield, continuing to South Dakota's Black Hills and beyond.

North–south routes include **Route 59**, which extends from Jordan through Miles City and Broadus to northeastern Wyoming; and **Route 87**, which links Billings with Great Falls via Roundup and Lewistown.

Billings-Logan International Airport is Montana's largest. Two national airlines—Northwest and United—and three regional airline carriers—Big Sky, Frontier, Horizon and SkyWest—schedule regular arrivals and departures. ~ 406-238-3420; www.fly billings.com.

AIR

Big Sky Airlines has commuter service between Billings and seven other eastern Montana cities: Miles City, Glendive, Havre, Lewistown, Glasgow, Wolf Point and Sidney. ~ 800-237-7788; www.bigskyair.com.

Billings-based **Rimrock Trailways** serves all of Montana's major cities and many of its smaller ones. ~ 5044 Midland Road, Billings; 406-245-5392, 800-255-7655.

BUS

Larger towns along the Route 90/94 corridor also greet buses of the nationwide **Greyhound Bus Lines**. ~ 2502 1st Avenue North, Billings; 406-245-5116, 800-231-2222; www.greyhound.com.

There are 16 car-rental agencies in Billings. Those serving Billings-Logan International Airport are **Avis Rent A Car** (800-831-2847), **Budget Rent A Car** (800-527-0700), **Hertz Rent A Car** (800-654-3131) and **National Car Rental** (800-227-7368).

CAR RENTALS

Billings Metropolitan Transit, better known as "The MET," has an extensive bus network throughout the metropolitan area. ~ 406-657-8218; ci.billings.mt.us/met.

PUBLIC TRANSIT

For taxi service and airport shuttle service in Billings, call **City Cab**. ~ 406-252-8700. Or try **Yellow Cab**. ~ 406-245-3033.

TAXIS

NINE

Northeast Montana

Montana's vast northeastern quadrant is its most sparsely populated. Only three states (Alaska, Texas and California) are larger than Montana, yet only two (Alaska and Wyoming) have a lower population density. Statewide, only about 902,000 Montanans live on 147,000 square miles of land—about 5.4 people per square mile. In the northeast, the density is far lower than that.

The eastbound Missouri River is the tie that binds the region together. This broad, slow-flowing stream provides water for the arid farmland, habitat for waterfowl and other wildlife, recreation for the sportsman and sportswoman. Members of the Lewis and Clark expedition were the first white men to travel upriver in the very early 19th century. A generation later, steamboats were plying the Missouri as far as Fort Benton, providing Montana's principal lifeline to the "civilized" East. The Great Northern Railroad arrived around 1880, its way cleared by the mass relocation of American Indians to reservations and the mass slaughter of bison by white hunters. Cattle ranching soon became the economic mainstay of the eastern plains; it remains so today. Montana is among the national leaders in cattle and sheep production and is a major grower of barley and wheat.

For someone studying a map of northeastern Montana, the most prominent features are two Indian reservations (Fort Peck and Fort Belknap) and the enormous Charles M. Russell National Wildlife Refuge, encompassing the Missouri's manmade Fort Peck Lake. But for the person passing through—on Route 2, for instance, which follows the Milk River through the grain country of the Hi-Line, or on Route 200, dubbed "the loneliest road in America"—it is the spaces between the small towns, the incredible openness of the prairie skies, that will live longest in memory.

The Hi-Line

From the Rocky Mountain Front to Montana's eastern boundary near the confluence of the Missouri and Yellowstone rivers, Route 2, "the Hi-Line," follows a course between the Missouri Valley and the Canadian border. Paralleled by the Great Northern Railway line, the highway cuts a swath through often-bleak wheat-and-cattle country, first along the Milk River valley (175 miles from Havre to Fort Peck), then following the Missouri (another 125 miles to the Dakotas).

Leaving Havre, the first community of interest is the small farming town of **Chinook**, 21 miles east. Chinook was named not for salmon but for the warm winter winds that can raise temperatures from 0° to 50°F in a matter of minutes.

SIGHTS

Stop at the **Blaine County Museum** to see pioneer re-creations and a multimedia presentation on famous Chief Joseph. Closed weekends in winter. ~ 501 Indiana Street, Chinook; 406-357-2590. Then drive 16 miles south to the **Bear Paw Battlefield**, the northeasternmost of 38 Nez Perce National Historical Park sites and one of three units in Montana. This is where Chief Joseph and his band of Nez Perce surrendered to U.S. government forces on October 5, 1877, and where Joseph is said to have uttered his famous words: "From where the sun now stands, I will fight no more, forever." ~ Route 240; 406-357-3130.

Route 2 enters the **Fort Belknap Indian Reservation** at Harlem, about 42 miles from Havre. Roughly 5000 Assiniboine and Gros Ventre tribespeople live on the 700,000-acre reservation. Tours focus on the historic Hays district; arrangements can be made through the **Fort Belknap Fish and Game Office**. ~ Route 2, Harlem; 406-353-2205 ext. 470.

Travelers with time on their hands can visit the southern part of the reservation and take in a couple of old mining communities in the Little Rocky Mountains at the same time. It's about 35 miles from Route 2 at Fort Belknap Agency to Hays. In 1887, the St. Paul's Mission Church was established here; today it serves as a school for kindergartners through eighth graders. A couple more miles south, scenic Mission Canyon includes a variety of sites of geological intrigue, including Natural Bridge, Needle Eye and Devil's Kitchen.

Outside the reservation boundary, the **Little Rocky Mountains** rise about a half-mile above the surrounding country to the summit of Antoine Butte at 5610 feet. Notorious outlaws Butch Cassidy and Kid Curry are rumored to have maintained hideouts in this semiwilderness.

◄ HIDDEN

Gold was discovered in the Little Rockies in 1884; about $25 million had been taken from these mountains by the end of World War II. While the mines have now closed around **Zortman**, gold-panning still takes place on a modest scale. Beware—gold panning can be addictive. Most folks think they'll spend an hour at it and can't believe when a whole day has passed. Although panning occurs year-round, May to October is best for long days in the gully.

HIDDEN ▶ You can rent pans, screens and scoops from the **Zortman Garage, Motel & RV Park** and pan for gold on their claims. Call in advance to arrange for lessons or a personal guide. ~ Zortman; 406-673-3160, 800-517-0372.

From Zortman, you can return to Route 2 via Route 191, crossing 50 miles of semiarid grassland to **Malta**. A ranching center for a century, Malta is named for the Mediterranean island with which it has virtually nothing in common. Seven miles east is the **Bowdoin National Wildlife Refuge**, a nesting place for migratory waterfowl, including the white pelican, and upland game. A brochure on a 15-mile, self-guided auto tour is available from refuge headquarters. ~ Old Route 2; 406-654-2863; bowdoin.fwf.gov.

The tiny town of **Saco**, almost midway from Havre to the Dakota border, is an unlikely place for a nationally acclaimed broadcast journalist to have begun his childhood education, but it is indeed where late newsman Chet Huntley learned his ABCs (or was that NBCs?) in the early 20th century. In fact, the one-room **Huntley School** has been restored and is open for visits. Inquire locally.

Glasgow was once best known for its U.S. Air Force base. Today there are only memories. Many of them are displayed in the **Valley County Museum**, along with a wildlife collection, artifacts and the historic Buffalo Cody bar that still sports a bullet hole and lead slug. Closed Labor Day to Memorial Day. ~ 816 Route 2 West, Glasgow; 406-228-8692; www.valleycountymuseum.com.

Engineering is, indeed, important to the area: **Fort Peck Dam**, on the Missouri River, is just 18 miles south of Glasgow. Built by the U.S. Army Corps of Engineers during the peak of the Great Depression (construction began in 1933 and was completed in 1940), it is, at 250 feet high and four miles across, one of the largest earth-filled dams on Earth. Free guided tours of the powerhouse are offered from Memorial Day to Labor Day. ~ Route 24; 406-526-3411; e-mail michele.l.frondahl@usace.army.mil.

Fort Peck Lake—the reservoir created by the dam—is 134 miles long with 1520 miles of shoreline. Thirteen recreation areas with boat launch sites and campgrounds surround its shores; the vast majority of adjacent land belongs to the **Charles M. Russell National Wildlife Refuge**. Hundreds of species of birds as well as elk, deer, pronghorn antelope and smaller animals make their homes in this million-acre refuge of forests, prairies and badlands (see "Parks" in the Heartland section below). Within the Russell refuge is another, more primitive reserve: the **UL Bend** area, located on a prairie peninsula about 75 miles west of the dam. Elk don't need to migrate from this native prairie; it capably supports them year-round. ~ Refuge headquarters in Lewistown; 406-538-8706, fax 406-538-7521; cmr.fws.gov, e-mail cmr@fws.gov.

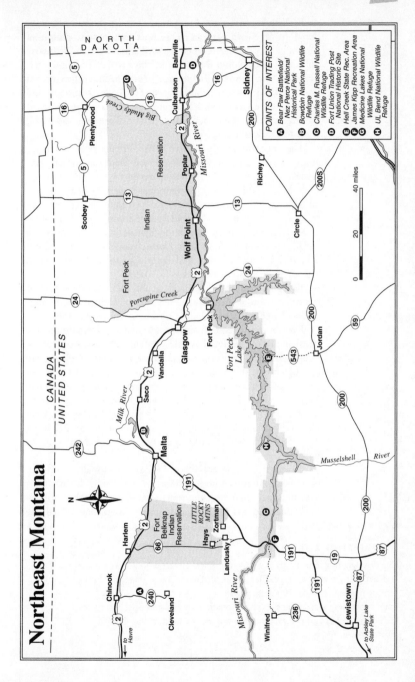

POINTS OF INTEREST
- **A** Bear Paw Battlefield/ Nez Perce National Historical Park
- **B** Bowdoin National Wildlife Refuge
- **C** Charles M. Russell National Wildlife Refuge
- **D** Fort Union Trading Post National Historic Site
- **E** Hell Creek State Rec. Area
- **F** James Kipp Recreation Area
- **G** Medicine Lakes National Wildlife Refuge
- **H** UL Bend National Wildlife Refuge

Northeast Montana

Fort Peck is still a good two-hour drive (in the best of conditions) from North Dakota. This northeasternmost region of Montana is dominated by the two-million-acre (550-square-mile) **Fort Peck Indian Reservation,** home to 10,700 mainly Assiniboine and Sioux tribespeople. Tribal headquarters are in Poplar, 21 miles east of Wolf Point. Its **Fort Peck Assiniboine and Sioux Culture Center and Museum** has permanent exhibits of arts and crafts. Closed weekends. ~ Route 2 East; 406-768-5155; www.fortpecktribes.org.

The reservation's largest town is **Wolf Point,** site of two major annual tribal celebrations: the Wild Horse Stampede, which takes place in mid-July, and the Wadopana powwow, held in early August. The **Wolf Point Area Historical Society Museum** focuses on regional farm and ranch history. Open June through September. Closed weekends. ~ 220 2nd Avenue South, Wolf Point; 406-653-1912. Farm machinery buffs will definitely want to call ahead to see **Louis Toav's John Deere Tractor Collection,** about a 15-mile detour north of Wolf Point. Call for an appointment. ~ Route 250, Lustre Road; 406-392-5294.

Just across Big Muddy Creek at the southeastern corner of the reservation is the agricultural town of **Culbertson,** famous statewide for its late-September threshing bee.

Even if you aren't a birder, consider a drive through the **Medicine Lakes National Wildlife Refuge,** which has one of the largest white pelican rookeries in America. About 24 miles north of Culbertson, the refuge is home to as many as 230 different species of resident and migratory waterfowl and shorebirds. Motorists can make a 14-mile self-guided drive through the reserve during the warmer months; fishing and picnicking are popular recreational activities here. ~ Route 16; 406-789-2305, fax 406-789-2350; www.medicinelake.fws.gov, e-mail r6rw_mdl@fws.gov.

On the north side of the Fort Peck reservation are a series of small towns that seem to have more in common with Saskatchewan province than with the rest of Montana. Worth visiting is the **Daniels County Museum and Pioneer Town,** a re-created, 42-

SURPRISING ZORTMAN

Surprisingly, tiny **Zortman** boasts several nearby attractions that beckon return visitors year after year. It's prime birding country, especially during spring nesting season when sage grouse and sharp-tailed grouse perform their courtship displays and dances. Rockhounds and geologists come in search of fossils and hikers come for the treks to old mining and historic sites in the hills.

building frontier town with stores, homesteads, churches, a library and many antique vehicles. Open Memorial Day through Labor Day. Admission. ~ 7 West County Road, Scobey; 406-487-5965.

Resting almost exactly on the Montana–North Dakota border, 16 miles southeast of Bainville, is the **Fort Union Trading Post National Historic Site.** The Missouri River's principal fur-trading post from the late 1820s until the Civil War has been restored to depict that era of America's westward expansion. Only the foundations of the original fort remain, but many buildings have been reconstructed and refurbished to their 1850s appearance. A visitors center is open daily, and the site has picnic tables and hiking trails. During summer, a trading post is open, too. ~ 15550 Route 1804, Williston, North Dakota; 701-572-9083; www.nps.gov/fous.

LODGING

One of the more charming places to stay along the Hi-Line is **Buckfield Bed & Breakfast,** just off Route 2 about 13 miles west of Glasgow. The 5000-square-foot house, a hit among outdoor recreationists, has a swimming pool, hot tub and satellite TV, and the hosts serve up generous home-cooked meals. There are four double rooms, two singles and one twin; all have shared baths. ~ P.O. Box 74, Vandalia, MT 59273; 406-367-5353, fax 406-367-5354; www.buckfieldbedandbreakfast.com, e-mail buckfld@ nemontel.net. MODERATE.

◀ *HIDDEN*

On the Fort Peck Indian Reservation, less than an hour's drive east of Fort Peck Dam and Lake, the **Sherman Inn** is a clean and comfortable three-story property. Its 46 ample rooms have queen-size beds, and desks; there's also a lounge/casino and a restaurant open for three meals daily. ~ 200 East Main Street, Wolf Point; 406-653-1100, 800-952-1100, fax 406-653-3456; www.sherman inn.com, e-mail sherman@midrivers.com. BUDGET.

The **Cattle King Motor Inn** has 30 units just 15 miles south of the Canadian border. All rooms are air-conditioned and have queen-size beds and standard amenities. Three bonuses: The continental breakfast features homemade treats, the guest laundry facility is free, and a restaurant and lounge is next door. ~ Route 13 South, Scobey; 406-487-5332, fax 406-487-5595. MODERATE.

DINING

Sam's Supper Club specializes in charbroiled steaks from the surrounding cattle country and filets of walleye pike. The low-lit restaurant, just off Route 2, also makes its own ice cream and other desserts. Lunch is served Wednesday through Friday, dinner Tuesday through Saturday. ~ 307 Klein Road, Glasgow; 406-228-4614. MODERATE TO DELUXE.

For a slice of 1950s-vintage Americana, stop by the family-style **Old Town Grill.** It's probably one of the few restaurants in the nation where you can sit in a booth decorated with historic

Text continued on page 292.

The Sport
of Rodeo

The most popular sport in Montana isn't fishing, golfing or skiing. It is rodeo, a cowboy tradition in which few might actually indulge, but all can enjoy watching.

The state's longest-established rodeo is the Wild Horse Stampede, which takes place each July at Wolf Point on the Fort Peck Indian Reservation. But roundups take place throughout northeastern Montana and indeed the entire state, all summer long. Full weekends are devoted to the sport, with parades, barbecues, street dances and country entertainment complementing the main event.

Some of Montana's top annual rodeos include the Professional Rodeo Cowboys Association circuit finals in Great Falls in January; the Last Chance Stampede (Helena, July); and the Northern International Livestock Exposition (Billings, October).

Rodeo evolved in the late 19th century from cowboys' macho desire to see who was the best calf roper, bronc rider or steer wrestler. Prize money and silver belt buckles were awarded to the winners, who often reinvested their earnings into next year's circuit. Losers usually gained nothing but broken bones.

A rodeo has six principal events: saddle bronc riding, bareback bronc riding, bull riding, steer wrestling, calf roping and women's barrel racing. Scoring is based on difficulty (stronger, more temperamental animals earn the riders higher points) and, in the latter three events, speed. Thus, while skill and courage are essential ingredients, winners also take the luck of the draw in being matched with higher-scoring livestock. Rides on bucking broncos last but eight seconds: horses are released from chutes (fenced-in enclosures) with riders already aboard. With saddle broncs, cowboys dig in with stirrups and hold onto a thick rope rein; with bareback broncs, there are no stirrups and no reins, only a pair of tightly cinched straps to which the rider clings. The horses buck wildly to throw their passengers off; cowboys who succeed in staying aboard do so with a rhythmic rocking motion. A pickup man rides alongside the bucking horse when the eight-second clock has sounded, and the rider slides off to safety.

Bull riding is considerably more dangerous. Riders must attempt to remain on the back of a 2000-pound bull for eight full seconds while clenching a single thick rope wrapped around its chest. The bull jumps, kicks and rams the wall to throw its rider, then it may turn and attack with its horns or hooves. Some riders have died, and many have been seriously injured. As fallen bull riders attempt to escape their foes, they put their faith in foolish-looking but daring rodeo clowns who put their lives on the line to lure bulls away from the cowboys until they can be recaptured.

In steer wrestling (also known as bulldogging) a cowboy must leap from his horse onto the back of a full-grown steer, grab his horns, and wrestle him to the ground with his feet and head facing the same direction. This involves a two-man team: a mounted "hazer" forces the steer to run straight ahead while the "dogger" gets into position for his leap. A good team can take down a 700-pound steer, running at 25 miles per hour, in less than seven seconds.

Calf roping, perhaps the truest test of a cowboy's skill, is the most highly contested of all events. Riding trained horses, two riders lasso a young heifer (which may weigh 250 to 300 pounds)—one by the neck, one by the hind legs. They quickly leap from their horses and tie it (as if for branding); if the calf cannot free itself within six seconds, the time stands and an "untie man" frees the animal.

Barrel racing is a speed and agility event. Competing women ride their horses in a set pattern around a triangular course of three barrels spaced 100 feet apart. Penalty seconds are added to times for any barrels that are knocked over.

photos and place your order by telephone. Locals particularly like the Mexican fare such as fajitas, enchiladas and chimichangas. But then again, they're mighty partial to the Grill's chicken-fried steak, fried chicken and homemade soups. No dinner on Sunday. ~ 400 Route 2, Wolf Point; 406-653-1031. BUDGET.

NIGHTLIFE   The most prominent stage association between the Rocky Mountain Front and the border of the Dakotas is the **Fort Peck Summer Theatre**. The summer repertory presents musicals and dramas every weekend of summer at its historic theater near the eastern Montana dam. ~ Missouri Avenue, Fort Peck; 406-526-9943.

A popular spot in the Fort Peck Indian Reservation is the **Stockmen's Bar**. ~ 220 Main Street, Wolf Point; 406-653-1248.

▼▼▼▼▼▼▼▼▼▼▼▼
The Heartland

Route 200 spans Montana's "Heartland," the state's geographical center, more or less paralleling the Hi-Line. Running east from Great Falls between 50 and 110 miles south of Route 2, it crosses the Judith Basin to Lewistown, the region's largest town; drops to the Musselshell River valley; then races through a couple of hundred miles of "great wide open" before hitting another town with a population of more than a thousand: Sidney, on the Yellowstone River at the North Dakota border.

SIGHTS   The Heartland really begins in the **Judith Basin**, in the ranching country immortalized by Charlie Russell's art, on the eastern flank of the Little Belt Mountains. Naturally blue Yogo sapphires are mined here; they were first discovered by Russell's friend Jake Hoover.

Lewistown, whose 6000 people live in the exact center of Montana, 105 miles east of Great Falls, is a ranching and wheat-farming center. The town is rich in late-19th-century pioneer history: Its downtown, Courthouse Square and Silk Stocking District are listed on the National Register of Historic Places. Self-guided tour brochures can be obtained at the **Lewistown Area Chamber of Commerce**, which chronicles the area. Closed weekends. ~ 408 Northeast Main Street, Lewistown; 406-538-5436, fax 406-538-5437; www.lewistownchamber.com, e-mail lewchamb@lewistown.net.

Popular recreational sites in the area include **Ackley Lake State Park**, 30 miles southwest, a favorite of trout anglers. ~ Route 400. **Crystal Lake**, 20 miles south in Lewis and Clark National Forest, features hiking to nearby ice caves. ~ Forest Road 275; 406-566-2292. **Judith Peak Recreation Area**, 20 miles northeast, offers 100-mile summit views and no facilities. Inaccessible in winter. ~ Route 81; 406-538-7461, fax 406-538-1904. **War Horse National Wildlife Refuge**, which is located about 40 miles east, is noted for its spring waterfowl viewing. ~ Blakeslee Road; 406-538-8706, fax 406-538-7521. Another portion of the refuge is the **Yellow Water** area. ~ Located 15 miles southwest of Winnett.

Perhaps most interesting to visitors, Lewistown is the headquarters of the **Charles M. Russell National Wildlife Refuge**. The million-acre refuge, which surrounds Fort Peck Lake, supports a rich variety of wildlife and such recreational activities as camping, boating and fishing. Call the refuge headquarters for maps and regulations. ~ Airport Road; 406-538-8706, fax 406-538-7521. The primary access point is at the **James Kipp Recreation Area**, 65 miles northeast of Lewistown; the site is also a favorite departure point for boat tours and floats of the Upper Missouri National Wild and Scenic River from Fort Benton 49 miles upriver. There's primitive camping during the summer. Overnight fee, $6. ~ Route 191; 406-538-7461, fax 406-538-1904.

Unlike other sapphires, which must be heated to achieve a blue color, Yogo sapphires are naturally cornflower blue.

East from Lewistown on Route 200, it's 130 miles to **Jordan**, once called "the lonesomest town in the world" by a New York radio station. Its **Garfield County Museum** is worth a look for its homesteading-era exhibits and the full-size replica of a triceratops discovered in nearby Hell Creek fossil beds. Closed September through May. ~ Route 200, Jordan; 406-557-2517; www.garfieldcounty.com/museum/museum.html, e-mail mareta@midrivers.com.

Another 26 miles north is the lone state park on Fort Peck Lake: **Hell Creek State Recreation Area**. Despite its isolation, this is a popular area, especially for boaters. It has a marina and offers camping and motel lodging. Admission. ~ Hell Creek Road; 406-234-0900, fax 406-234-4368.

Jordan gained national notoriety in 1996 as the stronghold of the isolationist Freemen, whose compound—where members engaged in a two-month armed standoff with the federal government—is several miles northwest of the town, near Brusett.

From Jordan, Route 200 continues east through **Circle** (67 miles) and **Richey** (96 miles) to **Sidney** (142 miles), on the Yellowstone River just inside the North Dakota border.

Circle, named for the brand of a long-defunct cattle ranch, is a small ranching center midway between Glendive and Wolf Point. Its **McCone County Museum** is noted for a fine taxidermy collection. Closed weekends. Admission. ~ 1507 Avenue B, Circle; 406-485-2414.

The center of a sugar beet–growing area, Sidney is home to the **MonDak Heritage Center**, a re-created pioneer street scene featuring 17 buildings, all displaying historical artifacts. It's a superb exhibit. There are also three art galleries here with changing exhibits. Closed Monday in summer; closed in winter. Admission. ~ 120 3rd Avenue Southeast, Sidney; 406-433-3500, fax 406-433-3503; e-mail mondakheritagecenter@hotmail.com.

If you have a particular interest in agricultural science, you may want to pay a visit to the **Northern Plains Agricultural Research Laboratory** in Sidney. Call ahead for tours. Closed weekends. ~ 1500 North Central Avenue, Sidney; 406-433-2020, fax 406-433-5038; www.sidney.ars.usda.gov. The **Sidney Chamber of Commerce** is happy to provide information year-round. ~ 909 South Central Avenue, Sidney; 406-433-1916, fax 406-433-1127; www.sidneymt.com, e-mail chamber@sidneymt.com.

LODGING

The Heartland's finest lodging is the **Yogo Inn**. Occupying most of a city block in the downtown hub, the two-story inn has 122 rooms, their spaciousness accented by high ceilings. Facilities include an indoor swimming pool and hot tub, a laundry room, a dining room, a coffee shop and a lounge. ~ 211 East Main Street, Lewistown; 406-538-8721, 800-860-9646, fax 406-538-8969; www.yogoinn.com e-mail yogo@yogoinn.com. MODERATE.

Twenty-one miles north of Jordan, just outside the Charles M. Russell National Wildlife Refuge, is the **Hell Creek Guest Ranch**. Cattle and sheep are raised at this working ranch, which offers a central location for exploring the region's wildlife-rich prairies and fossil beds. Closed December to mid-May. ~ P.O. Box 325, Jordan, MT 59337; 406-557-2224, 406-557-2244, fax 406-557-2234; e-mail jfstrumbo@midrivers.com. MODERATE.

DINING

You can take the whole family to **Whole Famdamily** for healthy home cooking. Savory soups, giant sandwiches and "international" dinner specials are presented in a golf-inspired atmosphere. Don't miss the rich desserts. Closed Sunday. ~ 35 Country Club Road, Lewistown; 406-538-5161, fax 406-538-3645. MODERATE.

RAMBLIN' ROADS

For a scenic backcountry driving tour of the **Upper Missouri River Breaks National Monument** and a small portion of the Russell wildlife refuge, depart east from Winifed on Secondary Road 236, 38 miles north of Lewistown. You'll travel through remote, rugged badlands country. Use caution as some portions of this byway are gravel, while others are not, becoming impassable when wet. Since much of this land is privately owned, permission is required prior to entering these lands. ~ Contact the Bureau of Land Management (406-538-1900, fax 406-538-1904) for information.

Eastern Montana ranchers may not be anxious to ride out to their own south 40 (acres), but they'll make a beeline for Sidney's **South 40**. Huge cuts of prime rib are served in a ranch-style atmosphere, along with hearty homemade soups and a salad bar. ~ 207 2nd Avenue Northwest, Sidney; 406-482-4999, 800-788-4419, fax 406-482-1342; e-mail home@midrivers.com. MODERATE TO DELUXE.

Take a look at the **Lewistown Art Center** for work by regional artisans. Closed Sunday and Monday. ~ 801 West Broadway, Lewistown; 406-538-8278.

SHOPPING

Moccasin Mountain Art Gallery specializes in Western and wildlife scenes by local and national artists. Closed Sunday. ~ 408 West Main Street, Lewistown; 406-538-5125.

ACKLEY LAKE STATE PARK Named for an early settler, this lake, at the northern foot of the Little Belt Mountains, is one of the most popular destinations for Heartland watersports lovers. In the winter enjoy ice skating and fishing. You'll find picnic areas and restrooms. ~ From Lewistown, take Route 200 west 22 miles to Hobson; turn south on Route 400 for five miles, then southwest on gravel-surfaced Ackley Lake Road for two miles; 406-454-5858, fax 406-761-8477.

PARKS

▲ There are 23 primitive sites; free; 14-day maximum stay. Water available May to the end of September.

CHARLES M. RUSSELL NATIONAL WILDLIFE REFUGE Encompassing one million acres of forest, prairie and badland surrounding 134-mile-long Fort Peck Lake, this refuge provides a home for hundreds of species of birds and a great many large animals. Thirteen recreation areas along its shores have boat launch sites and campgrounds, including the James Kipp Recreation Area, the main takeout point for floats of the upper Missouri River. The Russell Refuge surrounds the **UL Bend National Wildlife Refuge**, noted as a wilderness sanctuary for endangered species. Facilities include picnic areas and restrooms. ~ Headquarters are in Lewistown; easiest road access, besides Fort Peck Dam, is at the James Kipp Recreation Area on Route 191, 65 miles northeast of Lewistown; 406-538-8706, fax 406-538-7521; e-mail cmr@fws.gov.

▲ There are 87 RV/tent sites with hookups at two campgrounds ($12 per night) plus 219 primitive sites at 14 recreation areas (no charge).

HELL CREEK STATE RECREATION AREA The only state park on huge Fort Peck Lake, Hell Creek is located about midway down its southern shore. Probably as many visitors arrive by motorboat as by car. Picnic areas, restrooms, a marina, boat rentals, a store and concessions round out the amenities. Day-use fee, $4. ~ Take Hell Creek Road north from Jordan 26 miles to the Hell Creek Arm of Fort Peck Lake; 406-234-0900, 406-557-2345 (summer only), fax 406-234-4368.

▲ There are 55 RV/tent sites (no hookups); $15 per night; 14-day maximum stay; 406-557-2280.

Outdoor Adventures

Fort Peck Lake is the focal point for anglers in northeast Montana. In this fast body of water can be caught such coldwater species as mountain whitefish and brook and rainbow trout, as well as walleye and northern pike, sauger, burbot, smallmouth bass, channel catfish, and the prehistoric sturgeon and paddlefish.

FISHING

In the far north, the Milk River has an excellent fishery for trout, catfish and perch.

BOATING

The Upper Missouri National Wild and Scenic River is a major draw for river lovers who don't need whitewater to enjoy the scenery. For 149 miles, from Fort Benton to the James Kipp Recreation Area on Fort Peck Lake, this broad, slow-flowing stream meanders past striking geological features and abandoned homesteads, and through the Charles M. Russell National Wildlife Refuge.

Ask about commercial boat tours, or get information about renting a vessel and navigating downstream, at the **Fort Benton River Management Station**. ~ 1402 Front Street, Suite C, Fort Benton; 406-622-3839. Or try the **Fort Benton Visitors Center**. Closed Labor Day to Memorial Day. ~ 1718 Front Street, Fort Benton; 406-622-5185 (summer), 406-538-7461 (winter). One of the leading commercial operators is **Missouri River Outfitters**, which offers guided canoe trips up to seven days for groups of ten or more as well as multiday cruises in a canopied craft. ~ P.O. Box 762, Fort Benton, MT 59442; 406-622-3295, 866-282-3295; www.mroutfitters.com.

The 13 boat launch sites around the 1520-mile shoreline of vast Fort Peck Lake are administered by the Russell Wildlife Refuge. Contact the refuge office for information. ~ Airport Road, Lewistown; 406-538-8706.

RIVER RUNNING

Most of the rivers of northeast Montana are too slow for whitewater rafting, and many of them are quite muddy. Independent Missouri River floaters, however, have plenty of river opportunities.

Start your float in the Fort Benton or Virgelle area of the river, northeast of Great Falls, by consulting **Missouri River Canoe Co.** ~ 7485 Virgelle Ferry Road North, Virgelle; 406-378-3110, 800-426-2926. **Montana River Outfitters** offers half-day, full-day and overnight trips. ~ 923 10th Avenue North, Great Falls; 406-761-1677, 800-800-8218; www.montanariveroutfitters.com.

GOLF

Northeast Montana has a few golf courses, some of them semi-private but open to nonresident visitors. Green fees are $7 to $15 at the **Sleeping Buffalo Resort Golf Club** ~ Route 2, Saco, 406-527-3233; the **Sunnyside Golf & Country Club** ~ Cherry Creek Road, Glasgow, 406-228-9519; the **Airport Golf Club** ~ Route 25 East, Wolf Point, 406-653-2161; the **Scobey Golf Club** ~ Route 13, Scobey, 406-487-5322; the **Plentywood Golf Club** ~ 709 Sheridan Street, Plentywood, 406-765-2532; and the **Sidney Country Club** ~ Route 16, Sidney, 406-433-1894.

BIKING

The highways and byways of northeastern Montana can be very hot, very cold, and exceedingly windy. They are not regarded as the most favorable geography for bike riding.

HIKING

There's not much in the way of designated hiking trails in northeastern Montana. Backcountry wanderers often make their own paths through the Charles M. Russell National Wildlife Refuge or the Little Rocky Mountains near Zortman. A few suggestions follow. All distances listed for hiking are one way unless otherwise noted.

Beaver Creek Trail (.5 mile) is a self-guided nature trail off Route 24 near Fort Peck Dam. It offers visitors an opportunity to see wildlife in native habitats, including beavers, muskrats, deer and antelope.

Crystal Lake/Crystal Cascades Trail (6.2 miles) combines an easy 1.7-mile loop around a wooded Lewis and Clark National Forest lakeshore with a moderate climb up a small creek into the Big Snowy Mountains. The cascades flow from a cave and gurgle over a stairstep ledge for nearly 100 feet. The trailhead is 30 miles south of Lewistown on Forest Road 275.

AUTHOR FAVORITE

Trekking over the **Mission Canyon Trail** with your American Indian guide is an experience you'll not soon forget. This eight-mile trail takes in a natural rock bridge in the Fort Belknap Indian Reservation, as well as historical and sacred Assiniboine sites around Snake Butte. Arrangements to visit must be made through the reservation office (Harlem; 406-353-2205 ext. 470).

Transportation

CAR

The two primary routes through northeastern Montana both have east–west orientations. **Route 2** (the Hi-Line) links Williston, North Dakota, with Wolf Point, Glasgow, Malta, Havre and Glacier National Park. **Route 200** runs west from Sidney through the Heartland to Lewistown and Great Falls.

The main north–south roads are **Route 191** (Malta–Lewistown), **Route 87** (Lewistown–Billings), **Route 24** (Glasgow–Fort Peck north to Canada and south to Route 200), **Route 59** (Jordan–Miles City), **Route 13** (Circle–Scobey) and **Route 16** (Sidney–Culbertson–Plentywood).

For road reports—especially important during the unpredictable winter season—call 800-226-7623; or check www.mdt.state.mt.us/travinfo.

AIR

Most of the region's small airports have direct connections to Billings via the commuter aircraft of **Big Sky Airlines**. Service is available to Havre, Helena, Wolf Point, Miles City, Glendive, Lewistown and Sidney.

TRAIN

Amtrak's (800-872-7245; www.amtrak.com) Seattle–Chicago "Empire Builder" makes a few stops on the Hi-Line east of Glacier National Park. Contact the depot in Wolf Point for more information. ~ 51 South 1st Street, Malta; 320 Front Street, Wolf Point, 406-653-2350.

CAR RENTALS

Rentals are available at regional airports in Glasgow, Wolf Point, Lewistown and Sidney, as well as nearby Havre and Glendive.

Index

Lodging Index

Dining Index

HIDDEN GUIDES

Adventure travel or a relaxing vacation?—"Hidden" guidebooks are the only travel books in the business to provide detailed information on both. Aimed at environmentally aware travelers, our motto is "Where Vacations Meet Adventures." These books combine details on unique hotels, restaurants and sightseeing with information on camping, sports and hiking for the outdoor enthusiast.

PARADISE FAMILY GUIDES

Ideal for families traveling with kids of any age—toddlers to teenagers—Paradise Family Guides offer a blend of travel information unlike any other guides to the Hawaiian islands. With vacation ideas and tropical adventures that are sure to satisfy both action-hungry youngsters and relaxation-seeking parents, these guides meet the specific needs of each and every family member.

Ulysses Press books are available at bookstores everywhere. If any of the following titles are unavailable at your local bookstore, ask the bookseller to order them.

You can also order books directly from Ulysses Press
P.O. Box 3440, Berkeley, CA 94703
800-377-2542 or 510-601-8301
fax: 510-601-8307
www.ulyssespress.com
e-mail: ulysses@ulyssespress.com

HIDDEN GUIDEBOOKS

____ Hidden Arizona, $16.95
____ Hidden Bahamas, $14.95
____ Hidden Baja, $14.95
____ Hidden Belize, $15.95
____ Hidden Big Island of Hawaii, $13.95
____ Hidden Boston & Cape Cod, $14.95
____ Hidden British Columbia, $18.95
____ Hidden Cancún & the Yucatán, $16.95
____ Hidden Carolinas, $17.95
____ Hidden Coast of California, $18.95
____ Hidden Colorado, $15.95
____ Hidden Disneyland, $13.95
____ Hidden Florida, $18.95
____ Hidden Florida Keys & Everglades, $13.95
____ Hidden Georgia, $16.95
____ Hidden Guatemala, $16.95
____ Hidden Hawaii, $18.95
____ Hidden Idaho, $14.95
____ Hidden Kauai, $13.95
____ Hidden Los Angeles, $14.95
____ Hidden Maine, $15.95

____ Hidden Maui, $13.95
____ Hidden Miami, $14.95
____ Hidden Montana, $15.95
____ Hidden New England, $18.95
____ Hidden New Mexico, $15.95
____ Hidden New Orleans, $14.95
____ Hidden Oahu, $13.95
____ Hidden Oregon, $15.95
____ Hidden Pacific Northwest, $18.95
____ Hidden San Diego, $14.95
____ Hidden Salt Lake City, $14.95
____ Hidden San Francisco & Northern California, $18.95
____ Hidden Seattle, $13.95
____ Hidden Southern California, $18.95
____ Hidden Southwest, $19.95
____ Hidden Tahiti, $17.95
____ Hidden Tennessee, $16.95
____ Hidden Utah, $16.95
____ Hidden Walt Disney World, $13.95
____ Hidden Washington, $15.95
____ Hidden Wine Country, $13.95
____ Hidden Wyoming, $15.95

PARADISE FAMILY GUIDES

____ Paradise Family Guides: Kaua'i, $16.95
____ Paradise Family Guides: Maui, $16.95
____ Paradise Family Guides: Big Island of Hawai'i, $16.95

Mark the book(s) you're ordering and enter the total cost here ⇨ [____]

California residents add 8.75% sales tax here ⇨ [____]

Shipping, check box for your preferred method and enter cost here ⇨ [____]

❑ BOOK RATE   **FREE! FREE! FREE!**

❑ PRIORITY MAIL/UPS GROUND   cost of postage

❑ UPS OVERNIGHT OR 2-DAY AIR   cost of postage   [____]

Billing, enter total amount due here and check method of payment ⇨ [____]

❑ CHECK   ❑ MONEY ORDER

❑ VISA/MASTERCARD _____ EXP. DATE _____

NAME _____ PHONE _____

ADDRESS _____

CITY _____ STATE _____ ZIP _____

MONEY-BACK GUARANTEE ON DIRECT ORDERS PLACED THROUGH ULYSSES PRESS.

ABOUT THE AUTHOR

JOHN GOTTBERG is also the author of Ulysses Press' *Hidden Wyoming* and a co-author of *Hidden Pacific Northwest*. Formerly chief editor of the Insight Travel Guide series and travel news editor and graphics editor for the *Los Angeles Times*, he has traveled and worked all over the world. He has written ten other books and co-authored nine more, and his credits in more than 50 magazines and newspapers include *Travel & Leisure* and *Islands*.

ABOUT THE ILLUSTRATOR

DOUG McCARTHY, a native New Yorker, lives in the San Francisco Bay area with his family. His illustrations appear in a number of Ulysses Press guides, including *Hidden Wine Country*, *Hidden Tennessee*, *Hidden Kauai* and *Hidden Georgia*.